GABAM STUDIES 2

ALAKENT CHURCH
A Byzantine Monument at Myra
(12TH–13TH Centuries)

ORIGINAL TITLE

ALAKENT KİLİSESİ
Myra'da Bir Bizans Yapısı
(12.–13. Yüzyıllar)

Koç University
College of Social Sciences
and Humanities

Rumelifeneri Yolu
34450 Sarıyer-İstanbul
T +90 212 338 30 67
gabam.ku.edu.tr
gabam@ku.edu.tr

EDITOR

Engin Akyürek

PUBLICATION
COORDINATOR

Barış Altan

TRANSLATED
FROM TURKISH

Yiğit Adam

BOOK DESIGN

Burak Şuşut, FİKA

PRE-PRESS PRODUCTION

Beste Miray Doğan, FİKA

PROOF READING

Mark Wilson

PRINTED BY

Mas Matbaacılık San. ve Tic. A.Ş.

Hamidiye Mahallesi

Soğuksu Caddesi, No: 3

34408 Kağıthane/İstanbul

book@masmat.com.tr

Certificate No: 12055

First Edition

Istanbul, January 2018

ISBN 978-605-2116-15-9

KOÇ UNIVERSITY PUBLICATIONS
Certificate No: 18318

PHOTOS

© Myra-Andriake Excavations
Archive

ARCHITECTURAL
DOCUMENTATİON

Rekare Mimarlık

CONSERVATION PROJECT

Sebahattin Küçük, ARKİSTANBUL

ALAKENT CHURCH
A Byzantine Monument at Myra (12TH–13TH Centuries)

KOÇ UNIVERSITY
STAVROS NIARCHOS FOUNDATION
CENTER FOR
LATE ANTIQUE AND
BYZANTINE STUDIES

Koç University Suna Kıraç Library
Cataloging-in-Publication Data

Alakent Church : A Byzantine Monument at Myra (12th–13th Centuries) / editor Engin Akyürek ; publication coordination Barış Altan ; translation Yiğit Adam ; book design Burak Şuşut ; pre-press production Beste Miray Doğan ; proof reading Mark Wilson.-- İstanbul : Koç University Stavros Niarchos Foundation Center for Antique and Byzantine Studies, 2017.

281 pages ; 23,5x28 cm.-- GABAM Publications ; 1

Includes bibliographical references and index.

ISBN 978-605-2116-15-9

1. Alakent Kilisesi (Demre, Turkey). 2. Demre (Turkey)--Antiquities, Byzantine. 3. Church architecture--Turkey--Demre. 4. Excavations (Archaeology)—Turkey--Demre. 5. Church buildings—Turkey--Demre. 6. Myra (Extinct city). 7. Turkey--Antiquities, Byzantine. I. Akyürek, Engin. II. Altan, Barış. III. Adam, Yiğit. IV. Şuşut Burak. V. Wilson, Mark. VI. Title.

NA5871.D4 A5313 2017

CONTENTS

ALAKENT CHURCH
A Byzantine Monument at Myra (12TH–13TH Centuries)

Edited by
Engin Akyürek

PREFACE

The presence of this small Byzantine church in the Alakent neighborhood of Demre has been known to archaeologists and art historians for quite some time. Revealing the structure from under the five-meter deep alluvial fill in which it was buried was only possible as a result of the excavation work carried out in 2010 as part of the "Myra–Andriake Excavations." The excavation process, which proved to be extremely difficult due to technical and timing-related reasons, could be completed by channeling all available resources of the Myra–Andriake Excavations to this structure, and through the dedicated work of the excavation team. The church was not only revealed through the excavations but also after conservation treatments and a master plan for the area surrounding the church were completed, Demre was presented with a new monument – its museum. The archaeological data obtained from the excavations provided an invaluable source of information about the Byzantine architecture of the period, as well as led to significant conclusions about the history of Byzantine-period Myra.

The realization of this excavation was, above all, made possible by the encouragement and purposeful drive of the director of the Myra–Andriake Excavations, Prof. Nevzat Çevik, and his ability to procure the necessary resources. Scientific suggestions by Prof. Nevzat Çevik and Lecturer Süleyman Bulut were also very valuable for me. The nearly twenty-person scientific team of the excavation as well as students and a large number of workers all toiled with great devotion. The project was also privileged to receive a great deal of support from the then Minister of Culture and Tourism, Mr. Ertuğrul Günay throughout the process. The contributions of the Mayor of Demre, Mr. Süleyman Topçu, who strived to meet all our wishes and needs, and the support of the people of Demre who followed our progress with pleasure, were invaluable to us. I would like to thank everyone involved in and providing support to the excavations at this Byzantine-period church that we have named Alakent Church after the name of the neighbourhood. On behalf of the excavation team, I also thank to Dr. Nicholas Kontogiannis, Dr. Çiğdem Maner, Dr. Ekin Öyken, Architect Barış Altan and Merve Özkılıç for their contributions to the publication of this book in the form of translations and editorial input, and the current Metropolitan of Demre, Dr. Hrisostomo Kalaycı, who allowed us to include in our publication a complete list of the Bishops of Myra that he had prepared.

Engin Akyürek
GABAM Director

LIST OF THE ILLUSTRATIONS

VI. **CERAMIC FINDS**

VII. **INSCRIPTIONS**

VIII. **BURIALS**

IX. CONSERVATION TREATMENTS

I.
The Story of the Excavation

Nevzat Çevik
Excavation Director, Akdeniz University

This is the story of the rebirth of a small church that has slept in a bed of alluvium of the Myros River for 700 years. It is the story of the excavation of a small but significant church that informs us about the state and existence of hundreds of unknown structures that have been covered by alluvium for a thousand years.

Almost totally covered by alluvium as high as four to ten meters and having the modern-day town of Demre established on top of it, the metropolis of Lycia, Myra, hides thousands of secrets buried deep beneath the soil. Concealed underneath natural veils, it is in some way an "Anatolian Pompeii." Even the smallest of finds from this settlement, which is spread over an area of about 1.5 kilometers in diameter as a result of the research that we carried out, is of great importance in terms of rendering this invisible city apprehensible. Until 2010, when we began excavating Alakent Church, the only source of information regarding the city was derived from the excavations of the Church of St. Nicholas and the theater, which we had expanded through the research at Andriake, the harbor of the city. The accumulated sediment was approximately five meters high at the Church of St. Nicholas and nearly nine meters at the stage of the theater. The ancient topography of the city, for which we did not have a comprehensive picture, had been now transformed into an alluvial plain and so must contain other surprises. Furthermore, both the sediment fill of the last 700 years and the character of the earlier alluvial strata should provide us with the story of how the settlement was buried. Filled with curiosity, we started the excavation of Alakent Church. A lot of the answers that we thought to acquire through this excavation would also shape the future excavations. And to everyone, we would present a concrete, visual explanation of how Myra was buried. We would also save Demre from the present state of this site, an ugly dump in the immediate vicinity of the theater and on a well-traveled tourist route. Aside from saving a medieval church from heaps of rubbish and floods, the preserved scientific data that would be acquired from this site was at the forefront of the scientific and professional goals of the excavation.

The first account regarding the presence of the church originates from two photographs published in the 1975 book *Myra* by J. Borchhardt. During his research carried out in the 1960s, some parts of the chapel became visible due to the powerful surges of floodwater and so were included in Borchhardt's publication. The first assessment, which we now know to be wrong, was also arrived at through the parts that were visible at the time. In that publication, based on the way the northeastern corner and the northern arch looked, Otto Feld concluded that this was a "church with a cross-in-square plan." This initial mistake was repeated in publications that followed. However, as a result of our excavations, it was understood that the building was a domed-hall church. The building was also included in the cultural inventory of the province of Antalya, prepared by the Governorship of Antalya, and the comments in this publication also contained incorrect information since no excavation had been carried out at the time of its publication. For instance, the arch of the arcosolium in the northeast corner was described as a "doorway" (Pehlivaner 2004, p.23).

In the field surveys we carried out at the beginning of the excavation in 2009, we saw several of the roof tiles of the northeastern corner of the church preserved and in their original place. Apart from this survey, we gathered important information through our oral history research with the elderly inhabitants of Demre residing in the surrounding area. The stories revealed that, owing to the state of the alluvium carried by the floods, the northern and eastern parts of the structure were from time to time partly visible during the childhood of these elderly people. Some of these observations, largely based on childhood memories and sometimes with blurred boundaries between imagination and reality, ended up being transformed into local legends such as "a tunnel extended from here to the Church of Nicholas, three kilometers away." After eliminating some of this information, we also confirmed the validity of other accounts during our excavation. For instance, Mr. Nuri Gezer, who lived in a house immediately to the west of the church, reminisced about his earlier memories about the church and spoke of a large archway, at that time invisible, on the southeastern corner of the structure that he and an older friend had seen while playing as children. As a result of the excavation, an arcosolium was unearthed at that spot. Pointing to the place where the apse was located, they had said: "There is a round roof here," and this information came to light as the semi-dome of the apse. It was also understood that "the narrow door that was bricked up," which they had mentioned to be in front of the apse, was the arched window of the apse blocked up at a later date.

In the same years we were also conducting the Myra geophysics project, and through it we determined that the building extended further. With the scientific foundations laid in our 2009 research, we prepared an excavation and conservation project to be carried out in 2010. We were very excited about the chance of finding a place of interest buried safely under five meters of alluvium, about the possibility of adding new and important data regarding the Byzantine architecture of that period, and the opportunity to save and conserve another building. In fact, we were so optimistic about how good the structure would be preserved under the alluvium that – the altar and the frescoes aside – we were making jokes that we would find the priest at the bema. It was time to start the excavation.

However, the church was under the modern-day settlement of Demre, and on that site ran the streets with their water and electrical supply infrastructures of today. Over it flowed the floods of rain that streamed down from the acropolis of Myra. Although the land of the church was privately owned, it was used entirely as a dumping ground. We faced every conceivable problem that could hinder the realization of the project. The biggest of them all was private ownership, and it was very improbable that the Ministry of Culture and Tourism would exercise expropriation. So we requested excavation consent from the landlord and signed a protocol formalizing our prospect of excavating. He also acknowledged that this land, which has become useless as a dumping ground in a flood zone, was concealing the mysteries of history underneath. By revealing it through an excavation, it would add meaning and beauty to its surroundings: the beauty of the past would enwrap the ugliness of today.

In framing the project during long team discussions, we defined the possible problems in detail and then decided to proceed with the excavation. We identified the primary factors that would shape the work program as follows:

1. The structure is buried in five-meter deep alluvium.
2. The floodwaters have been passing over the structure for hundreds of years.
3. The drinking water and electricity infrastructures as well as a neighborhood street pass through the structure/excavation site.
4. All conservation measures after the excavation must be carried out before the winter.

All these determining factors necessitated the completion of the excavation in the summer season and the completion of the conservation measures in the autumn season. Because once the rains begin, the five-meter deep pit that would be formed by the excavation would fill with floodwaters which would harm the structure. Therefore, the conservation measures had to be finalized before the winter rains. We also determined the needs of the work program: a highly efficient schedule; a large enough team with appropriate credentials; efficient logistics; and sufficient funding. There was no room for failure.

We set out to determine the work schedule following some fundamental conditions. This would be the principal excavation of the season; it would commence immediately at the beginning of the season; it would be completed by the end of the season; and therefore, the work would continue without interruption throughout the day in two shifts. There would be as many workers and students as possible, and the team would be led by Prof. Dr. Engin Akyürek whose responsibility was the Byzantine sector of our excavation along with two Byzantine specialists, Assoc. Prof. Dr. Özgü Çömezoğlu and Assoc. Prof. Dr. Ayça Tiryaki. Should the need arise for any equipment or tools apart from the ones that the excavation team possessed, the Municipality of Demre would provide all the necessary logistical support. And sufficient financial resources would be arranged for these occasions.

At the beginning of the 2010 season, we started the excavation by fulfilling all the conditions mentioned above. During the excavation we demolished the old flood control channel, which required that a new closed rainwater canal be built running further east away from the church. The 130,000 liras, which we obtained from the Governorship of Antalya and spent through the Municipality, was expended solely on this work. A new vehicle route needed to be built on top of the closed canal, thus providing an alternative to the east of the Matarlar Street passing over the narthex, which could no longer be used. The water and electricity infrastructures passing through the excavation site were also redirected via other routes through the resources of the municipality. The needs of the community were met at a higher standard than previously without causing any inconvenience. It was time for us to carry on with the excavation in peace of mind.

The first thing we did was clear the rubbish. Clearing the rubbish and waste accumulated over the years took a lot of our precious time: we were getting rid of heaps of plastic greenhouse tarpaulins, greenhouse glazing, iron greenhouse construction bars, piles of nylon and rope, empty agricultural pesticide and fertilizer packages, car tires, uprooted plants, rotten vegetables, and various sorts of debris carried by the stream. From the two acres of land on which the building stood, twelve trailers of garbage was removed.

Then the actual excavation began. We dug trenches covering the whole site, clarifying the boundaries of the structure to comprehend the area where we would work. The initial view of the site was pitiful: the upper part of the dome was destroyed at the street level. As we descended further, we saw that the other sections of the building were still standing firmly; and that was our first cheerful moment. After seeing the exact boundaries of the structure, we recalculated the perimeter of our excavation trenches to make them much wider than the building. Otherwise, when the excavation was over, the chapel would remain in a deep and narrow well, and it would be impossible to preserve it. A situation arose that facilitated our work. The interior of the church and its surrounding area were filled with very soft alluvial soil, and local greenhouse owners almost competed with each other to take this fine-grained silty soil with their tractors so as to spread it in their greenhouses. The character of this fill did not change almost down to the floor level. And this was no surprise for us; on the contrary, it was exactly what we expected. This was because the Church of St. Nicholas, excavated earlier, was buried at the same depth and had a similar fill. The theater of Myra, next to Alakent Church, was covered with alluvium of a height of almost ten meters.

The geophysical results also did not indicate the existence of any other structure around the church. First, we started to uncover the walls of the church by making excavations in a wide corridor around the walls. After isolating the structure from the alluvial fill and seeing a full cross section of the fill, we cleared the upper layers of alluvial soil located at a distance from the structure in a controlled manner with an excavator to gain time and spare financial resources.

When the exterior shape of the church became clear as we carried on with the excavation, we also began to haul stones with the excavation's tractor to build a wall around the perimeter. These stones consisted of a lot of rubble from the Andriake excavations. In this way, we were able both to clear Andriake of this rubble and to obtain stones to build a retaining wall around the church without paying for them.

Another task in progress was to create a master plan for the area around the church. We managed to complete this project with the help of a benevolent architect, but it remains to be implemented by the Municipality of Demre. The plan still awaits execution mainly because the expropriation of the church land could not be completed.

While the alluvial fill outside the church was being removed, the interior of the building was simultaneously excavated. Through this, the risks that could arise from the inward or outward pressure created by the alluvial fill were eliminated. The work progressed downward from the void left by the already destroyed dome. The inside of the building was also completely filled with alluvial soil. What actually kept the structure standing firm for 700 years was this impermeable fill. As we removed the alluvial fill from outside the building and saw that all the walls were preserved intact, this was a cause for joy. But as we kept clearing the silt/soil fill inside the church, we became dismayed when we saw that the frescoes on the naos walls were damaged by thousands of fine tree roots. Still, it was a relief to see the presence of enough remains to be able to understand the contents of the painting program.

The remains of the top cover were secured with wooden support, and the removal of the alluvium inside the church continued. As the excavation moved on, the idea that there would not be too many small finds was confirmed: there was only the alluvial fill. We only recovered a few small finds, such as the medieval ceramics, from the alluvium layer above the floor level. These solitary finds were also important as determining elements in dating, because they provided evidence that the structure was in use until the 14th century. So, the church dated back to the beginning of the 12th century by Akyürek due to its architectural characteristics, was in use for almost 200 years. Apparently, in those centuries the Christian population of Myra had shrunk to such an extent that churches this small were sufficient to accommodate them. The Christian settlement that had continued for centuries was facing its final years. In its final days the church was used for a different function, and completed its cycle of life in the early 14th century. The most exciting thing was that we were uncovering one of the churches that must have existed apart from the Church of St. Nicholas. It was perhaps one of the latest churches to be built in the metropolis of Byzantine-era Lycia.

Clearing the soil from the surfaces of the walls was very time consuming. This was because the remaining fragments of the substantially damaged frescoes were fused with the tree roots and partially disintegrated due to vegetative pressure. As soon as we realized this, we started working together with the restoration team. We understood that in a case like this the rapid changes in humidity posed great risks. It would be an impossible task to place the tiny fragments of fallen frescoes where they belonged, and to keep in place the parts of frescoes prone to falling would be equally difficult. For this reason, we began to strip carefully the interior walls covered with silty soil with immediate and instantaneous conservation interventions. The workers excavating the interior did not strip the walls completely, but left a few centimeters of alluvium in place. The team of archaeologists, restoration experts, and students who made up the afternoon shift then cleaned the alluvium attached to the walls completely. At the same time they implemented the emergency interventions and stabilization applications on the fragments of frescoes that were revealed. Although much of the frescoes had disintegrated to a great extent, many fragments were still in place.

Except for a few pieces of ceramics, there were no finds buried in the alluvium, and the state of the frescoes at the naos was discouraging. But as the excavation at the naos descended further down, we were in for a pleasant surprise. The elements of the interior architecture/liturgical furnishings were intact. The interior architecture of our tiny church, with its ornamented parapets, templon columns, and altar table, was also unearthed in a very well-preserved state.

Matarlar Street, which passed above the narthex before the excavation began, fortuitously did not cause any serious damage to the structure underneath. In other words, the soil had done its duty for hundreds of years and preserved, while man destroyed all he could see. The walls of the narthex, which were under the road and were 1.5 meters lower than the walls of the naos, remained intact, but its roof was completely destroyed. When Matarlar Street was demolished and the excavation continued under its former path, it was seen that the western wall and the entrance of the narthex was right at the border of the house located to its west. For this reason, the excavation was forced to be confined within this boundary. We would never be able to enter the church from the western door of the narthex. So we reinforced the doorway with steel construction and left it without excavating any further. As the excavation of the narthex progressed and the structure was stripped of alluvium, we began to catch a glimpse of a terrific surprise. On the right side of the doorway leading from the narthex into the naos we uncovered a life-sized *Deesis* scene that was preserved in immaculate condition. As we stripped the alluvium, Christ stood staring at us with Mary on one side and John the Baptist on the other. Moreover, with scrolls in their hands and in an unparalleled *Deesis* dialogue never before seen at any church in Turkey: Mary was in supplication asking Jesus for forgiveness on behalf of humanity. This unique fresco, along with other frescoes on the inner walls of the naos, was carefully cleaned and conserved by the team of restoration experts. Their goal was to keep it from drying out too quickly and becoming damaged in the intense summer heat while making it stable enough before winter. We were unfortunately not as lucky with the naos frescoes as with that in the narthex. Thousands of fine roots crept under the frescoes and caused great damage. But still, the presence of enough fragments to give us an idea about the painting program was a relief. At the end of the day, the painting program of the naos could be established to a great extent. Without attempting to repaint any missing parts, we only stabilized and conserved the frescoes. With a specially made, transparent plexiglass panel, the *Deesis* scene was completely shielded from possible hazards.

As the excavations progressed further down inside and outside the church, the building started to emerge. Before the excavation was completed and the conservation was finalized, the entire structure was covered with a special textile to prevent drying and flaking due to changes in humidity. The textile was dampened twice a day to keep the frescoes and other sensitive plaster from drying. In addition, the four arches carrying the dome were reinforced with wooden supports to strengthen temporarily the building for operational and structural safety. Immediately afterwards, stainless steel beams were placed on the missing upper parts of the arches that used to carry the dome no longer in existence, thus preventing the arches that the alluvial fill had kept standing for centuries from collapsing.

As the excavations progressed down to the floor level inside and outside of the church, the perimeter and the boundaries of the structure became definite. We were at a depth of five meters below the walking level of Demre. A five meter-high alluvial cross-section was formed all around the church. Demre's houses, greenhouses, roads, rainwater channels and all other modern-day elements were forming the latest strata 5 meters above the floor level of the era of the church. Therefore, to be able to keep the building unaffected by Demre's famous gushes of rain and the church from being buried in water and silt again, a wall with a total height of 5.5 meters, at least 50 centimeters above the present ground level was required. Parallel to the excavation we had already begun to build walls with the rubble stones that we were hauling from the Andriake excavation. The wall was built by a team of stonemasons from Konya completely out of stone, with the necessary slant and at the required strength. From that day on, this wall continues to protect the church. Another project we urgently started working on was the protective roof above the church. To prevent rain falling on the building and to keep the rainwater from forming a giant pond in the trenches where the church was located, this cover had to be built before the rains came. The features considered in the design of the roof that would cover a very large area including the church and its surroundings were: sufficient width and height, stability, suitability for visitor traffic, channeling the winter rain away from the site through the gutters connected to the roof, and preventing overheating and greenhouse effects that would be caused due to intense sun light. We managed to complete the roof, meeting these requirements together with the surrounding retaining walls that same year before winter. We would no longer worry about leaving a job half-done, and we had no anxieties about the conservation process. Due to the priority of emergency consolidation and conservation work, we postponed the completion of the excavations around the church and the implementation of the long-term conservation and preservation measures to the following years. The work carried out on a number of tombs within the site was also completed during the 2011 and 2012 seasons.

The Alakent Church excavation, conservation, and preservation project, which started at the beginning of the 2010 excavation season, was to a great extent completed in early November of the same year before the winter rains began. The site was excavated, cleaned, and emergency consolidation and conservation measures were taken. The perimeter wall and the roof were completed, the stream bed to the east of the building was rerouted into a large concrete canal, the Matarlar Street was replaced with a road over the canal, and the scientific documentation of the excavation process was completed without exception. The detailed architectural drawings of the building were completed the following year in 2011. And now you are holding the publication in your hands. We consider the loss of several years that caused disruptions in publications and in field work as an unfortunate accident, and since 2016 we have been trying to compensate for our loss. Now the important thing to be done regarding the church is to finalize the expropriation of the land and to implement the master plan so as to reach the complete conclusion of the project. Our actual dream is to be able to see a completely excavated area extending from Alakent Church to the theater.

This project is an exemplary project for archaeological fieldwork. It has been a good example both in terms of preparation and programming, as well as implementation. The important outcomes of the project can be summarized as follows:

Scientific: Preserving a medieval church with its architecture, ornamentation, and frescoes and unearthed in the ancient center; the presence of a unique inscription in Mary's hands in the supplication scene with no known parallel in any of church in Turkey; the scientific contributions of the project such as the discovery of a probable Church of Mary in Myra, and a further understanding of the 12th–13th century Byzantine period in Myra: the fact that one of our fundamental principles about the responsibility of presenting the finalized parts of the project to the academic community through publications was also accomplished in a timely manner.

Conservation: Carrying out the excavation and conservation work and other relevant preservation work within the same season, in good time and meeting the necessary standards; not attempting to add any complementary elements to the structure, only carrying out consolidation and conservation work; having the permanence and safety of the conservation implementation repeatedly tested in the winter rains and summer heat during the last seven years until the preparation of this publication.

Urbanism: Improving –both at the excavation site and in the surrounding area– some aspects of the urbanization of the settlement of Demre, which seemed underrepresented in comparison to the magnificent history of this area.

Social: Presenting a new source of visual information to the public through excavating and unearthing a structure in Demre; making a point of the importance of preserving historical assets through carrying out a delicate conservation at a small church.

Touristic: Revealing another piece of the composition around the magnificent theater at Demre, a district of Antalya province that draws one of the highest number of tourists to Turkey, and providing new clues to the visitors of Myra about this city buried under alluvium,

Organizational: The excavation was a total success in terms of organization. We managed to change the infrastructure and road relocation of the present-day urban settlement as well as to carry out the excavation and conservation implementation within a single season. This was only possible through having a number of institutions working side by side as part of a single operation. This collaboration provided the necessary power both in terms of logistics and financial resources. The Myra–Andriake Excavations directorate managed to accomplish the task of bringing the Ministry, the Governorship, the Municipality, the University, and the public together as parts of a thriving program, and this led to a pleasing outcome for all.

Therefore, just like many other structures we have unearthed and conserved at Myra and Andriake, we are much indebted and grateful to many people and institutions for their exemplary cooperation at the Myra Alakent Church. At the end of the day we are all working for this country and its people. All institutions and persons who have been great collaborators, while being aware of this fact, deserve the highest praise. The work that was achieved belongs to us all.

Figure 1: Site was a dumping ground before the excavation

Figure 2: Structure becoming visible after clearing tons of rubbish

Figure 3: Perimeter of the structure dug out first

Figure 4: Team committed to the work

Figure 5: Short break at the narthex

Figure 6: Mid-session ice cream refreshment in Demre's scorching heat

Figure 7: Excavation begins inside the dome's cavity

Figure 8: Well-deserved rest under the apse's semi-dome

Figure 9: Hand reaching out from the narthex towards the naos

Figure 10: Bema begins to emerge with its altar table and templon

Figure 11: Workers, archaeologists and students working together

Figure 12: Soil covering church for 700 years is removed

Figure 13: Alakent Church excavation site

Figure 14: Floodwaters run through it, and above is Matarlar Street

Figure 15: Shift of workers is over, next are the archaeologists and students

Figure 16: Excitement as the ceramics are emerging

Figure 17: Face of Christ is slowly being revealed

Figure 18: One restoration expert for each saint

Figure 19: Restoration requires attention

Figure 20: Restoration requires love

Figure 21: Pleasure of the work

Figure 22: We achieved a marvelous result

II.
Myra: The Metropolis of Lycia

Engin Akyürek
Koç University

The geographical region known in history as Lycia is the ancient name of the Teke Peninsula located on the western part of the Anatolian Peninsula, roughly extending from the western side of the Gulf of Antalya to Fethiye. A large section of the Lycian region is covered by the Western Taurus Mountains (Teke Taurus), which almost immediately start to rise from the shoreline and reach a height above 1500 meters at certain points.[1] The Western Taurus runs east to east in a sequence of three principal ranges: Bey, Ak, and Üzümlü. These mountain ranges stretch parallel to the sea and meet the seashore at a steep angle, not allowing settlement on a large proportion of the coastline. However, the rivers reach the sea by flowing through these mountain ranges and the valleys that they form. They both connect the mountainous interior with the shore and constitute fertile alluvial plains, suitable for settlement along the coasts. The most important of these plains suitable for agriculture and urban settlements are: Kumluca Plain in the east formed by Alakır Creek and Karasu Creek, Kınık Plain in Western Lycia formed by Eşen Creek, and Demre Plain in Central Lycia formed by the Demre Creek (Myros).

This geographical region was also the source of the birth and development of three important coastal or proximate coastal settlements in Lycia: Phoinix, Limyra and Rhodiapolis in the east, Xanthos and Patara in the west, and Myra in Central Lycia.[2] These coastal cities have had the possibility to develop by utilizing the opportunities provided by their harbors in maintaining a close contact with the world of those days.[3] Through the rivers and the deep valleys in which they flow, these harbors were able to connect a large inland hinterland in Lycia with the network of the Mediterranean trade, thus integrating a large part of the Lycian region –not easily and economically accessible by land– with the bustling world of the Mediterranean by sea.

From a geological point of view, the settlement of Myra (Demre) is located on a plain of loose alluviumal plain, carried from the high mountainous regions by Myros, and is surrounded

1 Kahraman, Softa, and Akan 2010, pp. 329.

2 For the origins of the name Myra, see Çevik 2015, pp. 359.

3 Fowden 1990, pp. 347–348, 362.

by topographically high areas.[4] The deep valley of the Myros Creek provided major agricultural and economic access from the hinterland to Myra and the harbor of the settlement, Andriake.[5] It served as the gateway of this potential market to reach out to the world. However, this favorable geographical location also has had a serious negative aspect for Myra. The Lycian coasts are located on one of the two major earthquake zones of the earth's crust: the Mediterranean-Himalayan earthquake zone. Demre and its immediate surroundings are located in an active first-degree seismic zone with a high risk of seismicity in Anatolia,[6] and the most significant evidence of this risk are the great earthquakes experienced in the region throughout history.[7] On the other hand, a typical Mediterranean climate prevails in the region, therefore exposing it to heavy rainfall, especially during the winter months. From time to time this causes substantial floods.[8] As a city, the fate of Myra was mainly determined by its geographical setting.

The cities of Lycia, which to a degree have remained outside the networks of important land routes, established their ties with the world mainly by sea. Transportation by sea was much more efficient and therefore less costly than land transportation. The distance traveled on sea on a good day could only be covered in a week on foot on the land route.[9] Due to its geographical location the Lycian coasts were inevitably used in Mediterranean Sea transport leading to the Lycian region, which was difficult to reach by land. It thus became part of the Mediterranean transportation network since ancient times, and integrated the region with the world of those days. The earliest maritime documents in the Mediterranean world go as far back as the period of the Old Kingdom of Egypt (3rd millennium B.C.).[10] The seaborne trade ships of the Bronze Age, such as the Cape Gelidonia and Uluburun shipwrecks dated to the 14th and 12th centuries B.C.,[11] are evidence that the Lycian coasts were on the maritime trade routes of the Mediterranean even in those times. Underwater finds and various shipwreck or harbor excavations also show trade routes from the Bronze Age to the Byzantine period extending from Egypt, Syria, southern Anatolia, Cyprus, Rhodes, and Crete in the Eastern Mediterranean to the Aegean, Constantinople, and Rome.

Especially in the early periods, as seafaring could be done on routes divided into day trips, it was mainly in the form of coastal navigation. The ships did not have without the ability to navigate for extended periods in the open sea and so sailed parallel to the coastline. After a day's cruise the mariners had to moor at a harbor to spend the night, do maintenance on the ship, and refresh their supply of food and water.[12] In the Eastern Mediterranean basin, with its extensive commodity and passenger mobility, the trade vessels had to moor at a number of harbors along their routes. During Late Antiquity and the Early Byzantine periods, the most intensive maritime traffic in the Mediterranean was along the routes extending from the Eastern Mediterra-

4 Kahraman, Softa, and Akan 2010, pp. 329–330; Öner 2000, p. 2 passim.

5 For the Andriake harbor during the Byzantine period, see Akyürek 2014; Akyürek 2016; Çevik 2015, pp. 377–392.

6 Kahraman, Softa and Akan 2010, pp. 333–334.

7 Duggan 2004; Duggan 2005.

8 With an average annual precipitation of 1200 millimeters, Antalya is one of the provinces receiving the most rainfall in Turkey. The rains follow an irregular pattern, and 54.2% of the rainfall comes in the winter months. In some years these rains can be well over the average. This situation often causes floods and inundations on a disastrous scale; see Kafalı Yılmaz 2008.

9 Avramea 2002, p. 77.

10 Khallilieh 2006, p. 1.

11 For the Gelidonia shipwreck, see Bass 1961; for the Uluburun shipwreck, see Bass 1986.

12 Aslan 2010, p. 257; Çevik 2010a, p. 22.

nean to Rome and Constantinople. Particularly, the declaration of the city of Byzantion as the new capital of the Roman Empire under the name of Constantinople by Constantine I in A.D. 330 breathed new life into the Eastern Mediterranean trade. The increase in population and the continued implementation of the distribution of free bread for about 80,000 people until the beginning of the 7th century created a serious demand for grain in the city. Approximately 31,200 tons of grain were transported annually from Egypt to Constantinople, estimated to be shipped in over 620 journeys to Constantinople then referred to as the "New Rome."[13] Palestine, Syria, and the southern and western coasts of Anatolia were the shores along which this intense traffic passed. This route kept being busy until the 7th century, when the sway of the Arab ships was felt in the Eastern Mediterranean.[14] This economic development becomes evident through the commercial wrecks located on the maritime route between Egypt and Constantinople, a significant part of which can be dated to the 4th-7th centuries, and especially to the 5th-6th centuries.[15]

Although located in the middle of the Egypt to Constantinople maritime route, Lycia had only very few places on its steep coasts that could be considered a convenient harbor for such a bustling maritime activity.[16] The harbor of Andriake had a favorable geographical location among the Lycian harbors and accommodated the biggest granary (*horreum*) of the region. Along with the harbor of Patara, which had similar advantages, the two became the leading harbors in the interregional trade. From the beginning of its history Lycia has been shaped by the relationship between the coastal port cities and the inland agricultural hinterland. Generally, the ports of Western Anatolia served as marketplaces for the products produced in their hinterlands, as well as places providing logistical support for transit merchants.[17] The products produced in the mountainous parts of Lycia and at the vast plateau in the north were especially the cedar and pine timbers in high demand for shipbuilding. These could not be transported by land so were brought down along the valleys to the harbors and transported by ships to the world markets from there.

The city of Myra in Central Lycia became a stopover between the other two ports of Lycia – Phoeinix (Finike) and Patara. Because it was able to connect a vast hinterland to a suitable port such as Andriake with the help of the Myros Creek and its valley, Myra managed to develop and become one of the most important and prosperous cities of Lycia. The valley of the Myros Creek connected Myra to the vast Kasaba Plain on the inland, and in the Roman period an ancient road passed through this valley.[18] This stone-paved road was built to transport the products of the Kasaba Plain, such as grain, wine, and timber to Myra, and therefore to the Andriake harbor. For the safety of the road, towers were built along the valley.[19]

The strategic advantage of Lycia in terms of seaborne trade has continually turned the region into a field of rivalry between great powers. During the 1st millennium B.C., in the period of Doric colonization, the region saw the establishment of various cities.[20] Between 547 and 541 B.C., the Persian Empire expanded all the way to the Aegean, and with the fall of Xanthos that

13 Kingsley 2009, p. 34.
14 Avramea 2002, pp. 83–84.
15 Kingsley 2009, p. 35.
16 Aslan 2010, p. 258.
17 Jacoby 2001, I. p. 89.
18 Şahin and Adak 2007, p. 259.
19 French 1993, pp. 87–90.
20 See Akşit 1967, p. 95 passim.

was resisting the Persians, other Lycian cities also submitted to Persian rule without much resistance.[21] In the mid-5th century B.C. Lycia was a contested area between the Persians and Greeks who both wanted to dominate the maritime transportation in the Mediterranean as well as the Western Taurus, which was the most important source of timber used in shipbuilding.[22] Remaining under Persian rule until 333 B.C., Lycia was occupied by Alexander the Great in 333 B.C.[23] Later ruled by the Ptolemaic Kingdom for about a hundred years until 197 B.C., it became acquainted with Hellenistic culture. The Seleucid king Antiochus III, who seized Lycia in 197 B.C., was defeated by Rome seven years later, and in 188 B.C. Lycia was given to Rhodes, an ally of Rome.[24] In 167 B.C. Lycia was taken back from Rhodes and became a protectorate of Rome, and in A.D. 43 by an edict of the emperor Claudius, it became a Roman province.[25]

In the Lycian League founded in 167 B.C., Myra was one of the six cities entitled to three votes, as the representative of Central Lycia.[26] At the end of the 1st century and in the 2nd century A.D. during the course of Pax Romana (Roman Peace), especially under the reign of Hadrian and Antoninus Pius, Myra developed rapidly due to the growing importance of Andriake's harbor.[27] However, the main splendor of Andriake's harbor was during the reign of Emperor Hadrian. In the year A.D. 129 important port structures were built, especially the granarium (Horrea Hadriani) that is still standing today. The capacity of the port was increased, and Andriake became the most important harbor of the region.[28]

Although Christianity had been born in Palestine, it soon spread to the major urban centers of the Mediterranean.[29] The apostles spread the new religion initially in these centers, especially the port cities with extensive connections with the world of those days, and among the Jewish communities.[30] This, in fact, is true for the whole Mediterranean basin as well as for Lycia where communication was mainly by sea. As such, the new religion had the possibility of spreading faster, and it was then disseminated into the rural areas from these cities. For Christianity the first event that lifted Myra to a site of significance occurred when the apostle Paul was brought by ship to Andriake's harbor, and thus to Myra, on his way from Caesarea to Rome in the year A.D. 60. He and other prisoners were transferred onto a ship carrying corn from Alexandria to Rome.[31]

As early as the 3rd century, before the "Great Persecution" started by the Edict of Diocletian on 23 February 303, Anatolia had a considerable Christian population, mostly concentrated

21 Childs 1981, p. 55; Akşit 1967, pp. 112–122.

22 Childs 1981, pp. 61–62.

23 Akşit 1967, p. 126.

24 Akşit 1971, p. 56 passim.

25 Akşit 1971, p. 119.

26 Strabon, XIV–III; Çevik 2015, p. 360; Çevik and Bulut 2010, p. 27. The other cities were Xanthos, Patara, Tlos, and Pinara in Western Lycia, and Olympos in Eastern Lycia.

27 Çevik and Bulut 2010, p. 27.

28 Çevik 2015, p. 361.

29 Herrin 1989, pp. 57–58.

30 This is seen when the apostles' trips to spread the new religion are examined: "Now those who were scattered after the persecution that arose over Stephen traveled as far as Phoenicia, Cyprus, and Antioch, preaching the word to no one but the Jews only. But some of them were men from Cyprus and Cyrene, who, when they had come to Antioch, spoke to the Hellenists, preaching the Lord Jesus" (Acts 11:19–20). The apostle Paul also made his speeches to spread the new religion at synagogues in the cities he visited. These are also mentioned in Acts: Salamis (13:4–5); Pisidian Antioch, Yalvaç (13:14–15), Iconium, Konya (14:1), Thessaloniki (17: 1–2), Athens (17:17), Corinth (18:4), and Ephesus (19:8).

31 Acts 27:5–6.

in Cilicia and on the Mediterranean coasts including Pamphylia and Lycia.[32] After the granting of a legal status to Christianity by Constantine I with the Edict of Milan in A.D. 313, Christianity rapidly spread in the region. In the Byzantine period the importance of Myra increased even more. In addition to the important role of Myra in the interregional trade mentioned earlier, Christianity began to develop and spread as a new religion, thus having an immense part to play in this growth. At the Council of Nicaea in 325, the Lycian Church was represented by Eudemus of Patara. The absence of the envoy from Myra, the metropolitan of Lycia, is significant. This weak representation might be due to the strong support of Arius' doctrine in Lycia, and particularly in Myra. Arianism was declared heretical at the Council.[33] Later, at the council held in the year of 359 at Seleucia ad Kalykadnos (Silifke) where Arianism was discussed, the representatives of Lycia supported the Arianists. As a result, towards the 370's Basil of Caesarea asked Amphilochos, the bishop of Iconium (Konya), to contact people in Lycia who could defend the Orthodox line of belief. Apparently, the bishop of Myra was deemed not very dependable and skipped, so a priest named Tatianus was chosen as one of the people for this task.[34] Tatianus later became the bishop of Myra and participated in the Council of Constantinople in 381 as the bishop of Myra.[35] The banning of paganism by a decree of Emperor Theodosios I in A.D. 395 strengthened the position of Christians in the city. In Myra the bishop had "the temple of Artemis, destroyed down to its foundations."[36]

The elders, or leaders, of the first congregations formed in the cities became bishops in time. Thus, the church that organized in the city centers formed a church government parallel to the civil bureaucracy. And in the rural areas where the church spread later, it developed with a different understanding having monasteries at its foundation.[37] As far as Myra is concerned, Church B in the Andriake harbor settlement, which is still undergoing archaeological excavations, dates to the beginning of the 5th century.[38] Most of the religious buildings in the mountainous hinterland of Myra date to the 6th century and later.[39]

Just like many cities in Anatolia, Myra also had an important Jewish population that existed before Christianity. The synagogue unearthed in 2009 within the scope of the Myra–Andriake Excavations has provided concrete proof of the Jewish presence in Myra and its environs.[40] The synagogue was not only serving a small, settled population at the harbor of Andriake, but also serving a large number of Jews who came to the port for trading. The special position of the synagogue –within the port area located at the center of the Andriake harbor in front of the granarium– is also important in displaying that the Jewish community was a powerful community in Andriake and Myra. It would not come as a surprise to find another synagogue in the excavations to be carried out in Myra in the future.

32 Clarke 2008, p. 612.

33 Bennett 2015, p. 270.

34 Harrison 1963, p. 119; Hellenkemper and Hild 2004, p. 344.

35 Le Quien 1958, I, p. 968. I would like to thank Ekin Öyken for his fastidious translations of the related sections from the book in Latin (E.A.).

36 Jacobek 1999, p. 111.

37 Herrin 1989, pp. 59–62.

38 Akyürek 2016, p. 476.

39 İşler 2010, pp. 244–247.

40 The Andriake Synagogue is the first synagogue of the Anatolian Mediterranean to be unearthed through excavations. For this synagogue, see Çevik, Çömezoğlu, Öztürk and Türkoğlu 2010.

However, it was Nicholas, the bishop of Myra in the 4th century, who established the reputation of Myra in the eyes of the Christians.[41] Born in Patara, Nicholas later became the bishop of Myra and established his church here. In due time he was elevated to the rank of sainthood and accepted as one of the six founding bishops of the Byzantine Church. He is placed among the founding fathers of the Church, like Basil and John Chrysostom, in the painting programs of churches built after the iconoclasm. In the "painter's manual" also known as *Hermeneia*,[42] Nicholas is considered one of the six most important bishops to be depicted on church walls.[43] The very limited information we have on Nicholas comes from the life story (*vita*) of the abbot of Sion monastery, Nicholas (d. 564), an important monk who lived in Myra in the 6th century.[44] It would be right to say that our only source of information about St. Nicholas is this life story of Nicholas of Sion. In the following periods, the "two Nicholases" were merged, their miracles intertwined, and they became indistinguishable from one another and molded into a single cult of Nicholas. That Nicholas of Sion mentions Bishop Nicholas as a saint of a superior order suggests that the cult of St. Nicholas was quite prominent in the 6th century. The Church of St. Nicholas, visited by tourists in Demre today, was probably built in the 6th century in place of a preexisting church.[45] However, the possibility that a church named after Nicholas, considered to be the patron saint of seafarers, might have been built in Andriake, the port of Myra, cannot be disregarded.

The reason why the cult of Nicholas became so important to the Christian communities around the Mediterranean throughout Late Antiquity and the Middle Ages were the miracles that Nicholas was believed to have wrought. And at the center of this cult was the Church of St. Nicholas where the grave of Nicholas was located. It was believed that a sacred oil called myrrh (*myron*), exuding from the bones of the saint in the grave at the church, had miraculous medicinal properties. This oil was especially important for Christian pilgrims. It obtained from the myrtle tree that was referred to as *myron* and was also associated with the name of Myra.[46] The word *myron* was later on treated synonymous with "holy oil" and widely used as a term meaning holy oil.[47] The cult of Nicholas in Myra has also become a prototype for various similar cults.[48] The expectations for miraculous healing that people had have always been an important factor in movements of pilgrimage. And this miracle of healing is usually made possible by a healing oil that exudes from or is in some sort of contact with the body

41 On Nicholas, see Anrich 1913–1917.

42 This text that A. Didron saw in the hands of the monks painting the walls of a monastery in Mount Athos in 1839, is a sort of a "guide book" that contains wall-painting techniques, painting schemes to be implemented at churches, and iconographic information. The text was written by the priest, Dionysius of Phourna (d. 1745), but it is generally accepted to be an 18th century replication of a type of book believed to have been common in Byzantium. It was translated into English under the title, *The Painter's Manual of Dionysius of Fourna*. See *Dionysius of Fourna*.

43 These were arranged in order as Basil, John Chrysostom, Gregory Theologos, Athanasios, Cyril of Alexandria, and Nicholas of Myra: *Dionysius of Fourna*, p. 54 (154). And they were included in this order in many monumental wall painting schemes such as in the apse of the south chapel at Chora Church.

44 See *Nicholas of Sion*.

45 Ötüken 2006a, p. 524. For detailed information about the architecture of the Church of St. Nicholas, see Peschlow 1975b.

46 Çevik and Bulut 2010, p. 25; Çevik 2013, pp. 40–41; Ruge 1933, p. 1134; Foss 2002, p. 142.

47 Talbot 2002, pp. 160–161.

48 Foss 2002, p. 142.

of a holy person, or by directly being in close proximity to the relics of a saint.[49] This belief has made the graves of holy persons, such as Nicholas in Myra and Church of St. Euphemia in Constantinople[50] favored centers of pilgrimage. As the fragrant oil exuding from the holy person's relics could be filled into small bottles, the healing power of that holy person could be "transported."[51] In Myra, especially on the feast day of the saint on the 6th of December, large crowds would gather in order to procure the holy oil flowing from the saint's grave. This fragrant oil, which was believed to be a cure for all kinds of maladies, would be put into small vessels (*ampullae*) and taken away to be used later, or for patients far away. This grave that had wrought miracles has been known around the Mediterranean since early times. There is no doubt that the seafarers coming to Myra played a very important role in the spreading of this cult around the Mediterranean. In time, this grave became a place frequented by pilgrims and people who wanted to take their share of the holy oil of myrrh. So, and its reputation spread throughout the Christian world. Myra continued as one of the most important cult centers of Anatolia throughout the Middle Ages.[52] Despite the fact that the relics of Nicholas –the reason behind the existence of the cult of Nicholas– were smuggled by merchants from Bari in 1087, the interest of Christian pilgrims in the church at Myra has continued.[53]

Being a center of pilgrimage was important for Myra in various ways. The arrival of large numbers of wealthy and upper-class people from places far away would have been a considerable source of revenue for the region. On the other hand, this important center of pilgrimage also became a focus for the patronage of the empire[54] and drew investments into the city. Important centers of pilgrimage were also places where regional fairs and festivals, at which large-scale transactions took place, were held. And Myra continued to be an important center for these fairs and festivals during the Byzantine era.[55]

Pilgrimage movements in Anatolia declined after 1071 compared to the early Byzantine periods. Although this movement has fluctuated at times, it has never completely ceased. Sources from the Byzantine period indicate that the pilgrims' interest, especially in centers of healing, was concentrated in three periods: the beginning of the 5th century to the beginning of the 7th century; after the Iconoclastic period roughly between the years of 850–1000, and after 1261 when Constantinople was liberated from the Latin invasion.[56]

The 5th century was one of the turning points in the history of Myra. During the period of Emperor Theodosios II (408–450) Lycia was separated from Lycaonia and designated as a new province, and Myra was declared as the metropolis of Lycia. Malalas had expressed this with the following words:

"The emperor [Theodosios II] created a province which he called Lykia, by dividing it off from Lykaonia, giving the status of a metropolis and a governor to the city of Lykia known as Myra..."[57]

49 Foss 2002, pp. 129–151.

50 For the Church of St. Euphemia, see Naumann and Belting 1966; Akyürek 2002.

51 Talbot 2002, pp. 159–160.

52 Vryonis 1971, p. 36.

53 Foss 2002, p. 132.

54 Foss 2002, p. 139.

55 Foss 2002, pp. 145–147.

56 Talbot 2002, p. 168.

57 According to Malalas, the establishment of Lycia as a separate province happened during the reign of

Thus, Myra was raised to the position of both the civil and religious center of the province of Lycia. In this period, the borders of Lycia extended from Phaselis in the east to Telmessos (Fethiye) in the west, and to Balbura (Burdur) in the north. During the reign of Emperor Marcianus (450–457), upon the advice of governor Artemon and the *praetorian prefect* Palladius, the walls of Myra were expanded.[58]

The names of the two bishops who participated in the councils held in the 5th century and represented the Metropolis of Myra are known. The first is Seretianos who attended the First Council of Ephesus in 431.[59] The other bishop Romanos represented the metropolis of Myra at two important council meetings: the heretic Second Council of Ephesus convened in 449 and the following Council of Chalcedon in 451. There he renounced the Council of 449 with regret and signed the decrees as "Bishop Romanos of the Metropolis of Myra."[60] The letter sent by Emperor Leo I (457–474) to all the metropolitans in the East in the 5th century is evidence of the importance of the metropolis of Myra. In the letter, written on the occasion of the murder of St. Proterius of Alexandria, all metropolitans were requested to send letters attesting to their commitment to the canons of the Council of Chalcedon held in 451, which were to be collected by "the Right Reverend Peter, Bishop of Myra."[61]

In the beginning of the 6th century, Lycia was among the densest urban settlements on Byzantine lands, such as the Nile Delta and Palestine.[62] This century was also a time when the interregional trade system was at its prime and the city of Myra was having its most glorious period. In the Byzantine period, the most important building activity in the city was in the 6th century during the reign of Emperor Justinian. After the earthquake of 529, which caused great destruction in the city, Myra and its port Andriake were almost entirely rebuilt. Interestingly, Prokopios does not mention the construction activities in Myra, but Malalas mentions the aid given by Emperor Justinian to the city after the earthquake of 529:

"In that year Myra, the metropolis of Lykia, suffered through the wrath of God, and the emperor gave generously to the survivors and the city for building purposes."[63]

Although the information here does not clarify which structures in Myra were repaired or rebuilt after the earthquake, it can be assumed that the aid provided by the emperor to reconstruct the city was used to rebuild important public structures.

Nicholas, the abbot of Sion Monastery, provides important information on 6th- century Myra. Nicholas of Sion refers to Myra as "holy city" and states that there are many sacred places in this city.[64] He mentions an epidemic of plague coming from Egypt by sea in 542, taking hold of the city that he calls "the splendid metropolis of Myra."[65] From fear of the plague the villagers did not go down to Myra, so the flow of products such as wheat, flour, wine, and timber from the rural areas into the city came to a halt, and the urban population faced hunger.[66] This text is interesting

Theodosios II; see Malalas, pp. 199–200 (Book 14, pp. 364–365.24). However, Clive Foss attributes the establishment of Lycia as a separate province to Constantine I; see Foss 1991c.

58 Foss 1994, p. 23.

59 Le Quien 1958, I., p. 968.

60 Le Quien 1958, I., p. 968; Harrison 1963, p. 119.

61 Le Quien 1958, I., pp. 968–969.

62 Haldon 2001, pp. 7–8, Map. 1.5.

63 Malalas, p. 262 (Book 18, 448.40).

64 Nicholas of Sion, 8.29.

65 Nicholas of Sion, 58.93.

66 Nicholas of Sion, 52.83

in that it shows the interdependence between the city of Myra and the Andriake harbor and their hinterland in the countryside. One of the four bishops from Lycia who participated in the Council of Constantinople convened in 553 was Philip, the bishop of Myra.[67] In the life story of Nicholas, the abbot of Sion Monastery, the name of "Philippus the holy bishop of the metropolis of Myra" was mentioned.[68] At the Council held in 553, Philip signed his name as "by the grace of God, the bishop of the Myrans and the metropolitan of the province of Lycia, Philippus".[69] We hear of two more bishops from the 6th century: Nicholas (first half of the 6th century) and Modestos.[70]

The economic hinterland of the city of Myra covers the relatively nearby settlements of Muskar, Karabel, Belören, and Çağman in the north, extends to Gömbe and the Elmalı plateau further to the north, and contains Sura, Gürses, Kaş in the west, and the Kasaba Plain in the northwest. In the east, the area extending to Beymelek, Belen, and Arykandos Creek could be taken into account. This economic hinterland also determines the social and religious realm of authority under Myra in the Byzantine period.[71] Myra and its harbor Andriake served as a center linking this broad hinterland of Central Lycia to the vast interregional trade system embracing Egypt, Syria, the Aegean, Constantinople, and Rome. The interdependence between Myra and its hinterland implies that the city and its hinterland would develop and prosper together or also become impoverished together. The harbor tied the dispersed rural hinterland through trade. Indeed, in the 6th century Myra and its hinterland were prospered and developed together. The magnificent structures such as Karabel in the mountainous region are evidence that the countryside, like Myra, enjoyed prosperity in the 6th century.[72]

By the beginning of the 7th century the Byzantine Empire was in a difficult situation throughout Anatolia. Although Herakleios had defeated the Persians in 628 and moved them out of the Byzantine lands, a new threat to the Byzantine territory began to emerge by the middle of the century: the Arabs. The Lycian coasts were important for Arabs, because in the 7th century the sea route that extended from Egypt, Baghdad, and Damascus to Constantinople passed through the Lycian shores. Towards the end of the 7th century, the harbor of Andriake had also lost its function to a great extent. In addition to natural disasters such as major earthquakes and outbreaks of plague,[73] this loss was also due to the shores of the East increasingly falling under the control of the Muslims in the 7th century and the adverse effects of the changes in international trade routes in the Mediterranean on Lycia. Muslims had taken control of Syria in 636, Palestine in 638, and Egypt in 642.[74] In addition to its decline in terms of function due to these factors, the port of Andriake was also filling with alluvium and sea sand over time. In the excavations carried out at Andriake's harbor since 2009 as part of the Myra–Andriake Excavations, no evidence showing that the port was used after the 7th century was found. After the port of Andriake was abandoned, the port of Stamira, now known as Taşdibi, was used for small-scale local trade. Until the middle of the 20th century, this port was used between Demre and Finike and other nearby

---

67 Harrison 1963, p. 120.
68 Nicholas of Sion, 68.101.
69 Le Quien 1958, I., p. 969.
70 Hellenkemper and Hild 2004, p. 344.
71 İşler 2010, pp. 236–237.
72 Foss 1994, pp. 29–30; Foss 1993, pp. 22–23.
73 For the earthquakes and epidemics in the region, see Duggan 2004 and Duggan 2005.
74 Ostrogorsky 1991, pp. 102–108.

areas that had very limited land connections.[75] Although we do not have much information about 7th-century Myra, then going through a difficult period, the name "Polydectus, the bishop of Myra of the province of Lycia" was mentioned in the Third Council of Constantinople that convened in the year of 680.[76] Additionally, the name of the two more bishops from the 7th century have also reached our day: Anastasius and Theodore.[77]

In the beginning of the 8th century, between 716–717 the preliminary preparations for the siege of Constantinople by the Arabs were carried out mainly in Lycia. For the Arab navy, Lycia was midway to its final destination of Constantinople. It was therefore as much important for the Byzantines to keep control of the Lycian coasts both in commercial and military terms, as it was for the Arabs.[78] From the mid-7th century onwards, the provinces of the Byzantine territory were merged according to military needs, and vast themes were formed.[79] In the year of 717 during the period of Leo III, Lycia was combined with Pamphylia, Caria, and west Cilicia under the theme system to become an enlarged theme named Kibyrrhaiotai.[80] The theme of Kibyrrhaiotai was mainly established for military naval operations.[81] In the Mediterranean, referred to as *Bahrü'r Rum* ("Sea of the Romans") in Arab sources, the disruption of trade due to Arab attacks and other similar reasons also caused disturbances in the relations between Myra and other coastal cities.

After the city was damaged by the earthquake and reconstructed by Justinian, we do not hear much about Myra until the year of 790. Upon the arrival of the Arab fleet in Cyprus in 789–790, the Byzantine fleet was assembled and sent to intercept the Arabs. This fleet initially came to Myra, and after setting out from there, it navigated around Cape Gelidonia and arrived at the Gulf of Antalya. The Arabs also sailed out of Cyprus and arrived at a position off the coast of Attaleia. In this battle the *strategos* of the Kibyrrhaiotai, Theophilus, was taken prisoner by the Arabs.[82] In 807–808, Humeyid İbn-i Ma'yuf, a commander of Harun al Rasid, came to Myra on his way back from a raid in Rhodes. According to Theophanes, he wanted to destroy the grave of St. Nicholas, about whom he had heard so much, but instead he ended up destroying another grave next to it. Meanwhile, a fast-breaking storm destroyed many ships of the Arab fleet, and the "unbelieving" Arabs who were witnessing the power of the saint immediately fled from Myra.[83] After this event, the Church of St. Nicholas, which was a center of pilgrimage, was surrounded by a fortified wall. Visiting the region in 1842, Spratt and Forbes indicate that the Church of St. Nicholas (which they refer to as a monastery) was surrounded by a rectangular wall.[84]

The names of the bishops of Myra were also mentioned during the Iconoclastic (i.e., icon-breaking) period[85] (726–843), which has an important place in Byzantine history. At the Second Council of Nicaea convened in 787 which ended the First Iconoclastic wave,[86] the metro-

75 For the port of Stamira, see Duggan and Aygün 2010.

76 Le Quien 1956, I., p. 969.

77 Hellenkemper and Hild 2004, p. 345.

78 Küçükaşçı 2006, pp. 378–379.

79 Kazhdan 1991, pp. 2034–2035.

80 Haldon 2001, p. 70, Map. 6.2.

81 Foss 1991b, p. 1127.

82 Theophanes, p. 639; see also Harrison 1963, p. 121.

83 Theophanes, pp. 663–664, 664n2.

84 Spratt and Forbes 1847, p. 127.

85 For the Iconoclastic period, see Bryer and Herrin 1977.

86 The Seventh Ecumenical Council convened in Nicaea under the auspices of Empress Irene; see Ostrogorsky 1991, pp. 165–166.

politan of Myra, Theodore, who had supported the iconoclasts earlier but now regretted doing so, was present. At the same council meeting Nicholas, who had been dismissed by heretics earlier but then became the metropolitan of Myra again, was also present.[87] And in 821 Niketas (Hereticus), the bishop of Myra, was included in the Iconoclastic mission sent by Emperor Michael II to Louis the Pious and Pope Eugene.[88] At a later date in 879–880, Theodosios of Myra participated in the synod assembled in Constantinople to reinstate Patriarch Photios as the head of the Byzantine church.[89] In the 9th century Myra was still one of the most important metropolises of the empire. In light of the data included in the *Notitia Episcopatuum* in the 9th century, among the 51 metropolitanates of the whole empire, Myra, with its 33 bishoprics, ranked second in terms of importance and immediately followed Ephesus with its 34 bishoprics.[90]

In the second half of the 10th century, as a result of the military accomplishments of the emperors Nicephoras Phocas and John I Tzimiskes, and especially with the recapture of Crete in 961 and Cyprus in 965 from the Arabs, the Byzantine influence in the region once again increased.[91] The 10th century French coins unearthed at the excavations in the Church of St. Nicholas demonstrate that European pilgrims, taking advantage of the safe circumstances, were coming to Myra and visiting the tomb of St. Nicholas.[92] However, maintaining a stable state of security in the region in general was no longer possible to attain.

The 10th and 11th centuries were a period when piracy became more widespread in the Mediterranean. In 1034 Muslim pirates operating on the Lycian coasts landed at Myra and caused considerable damage to the city located slightly inland from the shore, and managed to take control of the city for some time.[93] In 1035 the brother of Emperor Michael IV, John the Orphanotrophos came to Myra to find a cure for epilepsy. He made a donation to the Church of Nicholas to help repair the damage inflicted by the Arabs.[94] Later in 1042–1043, a comprehensive restoration of the Church of St. Nicholas was carried out by Emperor Constantine IX Monomachus and Empress Zoe, and the complex was once again surrounded by a high wall. The inscription associated with this restoration was found during the Church of St. Nicholas Excavations.[95] Merchants from Bari, who came to Myra in 1087, removed the holy relics of St. Nicholas to their country without facing any resistance. This removal was regarded very highly by the Papacy and was celebrated in the Western Church by adding a feast day called the "Transfer of Relics" to the liturgical calendar. Considering this event as a theft rather than a "transfer," the Byzantine Orthodox Church rejected such a feast. Later however, the Russian Orthodox Church also began to celebrate this transfer alongside the Western Church. In a hymn composed in Kiev after the year 1091, the chant became: "The relics, like a star, were moved from the East to the West."[96] The smuggling of the bones of Nicholas to the West led to an increase in the popularity of the saint in the West, and eventually Nicholas of Myra was transformed into "Santa Claus". According to one

87 Le Quien 1958, I, p. 969.

88 Le Quien, 1958, I, p. 969; Harrison 1963, p. 121; Hellenkemper and Hild 2004, p. 347.

89 Le Quien 1958, I, p. 969.

90 Vryonis 1971, pp. 304–305. For the list of bishoprics related to Myra, see Kalaycı 2002, pp. 44-46.

91 Foss 1994, p. 34.

92 Ötüken 2006a, p. 525.

93 Jacoby 2001, I. p. 90.

94 Ötüken 2006a, p. 525.

95 Ötüken 2006a, p. 526; Ötüken 2002, pp. 401–414, Drawing 5.

96 Dvornik 1956, p. 241.

view, the bones of St. Nicholas are still at the church in Demre. Emperor Basil II considered moving the bones of St. Nicholas to Constantinople, but then gave up on the idea and hid the bones at the church in Demre where no one could find them.[97] According to this view, the bones smuggled by the merchants from Bari did not belong to St. Nicholas. In the 11th century, we have knowledge of the names of two metropolitans of Myra: Leo, whose name appears on a seal, attended the Council of Constantinople in 1054; and after 1079, Constantine, who stayed in the capital for a long time[98] due to his position as *synkellos*.[99]

The restoration of Byzantine rule in the region took place in the 12th century during the Komnenian dynasty, especially during the reigns of Alexios I Komnenos (1081–1118) and John II Komnenos (1118–1143). The Byzantine Empire once again dominated the region, especially Antalya.[100] The Lycian coasts were of vital importance to the empire, both in military concerns and matters of trade. Securing the Eastern Mediterranean maritime routes was important not only for ensuring the flow of goods that the empire needed, but also for the Byzantine fleet that wanted to have a presence in the region and for the Crusaders, who were going to Jerusalem by sea and relied upon halting the progress of the Turks in Anatolia. After relative stability was restored in the region, merchants and pilgrims started coming to Myra once again. In 1102 the English pilgrim Saewolf made a stopover in Myra on his way to the Holy Land, and prayed at the Church of St. Nicholas. In 1106 the Russian pilgrim Daniel visited Myra and the Church of St. Nicholas on his way to the Holy Land as well as on his return journey.[101] Architecturally, some small-scale repairs carried out at the Church of St. Nicholas and at some chapels in Beymelek, can be ascribed to this period.[102] According to Otto Feld, certain repairs were carried out both at the Church of Nicholas and at the port of Andriake.[103] However, the excavations at Andriake did not reveal any finds dating back to the 12th century. The Byzantine influence in the region did not last long, however. After the defeat wiping out almost the entire Byzantine army of Emperor Manuel I Komnenos in Myriokephalon on 17 September 1176,[104] the sovereignty of the Byzantine state in Lycia was also greatly impaired, as it was throughout Anatolia. With the conquering of Constantinople, the capital of the empire, by the armies of the Fourth Crusade in 1204, the power of Byzantine was diminished especially, and in time the region was taken over by the Turcoman. However, the presence and influence of the Christian community continued during the period of the Turcs. Starting in the 12th century, the Turcoman began to penetrate the Teke plateau in small independent groups. This did not happen in the form of a typical military invasion and occupation, but rather in the form of an ethnic migration of small, nomadic groups independent of the central states and moving together with herds of animals. This process continued for up to 200 years.[105] With the capture of Philethos, located to the north of Elmalı, in 1158 by the Turcoman,

97 Ötüken 2006a, p. 525 n19.

98 Hellenkemper and Hild 2004, p. 348.

99 The word *synkellos* literally means "one who lives in the same cell. It was the title given to the adviser of a patriarch, especially since the 5th century, who shared the same space with the patriarch. See Papadakis 1991, pp. 1993–1994.

100 Foss 1993, p. 23.

101 Foss 1994, p. 35; Hellenkemper and Hild 2004, p. 349.

102 Feld 1975, pp. 419–420.

103 Feld 1975, pp. 348, 386, 405.

104 Ostrogorsky 1991, p. 361.

105 Vryonis 1975, p. 50 passim; Vryonis 1971, p. 143.

the nomads began to settle around the inland sections of Lycia.[106] Although the Byzantine Empire had some control over the coasts, the inland sections were being taken over by the nomadic Turcoman tribes. It was at a much later period when the independent Turcoman groups who controlled the mountainous areas started to come down to the Lycian coasts.

Throughout the 12th century the appointment of bishops to the metropolitanate of Myra continued. In 1143 Bishop Theodore II signed the synod decree of the deposition of Cosmas Atticus, the patriarch of Bogomils, on the grounds of heresy, as "Theodore, the metropolitan of Myra."[107] Probably the same Theodore also attended the synod convoked by the patriarch in 1151. In 1166 Christopher of Myra attended the synod that the patriarch led with the patriarchs of Antioch and Jerusalem.[108] In 1178 the deacon of the church of St. Sophia and an eloquent orator Eustathios was elected the metropolitan of Myra. But as the territory was deemed unsafe, his appointment was postponed (*cheirotonia*). Instead he was sent by Emperor Manuel I Komnenos to the Metropolitan see of Thessaloniki, which was vacant at the time.[109]

With the Seljuks seizing Antalya in 1207, the importance of the Lycian ports for the Byzantines increased even further. Although the Byzantine presence in the region did not last long after that date, there is also no architectural or archaeological evidence that shows that the Seljuks permanently settled in the Lycian region.[110] Although the name Beymelek (Beğ Melik) –today is a town to the east of Demre– could suggest a Seljuk presence here, it was mostly independent Turcoman tribes that were active in Lycia rather than the Seljuks. The Seljuks did not have much of a presence in the Teke plateau except for Korkuteli. The fact that there are no caravanserais in the region also suggests that it remained outside the important transportation network of Anatolia.[111] The Turcoman started to become active in the coastal areas mainly towards the end of the 13th century. In the last quarter of that century Christian activity still continued in Myra. Loukas, the metropolitan of Myra, favored the idea of integration with the Western Church and was commissioned by Pope Gregory X in 1274 to establish a connection between Rome and the Orthodox Church. The name of Loukas also appears on an order of the Patriarchate of Constantinople dated 1283.[112]

In the mid-14th century the Beylik of Teke dominated a large section of Lycia.[113] The Turcoman, who first settled in Finike, Korkuteli and Fethiye, now settled in Elmalı, Kaş, Bayındır, and Gömbe by the end of the century.[114] They must have come to Myra during the same period. However, the existence of an important Turcoman settlement in Demre has not yet been documented. Gömbe, the present-day summer highland pasture of Demre, was a more important Turcoman settlement than Myra. In the 14th century Myra still had a significant Christian population. However, towards the middle of the century the region was largely taken over by the Turcoman, and the Christian population had lost influence to a great extent. In 1350 Ludolph von Suchem noted that Patara and Myra were in ruins due to the invasion of the Turcoman.[115] In 1362

106 Erdem 2006, p. 245.
107 Le Quien 1958, I, p. 970.
108 Le Quien 1958, I, p. 970; Hellenkemper and Hild 2004, p. 549.
109 Le Quien 1958, I, p. 970; Hellenkemper and Hild 2004, p. 350; Vryonis 1971, p. 205 n328.
110 Güçlü 2010, p. 307.
111 Erdem 2006, pp. 246–247.
112 Hellenkemper and Hild 2004, pp. 350–351.
113 Erdem 2006, pp. 247–248.
114 Erdem 2006, p. 248.
115 Vryonis 1971, p. 257.

the Cypriots attacked Myra in retaliation for the support that the Turcoman in Lycia offered to the Karamanids in their fight against Cyprus.[116] In the 14th century, although Myra was generally in a bad state according to the Order of the Patriarchate dated 1387, it was better off than Attaleia. For this reason, the Patriarch attached Rhodes, Kos, and the Cyclades islands to the Metropolis of Myra.[117] The last metropolitan that we have knowledge of living in Myra was Matthew between 1383 and 1393.[118] After the end of the 14th century or the beginning of the 15th century, the twenty-seven metropolitanates in Anatolia, including Myra, were no longer seen in the records of the synods of the Patriarchate. After the 14th century, the name of Myra also no longer appears in the *notitiae episcopatuum* containing the lists of bishops.[119] However, the assignment of metropolitans to Demre has continued up to the present day. The current metropolitan of Demre, Dr. Hrisostomo Kalaycı, utilized various sources including ordination records and letters in the archives of the Patriarchate to establish a list of the sixty-nine bishops of Myra up to today. His published list is presented at the end of the chapter.[120]

The Ottoman period, which started with Yıldırım Bayezid's capture of *Teke Eli* (Teke province) in 1393, was interrupted after the defeat of Sultan Bayezid I by Timur in the Battle of Ankara in 1402. Control of the region was handed over to Mehmet II of Karaman by Timur. Although the Karamanid rule in Lycia continued for some more time,[121] the Ottomans regained control over Teke in the 15th century. However, in this period, the coastal areas of Lycia remained almost unpossessed. The Ottomans endeavored to keep hold of these coasts because of their importance in Mediterranean trade, and repeatedly fought with the Genoese, Venetians, and Knights of St. John. The complete sovereignty of the Ottomans in the coastal areas of Lycia began with Sultan Suleiman the Magnificent's capture of Rhodes in 1522, which allowed him to take control of the Eastern Mediterranean.[122] This shows that to dominate Lycia, which was not really accessible by land at that time, one had to take control of the Eastern Mediterranean. Following the conquest of Rhodes by the Ottoman Empire, the Ottoman presence became more pronounced in the coastal areas of Lycia, and they were revived. The Şahkulu rebellions that erupted in the early 16th century involved Elmalı, Kaş, and Finike, and the mountainous sections were more affected by the uprising than the coastal sections.[123]

Demre was not an important settlement during the Ottoman period, and as a "village," from time to time, it was incorporated into Kaş or Finike. In the *Muhasebe-i Vilayet-i Anadolu Defteri* ("Register of Anatolian Provinces") dated 1530, Demre was recorded as a village of Kaş.[124] In the first half of the 16th century, Piri Reis mentions the ports of Finike and Kekova, but does not mention Demre and its port Andriake.[125] Although weakened during the Ottoman period, the Christian population still continued to exist in Demre.

116 Erdem 2006, p. 249.

117 Vryonis 1971, p. 296.

118 Hellenkemper and Hild 2004, p. 351. On the list of Dr. Kalaycı dates are 1388–1394.

119 Vryonis 1971, pp. 296, 302.

120 Kalaycı 2002, pp. 103–113.

121 Güçlü 2010, p. 307.

122 Güçlü 2010, p. 308.

123 Güçlü 2010, p. 307.

124 Güçlü 2010, p. 308.

125 Güçlü 2010, p. 308.

In 1831, in the first population census carried out during the period of Mahmud II, Demre was not included among the *kazas* (subdistricts) of the *Sanjak* (district) of Teke, and was presumably accounted for as a village of the Finike sub-district.[126] In 1876 a new administrative structure was established in the Sanjak of Teke, and Kaş was reestablished as a subdistrict. Demre was then made a village of Kaş. At this date, there were 59 households and a population of 169 inhabitants in the village of "Temre," which was included in the sub-district of Kaş. Around the same period, the population of Kaş was around 39,000.[127] After the Tanzimat (Reorganization), Demre was revitalized by a considerable Greek population resettling there from the island of Meis (Kastellorizo), who were mostly involved in trade.[128] On 23 July 1914, along with the Second Constitutional Era, the Sanjak of Teke was once again restructured administratively, and under the name of *Kal'a Nahiyesi* Demre was incorporated into the sub-district of Finike.[129]

European (British, German, and French) travelers who came to Lycia during the Ottoman period, especially in the 19th century, provided important information about the conditions of Demre and Andriake, the remains of buildings, daily life, and the natural world around the region.[130] Until the end of the 19th century, the most important areas of settlement of the Turcs in Lycia were still located inland, at places such as Elmalı and Korkuteli, rather than on the coasts. In 1811 Francis Beaufort came to Andriake while on his journey to prepare a map of the Mediterranean coasts of Anatolia. He published his impressions in 1818, stating that the plain of Demre was partially cultivated, but the timber that he saw on the shore was a sign that commercial activity was still ongoing in the region.[131] At the time the majority of the population in Demre consisted of Turcs with a small number of Christians. However the area did not have a bustling and lively population. The British traveler Sir Charles Fellows, who had come to the Lycian region and visited Myra during both of his trips in 1838 and 1840, provided interesting information about Demre in the mid-19th century. Setting out from Kasaba and walking along the Myros valley to reach Demre, Fellows mentions the remains that he saw there.[132] Fellows also visited the Church of St. Nicholas and notes that "a Greek priest alone remains within the holy walls." This old priest told him that since the middle of May, he was the only one to remain at the plain, and that everyone in the village (Demre) had gone up to the highland pasture to avoid the heat and the mosquitos.[133] Most of the people of Demre today also go up to high plateau around Gömbe and Elmalı in the mountainous regions during the summer months. The fact that someone was left behind to keep an eye on the Church of St. Nicholas shows that there was still a Christian community in the mid-19th century and that the church was functioning. Fellows also noted that St. Nicholas was revered here more highly than St. Peter.[134]

In 1842 a professor of natural science, Edward Forbes, and his assistant Lieutenant Thomas A. B. Spratt came to Lycia with the British HMS Beacon. Their diaries show that they were mainly concerned with the archaeological remains. They reach Demre by following the

126 Güçlü 2010, p. 310.
127 Güçlü 2010, p. 312 and the table at p. 313.
128 Güçlü 2010, pp. 314, 316.
129 Güçlü 2010, p. 315.
130 Bulgurlu 2010, pp. 273–291.
131 Beaufort 1818, p. 31.
132 Fellows 1852, pp. 355–358.
133 Fellows 1852, p. 360.
134 Fellows 1852, p. 360.

Myros valley from Kasaba.[135] There they visited the theater, the rock-cut tombs, the acropolis, Andriake, and Sura, and examined the ruins.[136] However, because they do not mention the small church, the subject of this publication, this shows that they could not see Alakent Church at that time because it was entirely buried in alluvium. Forbes and Spratt also visit the Church of St. Nicholas. According to their accounts, the "monastery" was surrounded by a rectangular perimeter wall. The priest and his family were residing there. In the evening they attended a service that they were invited to. They note that since the tolling of bells was banned by the Turcs, a hanging log was used instead of a bell. They joined a congregation of fifteen men, women, and children at the church.[137] This information gives us an idea of the Christian presence in Demre in the mid-19th century.

Professor Otto Benndorf, the Chair of Archaeology at the University of Vienna, arrived in the region in 1892. As far as we could trace from the album of Captain Ernst Krickl, who joined the Expedition of Asia Minor as a painter and photographer, they set out by sea. During their trip in Lycia they visited Xanthos, Letoon, Patara, Kaş, and Kasaba. They then followed the mountain routes via Arneai and Arykanda to descend to Kumluca without paying a visit to Demre,[138] proving that Demre was not an important settlement in the 19th century. During this tour Benndorf cut off and removed the relief frieze on the monument of Trysa and shipped it to Vienna.[139]

Within the framework of the new administrative arrangements carried out in the initial years of the Republic, once again *Kale Nahiyesi* (Demre) was incorporated into the sub-district of Kaş. Kaş and Finike were mentioned as the two most important ports of the Lycian region.[140] In 1987 *Kale Nahiyesi* was designated to become a *kaza* (subdistrict), and in 2005 it was re-named Demre.[141]

The deep gravel shore now known as Taşdibi, east of the cape of Kum Burnu and located two kilometers south of Myra, most probably has been used as the harbor of Myra since the port of Andriake was abandoned after the 7th century. The pilgrims who came to Myra by sea throughout the Middle Ages to visit the Church of St. Nicholas must have used the harbor of Taşdibi as well.[142] As far as we understand from the travelogue of Fellows, in the mid-19th century the logs harvested from the Taurus were transported to the coast by the Myros creek, which flows strongly in winters, and probably exported from the Taşdibi harbor. As Fellows left Myra and headed east towards Finike, he crossed over the creek and saw hundreds of logs being carried down by the river.[143] The pier at Taşdibi was actively used in the sea transportation of Demre until the middle of 20th century.[144] Besides, there was no proper motor way linking Myra to Finike and Antalya, until the 1970s.[145] The only remains of a harbor at Taşdibi today is the base of a lighthouse located on a cliff to the west.[146] A cubical

135 For the diaries of Demre, see Spratt and Forbes 1847, pp. 125–133.

136 Spratt and Forbes 1847, pp. 130–133.

137 Spratt and Forbes 1847, p. 127.

138 Krickl 2005, Album I and II, pp. 75–145.

139 Çevik 2015, pp. 342–343.

140 Güçlü 2010, pp. 315–316.

141 Güçlü 2010, p. 316.

142 Hellenkemper and Hild 2004, p. 290.

143 Fellows 1852, p. 361.

144 Duggan and Aygün 2010, p. 168.

145 Duggan and Aygün 2010, p. 168.

146 For the ruins of the lighthouse, see Duggan and Aygün 2010, pp. 163–165, Fig. 3–9. The authors identify these

base of stone masonry has survived, with traces of a tower with a cylindrical shaft on top of it. On the other hand, there are inhabitants of Demre who do recall a customs building at this location until recently. Here the water is deep, and the rocky coast to the west provides a sheltered spot from the sea.

The small church close to the theater of Myra, which had persevered until the beginning of the 14th century, is the last Byzantine remain that can be identified in the region.[147] In light of the archaeological data obtained from the excavations, this structure was buried under the silt that covered the city of Myra by the end of the 13th century or the beginning of the 14th century. Although the Church of St. Nicholas was also buried in silt probably up to the level of its gallery, it was never abandoned and kept attracting visitors and pilgrims in that state.[148] Considering that a church like this could be built in Myra and be in use until the disaster of flood which engulfed the city and caused its abandonment in the beginning of the 14th century, a substantial Christian population must have lived in Myra until the final days of the city. After the city was buried under the silt, some of this population would have settled in the acropolis, while others would have migrated. The acropolis of Myra is to the north of the city on a high and steep hill with rock-cut tombs on its skirts. Surrounded by walls, access to the acropolis is by the ancient road on the southern slope. The walls of the acropolis were used from the Hellenistic period to the Ottoman period, and the last phase of construction of these walls dates to the Byzantine period,[149] probably to the 7th or 8th centuries when the Arab navy was attacking the Mediterranean coasts. They were later renovated in the 12th century.[150] Some of the population might have migrated, but it is also possible that a large part was assimilated by being Islamized in the process. Especially since the 12th century, the assimilation of the local Christian population in Anatolia through Islamization was very common.[151]

Since the city of Myra is completely under alluvium today, there is a lack of satisfactory archaeological data on the physical structure and dimensions of the city.[152] Despite this shortage of physical data, through a combination of the study of ancient literature, field observations, sounding results, and a variety of research techniques, a significant amount of data on the breadth of the invisible presence of the city was gathered.[153] Additionally, the remains of the harbor settlement of Andriake, as well as the numerous, high-quality architectural structures in the mountainous sections, provide us with an idea about the population and size of the city of Myra. The period sources on the region of Lycia in general, and especially on Myra during the Medieval times, are truly insufficient. The history of the city could only become clearer by means of further archaeological data. For instance, no information either in Byzantine sources or other contemporaneous sources can be found about the alluvial deposits that were probably carried by powerful flood surges to cover the entire settlement in Myra. However, the excavations both

---

remains as a *manar* from the Seljuk period, but the ruins themselves are far from confirming this.

147 Akyürek 2010; Akyürek 2015a; Çevik 2015, p. 374.

148 Harrison 1963, p. 124.

149 For the acropolis of Myra, see Borchhardt 1975, pp. 45–47; Feld 1975, pp. 398–400, "Die Akropolis in christlicher Zeit"; Çevik 2015, pp. 365–366; Çevik and Bulut 2010, p. 32. For the walls of the acropolis, see Peschlow 1996.

150 Foss 1991a, p. 1428.

151 Vryonis 1975, p. 59.

152 The archaeogeophysical surveys conducted as part of the Myra–Andriake Excavations between 2009–2011 have shown that the ancient city stretches between the Roman theater in the north and the Church of St. Nicholas in the south. See Çevik 2015, p. 364.

153 See Çevik 2010b.

at the Church of St. Nicholas and at Alakent Church have shown that the stratum of culture beneath the approximately 5-meter deep silt[154] consistently ended around the beginning of the 14th century. The coin bearing the latest date in the excavations at the Church of St. Nicholas belongs to the period of Izzeddin Kaykaus II (1240–1250).[155] And the stratum of culture on top of the silt begins in the 18th century. Since the upper stratum at the Alakent Church excavation was scraped off during the modern era, no information was available on the stratigraphy of the layers above the alluvium. Therefore it would be possible to understand what cultural strata existed between the 14th century and today through excavations that might be carried out in other parts of the city. When did this alluvial flood happen? Why is a natural catastrophe of the dimension to cause a city to be abandoned not mentioned in any source? How long did it take for the entire city to be buried under the silt? These and other similar questions that could be posed about this final period of Byzantine Myra could only be answered by archaeological and geomorphological studies to be carried out. As a matter of fact, the Alakent Church excavations have managed to unveil the curtain of obscurity a little further in this regard. We now know that the last use of the church dates the end of the 13th century and the beginning of the 14th century. With new excavations to be carried out in Myra and as other parts of the city are unearthed, these questions too will be answered, and the history and morphology of the city of Myra will be better understood.

The List of the Bishops of Myra[156]

1. Nikander, 1st century, first bishop of Myra, made priest together with Ermaios by the Apostle Paul. Martyred and died after many tortures according to his martyrologion (source: Vita of Nikander).
2. Nicholas of Myron?[157]
3. St. Nicholas of Myra, 6 December 330.
4. Tatian, May–July 381.
5. Eretianos or Seretianos, June–July 431.
6. Romanos, 8 August 449–October 451.
7. Peter, 457–?
8. Modestos,* 6th century (source: inscription from Church of St. Nicholas in Demre).
9. Nicholas,* 6th century.
10. Theodore,* 536–541.
11. Philip, 5 May–2 June 553.
12. Anastasios,* 7th century.
13. Theodore, (?)* 7th century.
14. Nicholas,* 646–?
15. Polyeuktos, 16 September 681–?
16. Theophilos, 8th century or 754 (according to Prof. S.Y. Ötüken).

---

154 The depth of the silt differs according to the original topography: While it is 5-6 meters at the Church of St. Nicholas, it reaches well over 9 meters to the south of the theater.

155 Ötüken 2006a, p. 523.

156 The list is after Dr. Khrysostomos Kalaycı, the current Metropolitan of Myra (Kalaycı 2002, pp. 103–113). Those marked with an asterisk (*) are after S. Yıldız Ötüken. Because our aim was to provide only a list of the bishops of Myra, any other information except their name, date of office, and source of the information was excluded.

157 Myron accompanying name in the original text is Myra.

17. Theodore, 13 October 787.
18. Niketas,* 821–825.
19. Nicholas, 28 February 870–?
20. Theodosios, November 879–?
21. Ignatios, 10th century.
22. Basil,* 10th century.
23. Christopher, 10th century.
24. George, 10th–11th century.
25. (name unknown), 12 September 1019–?[158]
26. Timotheos, 10th–11th century.
27. Michael,* 1030–?
28. Leo, July 1054–?
29. Demetrios, 1071–1079.
30. Constantine,* 1079–?
31. George,* 11th century.
32. Nicholas,* 11th–12th century.
33. Theodore II, 22 February 1144.
34. (name unknown),* 1151–1153.
35. (name unknown),* 1156–?
36. Nicholas, 11th–12th century.
37. Christopher II, 20 March / 6 April 1166 – 6 May 1166 or July 1167.
38. John, 12th–13th century.
39. Eustathios,* 1143–1180 (did not assume his seat due to Turkish occupation).
    1200–1275 there is no evidence of Metropolitan of Myra.
40. Luke, April 1283–25 June 1310.
41. Arsenios,* 1352–1354.
42. (name unknown),* 1354–1364.
43. Dionysios,* 1364–?
44. Matthew, 20 June 1388 – January 1394.
45. (name unknown),* 22 March 1394.
46. (name unknown),* 1397–? (Last Metropolitan for the Middle Ages).
47. Gregory,[159] 1467–?
48. Matthew, 1596–?
49. Matthew, 1614–?
50. Jeremiah (Bores) 1633–1637.
51. Jeremiah (Preacher), 1644–? (Source: patriarchal letter, with patriarchal sigillion of 1651 Myra was given to the Metropolis of Pisidia, along with Side and Attaleia).
52. Silvester, 1659–? (Source: patriarchal catalogues, in the Catalogues of the Patriarchate he is mentioned in 1659 as "of Myra and Attaleia – vol. Γ", Manuscripts of the Theological School of Chalki, Catalogue of Aimilianos Tsakopoulos, p. 217).

---

158 In the sources we know there was a bishop, but his name is unknown.

159 The name was added to the list by Dr. Kalaycı during our meeting.

53. John, 1785–1792.
54. Benjamin, March 1817–? (Titular bishop;[160] source: Patriarchal Catalogues) *Codex of Patriarchal Correspondence,* vol. Θ΄, p. 372).
55. Anthemios, August 1833–? (Source: Patriarchal Catalogues; *Codex of Patriarchal Correspondence,* vol. ΙΔ΄, p. 226).
56. Chrysanthos, April 1834–? (Titular bishop; source: Patriarchal Catalogues, *Codex of Patriarchal Correspondence,* vol. ΙΔ΄, p. 233).
57. Gennadios, April 1857–1858 (Titular bishop; source:Patriarchal Catalogues, *Codex of Patriarchal Correspondence,* vol. ΚΒ΄, p. 323).
58. Jeremiah, 13 February 1860–? (Titular bishop; source: Patriarchal Catalogues, *Codex of Patriarchal Correspondence,* vol. ΚΒ΄, p. 359, and *Codex of Patriarchal Correspondence,* vol. ΛΓ΄, p. 116).
59. Cyril, 1870–? (Titular bishop; source: Patriarchal Catalogues).
60. Agathangelos (Stefanakis), 24 March 1875–? (Titular bishop; source: Patriarchal Catalogues, *Codex of Patriarchal Correspondence,* vol. ΞΖ΄, p. 160).
61. Ambrose (Kondos), 23 June 1880–26 August 1881[161] (Titular bishop; source: Patriarchal Catalogues, *Codex of Patriarchal Correspondence,* vol. ΞΖ΄, p. 238).
62. Gregory (Zerboudakis), 1 August 1887–1892 (Titular bishop; source: Patriarchal Catalogues, *Codex of Patriarchal Correspondence,* vol. ΞΖ΄, p. 346).
63. Germanos (Theotokas), 19 June 1893–? (Titular bishop; source: Patriarchal Catalogues, *Codex of Patriarchal Correspondence,* vol. ΞΖ΄, p. 451).
64. Stephen (Danielides) 19 February 1902–1903 (Titular bishop; source: Patriarchal Catalogues, *Codex of Patriarchal Correspondence,* vol. ΠΙΑ΄, p. 91).
65. Athanasios (Laskaris), 23 May 1905–? (Titular bishop; source: Patriarchal Catalogues, *Codex of Patriarchal Correspondence,* vol. ΠΙΑ΄, p. 134).
66. Alexander (Delanas), 22 June 1910–? (Titular bishop; source: Patriarchal Catalogues, *Codex of Patriarchal Correspondence,* vol. ΠΙΑ΄, p. 220).
67. Philotheos (Loukides), 22 December 1916–1924(?) (Titular bishop; source: Patriarchal Catalogues, *Codex of Patriarchal Correspondence,* vol. ΠΙΑ΄, p. 309).
68. Polykarpos (Demetriades), 17 December 1927–8 January 1936 (Titular bishop; source: Patriarchal Catalogues, *Codex of Patriarchal Correspondence,* vol. ΠΙΒ΄, p. 92).
69. Chrysostom I (Aimilios Constantinides), 1961–8 March 1990 (Titular bishop).
70. Chrysostom II (Kalaitzes), 14 November 1995– (Titular bishop).

160 He held the title of bishop but did not practically officiate in his see.

161 The date, 26 August 1881, was added to the list by Dr. Kalycı during our meeting.

Figure 1: Map of ancient Lycia, (TIB 8)

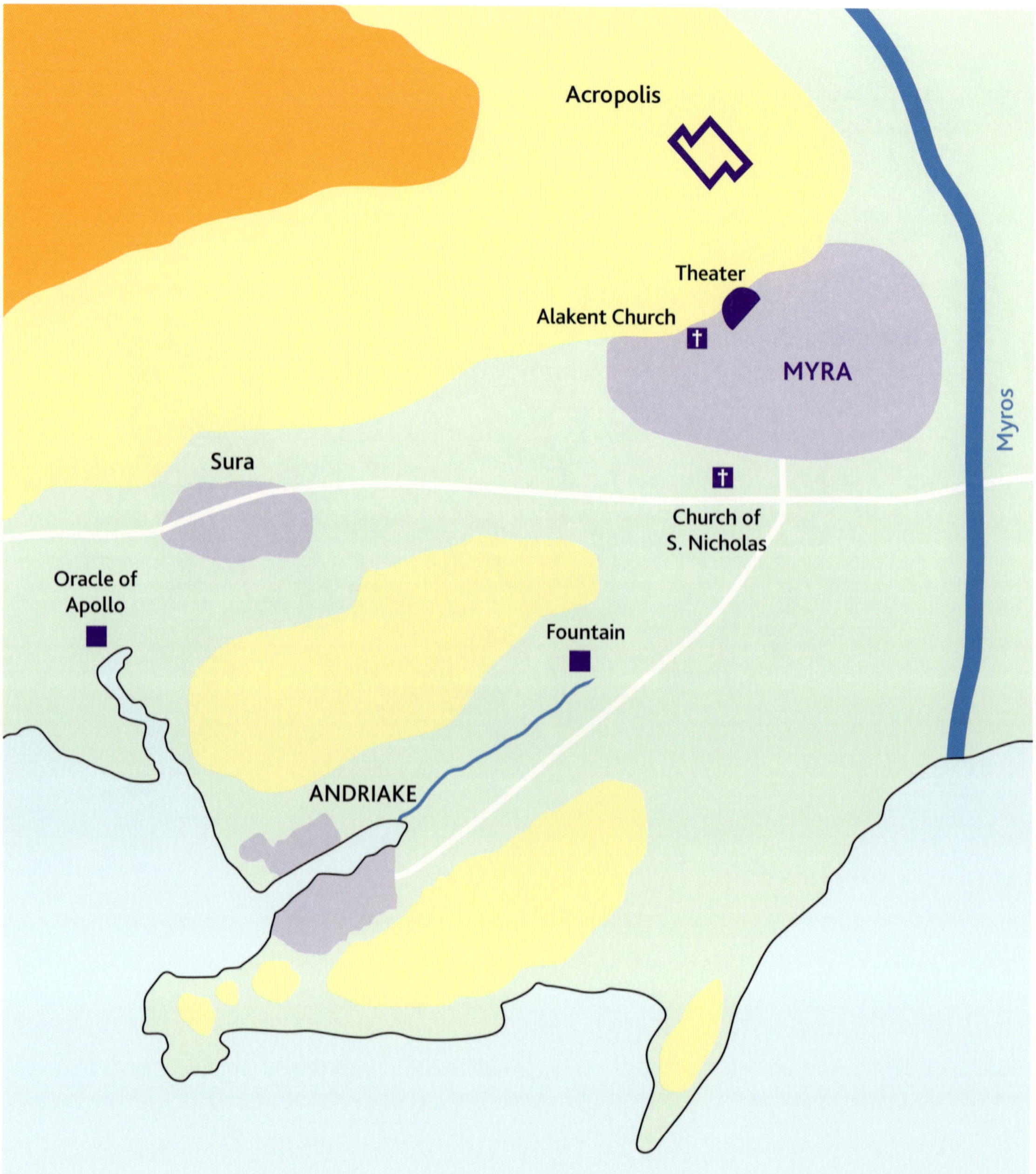

Figure 2: Myra settlement in Byzantine era

III.
Alakent Church: Location and Architecture

Engin Akyürek
Koç University

1. Location and Surroundings

Alakent Church is located in the district of Demre of Antalya province at the Alakent neighborhood for which it was named. The road extending north from the center of town of Demre, where the Museum of the Church of St. Nicholas is located, turns westwards after two kilometers and heads towards the center of the ancient city where the ancient theater and rock-cut tombs are located on the southern skirts of the acropolis. Continuing west along Alikahyalar Street, not taking the route that leads to the entrance of the theater to the north of the road, after about 130 meters Alakent Church is visible on the right. The church is located at the coordinates of 36°15’25.08” North, 29°59’5.04” East. The building sits 1500 meters straight north of the Church of St. Nicholas in Demre’s town center, and 200 meters directly southwest from the ancient theater. (Figure 1)

Matarlar Street, which is a blind alley perpendicular to Alikahyalar Street and intersects it to the west of the church, continues north and arrives at the area of greenhouses. The stream bed that follows the northern edge of Alikahyalar Street turns northwest as it draws near Matarlar Street. Passing under Matarlar Street, it heads west once again. Thus, Alikahyalar and Matarlar Streets and the stream bed that intersect it form a triangular area. The church is located on plot no. 1625 at the corner of the intersection of Alikahyalar Street and Matarlar Street. Although this piece of land is private property, it is not suitable for agricultural use since it is partially in the stream bed. Because it is a First-Degree Archaeological Site, any building activity on the plot is prohibited. For this reason, the plot has remained empty, and to a certain degree, been used as a dumping ground that also contains greenhouse wastes.

Because Matarlar Street passed over the western part of the church and its narthex, it was moved to the east of the building during the excavation process. The western side of the church was bounded by a residential building. The western wall of the narthex was located exactly under the border of the garden wall to the east of this house. For this reason, the excavation continued up to the inside face of the western wall at the narthex, but the outer side of the wall could not be reached. To the north of the building in the area all the way up to the slope where the rock-cut tombs are located –except for a small shed on the opposite side of Matarlar Street– there are greenhouses. After passing from the east and the north of the church and continuing northbound for approximately 200 meters, Matarlar Street comes to an end. There are greenhouses and a few sheds that are not constantly occupied on both sides of this dirt road. However, at the end of the dead-end street, there are a few buildings used for residential purposes. The southern side of Alikahyalar Street, passing from the south side of the church, is presently a settlement area.

The stream bed that follows the northern side of the road along Alikahyalar Street passes from the front of the apse on the east side of the church and continues northward. Running along the north side of the building, it carries on its westward journey. Today the stream bed acts as a flood channel that only has water flowing in it during the rainy seasons. According to data obtained from the excavations, this used to be a stream flowing in front of the apse before the area was covered with alluvial deposits. It was understood that some measures have been taken at the church to protect it from the floods of this stream. As the area was filled with alluvium and the ground level rose, the bed of the stream had also risen and was transformed into a water channel that has run at the roof level of the church in recent times. Today, during times of heavy rainfall, the quantity and intensity of the water flowing from this channel also increases. When the two drainage pipes under Matarlar Street through which the canal passes becomes clogged with waste, the neighborhood gets flooded. Although the risk has been reduced with the newly built channel to the east of the church, the problem of clogging persists because the rest of the channel still remains in its old bed. From time to time the layers of alluvium covering the building were partially washed away due to the intensity of the currents –especially in the northeast corner– and these parts of the structure became visible. Today, as part of the excavation program, the stream was moved away from the church to the east and was contained in a reinforced concrete channel 3.80 m wide and 2.30 m deep. And Matarlar Street, previously passing above the western side of the church, was rerouted to pass over this channel.

The core of the ancient city was located around the theater to the south of the acropolis with the rock-cut tombs on its slopes. The city spread mainly between the ancient theater and the Church of St. Nicholas to the south. The archeogeophysical studies carried out within Myra–Andriake Excavations have shown that the density of buildings were higher on the south side of the acropolis and around the theater.[1] Without a doubt, this area was the center of Byzantine Myra extending from the Church of St. Nicholas northward to the slopes of the acropolis. The fact that Alakent Church is located in this center indicates that it was one of the important buildings of Myra in the 12th–13th centuries. However, to learn more about the historical surroundings of the church, it was necessary to excavate a large area to the south and southwest of the theater.

1 Çevik 2015, pp. 363–364.

Figure 1: Location of Alakent Church relative to the Roman theater

2. Architecture

2.1. Naos: Plan and Structural Features

Alakent Church is a small church with a length of 12.73 m and a width of 5.50 m including the narthex. The single-naved naos is covered with a dome in the middle. (Drawing 1, 2 and 3) The narthex was added to the church at a later date, and is completely different from the naos in terms of masonry. The church, which was buried under alluvium up to the level of the dome, survived in a well-preserved state with its walls, its vaults up to the level of the dome, and its liturgical elements. (Figures 2 and 3)

The length of the external measurement of the naos is 8.90 m, the internal measurement is 7.30 m including the apse; its internal width is 4.02 m, and the depth of the apse is 1.30 m. The apse protrudes outwards, and is semi-circular both inside and outside. The central part of the single-naved naos is covered with a dome with an internal diameter of approximately 3.40 m. The central dome of the rectangular naos is supported by arches on top of piers abutting the walls. However, the two arches in the east and west were extended in the shape of a barrel vault, creating a longitudinal rectangular space. While the arches in the north and south are about 30 cm wide, the eastern arch (or the bema vault) is about 1.15 m wide and the western vault is about 1.50 m wide. The arches and vaults rest on corner piers that protrude approximately 30 cm from the walls of the naos. These piers continue along the barrel vaults to the east and the west, all the way to the walls at each direction. Thus, the wall thickness at these corners would reach approximately 1 m and have enough mass to bear the lateral loads of the roof. Pendentives were used in the four corners as transition elements to the dome. The dome, which could not survive as it was above the present-day ground level, was probably resting on a tall drum[2] with a sequence of windows, in line with the architectural characteristics of the period. (Drawing 6) The fact that all the windows on the main walls were bricked up in the final phase of the building indicates that the windows on the drum were the sole light source illuminating the naos.

A remarkable element in the architectural structure of Alakent Church is the use of pointed arches in the building. The four arches supporting the dome, the arch of the apse, and the arches of both windows were constructed as slightly pointed arches.

The structure type in which the dome covering the naos is supported by arches abutted to the inner walls and resting on four corner piers is often referred to as a ciborium-type plan in related literature.[3] Although some researchers have defined this plan type as a variant form of the cross plan,[4] the fact that the dome is supported by four corner piers connected to each other by arches substantiates the thought that it would be more accurate to call it a ciborium-type plan.[5] It would not be correct to accept the "cross plan" definition when the arches supporting the dome are too narrow to be perceived as a cross.

However, the fact that the arches in the east and the west parts of Alakent Church have been extended, lending an elongated rectangular plan to the structure, steers it away from the

2 In Middle Byzantine domed churches, the dome rests on a tall drum with a row of windows, although there are exceptions. See Ousterhout 1999, pp. 208, 214.

3 Eyice defines ciborium as a space that has a dome supported by four piers connected to each other with arches; see Eyice 1980, pp. 46, 109.

4 Ousterhout 1987, p. 38. In another publication, Ousterhout uses the term "atrophied Greek cross" with reference to Kariye: Ousterhout 1999, p. 97.

5 Eyice 1980, p. 46.

ciborium plan type. The ciborium definition would be more appropriate for structures such as the Chora Church at Istanbul, where the naos is in the form of a square or approximately a square. Buildings where a rectangular nave is covered with a single dome are more accurately defined as "single-naved domed" structures.[6] It would be more appropriate to categorize Alakent Church under this plan type. Extending the east and west arches in these directions was chosen as a means of expanding the building along the east–west axis without enlarging the size of the dome, and having to deal with structural problems that would arise from a large dome. Thus, the plan type that looks like a ciborium in terms of the logic of the structural design was transformed into another architectural plan. Although studying Byzantine religious architecture through typological categories proves easier for researchers, the accepted structural types should not be considered as patterns exactly repeatable in each and every instance. Otherwise it would become difficult to explain the rich diversity of Byzantine architecture and the variations between the structures considered to have the same plan type.

In the interior space, an ornamented stone cornice at 2.19 m above the floor level extends along the piers abutted to the walls. The cornices indicate the beginning of the arches/vaults that support the dome, and they do not appear on the surfaces of the walls other than the piers on which the arches rest. While there is no original window opening on the northern wall of the naos (Figure 4, Drawing 3), there is a large window with a pointed arch in the middle of the southern wall, starting at 1.46 m above the floor level and with a height of 1.33 m. (Figure 5, Drawing 2) It is possible to observe that the window was initially divided into two narrow windows with the use of a mullion, and that these two windows were completely bricked up at a later date. (Figure 6) Likewise, another small window opening with a pointed arch at the apse was also subsequently bricked up. On the western wall of the church there is a door with a height of 2.24 m and a width of 1.05 m, providing access from the narthex into the naos. (Drawing 4, Figures 3 and 7).

The average wall thickness is 0.70 m. Reinforced by four long corner piers and with the added benefits of a modest scale, these walls provide a statically balanced and robust structure. The walls were built with small rubble, with occasional use of ashlar, and with horizontal rows of broken tiles and brick –although not forming regular rows– placed between layers of stone. Even though pieces of tile/brick were used vertically between some stones, to mention the use of a proper *cloisonné* technique would be incorrect. (Figure 8) The pendentives were made entirely of bricks, (Figure 9) and then plastered and decorated with frescoes. Immediately above the cornice, at approximately 2.30 m above the floor level, the beam slots at the springing points of the arches could have been used for the wooden scaffoldings built to aid the workers during construction[7] or for wooden beams used to reinforce the walls and the arches.[8] (Figure 10) Since the region is prone to frequent major earthquakes, the use of wooden beams in wall masonry and arches was an important technique of reinforcement.

Similar small-scale, single-naved domed churches with a plan type like Alakent Church were becoming widespread in Cyprus, which had close links to Myra, especially during the 12th century and later.[9] One of the plan types resembling the naos of Alakent Church in Anatolia is

6 Buildings with a similar plan were defined as "the domed hall-church" by Megaw and Hawkins, 1962, p. 281.

7 Ousterhout 1999, pp. 184–188, Fig. 148.

8 In Byzantine architecture, wooden beams were used both in walls and at arches. The metal beams that we see in some structures today were introduced instead of the wooden beams in the modern era. See Ousterhout 1999, pp. 210–212.

9 Stylianou and Stylianou 1997, p. 422; Erel 2010, p. 381.

the Church of St. Abercius at Kurşunlu (Elegmi) in the Marmara Region.[10] Abercius, which is a single-naved structure, is covered by a dome of 5 m diameter, supported by pendentives resting on four corner piers connected to each other by arches. The western arch was built wider than the other three, slightly extending the space of the naos. However, with a difference, the plan of Abercius has protruding *pastaphoria* chambers.[11] Mango dated this building to the Komnenian period in the second half of the 12th century (1162).[12]

We see many examples of the single-naved domed plan type from the second half of the 12th century onwards in Cyprus. The Church of the Holy Apostles in Perachorio, an example very similar to Alakent Church, is dated later than 1150.[13] What makes this plan so similar to Alakent Church is that of its four arches supporting the dome, the western and eastern arches were extended as vaults, and the other two arches were built adjacent to the north and south walls.[14] However, what differs from Alakent Church is that, as an exception to the Byzantine churches, it has no drum below the dome.[15] The building is illuminated by a triple apse window and the large windows on the side walls. A more typical example of this plan type in Cyprus is the Church of Panagia tou Arakou in Lagoudera. The church, dated to 1192, constitutes a close parallel to Alakent Church not only because of its plan[16] but also because of its blunt pointed arches.[17] A tall-drummed dome rests on top of two blunt pointed arches adjacent to the northern and southern walls of the structure and on the eastern and western vaults. If we were to introduce a few other buildings in Cyprus that are counterparts of Alakent Church, we could consider mentioning the Church of Archangel Michael in Lefkara (second half of the 12th century)[18] and the Church of St. Euphemia in Lysi (early 14th century)[19] among them. Both churches are small-scale, rectangular-planned, single-naved structures.

The use of blunt pointed arches, such as the ones found in Alakent Church, began in the architecture of Cyprus towards the end of the 12th century and continued to be used later.[20] The churches of Panagia tou Arakou, Archangel Michael, and St. Euphemia, mentioned earlier, also have used such pointed arches. The Church of Panagia Phorbiotissa at Nikitari, dated to the third quarter of the 14th century, is one of the Late Byzantine examples of utilizing pointed arches on the island.[21]

The reduced building sizes and more compact design make sense of the fact that these buildings became more widespread as a precaution against the earthquakes that have caused massive devastation in the area.[22] The piers abutting to the walls –continuing all the way along

10 Mango 1968, pp. 169–172.
11 Mango 1968, p. 170 and Plan A.
12 Mango 1968, p. 172.
13 Megaw and Hawkins 1962, p. 284; Ćurčić 1999, Fig. 18.
14 Megaw and Hawkins 1962, pp. 281–282, Figs. 1–4; Stylianou and Stylianou 1997, pp. 422, 423, Fig. 254.
15 Megaw and Hawkins 1962, p. 283.
16 Stylianou and Stylianou 1997, pp. 158, 181–183, Figs. 99–101. Its difference from Alakent Church in the floor plan is that the wall piers supporting the dome are in the form of pilasters and that they separate the naos into three spatial units. See Winfield and Winfield 2003, pp. 57, 60, also Fig. 10. In the case of Myra, the piers extend all the way to the eastern and western walls.
17 Stylianou and Stylianou 1997, p. 169, Fig 92; Winfield and Winfield 2003, p. 38, also Figs. 3–4, also Plates 1–4.
18 Stylianou and Stylianou 1997, p. 447, Fig. 264.
19 Stylianou and Stylianou 1997, p. 492, Fig. 298.
20 Megaw and Hawkins 1962, p. 284.
21 Stylianou and Stylianou 1997, p. 130, Fig. 65.
22 Ćurčić presents such an evaluation about the Middle Byzantine churches at Cyprus: Ćurčić 1999, pp. 71–80.

the vaults in the east and the west until they reach the corners in both directions– were also designed as a means of strengthening the structural integrity of the building by increasing the thickness of the walls at Alakent Church by 30–35 cm. While the four piers supporting the dome at the Chortani Church in Cyprus, which has a plan type similar to Alakent Church, are in the shape of almost square pilasters that do not extend along the eastern and western walls,[23] the piers at Alakent Church extending along the walls in both directions all the way to the corners should be regarded as additional reinforcement. The use of tall and robust piers fused with the walls adds sturdiness to the structure. The use of blunt pointed arches in buildings also reduces the lateral loads applied to the walls by the canopy in favor of the vertical loads, and reinforces the structural integrity of the building. These practices are of vital importance in the Lycian region located in a particularly significant earthquake zone. The architecture of this region can not be fully comprehended without considering the reality of earthquakes. It is possible to see that this fact was taken into consideration in the architectural design. While churches with a cross-in-square plan type were more common in the Byzantine world during the 11th–12th centuries, in this region single-naved small structures were favored. If the structures had domes, the dome would be supported on piers rather than on single supports such as columns, since this was structurally more reliable. As in the case of Alakent Church, corner piers fused with the walls were opted for as they were deemed a more sound design.

Despite its relatively small dimensions, Alakent Church is one of the important buildings of the city, and architecturally a structure of considerable merit. During the same period (ca. 11th–12th centuries) several single-naved and barrel-vaulted simple churches and chapels, usually of a smaller scale, had been built in the vicinity of Myra. For example, the chapels at Beymelek are typical examples of these structures were generally dated to the 11th–12th centuries.[24] The use of spolia material in the structure is not an indication of it being second-rate. Even in first-class buildings built by the emperor himself, it is possible to see the use of spolia, not only the reuse of valuable architectural elements such as columns and capitals but also ashlar and even bricks.[25]

23 Compare the Alakent Church plan (Drawing 1 in this volume) and the Chortani Church plan; see Ćurčić 1999, Fig. 15.

24 Feld 1975, pp. 360–428, tables 139–140, see pp. 419–424; Hellenkemper and Hild 2004, part 2, 485.

25 For example, in the Monastery Church of Pantocrator built at the capital under the patronage of Emperor John Komnenos in the 12th century, a large number of bricks were used as spolia: Ousterhout 1999, p. 140.

Drawing 1: Floor Plan

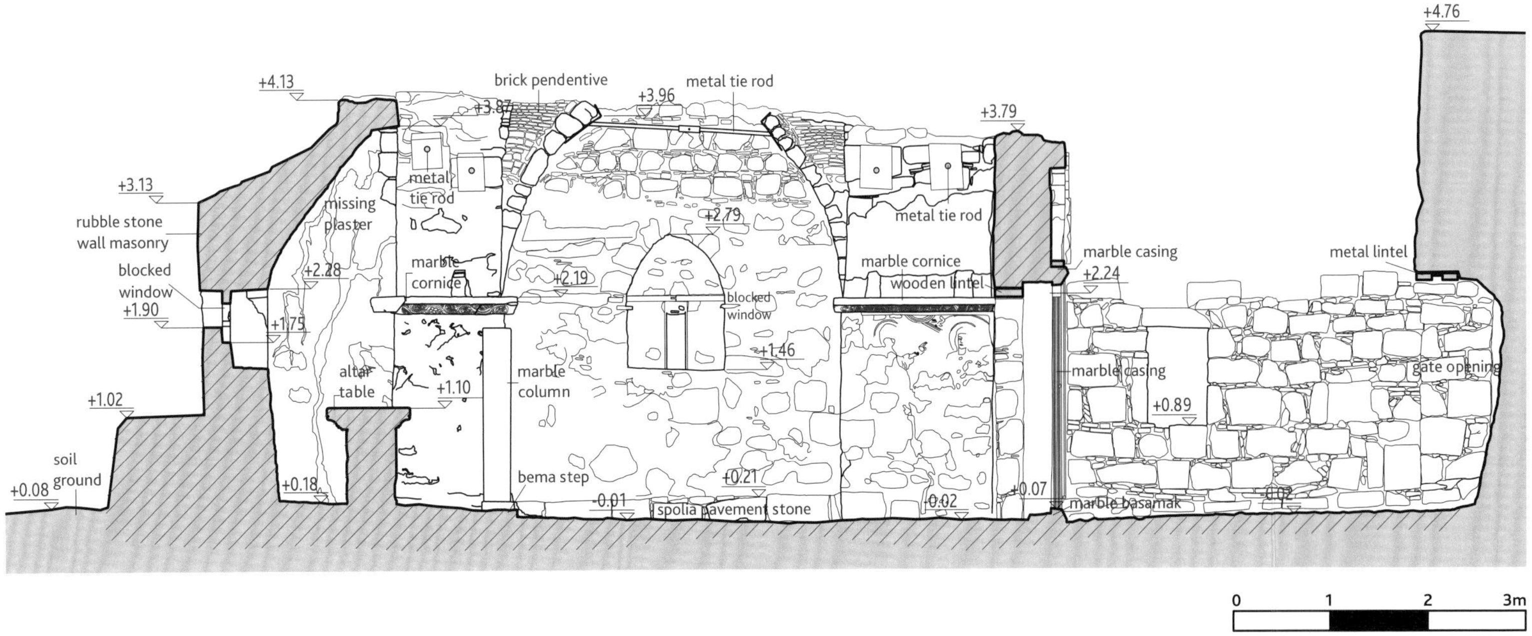

Drawing 2: Section A-A

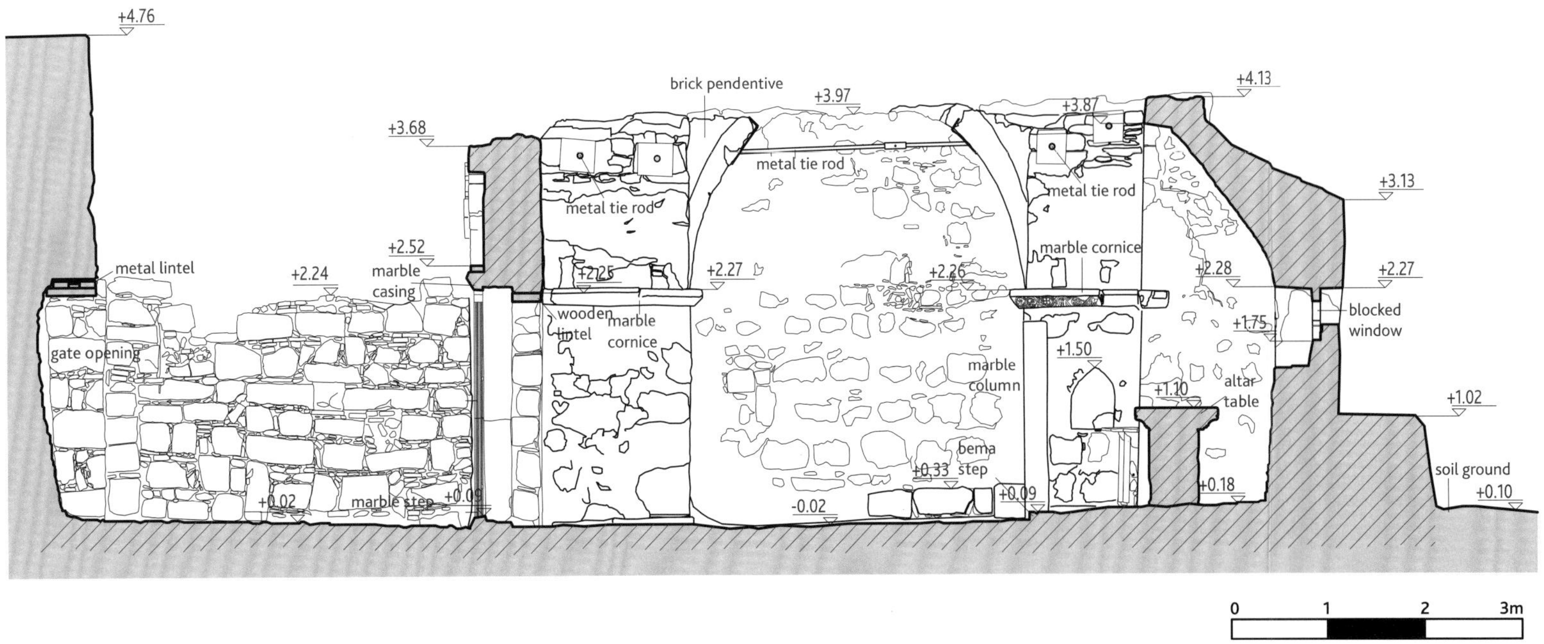

Drawing 3: Section B-B

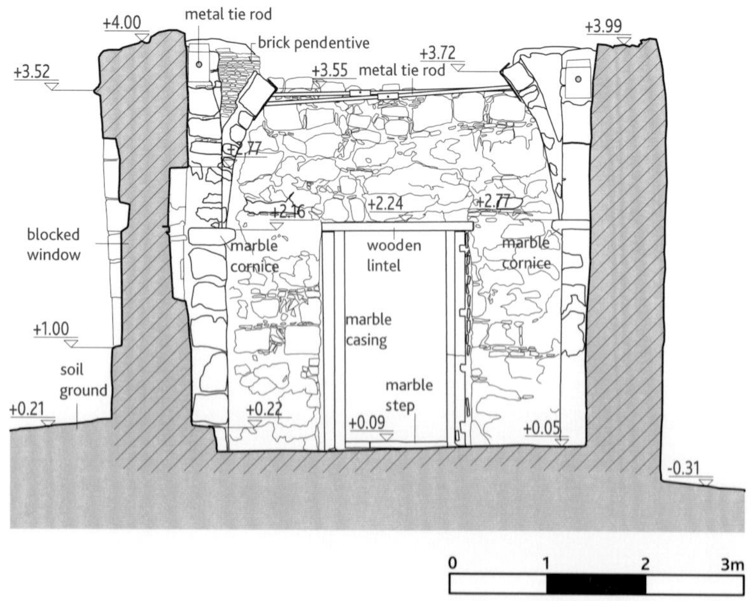

Drawing 4: Section C-C

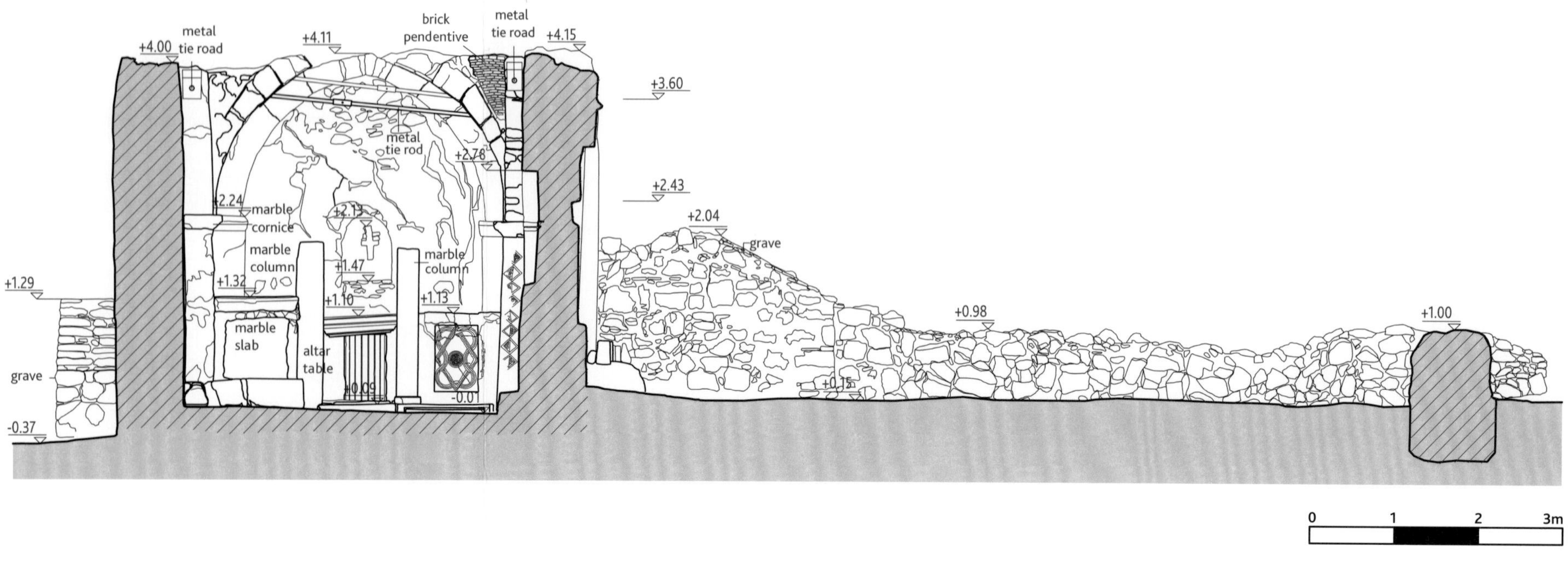

Drawing 5: Section D-D

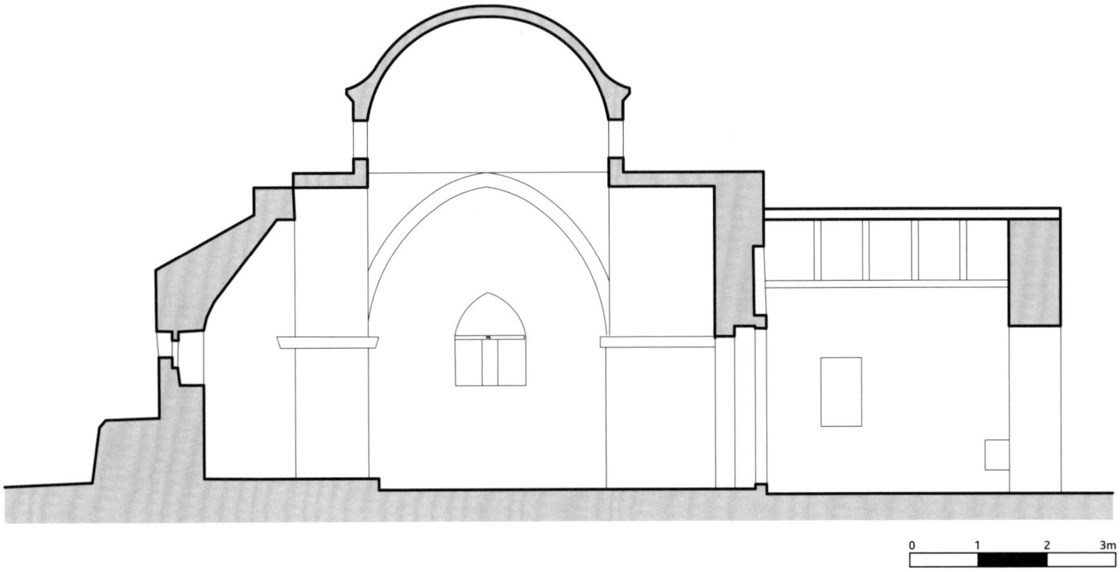

Drawing 6: Section of restitution of Alakent Church (Barış Altan)

Figure 2: Aerial view of Alakent Church

Figure 3: Naos, general view from the narthex

Figure 4: Naos, north wall viewed from inside

Figure 5: Naos, south wall viewed from inside

Figure 6: Southern window, viewed from inside

Figure 7: Naos, west wall viewed from inside

Figure 8: Texture of south wall, viewed from inside

Figure 9: Southeastern pendentive

Figure 10: Wooden beam slots, western part of the south wall

2.2. Roofing System

The naos is covered with a dome in the middle, two vaults on the east and the west, and a semi-dome on the apse. The arches and the vaults supporting the dome have survived except for one or two rows of stones at the top. This level is also the present-day walking level, and the top parts of the arches above the present ground level and the dome were destroyed. One of the important findings of the excavation is that a significant part of the tile roofing covering the arches/ vaults and over the semi-dome of the apse had survived *in situ*. The roof tiles on the northeast and northwest corners of the roof, and especially on the northern end of the eastern arch, were preserved at a better state. (Drawing 7, Figure 11)

In Byzantine architecture, roofs, whether wooden or masonary, were covered with various roofing materials to protect the building from rain as well as the heat of the sun. In buildings of major significance, although rarely large sheets of lead or bronze were used,[26] the roofing usually consisted of various types of roof tiles. These could be terracotta, fine-cut stone, marble, or copper roof tiles.[27] From the numerous roof tile pieces found at excavations, we understand that the vast majority of Byzantine structures were covered with terracotta roof tiles, which were a cheaper material. Based on the finds from excavations, reconstructions of these tile roofing systems have also been put together. However, since roofing on buildings has to be maintained frequently by replacing the roof tiles, the data available on the original roofing of Byzantine structures are very limited.[28] The roof tile coverings of Byzantine structures still in use today are not in their original state, they must have been replaced many times through the centuries. And the roof tiles found in the remains of buildings now in ruins are not found *in situ*, but as broken pieces scattered in the rubble. This situation makes the tile roofing of Alakent Church, which has managed to survive until the present-day in its original state, outstandingly valuable. The Alakent Church roofing is important as it provides information on the choice of the type of roof tiles, as well as the way the tiles were fixed in place in their original state.

Three types of roof tiles were used at the roof of Alakent Church. The first type are slightly curved, large rectangular tiles. According to measurements taken from intact specimens found in the northeast corner, these roof tiles have a length of 55 cm, a width of 33 cm, and a thickness of 1.7 cm. The thickness of the shorter sides was increased up to 2.2 cm to create a rounded flange. These flanges allowed the tiles to be held together on the sloped surface of the roof. In the middle of the tile is a groove (channel?) going all the way from the top of the tile to the bottom, most likely made by a finger when the tile was still wet. This application might have been done to facilitate the flow of water. There is a wavy line made with a sharp tool on either side of this groove. (Figure 12) This was done to let the tiles better bond with the mortar bed below. These roof tiles were placed side by side, without any gaps, following the direction of the slope of the roof, on top of a layer of mortar of about 4–5 cm thick. Each tile overlaps nearly 5 cm over the next tile placed below it.

The second type of roof tiles are roughly in the shape of a ⌃. However, their top parts are not pointed but flattened to a 1.5–2 cm ridge. (Figure 13) These tiles were placed all the way from the top of the roof to the bottom, on top of the lines where the slightly curved first type of tiles meet. These tiles, which are approximately 50–55 cm long, 17 cm wide, and 1.2 cm thick,

26 Ousterhout 1999, pp. 148–149.

27 Loerke 1991, pp. 1812–1813; Ousterhout 1999, p. 147.

28 Ousterhout 1999, pp. 147–148.

have a cavity depth of 5.5–6 cm on their concave side. They are placed from top to bottom, each overlapping a few centimeters on the tile below.

The third type are in the shape of a rectangular prism and resemble a brick. This type of tiles was identified in use in the roofing of the apse and the western vault (especially on its northern part). In these locations these tiles (bricks?) were used on top of the first type tiles to cover the adjoining parts, as a substitute for the second-type tiles with which they have approximately the same dimensions, except for their thickness. (Figure 14) This third type of roofing material was probably used as a replacement to repair the tiles of the apse and the western vault.

The roofing system could be observed best on the northeastern corner of the building, and especially on the northern part of the vault on the east side. In this section three rows of flat tiles of the first type, placed side by side along the width of the vault, and two rows of the second type placed between them were preserved *in situ*. (Figure 15) This system continues in four courses laid lengthwise along the vault down to the end of the eave. The tiles that descend down along the vault form an eave overhang by extending a few centimeters over the wall. Although the outward projecting sections of the tiles were broken and the extent of the overhang could not be measured, through a comparison with the length of the tiles that have remained intact, it is possible to propose that the overhang was at least 10 cm. At the western part of the building with a dogtooth eave, the roof tiles were placed to overhang 1–2 cm further than the eave. (Figure 16)

The sections of the roof to be covered with tiles were initially covered with a thick layer of tile fragments and a large amount of mortar as a base. The large tiles of the first type were embedded on top of this base. This is best seen on the eastern side of the north arch. This bed of tile fragments and mortar was used to fix the tiles in place and to even the surface of the roof to be covered. The second type of tiles were placed on a layer of mortar which was raised about 5–6 cm. Sometimes under one tile there was a second tile –usually one that was broken– which might have been utilized to render the mortar layer underneath this second type of tile thicker, essentially to raise the roof tile on top. (Figure 13) On the northern part of the western vault the mortar layer was raised by placing tiles of the third type (flat prismatic bricks) on a bed of mortar over the adjoining sections of the first type of flat tiles arranged side by side. The practice of raising the second type of tiles must have been an application allowing the formation of a deep water bed on top of the first type of flat tiles, so that water could flow faster. This way, a water channel with a width of at least 20 cm and a depth of 10 cm was formed on top of the sequence of flat tiles between the two strips of ∧ shaped tiles. Hence, we can see that a roofing system suitable for a geography with abundant and at times vigorous rain was constructed. On the northeastern corner of the roof where the courses of tiles meet a flat wall, a layer of mortar becoming gradually wider as it goes down from the wall to the top of the first type of tiles was applied. This transfered the water flowing from the wall directly onto these tiles. (Figure 17)

The tile roofing system was applied with a slightly different arrangement on the semi-dome of the apse. The tiles were arranged to spread out like a fan as they descend from the top of the apse to the eave. Only a few large tiles identified as the first type have survived *in situ* on the northern and southern sides of the apse roofing, while the rest were completely destroyed or remained as fragments in certain places. However, the mortar beds of the tiles on the apse have remained clearly visible, and from this we could form an idea about its tile roofing system. (Figure 18) Here it could be observed that, besides the first type of large tiles, the brick-like third type of tiles that are flat, rectangular, and thicker, which were also used in the roofing system of the western vault –mainly on the northern side– were used. There are also some remains of the second type ∧ shaped tiles on the southern part of the apse. It is not possible to see how the second and third types were integrated into the roofing system, but it could be assumed that the third type, which were placed over the joints of the first type, were also used here as a replacement for the ∧ shaped tiles, and possibly placed under the ∧ shaped tiles in some places. We should bear in mind that at other parts of the roof a 5–6 cm-high raised bed was put in place under the second type of ∧ shaped tiles.

Considering the tile fragments found during excavations and surveys, this tile roofing system was the most widely used system in Byzantine architecture. This system, still in use in traditional architecture, can also be seen in the architectural depictions in some Byzantine miniatures. A miniature included in the Menologion of Basil II depicts the relics of St. John Chrysostom being brought to Constantinople and buried in the Church of the Holy Apostles. In the miniature the church in the background displays flat and ∧ shaped tiles used in the same system on its dome and vaults.[29] (Figure 19)

The dome and the drum, which have remained above the present-day ground level, were in time completely destroyed after the building was buried under alluvium up to the level of its vaults. This destruction was not due to a natural collapse, but was brought about by the hand of man as these parts remained above the walking level of Demre. During the excavation process, when the interior was cleared of the debris by accessing from the top of the church, the upper layers contained small amounts of stone and tile material that could have belonged to the dome, but no material associated with the dome was found in the lower layers.

29 This miniature is at the Menologion of Basil II in the Vatican, Vat.gr.1613, fol.353.

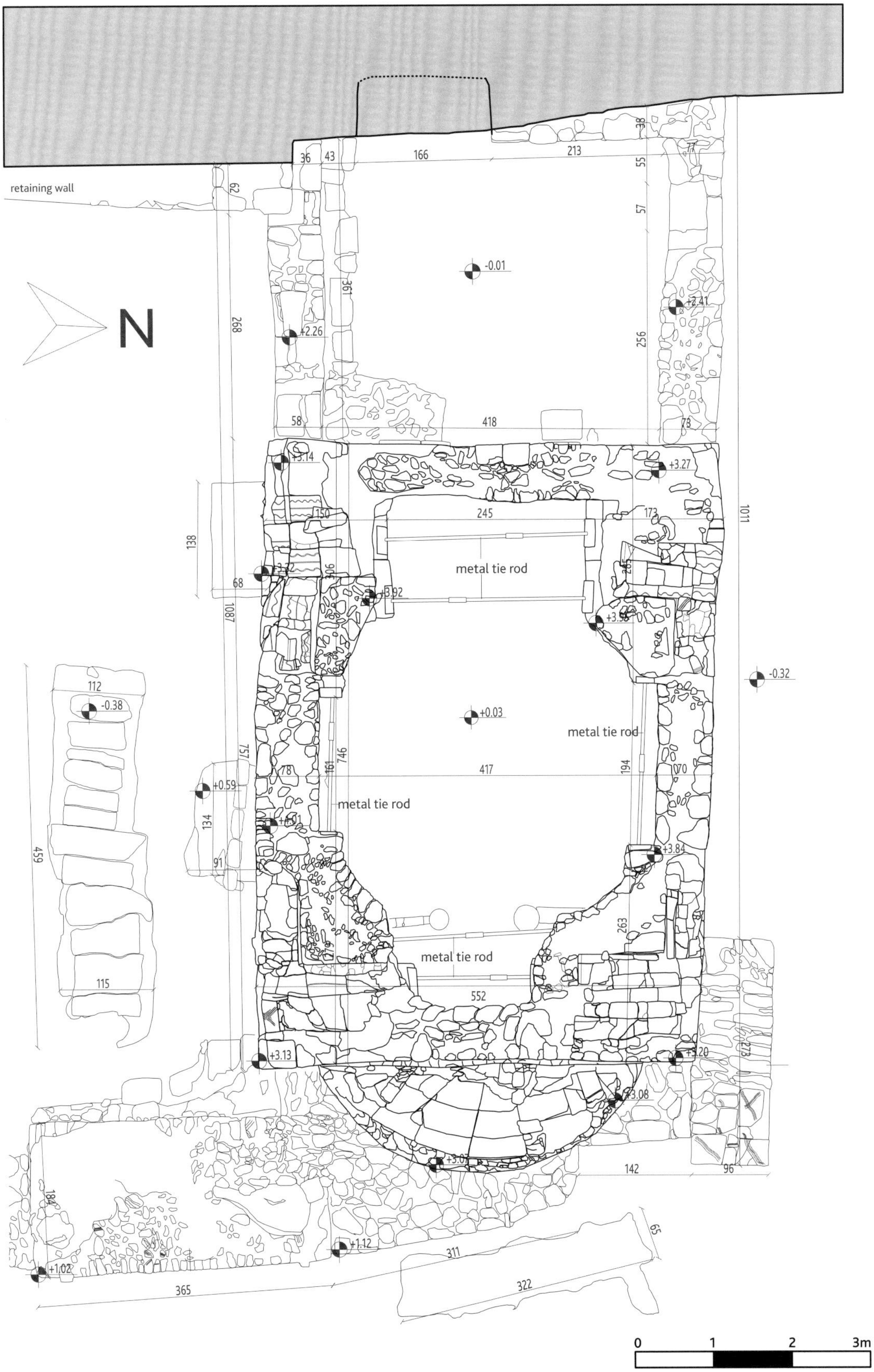

Drawing 7: Plan of the roof level

Figure 11: Tile roofing, northeast corner

Figure 12: Tile roofing, detail

Figure 13: Tile roofing, detail

Figure 14: Tile roofing, northwest corner

Figure 15: Tile roofing, general view from northeast

Figure 16: Dogtooth eave, northwest corner

Figure 17: Tile roofing, detail from northeast

Figure 18: Tile roofing, apse

Figure 19: Moving the relics of St. Chrysostom, Menologion of II. Basil (Vatican Library, Vat. gr. 1613.-f.353r)

2.3. Facades

North Facade

The north facade of the church consists mainly of two sections: the north wall of the naos and the north wall of the narthex on the west. These two walls are different from one another in terms of material and workmanship. A third unit that stands out in the north facade is the arcosolium with a pointed arch attached to the northeastern corner of the church on an east-west axis. (Figure 20)

Interestingly, the north facade of the naos is a bare wall with no window openings. The northern wall of the naos, which was preserved very well under the alluvium, does not even have cracks on it. From the corner where it joins the east wall, at roof level the north wall continues straight for 1.30 m towards the west. From there it follows the curve of the northern arch –one of the four arches supporting the dome. After the 3.40 m span of the arch, it continues along a straight line towards the west for another 1.70 m and meets the northwest corner of the building. At the eastern part of the northern wall the roof level is at 3.25 m, in the middle part at 4.19 m, and in the western part at 3.30 m. This plain wall in the western part was preserved in a good state up to the dogtooth eave.

On both corners of the north wall larger blocks of ashlar were used. The masonry in the remaining parts consists of smaller stones of varying sizes with their exposed surfaces roughly tooled. Nevertheless, it is possible to observe courses in the masonry. Although not very regular, fifteen courses of stone could be distinguished from the top of the wall to the floor. There are also courses of thin brick/tile of at least two rows placed horizontally on the wall from side to side, which are not as regular as a runner beam in appearance. However, these rows are thin and irregular, and hardly distinguishable. One of these runs at 1.30 m above ground level and the other at 2.60 m. Apart from these barely detectable rows, there are also tiles placed haphazardly between the stones. The grout was filled with white lime mortar, and the wide lines of grout also covering some of the stones was preserved almost without any loss. Although there were traces indicating that the north facade was finished with an even layer of plaster, the plaster on the walls did not survive.

The north facade of the narthex has a completely different appearance from the naos. (Drawing 8, Figure 21) This wall is not tied to the wall of naos and is understood to have been attached to the naos at a later date. It was not possible to view its western corner as it was under an existing residential building and could not be excavated. Even though some ashlar blocks – believed to be spolia– were used in the masonry, most of the material consists of partially tooled medium-sized stones and small, irregular rubble. From the top of the wall, eight more or less regular courses of stone could be distinguished. Among the rows of stone, plenty of thin brick and tile fragments, as well as small pieces of stone, were placed in certain spots forming two rows. In some places this material was used to fill the gaps created by stones with chipped corners. In contrast to the naos wall, there is no trace of grout between the stones or plaster on the surface on the exterior facade. There is no door or window opening on this facade; however, there is a section 2.20 m from the corner of the naos wall, 1.10 m in width, and 1.60 m in height which might have been a doorway bricked up at a later date. The absence of a lintel or an arch on its top indicates that this part of the building was probably destroyed at one time, and the doorway was closed off when it was rebuilt. The present top level of the narthex north wall is at 2.16 m, but its original height could not be determined as its upper part had been destroyed.

South Facade

The south facade of the church is similar to the northern facade in terms of masonry and materials. On the eastern and western corners of the wall of the naos section, bigger and smoother ashlar blocks were used. In other parts we encountered medium-sized stones with a tooled, exposed face and small, irregular rubble. Although thin brick or tile pieces were used among the stones, it was not possible to observe a regular course running from side to side, as on the north facade. This was probably due to the presence of a tall window on the south facade. (Drawing 9, Figure 22)

The most significant difference of the south facade, which has a profile similar to the north one, is the presence of a large window in the middle. The window, which starts about 1 m above ground level, is 2.05 m high and 2.40 m wide and rather large compared to the relatively small structure. (Figure 24) Its pointed arch consists of six finely dressed voussoirs. The section with the keystone is covered with plaster and cannot be seen clearly. The dogtooth frieze, located right above the pointed arch and formed with six bricks on either side, forms an elegant hood on top of the window with a single row of bricks above it. (Figure 25) This dogtooth eave was unearthed without loss and in a completely preserved state.

The window was made narrower at a later stage and turned into a double window with two pointed arches. The window openings were separated by a marble mullion of 1 m length and 13 cm diameter. The original window opening was also narrowed by a single row of stones on either side, making it into two long and narrow windows about 35 cm wide. The arches of the twin windows are pointed and made entirely of brick. But, compared to the stone arch of the original window, their workmanship is lower quality. The arch on the right is slightly wider and marginally slanted to the right. Above the middle of these two pointed arches a marble stone decorated with floral motifs inside three circles made of interlaced strips was placed.[30] (Figure 24) This spolia piece has no structural function and was inserted to fill the large gap on the pediment and to add an aesthetic value. On the southern window in the third phase, these twin windows were bricked up to be completely closed off. At the top level of the small stone block functioning as the capital of the colonette in the middle, the slot of a wooden beam spanning the whole width of the original window was identified. A wooden beam of the same dimensions was placed here by the restoration team to prevent possible stone loss or damage. (Figure 6) The reasons why the window was gradually closed off are discussed later.

In the eastern part of the south facade, there is a crack starting close to the roof and going all the way down to the floor. However, the crack is not visible on the inside of the wall and is not significant so as to affect the structural integrity of the building. The presence of *in situ* plaster fragments on the south facade, especially on the upper parts of the western half, indicates that the exterior of the building was originally completely plastered. The dogtooth eave visible on the western side of the facade at roof level has survived in a well-preserved state. (Figure 25)

The south facade of the narthex is not different from the north facade in terms of material and workmanship. (Figure 23) Spolia ashlar blocks were utilized in the masonry of the wall that is not tied to but stands adjacent to the south wall of the church. Brick and tile fragments, as well as smaller size rubble, were used to fill the gaps between these stones. The difference between this wall and the northern wall of the narthex can be seen in the composition of the wall. On this facade there is a window opening measuring 55 x 90 cm. There is also a small niche mea-

30 For this artefact, see the following Chapter IV, catalogue no. 3.

suring approximately 30 x 30 cm between the window and the naos wall. Just like on the north facade but to a greater extent, the western corner of this facade remains invisible under the modern residential building.

East Facade

Apse: The apse wall, 3.80 m wide and protruding 1.20 m from the east facade of the church, constitutes the dominant image of the east facade. On the north and south sides of the semi-circular curvature of the apse are two straight walls both measuring 75 cm wide. There is a dry stone wall extending southwards from the front of the apse. The facade of the apse, which mainly has a rubble masonry, also has ashlar blocks here and there. The use of stone blocks more regular in shape and relatively larger is noticeable, particularly in the north and south corners of the east facade. Plenty of mortar was used between the stones in the wall masonry, and although the grout is not regular, as the gaps between the stones were completely filled with mortar, the wall has a flat and even appearance. The traces of plaster remaining on the wall indicate that the exterior of the wall was completely plastered. (Drawing 10 Figure 26)

The apse has a window that is 1 m high and 65 cm wide. The top part of the window ends in a pointed arch made of three finely dressed voussoirs. Instead of a keystone, a piece of brick embedded in plenty of mortar was utilized. However at a later date, this window opening was bricked up with a thin wall 15 cm thick, leaving a cruciform crenel window at the top. In the third phase, this cross window was also closed off with mortar and small pieces of stone and brick, leaving the apse window, like the big window on the south wall, completely closed. (Figure 27)

Above the low semi-dome of the apse, the wall of the east facade continues to rise in the form of the eastern vault of the building. There are traces of the tile roofing on top of the semi-dome of the apse spreading out from the center like a fan. (Figure 28)

Arcosolium Tombs:[31] Viewing the structure directly facing the east facade, the arcosolium tombs –on both sides of the apse and attached to the north and south corners of the church– appear as components forming the defining characteristics of the east facade of the building. (Figure 26) To the north of the apse, on the northeast corner of the structure is the northern tomb built on an east–west axis and adjoining the wall. Viewed directly facing the facade, the gap between this tomb and the apse wall was filled with a dry wall at a later stage. In this masonry work ashlar blocks were used, and one of these measures 90 x 60 cm. This piece of wall was built separately after the church and the northern arcosolium tomb were built. It is also noteworthy that no mortar was used in this wall.

The arcosolium tomb, with a north–south axis on the south corner of the apse, plays a defining role in the appearance of the east facade after the apse itself. It is larger than the one on the north and has a facade facing the east. Due to its architectural design, this tomb resembles *aedicula* tombs. The gap between the southern end of the apse and the arcosolium is filled with a wall, as it was on the north. The interior and the exterior of the arcosolium was plastered, and the surviving remnants indicate that it was decorated with wall paintings.

Flood Bank: On the eastern side of the church, a featureless stone wall starting in front of the apse passes over the arcosolium tomb on the south and extends southwards for 9.20 m. Then with a sharp angle it turns to the northwest and terminates after continuing for 3.40 m in

31 The graves are explored in detail in Chapter VIII.

this direction. Thus, the wall bounds an area on the south side of the church from the east and south. (Drawing 1, Figure 26) The height of the wall in front of the apse is 90–100 cm on average, and the part visible today is the original top level of the wall. The wall continues towards the southern side of the apse by gradually rising and reaches the top level of the vault of the arcosolium at 2.18 meters. It then passes over the vault, descends back to 1.30 m in height, and runs from the south side of the arcosolium vault to continue southwards at an average height of 1 m. The wall was most likely slightly higher in its southern section too, but probably became lower with the destruction of these parts later.

The varying thickness of the wall is around 80 cm in front of the apse. As the exterior face follows a straight line towards the arcosolium tomb, the wall thickness increases on the other side due to the curvature of the apse. The wall thickness, reaching 1.80 m along the width of the vault above the arcosolium, decreases to 1.30 m immediately afterwards. It gradually becomes thinner as it extends towards the south with an average thickness of 80 cm and becomes even narrower after the bend, tapering to 70 cm. Since the section of the wall in front of the apse abutted the sturdy eastern wall of the church, not much extra thickness was needed here. The gap between the back wall of the north arcosolium –half of which was leaning against the northern wall of the building– and the apse was filled with a wall of 1 m height, in which a few large stone blocks were also used. (Figure 28)

Although there were some ashlar used alongside the rubble in the masonry of this wall, no binding mortar was found. The soil seen in the grout today was either used instead of a binding mortar, or the mortar in the grout of the wall dissolved and was destroyed as it was exposed to continuous currents of water and replaced by the soil carried by the stream. Although it bears the form of a wall with regular masonry in front of the apse, it becomes more of a stacked-up bank, especially in the southern section. Mortar was only used in the sections in front of the apse and passing over the arcosolium tomb. In front of the apse, a row of stones was removed from the exterior surface of the apse, or parts of the wall of the apse were slightly shaved with the aim of binding and integrating the bank with the wall of the apse. This way, on the east facade of the building, a sturdy bank enclosing the apse was formed between the two arcosolium graves. Likewise, the vault of the tomb on the south was also shaved at the top, providing a better bond between the surface of the vault and the bank. The section that runs southward after the arcosolium tomb is a dry stone wall with some ashlar blocks, but mainly with masonry of large rubble without mortar. We observed that stones from previously destroyed buildings and large wall fragments were also used in the masonry of the southern section. A large wall fragment was used as spolia at the south end where the bank was bending. This wall fragment must have been taken from the ruins of a substantial building that used to be there at an earlier date.

The examination of the apse wall revealed that the bricking up of the apse window preceded the construction of the flood bank. It is possible to observe that when the apse wall was shaved for the flood bank, the lower parts of the bricked-up apse window were also scored. (Figure 28) This indicates that the flood bank was built after the apse window was closed off.

It is clear that this bank was not intended as a simple "enclosure" after the church was no longer in use and that the building was going to be utilized as a workshop or animal shelter in a later phase of use. The fact that this bank passes over the arcosolium tomb and extends along the east facade of the church and that the wall of the apse was slightly shaved and scored to integrate the bank with the structure suggests that the bank was built while the church was still being used. Therefore, it had a function related to the use of the building. It seems that this wall was built to protect the church against the floods of water and mud coming from the east. (Figure 29) Looking at the fill inside the arcosolium tomb, it is possible to see layers of gravel apart from the alluvial silt, which indicates that the stream flowed only during the wet periods today, was perhaps flowed continuously in the period when the structure was in use, and overflowed from time to time as it does today. A similar layer of gravel was also found on the northern side of the church under the alluvial deposit. The fact that the apse window and the southern window were gradually bricked up at certain phases must signal efforts to tackle the floods coming from this direction. Additionally, it is also understood that the facade of the southern arcosolium overlooking the stream was completely covered with a thin wall at one stage. Later this wall was destroyed, probably due to a flood, and the interior was filled with silt. The materials of this wall were found in the alluvial fill inside the arcosolium.

West Facade

The west facade of the church stands to a height close to 4 m. (Drawing 11, Figure 30) In the middle of its facade is a doorway leading to the naos. The door measures 2.24 x 1.05 m, with a threshold at +0.09 m relative to the naos floor. The two ornamented jambs and the profiled lintel used here are spolia. The relieving arch above the lintel is at +3.68 m. Over this relieving arch is a triangular brick dogtooth eave overhanging around 10 cm from the wall. (Figure 31)

Archaeological evidence shows that the walls of Alakent Church, built with rubble, were plastered and decorated with paint. The plaster and the decoration of the church's west facade were preserved in a relatively good state to the present day. We owe this to the building being buried under alluvium up to the level of its dome. After the excavation when the wall was cleaned, red lines on the whitewash imitating an ashlar wall technique became visible at certain places.

The west facade was built with rubble and plastered. The plaster on this wall was almost complete from the roof level down to 30–40 cm above the narthex floor. After being plastered, whitewash was applied to the wall, a pattern of ashlar masonry was scored with a pointed tool, and the lines were enhanced with red paint. (Figure 32) This decoration, more evident on the wall on the north side of the doorway, continued on the wall to its south. Fragments of red lines made on a white background could be detected in various parts of the western wall. (Figures 33, 34) When these red lines detected during the work at the site were connected, the decoration of a pseudo-ashlar masonry covering the whole facade emerged. (Drawing 12)

On the wall south of the doorway a fresco mortar of 3–4 cm thickness was applied on the existing pseudo-ashlar masonry decoration, and on this layer the *Deesis* scene was depicted.[32] The scene, which starts about 40 cm above the narthex floor, goes up to the 2.40 m level and covers the entire wall up to the height of the lintel. This extensive scene has survived in a very well-preserved condition under the alluvium. The fact that this fresco was added later to the west facade could be deduced from the presence of the layer of plaster with the pseudo-ashlar decoration that continues underneath the fresco plaster.

Another example of a decoration representing a similar wall construction technique at Alakent Church could be found on the relieving arch above the lintel. The arch made of blocks of stone was plastered, and a faux-brick arch was drawn on it with a pointed tool. The faux bricks

32 For more on this scene, see Chapter V.

were painted white and red alternately. (Figure 35) Considered together with the ornamented spolia lintel, it can be assumed that this faux-brick arch decoration functioned to emphasize the entrance. The bricks constituting the dogtooth eave of the pediment above the doorway were also plastered, painted with whitewash, and given a border with red paint. (Figure 36) The inner part of the pediment eave was decorated with red zigzag lines. (Figure 37) A similar fragment of a dogtooth eave belonging to the roof has survived on the southern side of the facade. The triangular bricks of the dogtooth eave were plastered and painted with whitewash, and zigzag motifs were drawn in red paint on the white background. (Figure 38) A similar example of painted dogtooth eave bricks can be found on the west facade of the mortuary church in Smederevo (Serbia).[33]

There are wooden beam slots, one on each side of the arch of the doorway, approximately at the 3.10 level. In the middle of the wall on the northern side of the doorway is a rectangular marble stone with a cross with pellets in relief, used as spolia at approximately 1.40 m above the floor level.[34] (Figures 30, 33)

The issue of painted exterior walls poses a significant difficulty for Byzantine architectural historians. There is very little data and knowledge on this subject. Archaeological data is also very limited and fragmentary, and does not provide a comprehensive idea about the matter. The original exterior plaster of existing Byzantine structures has not survived to the present day. When we observe the buildings in use today, we either see walls without plaster or those with plaster that was renovated. However, through some surviving examples, although very limited in number and extent, we know there was a practice of plastering and painting exterior facades in Byzantine architecture.[35] The reason only a very small number of examples survive is because the buildings not in use are often in ruins, and the plaster on their exterior facades has long been destroyed. Those still in use today, especially in the Balkans, show paint on the exterior facades that has either been renovated during the centuries or lost as it was not renewed. Nonetheless, the few surviving examples in the Balkans indicate that the exterior facades of Byzantine structures were painted. Some of these decorations involve figures. The remnants on the west facade of Anargyroi Church in Kastoria[36] and the original figurative ornamentation fragments on the exterior of the Church of St. Nicholas Kasnitse[37] are among these examples. Examples where paint was utilized to imitate wall masonry techniques can be found in some churches in Mount Athos or in the 13th–14th century churches in Serbia and Macedonia.[38] The drum of the dome in the St. Nicholas Chapel of the Prodromos Monastery (Church of St. Theodores) in Serres was plastered and decorated with red lines imitating ashlar masonry. Similarly, the windows on the drum of the Chapel of the Archangel of Hilandar Monastery on Mount Athos are surrounded with a band of red and white triangles facing one another.[39] As these structures have been in use for centuries, the originality of the decorations might be doubtful, but we could consider this as the continuation of a tradition in existence since the Byzantine period. The closest matching example to Alakent Church can be seen on a few fragments of plaster from the Church of St. George (1191) in

33 Trkulja 2004, p. 126, Fig. 170.
34 For this slab, see the following Chapter IV, Catalogue no. 2.
35 Ćurčić 2010, p. 659.
36 Trkulja 2004, p. 130, Fig. 177. See also Hadermann-Misguich 1975.
37 Ćurčić 2010, p. 383.
38 Trkulja 2004, pp. 118, 123–127.
39 Ćurčić 2000, for Serres see p. 23, Fig 28; for Mount Athos see p. 79, Fig. 50.

Kurbinovo, which have survived in their original condition.[40] The exterior facade of the church probably had a stone masonry decoration in red paint on whitewash, similar to Alakent Church. According to Ćurčić, these examples might indicate that plastering and painting the exterior facades of Middle Byzantine churches was a routine procedure.[41] Similar exterior decorations can be encountered in Anatolia in 12th–13th century Seljuk structures such as pavilions, hunting lodges and baths. Zigzags, checkerboard patterns, or ashlar motifs painted in red and white similar to the Alakent example, were decorations widely used on the exteriors of these buildings.[42]

The closest matching example to Alakent Church can be found in Cyprus. The Panagias Phorbiotissa Church in Nikitari has a pseudo-ashlar wall decoration made with a sharp tip on small fragments of plaster and preserved in its original condition. The walls of the church were rubble masonry that was plastered, as in the case of Alakent Church, and the decoration was applied onto this plaster. There is also a decoration consisting of zigzag lines in red paint on this plaster.[43]

40 Ćurčić 2000, pp. 382–383, Fig. 411.

41 Ćurčić 2000, p. 383.

42 For these examples, see Redford 2000. For the ashlar decoration with red lines over a white background, see p. 158, the facade of the entrance of the building known as Gazipaşa Şekerhane; for zigzag facade decorations, see the Sugözü bath, p. 153, Fig. 98; Hasbahçe, pp. 149, 212, ill. 73–74.

43 Chotzakoglou 2005, see p. 522, Figs. 194–195.

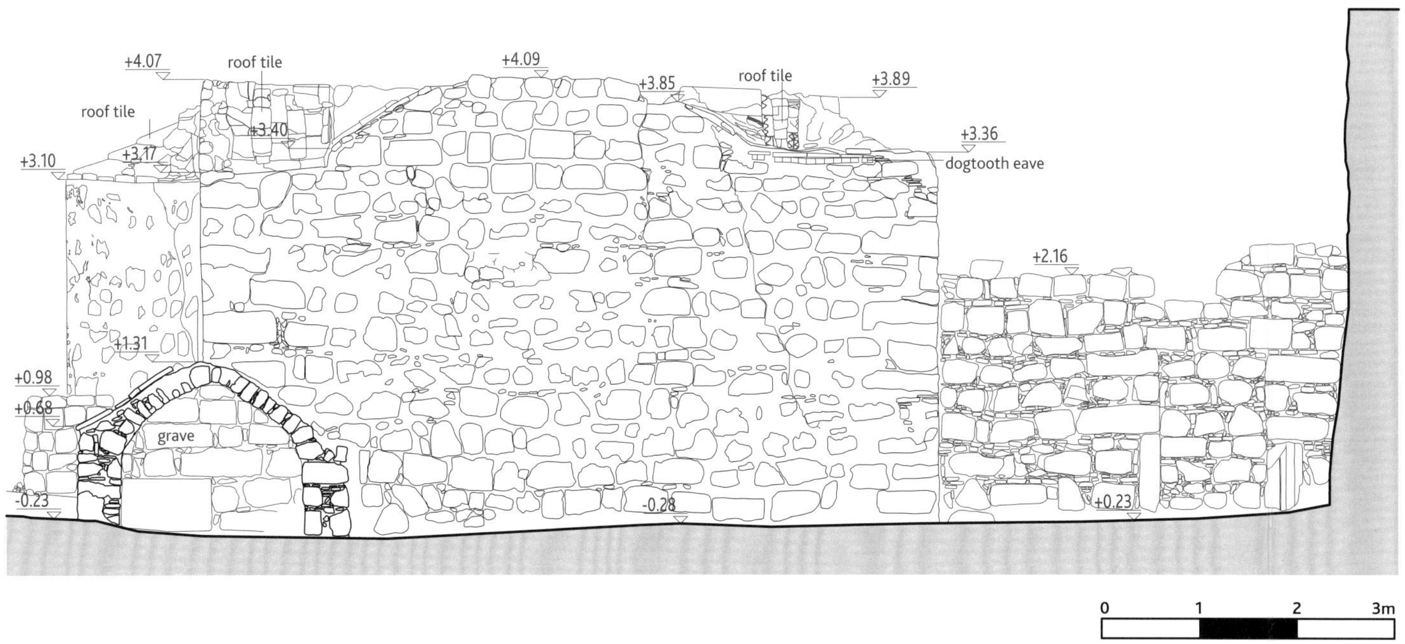

Drawing 8: North facade

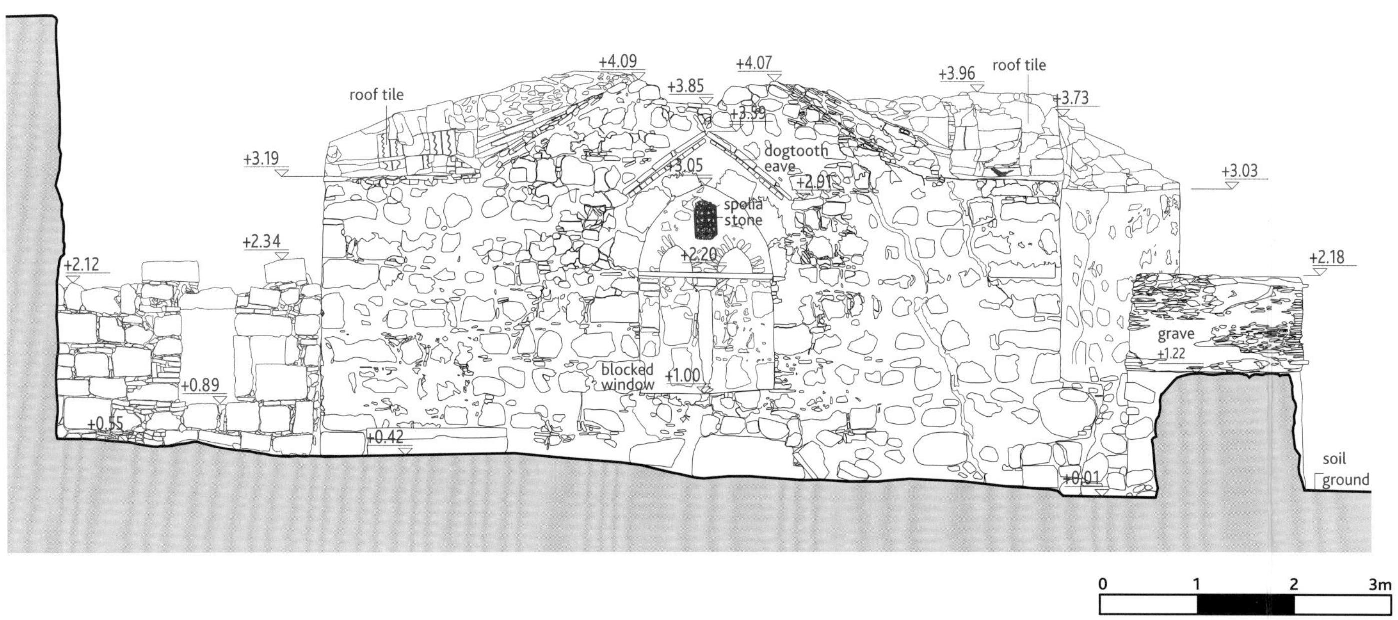

Drawing 9: South facade

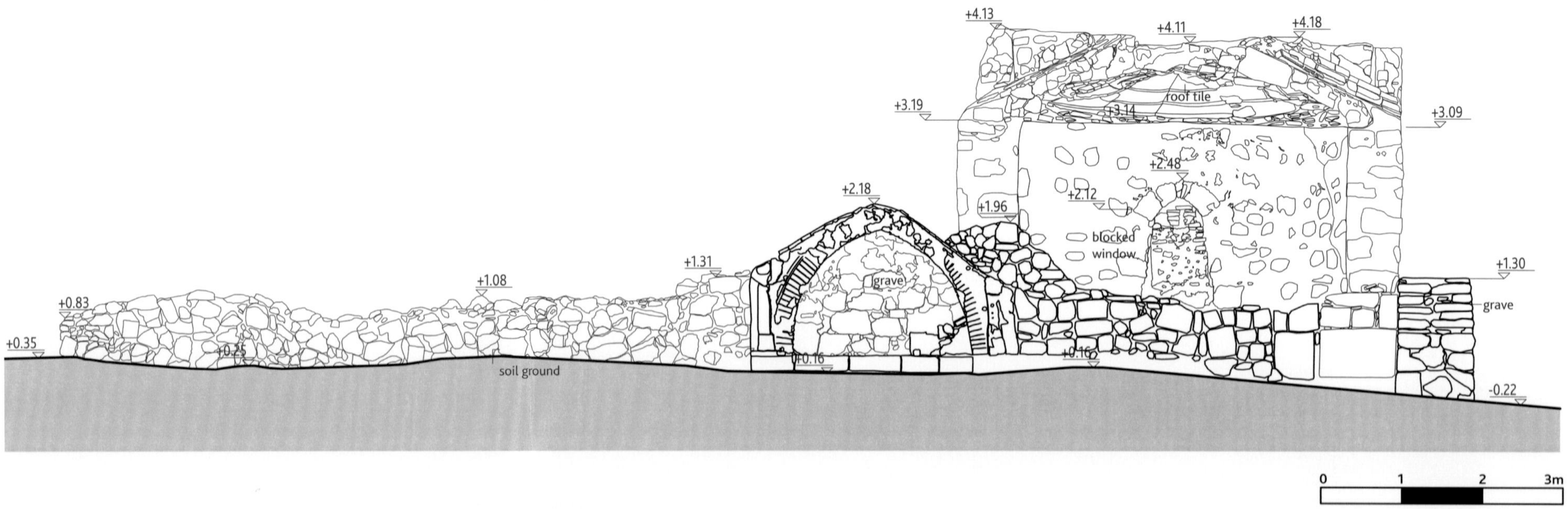

Drawing 10: East facade

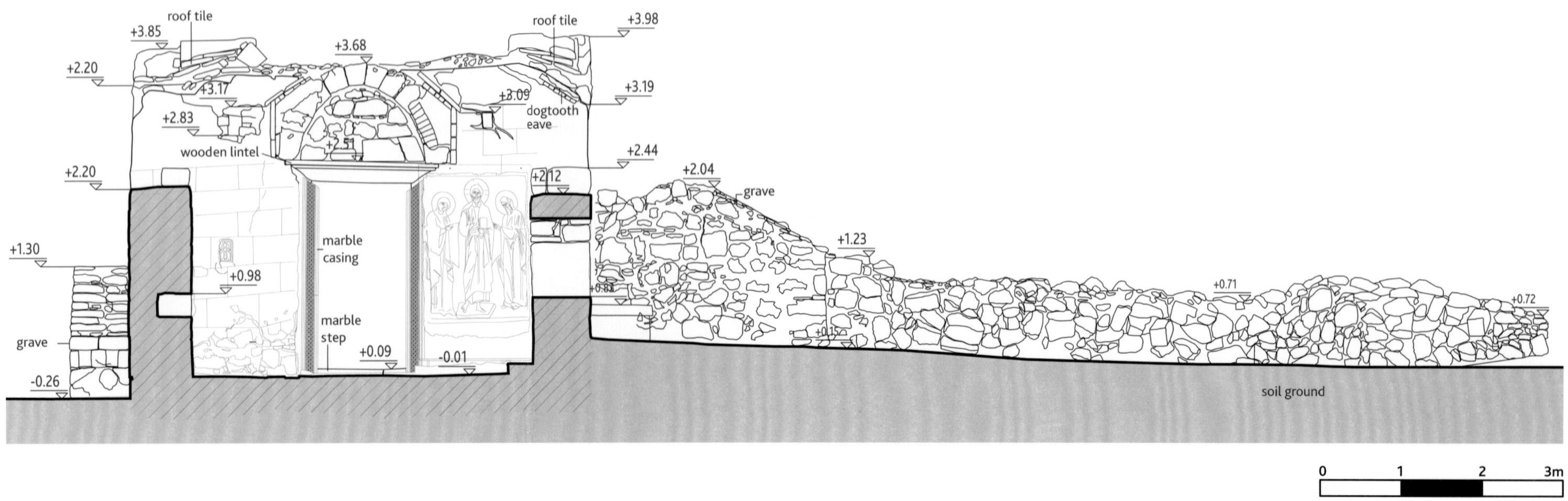

Drawing 11: West facade

Drawing 12: West facade wall decoration

Figure 20: North facade, naos

Figure 21: North facade, narthex

Figure 22: South facade, naos

Figure 23: South facade, narthex

Figure 24: South window

Figure 25: South window, eave above the arch

Figure 26: East facade, general view

Figure 27: Apse window, viewed from outside

Figure 28: Apse, viewed from outside

Figure 29: General view from northeast

Figure 30: West facade, viewed from the narthex

Figure 31: Entrance arch, southern half

Figure 32: West facade, north section, wall decoration

Figure 33: West facade, north section, red lines and a cross in relief

Figure 34: West facade, south section, red lines

Figure 35: Entrance arch, southern half, detail

Figure 36: Entrance arch, eave, detail

Figure 37: Entrance arch, north section, detail

Figure 38: West facade, dogtooth eave, detail

2.4. Bema: Liturgical Arrangement of the Church

The bema section of the church consists of the area covered by the semi-dome of the apse and the bema vault. This section is bounded by a templon consisting of two columns and two balustrade slabs. (Drawing 13, Figure 39) The floor of the bema section is approximately 10 cm higher than the floor of the naos and is paved with irregular stone slabs. There are fresco fragments on the semi-dome of the apse, the bema vault in front of the apse, on the north and south walls of the templon, and on the southern templon slab. The upper part of the bema vault in front of the apse has been destroyed. There are ornamented stone cornices on both sides of the bema walls extending from the arch of the apse to the outer edge of the templon. The cornices are at the height of the springing line of the vault approximately 2.20 m above the floor level.

Templon: Two spolia columns separated by the space of a door opening (80 cm) and two slabs between the columns and the walls of the naos, constitute the templon. This separates the bema section, where the altar table is located, and the naos. The column on the north side measures 30 cm in diameter and 1.90 m in height, and is made of white marble with gray veins. At its top section a bracelet was rendered with a fine profile. Except for a small fracture on the side facing the north wall, the column is intact and found *in situ* as it appears today. The column has a complete top section and was cut from the bottom that stands on the naos floor. Traces of a thin layer of plaster seen at the top sections of the column indicate that the column might have been plastered and possibly painted in its original form. On the south side, there is a slightly shorter and more slender column. This column, carved from a gray granite, has a diameter of 26 cm and a height of 1.70 m. Unlike the other column, which had been placed directly on the naos floor, this one rests on a spolia stone that raises the floor of the bema by 10 cm. It still stands *in situ* and vertically true. At the bottom of the column there is a bracelet protruding around 2 cm. The column tapers slightly upwards and was cut from the top. These two columns –completely different from one another in terms of material, thickness, and bracelet shapes– were adjusted to the appropriate height and used as spolia at the templon. The bema is accessed through the opening between these two columns. On the sides of the columns facing each other, there are no marks indicating door wings in this opening. A stone block was placed between these columns to act as a threshold, and paving stones covering the entire floor of the bema were placed level with the top of this threshold.

In the northern wing of the templon, between the column and the north wall, (Figure 40) a single thick slab, flat and unornamented on both sides and measuring 75 x 70 cm, was used. But as this block, probably a spolium, was not big enough, its right, left, and top were filled with bricks, small stones, and mortar. The resulting balustrade terminates at a height of 90 cm with a roughly dressed stone handrail placed on top of it. The two anchor holes at the top of the stone indicate that this block had previously been used with a different function. The part of the stone adjoining the column was trimmed with a curved form to fit the column, and the remaining gap was filled with mortar. At the northern wing of the templon, at its front facing the naos, there is a bench consisting of two regular-shaped stone blocks approximately 20 cm wide and an average height of 25 cm. This bench continues along the north wall of the naos for another 1.50 m.

In the southern wing of the templon a slab, ornamented on both sides, was placed between the granite column and the south wall. The granite column and the ornamented slab on this part of the templon were placed on top of a templon pier from an earlier church and used here in a horizontal position. (Figure 41) The slab, with a width of 1 m and a height of 1.05 m, is from an earlier structure and was used here as spolia. The front side of the slab facing the naos has an ornament in relief in the middle that is surrounded by a wide frame. This wide frame is plastered and decorated with frescoes. On the back side of the slab facing the bema is a cross motif in relief in the form of the tree of life.[44] The fragments of the broken upper section were found immediately in front of the slab, and during the conservation work the slab was restored by attaching these pieces back where they belonged. A similar motif was found at the Church of St. Nicholas in Demre.[45]

No architectural sculpture was found during the excavations that could have been the architrave stone on top of the templon columns, nor were there marks on the walls indicating the presence of an architrave stone. However, in accordance with the architectural characteristics of the period, the bema would have been separated from the naos by a "raised" templon (iconostasis).[46] We can assume that there was probably a wooden architrave on the templon columns and large icons hanging from it above the templon slabs.

Apse: At the front section of the semi-dome of the apse is a pointed arch formed by blocks of stone. The semi-dome, which is bound by the pointed arch, was built of rubble. There are a few rows of stone blocks missing from the top of the bema vault in front of the apse. (Figure 42) When viewed from the inside, the apse window –80 cm high, 60 cm wide, and about 40 cm deep– looks like a niche with a pointed arch. The window was closed off by a thin wall that was flush with the exterior facade, and a niche was formed within the thickness of the wall. In the middle of this niche is a cruciform crenel window. The length of the cross is 40 cm and its width is 22 cm. The upper and lower arms are of equal length at 16 cm, and the horizontal arms are 6.5 cm. The slit of the crenel is 9 cm wide. (Figure 43) The window, originally 1 m high, was filled with mortar and brick fragments for about 20 cm from the bottom. In the middle of this filling is a rectangular hole with a width of about 4 x 5 cm and a depth of 20 cm. The hole descends all the way down to the original base of the window opening. (Figure 44) It was not possible to determine its function, however. The niche created within the depth of the window would have been used as a niche to place liturgical items. Depending on the season and time of day, the sunlight entering the cross-shaped window would fall on the altar table, and a cross of light would appear on the table.[47] (Figure 45) The cruciform crenel opening was also completely blocked at a later stage. This later filling, done in a very cursory manner evidenced by its state of disintegration, was documented and removed during the excavation, and the cross-shaped window was exposed.

Altar table: The altar table, located in the center of the bema, is made up of two large spolia stones.[48] (Figure 46) Its base is a section of a fluted column from the Roman period with a diameter of about 54 cm and a height of 71 cm. On top of this base is a slab measuring 85 x 104 cm, with a thickness of 23 cm. Thus, the height of the altar table from the floor reaches 92 cm. Three sides of this slab are profiled, and its bottom is a flat without ornamentation. The surface forming the top of the altar table was trimmed to be flattened by a tooth chisel from all four sides at a width of 15–20 cm. The rough workmanship seen in the middle part was performed during

44 For this slab, see Chapter IV, Catalogue no. 8, Figs. 16, 17 and 18.

45 Peschlow 1990, pp. 235–236, plate 6; Alpaslan 1996, pp. 104–105, Figs. 30–31.

46 Especially after the 11th century onwards, the templon –with icons placed between the columns of the templon above the balustrade slabs– was screened off in such a way that the bema would not be seen from the naos. See Bouras 1991.

47 The photograph was taken on 31 July 2010 at 08:37 a.m.

48 For the artefacts constituting the altar table, see Chapter IV, Catalogue no. 9.

the Roman period so that the stone that would rest on top would fit better. According to this, it was understood that this block was used as an altar in this church in the Byzantine period. It had a corniced element visible from three sides that had belonged to the superstructure of the facade of a monumental building during the Roman period. The hole in the center of the slab with a measurement of 8 x 3 cm is the lewis hole made for transporting and lifting this block.

Niche: On the northern wall of the bema is a niche 90 cm above the naos floor, measuring 59 cm high, 42 cm wide, and 55 cm deep. (Figure 47) The niche with a pointed arch has a sill finished with bricks. In front of the niche to its right side, an ornamented stone pedestal set into the corner of the wall was found *in situ*. It has a shelf with a large brick on top of it. (Figures 48, 49) The square brick forming the shelf has an edge measurement of 35 cm. It is at the same height as the niche sill and adjacent to the niche. The ornamented stone that forms the shelf pedestal is spolia.[49] It was raised with a filling of mortar and small stone fragments, probably because it was not high enough. The two faces of the stone attached to the walls were also filled with mortar and rubble to fit it to the walls. The corner of the terracotta shelf, attached to the pedestal with mortar, is broken. Considering the location of the niche in the bema relative to the altar table, we believe that the niche was used for liturgical purposes during the rituals.

---

49 For more on this stone, see Chapter IV, Catalogue no. 7.

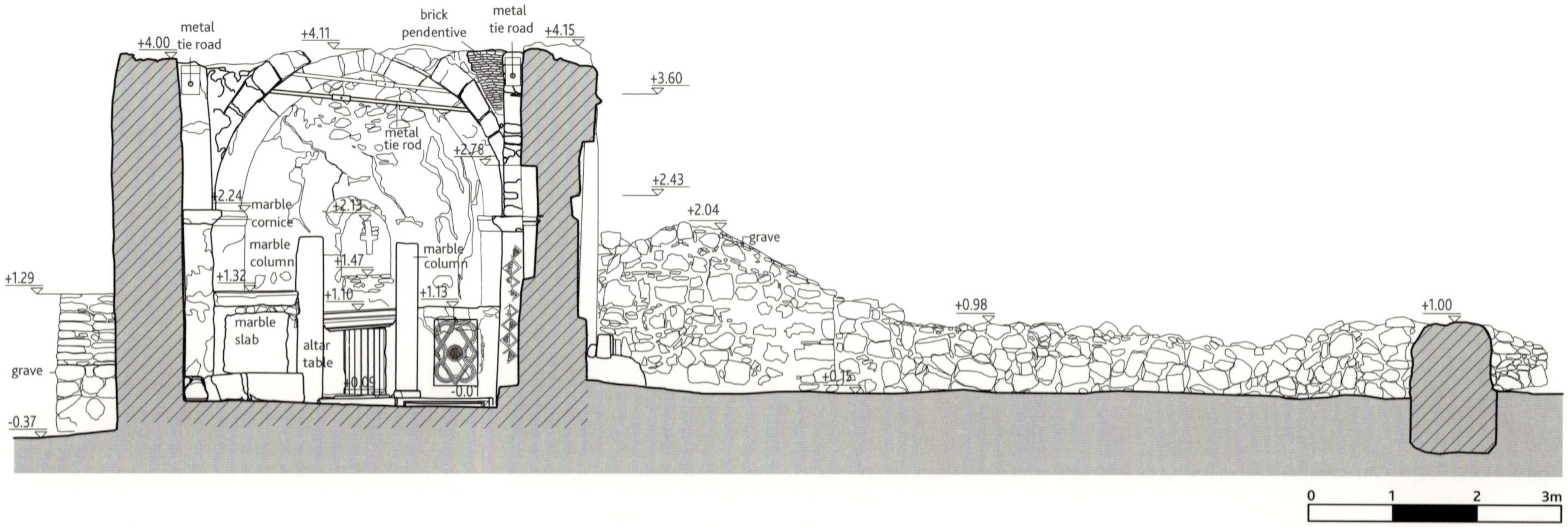

Drawing 13: Section D-D

Figure 39: Bema, general view

Figure 40: Templon, north section

Figure 41: Templon, south section

Figure 42: Semi-dome of the apse and the eastern arch

Figure 43: Cruciform apse window

Figure 44: Apse window, the infill bed

Figure 45: Sunlight falling on the altar table

Figure 46: Altar table

Figure 47: Liturgical niche, position relative to altar table

Figure 48: Liturgical niche

Figure 49: Liturgical niche, shelf and its pedestal

2.5. Narthex

The narthex was added to the church at a later date. The northern and southern walls of the narthex are adjoining but not tied to the western wall of the naos. They actually lean against the plaster on this wall. Moreover, the texture and workmanship of the narthex walls are entirely different from the naos walls. (Figure 50)

The interior length of the narthex along its east-west axis is 3.60 m and is the same width as the naos. Since the western wall of the narthex was under a residential building, only the inner surface of this wall could be unearthed. The upper section of the narthex was destroyed due to Matarlar Street pass over it in recent years. According to eyewitness accounts, as this street was levelled with a road grader from time to time, the top part of the church's narthex was scraped off. The walls that have survived to this day stand at a height of 2.00 m to 2.40 m. There is also no surviving architectural data that could lead to an understanding of the roofing system on top of the narthex. There is no trace of any kind on the western wall of the naos resembling a beam slot that might have belonged to the roof over the narthex. As the building was filled with alluvium while it was still intact, the parts that constituted the roof could not have fallen into the building when they collapsed. However, considering the width of the space and the thickness of the walls, we may think that the narthex was covered with a wooden roof. It is obvious that walls of 60 cm thickness –unsupported by the piers and without a sturdy stone masonry like the walls of the naos– could not have carried a vaulted cover of this width. Taking the door on the west wall of the naos and the arch above it into account, the narthex roof must have been at least at a height to accommodate this arch. And this might be the level of the vaults on which the dome of the naos rests. In that case, there would be a wooden roof starting from the level of the vault, rising at an appropriate angle and extending along the east-west axis. However, we do not have any archaeological data that would support the existence of such a roof. The narthex, as it is surviving today, probably was not covered by a roof, like a courtyard added to the church in its last phase.

Originally, access to the narthex was provided through a 1.70 m wide doorway on the west. This entrance was not in the middle of the western wall of the narthex but on its southern part. (Figure 51) Since the upper section of the entrance did not survive, the height of the doorway, whether with an arch or a lintel, remains unclear. This doorway has no jambs either, but regularly shaped stone blocks were used at its sides. It was not possible to see the exterior facade of the west wall of the narthex, because the eastern garden wall of the house west of the church runs on top of it, and hence the area could not be excavated.

On the eastern side of the south wall of the narthex, there is a window at a distance of 90 cm from the naos wall. (Figure 52) A rough-cut block of stone was used as a lintel on this window. The window is 60 cm wide and 90 cm high, and starts 90 cm above the narthex floor. On the inside of the south wall there is a niche at a distance of 50 cm from the west wall and about 90 cm high from the floor of the narthex. The width, height, and depth measurements of the cubic niche nearly match each another and are around 40 cm. On the exterior facade of the same wall, in the section between the window and the naos wall, at around 1.30 m level above the floor, there is another niche approximately the same shape and dimensions as the other. It is formed by four stone blocks. (Figure 53) On the north wall of the narthex there are also two niches in the interior. (Figure 54) Of the two cubic niches, the bigger one towards the naos measures around 37 cm in width and height, and the other slightly smaller one around 28 x 25 cm. The depths of the niches could not be determined precisely as they were collapsed on the inside. The niches are located on the eastern section of the wall and set at different heights from the floor. The larger niche on the east is 70 cm from the floor, while the smaller niche starts at the level of the top of the other niche. The sill of the small niche is a smooth brick. (Figure 55) It was understood that there was a doorway bricked up at a later date on the western section of the north wall. The traces of the doorway could be seen more clearly on the exterior facade of the wall. (Figure 21) There are no window openings on this wall.

In the masonry of the narthex walls some middle-sized ashlar blocks were used here as spolia. The gaps between the stones in the wall masonry were filled with thin, small stone fragments and pieces of brick. At the sides of the entrance in the west and around the window in the south, larger ashlar blocks were used. The niches were usually made up of four blocks of stone. Unlike the naos walls, there was no remaining plaster on the walls of the narthex, and most of the grout had fallen. However, there is no serious structural problems with the sections of the walls that have survived. There is no detachment or cracks in the walls, and no deviation from the plumb line. This shows how well the alluvium has preserved the building.

Although the narthex floor was excavated down to the level of the stone floor of the naos, no paving on the floor was found.

Figure 50: Narthex, general view from north

Figure 51: West wall and entrance, from inside

Figure 52: South wall, general view from inside

Figure 53: South wall, general view from outside

Figure 54: North wall, general view from inside

Figure 55: Niche on the north wall

3. Phases

By comparing similar examples and the techniques of construction utilized, we believe that the naos was built in the 12th century. Different phases of construction/repair are mainly seen at the narthex; on the wall built on the eastern side of the church extending southwards, which we have called the flood bank; and on the naos windows gradually made smaller and finally completely closed off. In fact, architecturally, the only two stages that can be mentioned as phases are the addition of the narthex as an extension and the construction of the flood bank. The others are actually modifications that should be considered as simple repairs and additions to the building rather than phases of construction.

The following phases could be identified in the construction and subsequent use of the church:

1. The construction of the naos was probably completed in the 12th century. At this stage, in the interior the bema, frescoes, the plastered west wall, and the stone with a cross motif applied to the northern part of this wall were present. Of course, the spolia lintel and jambs also belong to this phase. In all probability, the exterior facades were plastered and painted. On the west wall, close to the lower left corner of the carved cross, under the plaster that has fallen off, another layer of plaster was detected. This small fragment of plaster has the same finishing level as the stone with the cross motif and the jambs, and probably belongs to the first phase of construction. (Figure 56)

2. The west wall of the church was replastered, painted with whitewash, and given a pseudo-ashlar masonry pattern in red paint. The plaster layer that we see today is this one. The fact that there is another layer of plaster underneath it, and that the final layer of plaster was smeared over the stone with the cross motif and the jambs at some places, suggests that the layer existing today, was another phase of repair. We have no data concerning the other facades of the building at this stage.

3. At a later stage, on top of the plaster with the pseudo-ashlar masonry ornamentation on the southern side of the west facade of the church, a thick layer of plaster was applied and the *Deesis* fresco was painted on this layer. The pseudo-ashlar masonry ornamentation continues under the plaster of the *Deesis* fresco in this section. The plaster of the *Deesis* fresco was also smeared over the door jamb. (Figure 57) We have no idea on the narthex of this phase.

4. The narthex that we see today was added to the church as a different architectural phase. This is understood not only because the narthex wall was built with simpler workmanship, but also because the narthex wall was adjoined onto the plastered and decorated west wall of the church. The narthex walls adjoin the pseudo-ashlar masonry-decorated west wall of the church without being tied to it. They even cover a few centimeters of the *Deesis* fresco made later than the naos. (Figure 58) Therefore, when the narthex was built, the church was in use, the west wall was plastered and decorated with a pseudo-ashlar masonry motif, and the *Deesis* fresco was in place with its thick layer of plaster on top of this previous layer of plaster. Probably, either an existing narthex was renovated at a later date, or the narthex was built around the same time as the *Deesis* fresco, but subsequent to it.

5. In its final phase the building, after being vacated and filled with nearly 40 cm of silt, and no longer functioning as a church, it was used with a different, simple function for a short time. In the narthex section, a dry stone wall reaching 1.40 m above floor level was built. It adjoins the southern jamb and covers the figure of Mary close to the jamb in the *Deesis* scene on

this wall. (Figure 59) Although the wall was built with ashlar blocks, it does not have high-quality workmanship and stands on the alluvial deposit about 40 cm above the floor. It runs about 1 m to the west from the wall with the fresco, then bends slightly towards the north. To the west of this wall, towards the west wall of the narthex, another wall built of block stones and standing on the alluvial fill was found. And, in front of the doorway that provides access from the narthex to the naos, at a level higher than the original threshold, a two-treaded oval set of steps was made with a simple arrangement of stones placed on top of the alluvium deposit. (Figure 60) The ceramics in the narthex[50] were found approximately at the level of this stair. It was identified that in the interior, along the south wall of the narthex, regularly shaped stones were arranged in a row to form a bench. In the southwest corner, two stone blocks were placed vertically, raising this section of the bench. (Figure 61) The row of stones, which were not joined with mortar, belongs to the final phase of the narthex's use. At the naos, on top of the silt 35–40 cm above the stone-paved floor, six pieces of finely dressed thick stone slabs with profiled edges were found lying on the floor. The slabs were scattered on the silt with no particular arrangement and all located on the same level. (Figure 62) These stone slabs had probably been moved to the building after the church was vacated and filled with nearly 40 cm of alluvium. They belong to the final phase when the naos and the narthex were used with a different function. It was not possible to identify the structure these stones belonged to and the purpose of their use in the church.

This final phase of use is evidenced by traces found at the narthex and the naos on the alluvial deposit about 40 cm above the church's original floor. It is considered to be after the building no longer was functioning as a church and vacated, thus dates to the end of the 13th century, or more likely the beginning of the 14th century.

50 For ceramics see Chapter VI in this volume.

Figure 56: North wall of the narthex leaning on the plaster of the west wall

Figure 57: *Deesis* fresco overlaying the south jamb

Figure 58: South wall overlaying the *Deesis* fresco

Figure 59: Dry stone masonry in front of the *Deesis* fresco

Figure 60: Two-treaded set of steps on the higher level at the entrance

Figure 61: Bench adjacent to the south wall

Figure 62: Stone slabs on the higher level at the naos floor

IV. Architectural Sculpture

Ayça Tiryaki
İstanbul University

During the excavations at Alakent Church in 2010, thirty-six stone artefacts of fourteen different types were uncovered, fifteen of which could not be identified.[1] The twelve *in situ* architectural sculpture works are examined in detail in the following catalogue.[2]

1. Catalogue

Catalogue no. 1	Doorframe (lintel and jambs).
Illustration	Drawing 1.I, 2, Figure 1–3.
Position	Door leading from the narthex to the naos.
Material	Limestone.
Date	Lintel (?); Jambs 9th–10th centuries.
Dimensions	Lintel: Height 16 cm; length at top 1.67 m; length at bottom 1.20 m; depth 35 cm; depth at bottom 27.5 cm.
Jambs	Height 2.22 m; width 20 cm; depth 42.5 cm.
Description	The doorframe consisting of *in situ* lintel and jambs is in relatively good condition. The door lintel has a trapezoidal cross-section, with no ornamentation on its finely cut front face apart from the cross-shaped engraved motifs. A part of the lintel near its left side is broken. The geometric patterns and profiles utilized on the two jambs are the same. The pattern visible on the front face of both jambs consists of flowers with oblong leaves placed at the intersections. Among them is a series of circles arranged to form concave-sided squares between them. The low relief interlaced circles are framed with two plain profiled strips, one

1 The artefacts with an identifiable function consist of four cornices, six columns, two slabs and vessels/mortars, as well as a column base, a capital, an architrave, a pier, a doorframe (one lintel and two jambs), an altar (altar table and base), and finally a mortar.

2 The lintel and jambs, and the altar slab and altar base of the altar table were assigned a single catalogue number and not considered separately in the catalogue.

thicker than the other. On the side face of the jamb on the left side of the doorway, there are holes for the wooden doorframe. The lintel does not exactly fit the jambs, since there is a difference in size.

Catalogue no. 2 Slab with cross pattern.
Illustration Drawing 1.II, Figure 4.
Location On the eastern wall of the narthex north of the naos entrance.
Material Limestone.
Date 11th century.
Dimensions Width 18 cm; height 26 cm.
Description It was used as spolia in the wall. Its original function is unknown. Inside the two rectangular frames with a pointed profile is a low-relief Latin cross. At the intersection of the arms of the cross is a circle. At the ends of the arms of the cross, extending outwards from the central circle, are also two circular motifs. The ends of the cross are arc-shaped. In the longer lower arm –between the two circles– is a pointed component that acts like the handle of the cross. On the flat surfaces between the arms of the cross and the frame, Greek letters were engraved. On the two sides of the upper part of the cross it reads IC XC, and on the two sides of the lower part the letters NI KA can be distinguished.

Catalogue no. 3 Fragment of the templon architrave (?).
Illustration Drawing 1.III, 3, Figure 5.
Location Located on the south facade of the church, above the window.
Material Limestone.
Date 11th century.
Dimensions Length 36 cm; width 21 cm.
Description It is difficult to determine the original function of this piece as it was used as spolia in the wall. The stone piece broken on two sides has a rectangular frame consisting of three strips within which are circles, placed side by side. They are attached to one another and to the frame with loops. Inside the three-stripped circles is a rosette consisting of twelve sections and a cross-shaped flower motif with three-bladed leaves. On the almost completely destroyed third circle it is possible to distinguish the multi-petaled rosette motif. In the area between the circles, two strips twisting out of the loops stretch out on both sides to form stylized heart-shaped lotus motifs. There are drill holes on the loops and the filling motifs.

Catalogue no. 4 Cornice No. 1.
Illustration Drawing 1.IV, 4.1, Figures 6-8.
Location On the southwest wall of the naos.
Material Limestone.
Date 12th century.

Dimensions Length 1.65 m; height 19 cm; depth at top 43 cm; depth at bottom 16.5 cm.

Description The wide upper part of the cornice with a right-angled profile is unornamented, roughly levelled, and has visible pointed chisel marks. Its chamfered lower part is ornamented. On the bevelled surface is a relief consisting of an S-curved branch and stylized acanthus leaves arranged alternately facing up and down between the curves of the branch. The leaves are arranged to cover completely the surface between the curves and rendered with concave lobes and pointed tips. The leaves were executed in a slipshod manner, and no two are the same. Some of them were rendered with thick veins while the veins in some were altogether lost between a complex structure of lobes. Within the ornament consisting of a sequence of curved branch and leaf, two stylized animal figures were placed. At the left end of the cornice, inside the first curve of the twisting branch motif, there exists a disproportionately rendered representation of a predator. The lion-like figure has a head out of proportion to its body, and in this depiction its front paws and head with pointed ears were emphasized. It has a tail curled upwards and lines engraved on its mane. Towards the right side of the cornice is a bird figure, placed between the leaves with its head facing down. It has claws emphasizing its characteristic feature and wings with engraved lines. The head and the body of the bird are depicted in profile, while the claws are depicted in frontal view. It was rendered with an open mouth and large talons. At the right end of the cornice there is a half-acanthus leaf and two pine cone motifs.

Catalogue no. 5 Cornice No. 2.

Illustration Drawing 1.V, 4.2, Figures 9 and 10.

Location On the southeast wall of the naos.

Materials Limestone.

Date 12th century.

Dimensions Length 1.07 m; height 21 cm; depth at top 41 cm; depth at bottom 16 cm.

Description The upper part of the cornice is unornamented and wide, roughly levelled with the use of a point chisel. There is a crack near the right side of the cornice. There are pieces broken off on its left side. In the lower concave profiled and ornamented part, between the curved branches with buds and other branches, there are conifers, leaf, and flower motifs in relief. The branch collars of the curved branches are indicated by three fine lines, and by splitting them in two the branches form the curls. The spaces between the curved branches are filled with motifs of a compounded leaf consisting of seven smaller leaves, four-petaled flowers, and pinecones arranged in sets of two or three. The leaves of the four-petaled flower are rounded and concave, and the ones on top of the pinecones are angular. The triangular spaces between the curved branches and the frame are filled with small bud-like leaves. Amidst the curls on a wide leaf and pinecone is a bird figure. There are horizontal and vertical lines engraved on the body of the bird, emphasizing the feathers of the hardly visible bird.

Catalogue no. 6	Cornice No. 3.
Illustration	Drawing 1.VI, 4.3, Figures 11–13.
Location	On the northeast wall of the naos.
Material	Limestone.
Date	12th century.
Dimensions	Length 85 cm; height 21 cm; depth at top 41 cm; depth at bottom 16.5 cm.
Description	The upper part of the cornice with a right-angled profile is unornamented and roughly cut. The surface bares the marks of a pointed chisel and a fine-tooth chisel. Its lower part is ornamented on the bevelled surface utilizing a relief technique. The plant motifs featuring in the composition include single, double, and triple pinecones, four-petaled flower, and stylized leaf motif. The spaces between the curved branches and the frame are ornamented with small bud-like leaves. On the left side of the cornice is the figure of a bird depicted in profile and pecking at a pinecone. The bird depicted under the pinecone is rendered smaller than the pinecone. The bird has a very small head in comparison to its body and was rendered without any detail. For instance, it has no claws and only the feet on the pinecone were shown. While its eye and mouth could be distinguished, its body has deteriorated. The same composition repeats at the other end of the cornice. Here a relatively larger bird figure is depicted on another pinecone. The beak and eyes of the bird were depicted, and the feathers on its body were emphasized through horizontal and vertical lines. Its feet are visible but it has no claws.

Catalogue no. 7	Templon Pier.
Illustration	Drawing 1.VII, 5, Figures 14–15.
Location	On the north wall of the bema.
Material	Limestone.
Date	Middle Byzantine period.
Dimensions	Height 68 cm; width 16 cm.
Description	It is placed adjacent to the wall in front of a niche used for liturgical purposes on the northern wall of the bema. The stone was originally a templon pier and utilized here to support a terracotta shelf. The bottom part of the block was trimmed off evenly at a later date to fit its new place. It has a guilloche motif ending in a pointed form at both ends in low relief inside a rectangular frame. At the bottom of the stone piece the tip of what was probably another guilloche motif is visible. At the point where the two tips converge there is a circle motif. There are drill holes in the middle of the guilloche motif. At the center of the design, the trace of

a ruler mark left by the stonemason as part of a sketch is visible. Additionally, there are traces of other ruler marks that could be distinguished around the drill holes.

Catalogue no. 8 Templon Slab.
Illustration Drawing 1.VIII, 6-7, Figures 16-18.
Location On the south side of the templon.
Material Limestone.
Date 11th century.
Dimensions Height 1.02 m; width 1.00 m; thickness 11 cm.
Description Both sides of the spolia slab used in the southern part of the templon are ornamented. The upper part is broken and has cracks on its surface. On its front face, inside a horizontal rectangular frame in relief, is a three-striped rhombus and an interlaced arrangement of three stripes curving out of the diagonal axes of the rhombus to form semicircles. At the center of this geometric composition is a flower motif with six pointed petals inside a three-striped medallion. The large frame surrounding the ornamented surface was covered with a fresco having a geometric pattern painted red. Underneath the layer of fresco on the right side of the slab the ornamentation in relief was visible. On the back of the slab, inside a broad frame, is a Latin cross with leaves in relief. The slab was placed upside down so that the long lower arm of the cross would face upwards. The arms of the cross have a concave form and end with two circles. From each side of the long, lower arm of the cross an ivy vine sprouts and curls inwards. At the end of each branch is a stylized, heart-shaped ivy leaf. At the upper part of the slab, at the place where the branches converge, a triangular protrusion adjacent to the frame is noticeable. On the arms of the cross there are visible horizontal and vertical ruler marks left behind from the stonemason's sketch. On top of the broad frame on the rear is a layer of plaster, and on the side with the cross there are marks of a pointed chisel and a fine-tooth chisel.

Catalogue no. 9 Altar Table and Altar Base.
Illustration Drawing 1.IX, 8, Figures 19-20.
Location At the bema, in front of the apse.
Material Limestone.
Date Roman era.
Dimensions Altar table: Length 1.04 m; width 83–85 cm; thickness 23 cm.
Altar base: Height 71 cm; diameter 54 cm.
Description The front, back, and side faces of the altar table are made up of unornamented, inward-inclined profiles. Its fine-tooth chiseled, unornamented surface has fractures. The rectangular slab has a right-angled profile at the top that merges with the convex and concave profiles underneath. The flat strip located at the fourth level of the set of profiles concludes

the set by adjoining the concave profile underneath. On the fine-tooth chiseled upper side is a mortise 5 cm deep and measuring 7.5 x 3 cm. On the surface around it are pointed chisel marks. Its upper side has a lewis hole measuring 18 x 4 cm. It was used as spolia. A fluted column shaft from another ancient structure was utilized as an altar base. Its fluted surface is damaged and has fractures.

Catalogue no. 10 Column Base.
Illustration Figure 21.
Location Found in front of the apse.
Material Limestone.
Date 5th–6th centuries.
Dimensions Height 26 cm; diameter 31 cm; height of plinthus 8 cm; width of plinthus 40 cm.
Description The Attic-type column base consists of a convex, profiled torus and a necking ring on top of a flat, non-profiled *plinthus*. A corner of the *plinthus* is broken. There are marks of wear on the surface of the base. On its top, the cavity usually present in the center in which to pour molten lead is missing.

Catalogue no. 11 Water Basin.
Illustration Figures 22 and 23.
Location South of the building.
Material Limestone.
Date Undetermined.
Dimensions Height 46 cm; diameter at top 48 cm.
Description The profiled lower part of the basin remains partially preserved, with a small chip on its surface. The top was carved at a depth of 28 cm and 40 cm in diameter. The outer edges of the shaft bearing a hole in the middle are fractured. On the profiled lower section is a Maltese cross in a circle. However, only two elements of the cross remain. Inside the subsequently carved section are pointed chisel and coarse-tooth chisel marks. A pouring hole, bored at the bottom of the shaft to drain liquids, indicates that it was used as a water basin.

Catalogue no. 12 Column Shaft.
Illustration Figure 24.
Location Found located to the south of the building.
Material Limestone.
Date 5th–6th centuries.
Dimensions Height 68 cm; diameter 42 cm.
Description The upper and lower parts of the column with a polygonal sectioned shaft are broken. There are coarse-tooth chisel marks visible on its en-

tire surface. Its two faces were subsequently flattened to fit against a wall. The upper part of the shaft was carved 13 cm deep and 23 cm in diameter for its later use as a mortar.

2. Evaluation

At the entrance of the church leading to the naos is a doorframe that has incompatible elements in terms of pattern and profile (Catalogue no. 1). Although using the same pattern on lintels and jambs is not generally favored in the Byzantine period, the same profile would continue without interruption, and thus they would be compatible with one another.[3] However, at the entrance door of the church, although the jambs share the same profile and pattern, an unornamented lintel with a different profile was utilized (Figure 1). The pattern and two strips on the jambs do not extend onto the lintel. There is also a discrepancy between the lintel and the jambs in terms of their dimensions. This demonstrates that the doorframe was not designed for the church, and that these elements were brought from different structures and used here as spolia.

The four-leaf motif, formed by intersecting circles on the ornamented jambs of the door, was used extensively across a broad geographical area and throughout a long span of history. It is found in floor mosaics of the Roman period as well as in stone artefacts of the Byzantine period (Figure 2). Early Anatolian examples of this pattern in floor mosaics can be found in the Zeugma and Antioch mosaics of the 2nd and 3rd centuries.[4] It was also used in different kinds of products in Byzantine stonemasonry since the 4th century. For example, the front of a sarcophagus from the 4th–5th century used as spolia in the wall of Konya's Sahip Ata Mosque bears the same pattern in relief.[5] Another early example is seen in the basilica-plan church in Knossos, Crete. The limestone balustrade slab dated to the mid-6th century has the same motif carved on its back.[6]

The motif of intersecting circles was utilized in stone works of different types and prepared with different techniques in the early period within Lycia. It appears at Lebissos/Gemiler Island in a plaque with openwork technique,[7] and with a *champlevé* technique on the cladding slabs at Arykanda and Rhodiapolis.[8]

In the Middle Byzantine period, especially between the 9th and 12th centuries, different arrangements of the motif of intersecting circles were frequently used, in relief form mostly in stone works with a liturgical function. In the first instance of these arrangements, in contrast to the example at the church, the square spaces between the pointed leaves formed by the intersection of circles are filled with circular motifs in relief. Artefacts with similar arrangements have been found in various regions, first and foremost in Antalya and its surroundings, as well as in Izmir, Nevşehir, the Aegean Islands, and in Greece.[9] In another arrangement of the same motif,

3 On doors from Late Antiquity and the Byzantine era, see Özügül 2005.

4 For the mosaic dated to the 2nd century in the Euphrates House at Zeugma, see Önal 2008, p. 83, Fig. 5. For the 3rd century examples in Antioch, see Campbell 1988, pp. 25, 75–76, Pl. 77, 214. For different variations of the interlaced circles motif used in mosaic floors, see Balmelle et. al., 1985, Pl. 238–239.

5 Temple 2013, p. 206, Fig. 463.

6 Frend and Johnston 1962, pp. 213, 215, Pl. 52d.

7 For the example at Gemiler Island, see Asano 2010, Pl. 10/3, 60/6. The openwork implementation of the pattern also appears at the second construction phase of the Church of St. Nicholas in Demre during the Middle Byzantine period. See Ötüken 1999, p. 486, Fig. 7.

8 For the cladding slabs at Arykanda, see Tekinalp 2006, p. 794, Fig. 10. The champlevé cladding slab examples found at the Rhodiapolis Church have not been published yet.

9 A similar ornamentation was used as border ornamentation on the templon slab at the Church of St. Nicholas

the surface is divided into squares, and each leaf is placed inside one of these squares. Similar examples of this arrangement were found in Western Anatolian cities such as Izmir, Aydın, and Afyon, and other comparable examples have been identified in Central Anatolia.[10] The majority of these liturgical stone pieces utilizing a square variant are dated to the 10th–12th centuries.

In contrast to the above-mentioned arrangements, in the pattern on both jambs of the church the square areas between the leaves were left empty. This favors a simpler variation of the pattern with a deceptive effect. The closest match to this pattern has been found at the Church of St. Nicholas in Demre and at Kaleiçi, Antalya. The same features of technique and style were utilized on the entire surface of the templon architrave and the small pier fragment of the gallery of the Demre church. While S. Alpaslan dated both pieces to the 9th–10th centuries,[11] another architectural element of the same church exhibiting the same characteristics was dated to the 11th century by U. Peschlow.[12] The templon pier used as a building element at Kaleiçi, Antalya, has the same composition in a similar technique and style.[13] It is also be necessary to mention the two balustrade slabs and templon architrave at Selçuk's Ephesus Museum, dated to the 9th–10th century, as some of the closest matching artefacts in terms of style and technical characteristics.[14] Examples have been identified in Phrygia[15] and around Konya[16] that have a similar pattern in a different style.

The motif of intersecting circles was generally used as a fringe motif or an infill motif in Byzantine-period stone artefacts across a broad, extensive geographical area from the early Byzantine period through the 12th century, as mentioned earlier. This makes it difficult to date these artefacts accurately. Considering the most closely matched examples of the motifs in the church, these should be dated to the 9th–10th centuries.

On the west facade of the church, just to the right of the door, is a Latin cross in relief (Catalogue no. 2) on the wall, bearing the features of a ceremonial cross. The cross motif, usually placed at the entrance of a structure or on its lintel or jambs, was placed to the left of the doorway that provides the only entrance to the naos. This is in keeping with safeguarding the holy space.

in Demre. See Feld 1975a, p. 376, Lev. 122c. The templon slab dated to 11th century by U. Peschlow was identified to belong to 9th–10th centuries by S. Alpaslan. See Peschlow 1990, pp. 224–225, 240, Abb. 3; Alpaslan 1996, pp. 110–111, Fig. 39. For the molding fragment at the Antalya Archaeological Museum, see Alpaslan-Doğan 2008, p. 125, Fig. 4. The templon architrave utilizing a similar ornamentation at Side's Küçük Liman Church is dated to the 10th–11th centuries. See Yıldırım 2013, p. 101, Fig. 216–217. For the templon architrave at the Tire Museum and the architrave and archivolt pieces uncovered at the Kadıkalesi excavations, see Ermiş 2004, Fig. 11; Armağan 2010, pp. 40–41, 43. It is possible to see similar stylistic features in the pier and molding pieces at the city of Corinth in Greece, and the 11th century architrave at the Panagia Krina Church on the island of Chios. See Bouras 1981, Fig. 33a; Scranton 1957, p. 121, Pl. 24/41, 34/180. For the similar example in Nevşehir see Temple 2011, p. 540, Fig. 7.

10 For the architrave piece uncovered at the Agora in Izmir (9th–12th centuries) and the ambo slab fragments at Bergama Museum (11th–12th centuries), see Ermiş 2004, Fig. 12; Dennert 1995, Table 49/1–2. For the baluster drum at Didyma (10th–12th centuries), see Peschlow 1975a, p. 221, Table 42/4. For the architrave at the Afyonkarahisar Archaeological Museum (10th century), see Parman 2002, pp. 109–110, Plate 27; for the templon piers used as spolia at St. Helena's Church in Sille, Konya (10th–12th centuries), see Temple 2013, p. 168, Fig. 350–352.

11 Alpaslan 1996, pp. 210–211, pp. 262–263, Fig. 90, 91, 110.

12 Peschlow 1990, pp. 233, 238, 240, Table 44/7.

13 Alpaslan 2003, p. 253, Fig. 2.

14 Büyükkolancı and Öztaşkın 2010, pp. 41–42, 46–47, Fig. 3–4, 11.

15 For the balustrade slab at Amorium (9th–10th centuries) and the two templon architrave pieces at Çömlekçi Village around Kütahya, see Ivison 2008, p. 509, Fig. 15; Niewöhner 2008, p. 324, 328, Fig. 27, 37a–b.

16 For a similar example utilized as spolia in a wall at Beykonak Village near Konya, which has been identified as a lintel/jamb (10th–12th centuries), see Arslan 2014, p. 137, Plate 45, Fig. 128.

During the Byzantine period it was a common belief that the openings of windows or doors were potential points of access for hostile or evil spirits and that these openings should be safeguarded to keep such unwanted beings away.[17] For this reason, inscriptions or simple symbols used for apotropaic purposes were placed on door lintels.

The Latin cross in relief –with arms ending in the shape of arcs decorated with small circular motifs– has the features of a ceremonial cross as mentioned earlier (Figure 4). The main features of ceremonial crosses are the cross arms designed to broaden as they move from the center to the ends and generally have an arc-shape. The tips of the arms terminate in drops, elongated circles, spheres, or palmettes. Their most distinctive feature would be a handle on the lower long arm that aids carrying the cross.[18] In the example at the church, there is a component between the circle motifs at the ends of the lower arm, which acts as a handle. It is known that ceremonial crosses, especially in the period after iconoclasm, terminated in large circle motifs at the ends of their arms.[19] Crosses with this shape, also known as pearled crosses, were associated with the "True Cross." In the early 8th century it was believed that Constantine saw this same type of cross before his victory at the battle of Milvian Bridge.[20] There are many cross motifs depicted in works of stonemasonry bearing the characteristics of the ceremonial cross. While most of these have been depicted as Latin crosses, there are also Maltese crosses with arms of equal length.[21]

The Greek letters engraved next to the arms of the cross make it easier for us to date this slab used as spolia. The letters IC XC inscribed on the two sides of the upper arms are a ligature for Jesus Christ (IESOUC XRISTOC), which later developed into a monogram of Jesus' name.[22] With the addition of the letters NI KA inscribed on the two sides of the cross's lower arm, an expression that translates as "Jesus Christ conquers" emerges. This expression is used frequently from the Middle Byzantine period onwards in various contexts, first and foremost in miniature arts but also in stonemasonry, the metal arts, icons, and even on the bread (*prosphora*) offered during the Eucharistic service.[23] Crosses depicted together with the "IC XC NI KA" inscription are also called the "conqueror's cross" and believed to provide the most powerful protection against evil.[24] This inscription, which appears in 9th century miniatures for the first time, was widely used until the 11th century. For instance, while its earliest parallels in metal arts date back to the 9th century, the majority date to the end of the 10th and the 11th centuries.[25] Additionally, examples of grave architecture utilizing conqueror's crosses begain to increase in number in

17 As the cross was believed to be the only real weapon with apotropaic powers, which could keep the evil at bay, it was extensively used on everyday objects, on the facades of religious and civil buildings –even at quarries– and due to its safeguarding powers in all areas of daily life it has become a symbol of widespread use. See Karpozilos and Cutler 1991, pp. 550–551; Israeli 2000, p. 127; Spieser 2001, p. 1.

18 Acara-Eser 2010, p. 29. For Byzantine ceremonial crosses, see also Cotsonis 1994.

19 Bouras and Cutler 1991, 553.

20 Cotsonis 1994, 40.

21 For similar examples from Greece (Ano Volos, Corinth) and Anatolia (Yalvaç – Isparta, Miletus – Aydın, Eskişehir, Konya), see Androudis 2007, Fig. 11; Scranton 1957, Pl. 20/12; Ruggieri 2005, Photo 13; Niewöhner 2013, p. 198, Abb. 58; Parman 2002, pp. 166–167, Photo. 114a; Temple 2013, Fig. 360, 482.

22 Ševčenko 1991a, p. 438.

23 Sandin 1992, p. 132. The IC XC VC ΘV inscription used in early icons was replaced by the Greek letters of IC XC NI KA in Middle Byzantine period. See Weitzmann 1976, p. 85, Pl. CVIIIb.

24 For a detailed account of the apotropaic function of the conqueror's cross, its uses in Byzantine art, and its origins, see Walter 1997.

25 Sandin 1992, p. 132.

the 11th century.[26] Therefore, it would not be wrong to date the spolia slab at the entrance facade of the church to the 11th century, the era when the conqueror's cross was used most extensively. There is also a simple cross motif engraved with a pointed tool on the middle part of the lintel, which serves the same purpose. (Figure 3)

The spolia piece placed just above the window opening on the south facade of the church (Catalogue no. 3) points to the Middle Byzantine period with its drill workmanship and its pattern. (Figure 5) The interlooped circles –consisting of three angular strips and filled with rosettes– is a motif widely seen in the Middle Byzantine period. It was used on piers and mostly on templon architraves generally at institutions with liturgical functions. On the loops and circles there is clearly visible drill workmanship. The use of drills in architectural stone artefacts is a frequently encountered practice in the Middle Byzantine period from the 9th century onwards. Drills were used to carve stone and to apply openwork technique in stone decoration in the Early Byzantine period and for making holes between the motifs to emphasize the patterns in the Middle Byzantine period.[27] In the stone artefacts bearing this pattern, different motifs were used inside the interlooped circles, while different plant motifs and geometric patterns such as single leaf, lotus, palmette/triple leaf, arrowhead, and spearhead were used as filling patterns in the empty spaces formed above and below the loops connecting the circles.[28] In the example at the church with its high-quality workmanship, stylized lotus motifs were used as infill. Similar examples can be observed on templon architraves in Anatolia around Afyon, Kütahya, Izmir, and Konya.[29] These examples are dated to the 10th–12th centuries. We also encounter parallel examples outside Anatolia from the 10th and 11th centuries. For instance, it is possible to see a similar composition in a different style at Mani[30] and at the Athens Museum[31] in Greece, at the templon piers of the Church of St. Sophia in Ohrid,[32] and on a sarcophagus in Kiev.[33] Considering its parallels in terms of geographical proximity, we can see the use of a similar pattern with a different arrangement at the Dereağzı Church in Lycia.[34] In the piece of slab dated between the second half of the 9th century and 10th century, the motif of interlooped circles appears as the filling pattern surrounding the Latin cross. Another example close both in terms of geographical location and of style and technical features is found at the Eastern Basilica of Xanthos.[35] The architrave pieces of the templon dated to the 10th–11th centuries have interlooped circles composed of a set of three strips, just like in our example, and there are noticeable drill holes on the loop motifs. What differs from our example is the use of stylized palmette motifs between the circles. An-

26 Walter 1997, p. 205.

27 Alpaslan 2003, p. 255.

28 Yıldırım 2006, p. 154.

29 In these examples, the space between the interlooped circles are either left blank or filled with motifs of lotus leaf, single leaf or three-bladed leaf. Of the architraves belonging to the Middle Byzantine period at the Afyon and Kütahya Museums, only one was dated to the 11th century, while the others are undated. See Parman 2002, pp. 99, 103, 112, Photo. 2b, 3, 4b, 10, 24. For the similar 11th century templon architrave pieces at the Izmir Archaeological Museum, see Grabar 1976, p. 48, Pl. 13–14. Similar examples from Konya found at museums and used as spolia in Seljuk architecture have been dated to the 10th–12th centuries. See Temple 2013, pp. 173–174, 176, Fig. 370, 372–374, 377–378.

30 Drandakis 1976, πίν.6β, 13β–γ.

31 Sklavou-Mauroeidi 1999, p. 120.

32 Grabar 1976, pp. 71–72, Pl. 41b, d.

33 Grabar 1976, pp. 71–72, Pl. 58b.

34 Morganstern 1993, pp. 174-176, Pl. 28/3.

35 Sodini 1980, pp. 123–127, Pl. 31a, c, 34c.

other parallel of the Alakent example, with matching motifs, technique and stylistic qualities, is found at the Church of St. Nicholas in Demre. The two templon architrave pieces found at the gallery and the courtyard of the building have been dated to the 11th to 12th centuries.[36] The *in situ* architectural pieces dated to the 11th century at the church also display parallel characteristics with our example in terms of motifs and style.[37] Taking the style and motif characteristics of the closest matching examples into account and considering the construction date of the church, the templon architrave is believed to be an 11th century artefact, ornamented before the 12th century.

The fact that the spolia described in Catalogue no. 3 was placed right above the southern window, one of the few openings of the church, suggests that this architectural piece was not just used as building material or as a decoration. Rather there was another reason behind its placement here. Since the Early Byzantine period, it was believed that these types of interlaced patterns, such as the motif on this piece, acted as an apotropaic talisman against evil, and especially that such patterns formed an infinite loop to ward off the devil.[38] There are three openings in the building that allow access to the naos. One of these is the doorway on the western wall, another is the apse window on the eastern wall, and the third is the twin window opening on the southern wall blocked at a later date. This is where piece No. 3 is located. Next to the doorway on the west side a spolia slab with a conqueror's cross was placed, and a cross motif was engraved on the lintel. And the window on the east – in the form of a cross – constituted the most powerful talisman.

There are four ornamented cornices on the walls of the naos. Since the cornice on the northwest wall was plastered over, it was not included in the catalogue. On Cornice No. 1 on the southwest wall (Catalogue no. 4), a composition frequently used on horizontal and vertical load-bearing stone works in both the Early and Middle Byzantine periods could be seen. It consisted of curved branches and leaves. (Figure 6) The examples utilizing this pattern can be found on the capital. Those closest to the site are located in the mountainous part of Lycia: the marble capitals of Church A at Beyazıt,[39] the marble architrave of the capital of the Monastery Church of Stoudios,[40] the stone works in the basilica at the Alakilise settlement,[41] and the church in Asarcık East.[42] These are examples found in Lycia that utilize openwork with outstanding workmanship in the Early Byzantine period. At the Monastery Church of Stoudios and at Alakilise, just like on Cornice No. 1, a bird figure was placed between the acanthus leaves. Compared to these examples, Cornice No. 1 appears to mimic the decoration of the curved branch in local style, produced with a rather simple workmanship. Unlike these examples from the early period, in this cornice

36 The architrave pieces were dated to the 11th century by Feld and Peschlow, while S. Alpaslan has identified them as belonging to the 11th–12th centuries. For the two pieces of the architrave which were uncovered, see Feld 1975a, p. 372, Table 119–120; Alpaslan 1996, pp. 214–215, drawing. 34–35, Fig. 97–98. For the templon architrave with six different pieces uncovered at the gallery and courtyard, see Peschlow 1990, p. 240, Table 42/5–10; Alpaslan 1996, pp. 215–217, drawing. 36–41, Fig. 99–105.

37 Three-bladed leaves were used as filling motifs between the looped circles. See Peschlow 1990, pp. 238, 240, Table 43/5–6, 44/2.

38 Kitzinger states that as the looping compositions were believed to ward off evil they were used as a protective talisman in various cultures since antiquity. This continued in the Middle Ages. Similarly, Gombrich, too, expresses that interlaced arrangements were believed to provide the best protection against evil forces. See Kitzinger 2003, p. 802; Gombrich 1994, pp. 262–263.

39 Mathews 1976, p. 31, Fig. 5–3, 5–4.

40 Mathews 1976, pp. 156–157, Fig. 15–21, 15–24.

41 The architrave piece at Alakilise also have a bird figure among the leaves. See Harrison 1972, pp. 191–192, Fig. 10, 12.

42 İşler 2009, p. 140.

there is also a lion motif carved inside a curved branch. The lion is considered to be a symbol representing Jesus.[43] (Figure 7) On this piece from the church, the animal figures are not depicted in a realistic manner as they had been in the early period. They are rendered in a superficial and simple style without any detail. With its stylized approach characteristic of the Middle Byzantine period, no examples similar to Cornice No. 1 in terms of style have been identified. So, it is clear that this was produced by a local workshop. The leaves give the impression of being carved casually on the surface of the cornice. They were rendered with pointed tips and a concave form. This type of leaf appears to have been used during the Middle Byzantine period, and more extensively between the 9th and 12th centuries.[44] The closest matching examples of this type of stylized acanthus motif can be seen on slabs at Arneai[45] and at the Church of St. Nicholas in Demre.[46]

Cornices on the southeast and northeast walls of the naos (Catalogue nos. 5 and 6) were produced with similar motifs and in a similar style. They were rendered with curled branches with collars and motifs of different plants (leaf, flower, pine cone) between them. (Figures 9-13) The same local style can be seen in the bird figures placed between the leaves. This similarity indicates that the other cornices were also made by the same stonemason.

That the pinecones on cornices no. 2 and no. 3 were rendered in sets of two and three is noteworthy. (Figures 9, 10 and 12) The pinecone motif was used in the Early and Middle Byzantine periods, especially as an infill motif at the corners of column capitals. It was depicted as a single cone,[47] and often also appears as a single motif in various types of sculptural pieces. For instance, it is utilized as an infill motif with single elements on the templon architrave at the Afyonkarahisar Archaeological Museum in a composition with an arcade from the Middle Byzantine period.[48] It is likewise found on a balustrade slab from the 9th–10th centuries at the Istanbul Archaeology Museum. It is also used at the end of a column depicted as the Tree of Life.[49] Three pinecone motifs at the tip of a tree clasped by a lion figure on a slab piece dating from the 10th century is found at the Byzantine And Christian Museum in Athens.[50]

The vegetal motifs used in the curled branch compositions of Byzantine stonemason-

43 Karpozilos, Kazhdan, and Cutler 1991, p. 1232. It is believed that “as the lion sleeps in its den with eyes open, so Christ is vigilant for the salvation of Man, whom he saved with his death on the cross and with his resurrection and whom he freed from the error of sin”. See Pitarakis and Merantzas 2006, p. 150. For the lion figure in Christian iconography, see Bloch 1968, pp. 112–119.

44 Alpaslan 2003, p. 254.

45 Alpaslan 2003, p. 254.

46 Peschlow dates the slab to the Early Byzantine period, while Alpaslan states that it belongs to the 8th-9th centuries. See Alpaslan 1996, pp. 254–255, drawing 26, Fig. 50; Peschlow 1990, p. 234, Table 44/8.

47 For the 6th century column capitals with cone motifs at the Church of Metamorphosis in Burgazada, at the St. Sophia, and at the Istanbul Archaeology Museums, see Zollt 1994, p. 89, Table 35/220, 222. In the Middle Byzantine period, the motif appears in buildings at the capital and in Greece, especially between the 10th and 12th centuries. Examples include the column capitals of the Church of St. George in the Mangana Quarter in Constantinople (11th century); capitals of the Monastery Church of Pantocrator (12th century), currently in Berlin; in Greece, the two column capitals of the Hosios Loukas Katholikon (10th century), the capitals at Hosios Meletios (11th century), and the capitals in Serez (end of 11th to beginning of 12th century). All have single pine cone motifs at the corners of the capitals as infill motifs. See Dennert 1997, pp. 93–97, Table 201–211. During the restoration of the Pantocrator Monastery of Constantinople, an *in situ* column capital with pine cones was uncovered. See Ousterhout, Ahunbay and Ahunbay 2009, p. 252, Fig. 23. Another example from the second half of the 10th century to the second half of the 11th century can be found at Alanya Museum. See Doğan 2009.

48 Parman 2002, pp. 100–101, Fig. 5a.

49 Fıratlı 1990, pp. 163–164, Pl. 99/324.

50 Sklavou-Mauroeidi 1999, p. 106.

ry generally feature various leaves, flowers, and grapes. The use of the pinecone motif in the curled branch arrangement was identified only in one other example. This templon architrave, no longer in existence, belonged to the Church of St. Nicholas in Demre.[51] This artefact, which displayed signs of high-caliber workmanship, had vine leaves, pomegranates, and pinecones in its curvilinear composition of acanthus leaves. Additionally, the bird figures in the curled branch compositions are generally depicted eating grapes. A bird figure pecking at a pinecone, as in cornices no. 2 and no. 3, was encountered only in one other example: a slab piece from the 9th–10th centuries in the Byzantine And Christian Museum in Athens.[52]

As mentioned earlier, in terms of composition and style no matching examples of the cornices described in the catalogue have been identified. Therefore, it is believed that these works, rendered with a simple style yet differing from the other pieces, are not spolia but may have been produced specifically for Alakent Church.

It is difficult to determine the exact function of the spolia piece with a refined workmanship that supports a niche shelf adjacent to the wall of the bema (Catalogue no. 7). Based on its dimensions and shape, we deduced that this was used as a templon pier (Figure 14, Drawing 5). The guilloche motif with a drill-work center was an ornament frequently used in different types of stone artefacts in the Middle Byzantine period (Figure 15). In the example at the church, after a single strip was carved, its center was left flat. That this single strip has a pointed profile indicates that the spolia belongs to the Middle Byzantine period.[53] However, it was not possible to identify a guilloche motif with pointed tips on both ends at any other location, and no similar examples were found.

Both the front and back faces of the balustrade slab (Catalogue no. 8) –placed in an inverted position in the south section of the templon– are ornamented. On its front is a basic application of one of the frequently used compositions in the Middle Byzantine period. (Figure 16, Drawing 6) This sort of geometric arrangement with rhombus connected to an interlocking curling motif is often used as the main pattern covering an entire surface, as on the slab at the church. Yet it is also commonly used as an infill motif on templon architraves. Similar examples of this simple geometric arrangement were used as spolia in architectural pieces dated to the 9th–11th centuries in buildings in and around Konya,[54] and on the templon architrave from 11th century at the Izmir Archaeological Museum.[55] Other more ornate and intricate variations of this pattern could be seen on a slab dated to the 10th–11th centuries at the Akşehir Archaeological Museum[56] and on the liturgical slab and architraves at the Afyonkarahisar Archaeological Museum.[57]

On the back of the balustrade slab is a cross with leaves in relief, symbolizing "life, born of death, through the torment and resurrection of Jesus."[58] (Figure 17, Drawing 7) This symbolic

51 Rott 1908, p. 333, Fig. 125.

52 Sklavou-Mauroeidi 1999, p. 90.

53 The strips of interlaced motifs were rendered flat in the Early Byzantine period and pointed in the Middle Byzantine period. See Alpaslan 1996, p. 351.

54 For two similar pieces of slabs found near Konya, see Arslan 2014, pp. 155–156, Fig. 201–202. The templon architrave (9th–10th centuries) and the sarcophagus slab (10th–11th centuries) were used in the walls of Konya Zazadin Han in the arches of an arcade design. See Temple 2013, p. 179, Fig. 382,

55 Grabar 1976, p. 48, Pl. 13.

56 Yıldırım 2006, pp. 104–105.

57 Parman 2002, pp. 99, 101–102, 123, Lev. 3/2d, 11/6–7, 47/47.

58 Pitarakis and Merantzas 2006, p. 161.

motif –associated with the Tree of Life[59] in the Garden of Eden and called the "Cross of Life" in Byzantine art– has been extensively used in various fields of art: from metal art to wall paintings and manuscripts, as well as for architectural and liturgical stone artefacts.[60] The earliest known example of the cross with leaves in Byzantine art is on the balustrade slab at the Church of Sergius and Bacchus in Constantinople, dated to the 6th century.[61] However, it was widely used in the Middle Byzantine period, especially in the 10th and 11th centuries. It continued in use on coins and seals in the post-Byzantine period.[62] The closest matching example of the cross with leaves found at Alakent Church is from the Church of St. Nicholas in Demre. On this slab, the cross with leaves has the form of a Maltese cross with arms ending in circle motifs. The leaves climbing on both sides have similar characteristics with our example.[63] Similar examples in terms of motifs and style, especially leaf styles, can be seen on sarcophagus slabs from the 11th century on the Greek islands of Leros and Kos, and on the balustrade slabs at the Basilica of San Nicolas in Bari.[64] Therefore, like similar other examples, the templon slab would have been produced in the 11th century and later used as spolia in this building.

The altar table and base (Catalogue no. 9) unearthed *in situ* in front of the apse consists of spolia pieces used as architectural elements in other buildings. (Figure 19, Drawing 8) The piece of a column utilized as the altar base must have been taken from an ancient structure and reused here. This practical approach can also be seen in larger-scale basilical churches.[65] The piece used as the top plate of the altar table is profiled on three sides and has a flat back. Taking into consideration the central mortise (lewis hole) on its top face, this piece was originally used on the facade of a building from the Roman period as part of the superstructure.

The artefacts examined in the catalogue are spolia utilized as building materials on the walls, or elements reused in their original function. However, the cornices (Catalogue nos. 4,5 and 6), which are considered contemporareous with the building, are not spolia. No similar elements could be identified elsewhere. At first glance the ornamented pieces on the facades (Catalogue nos. 2, 3) give the impression of being simply used as building materials on the walls. However, they are thought to have acted as talismans protecting the sacred space.

The ornamentation seen on these artefacts consists of vegetal, geometrical, and symbolical motifs, frequently used in the Middle Byzantine period. The geometrical motifs were interlooped circles (Catalogue no. 3), interlaced geometric patterns (Catalogue no. 1), and guilloche motifs (Catalogue no. 7), while the symbolical motifs are the ceremonial cross (Catalogue no. 2) and the cross with leaves (Catalogue no. 8). All of these motifs were extensively used during

59 Genesis 2:9.

60 Doğan 2009, p. 139; Osborne 1997, p. 10.

61 Rice 1950, p. 71, Pl. 1. G. Mendel, although not definitively, dates the slab to 6th century. See Mendel 1914, p. 524.

62 Doğan 2009, p. 139; Pitarakis and Merantzas 2006, p. 161.

63 U. Peschlow dates the slab to 11th century, pointing out that due to its size this would be a sarcophagus slab. The same slab was dated to 9th–10th centuries by S. Alpaslan. See Peschlow 1990, pp. 235–236, Fig. 6, Tab. 45/2, 4; Alpaslan 1996, pp. 104–105, Drawing 11, Fig. 30–31.

64 For the 11th century sarcophagus slabs at Leros and Kos, see Katsioti and Papavassiliou 2002, pp. 122–123, Fig. 4–5; Militsi 2009, Fig. 6. The slabs at Bari were dated to be between the end of 10th century to the first half of the 11th century by M. Salvatore and N. Lavermicocca. And M. M. Lovecchio dates them to 11th century. See Salvatore and Lavermicocca 1980, p. 109, 111, Fig. 17, 20; Lovecchio 1981, pp. 25–29, Fig. 7–7a, 8a, 8c. For other variations of this motif in stonemasonry, see also Doğan 2009.

65 In the ancient city of Letoon, at the church with a basilical plan located south of the temples, there is a column shaft taken from Temple A and used as an altar base. See Metzger 1966, p. 109, Fig. 9.

that period. On the cornices (Catalogue nos. 4, 5 and 6), believed to belong to the Middle Byzantine period because of their simple workmanship, the use of animal figures alongside plant motifs with curled branches is noteworthy in the compositions. In those with curled branches, frequently seen in the Early Byzantine period onwards, the unusual use of a number of pine cone motifs and the absence of any matching examples of such motifs rendered in a simple style suggest that these pieces, unlike the others found on site, were not spolia.

The artefacts found *in situ* at the church and the other stone artefacts unearthed in the excavations indicate a predominant use of limestone produced in local quarries, These stone artefacts were produced at workshops in the region between the 9th–12th centuries, although the majority belong to the 11th century.

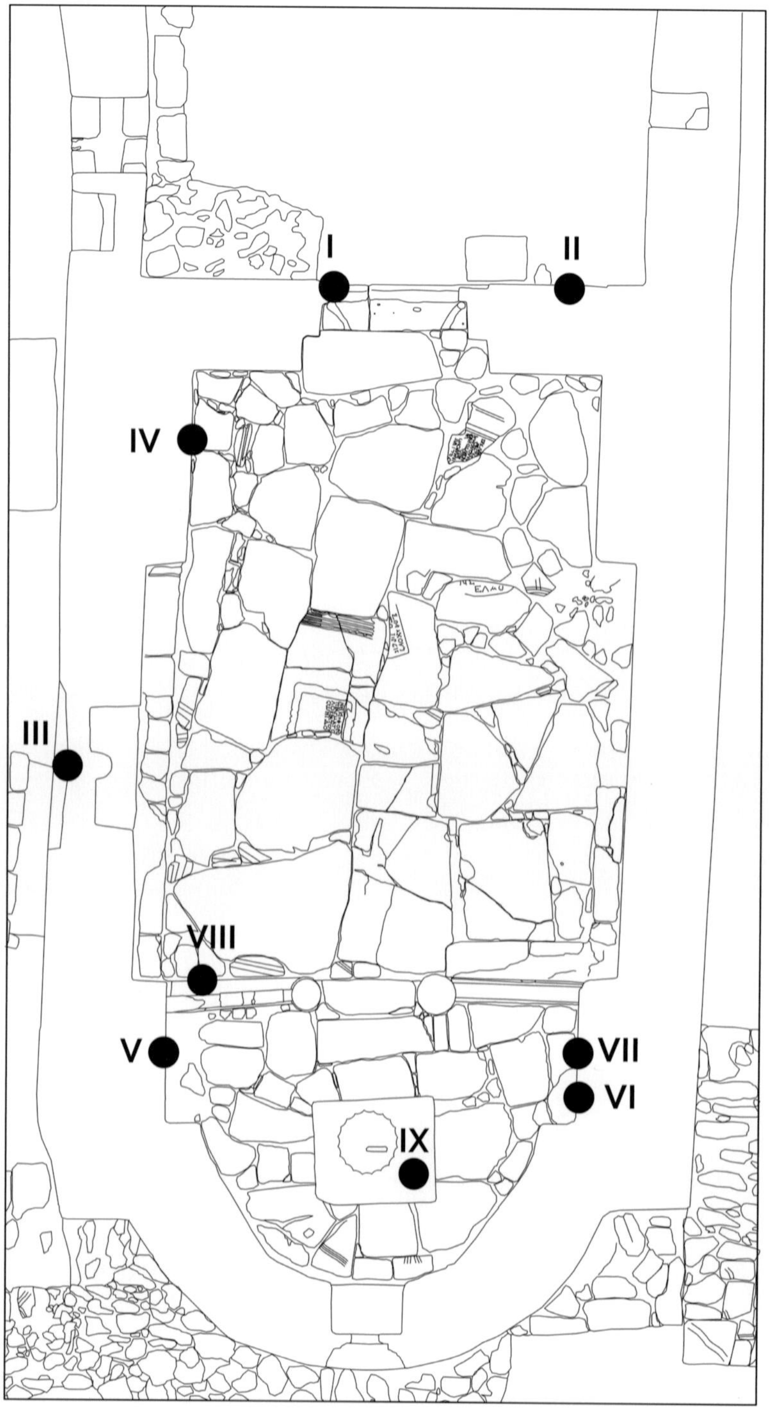

Drawing 1: Key to architectural sculpture

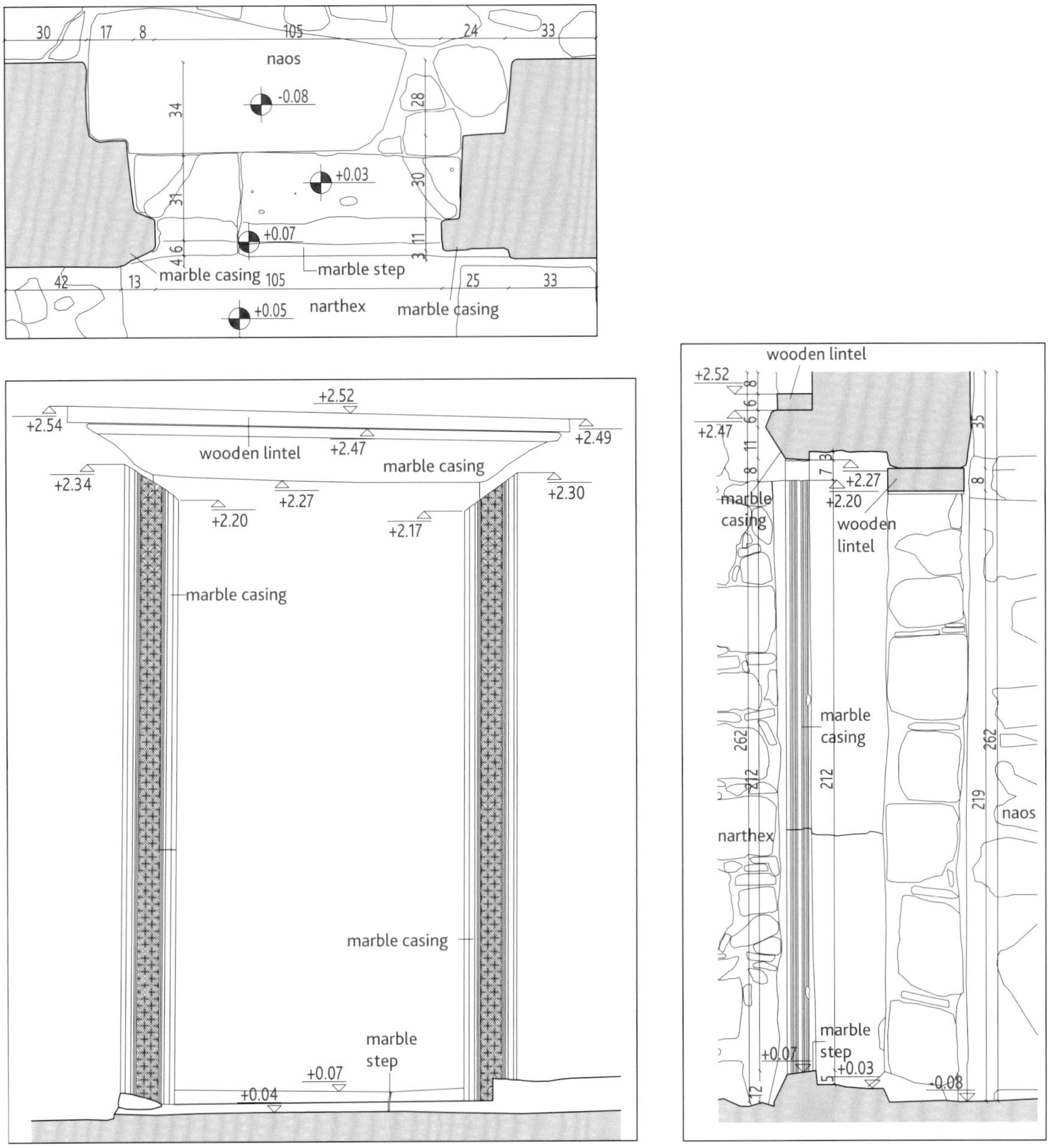

Drawing 2: Door lintel and jambs

Drawing 3: Templon architrave fragment

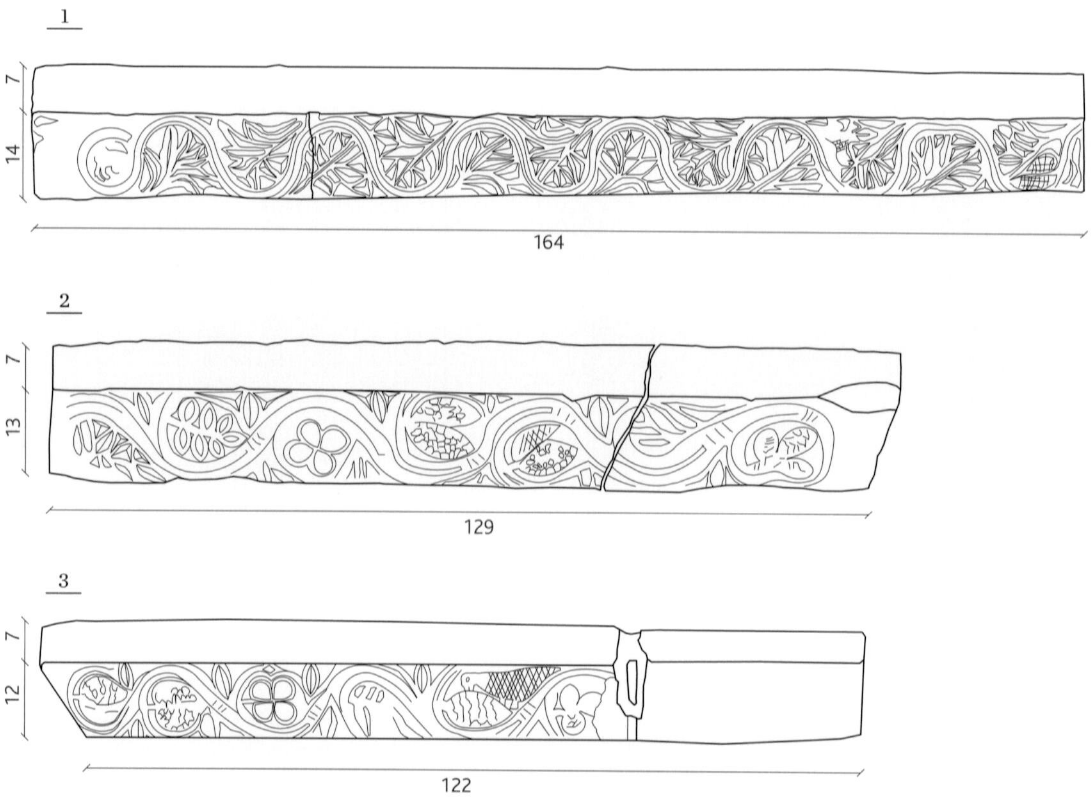

Drawing 4: Cornice fragments No. 1, 2 and 3

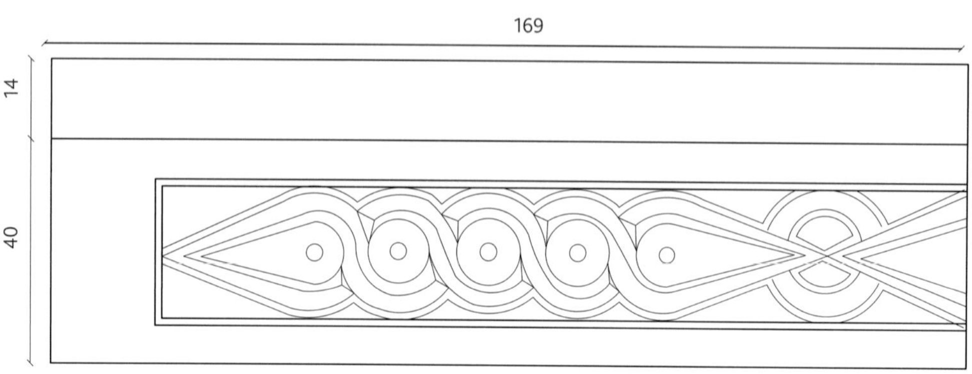

Drawing 5: Templon pier

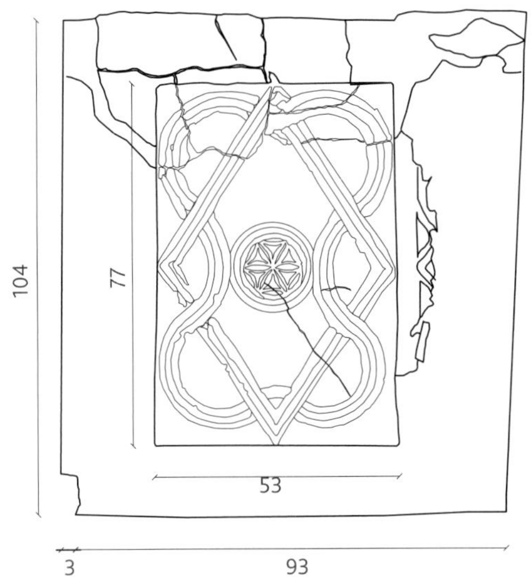

Drawing 6: Templon slab, front

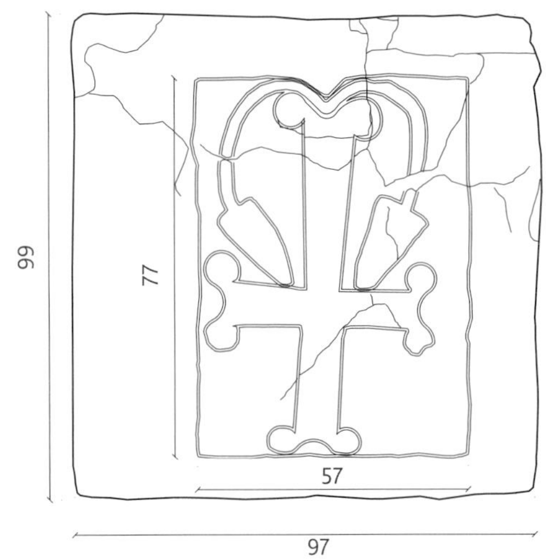

Drawing 7: Templon slab, back

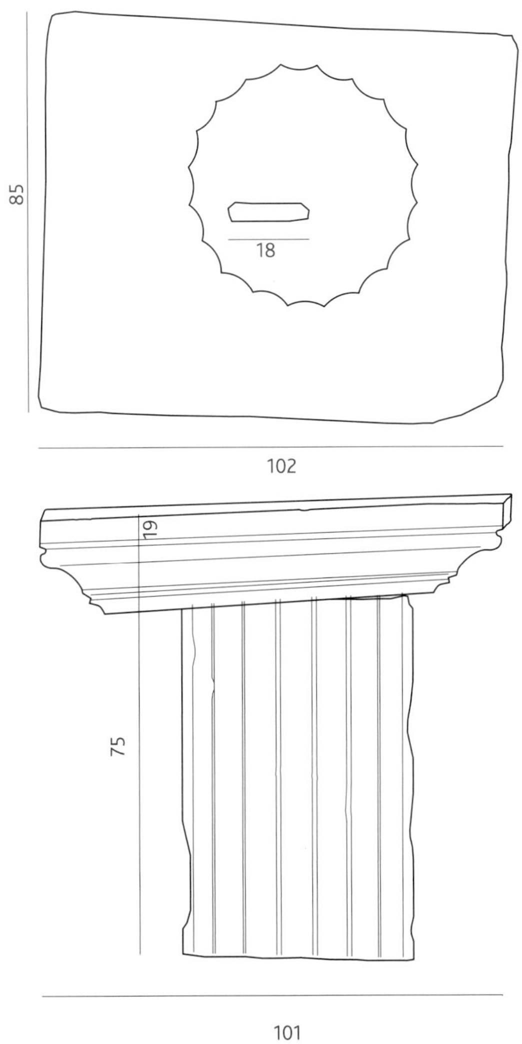

Drawing 8: Altar table and base

Figure 1: Door lintel and jambs

Figure 2: Detail of north jamb

Figure 3: Detail of lintel

Figure 4: Slab with cross pattern

Figure 5: Templon architrave fragment

Figure 6: Cornice No. 1, southwest wall

Figure 7: Cornice No. 1, detail

Figure 8: Cornice No. 1, detail of bird ornamentation

Figure 9: Cornice No. 2, southeast wall

Figure 10: Cornice No. 2, detail

Figure 11: Cornice No. 3, northeast wall

Figure 12: Cornice No. 3, detail

Figure 13: Cornice No. 3, detail

Figure 14: Templon pier

Figure 15: Templon pier, detail

Figure 16: Templon slab, front

Figure 17: Templon slab, back

Figure 18: Templon slab, back, detail

Figure 19: Altar table and base

Figure 20: Altar table, viewed from top

Figure 21: Column base

Figure 22: Stone water basin, viewed from top

Figure 23: Stone water basin, viewed from side

Figure 24: Column shaft

V.
Wall Paintings

Nilay Çorağan
Erciyes University

1. The Painting Program

The church, unearthed in the excavation west of the entrance of the ruins of Myra on the southwest side of the ancient theater, sheds light on the ancient city and the art of the period not only through the architectural data it provides but also with its wall paintings.[1] Although much of them was either destroyed or damaged extensively, the limited iconographic and stylistic features of the wall paintings provide us with important insight into the building. The relatively small-sized church has a specific painting program in the naos and the narthex. It is possible to observe that there is an emphasized presence of feast scenes in the building. Of the nine scenes that have survived, the Annunciation to the Virgin from the infancy of Christ, and the Baptism of Christ from the ministry of Christ could be identified due to their distinctive features. (Drawing 1) The limited iconographic data from the other fragmentary surviving scenes allow us to speculate about their themes. These scenes should be the Nativity or apocryphal Dormition of the Virgin (*Koimesis*) and the Presentation of Christ to the Temple from the infancy of Christ; the Transfiguration of Christ (*Metamorphosis*) from the ministry of Christ and the Crucifixion of Christ and the Harrowing of Hell (*Anastasis*) from the sequence of the Passion of Christ. Therefore, there are seven feast scenes in the church, and two symbolic scenes including the Virgin as *Platitera*, *Blachernitissa*, or *Nicopoia*, as well as the *Deesis* scene. (Drawing 1) It is noteworthy that the program includes extensive use of floral and geometrical decoration.

1.1. Scenes

In the middle of the semi-dome of the apse, Virgin Mary was depicted on a throne with archangels on both sides. (Drawing 1.I, Drawing 2, Figures 1–3). In the center of the scene, Mary was portrayed frontally seated on a throne. The figure, now almost entirely destroyed, has only the reddish-brown paint of her *maphorion* remaining. To the lower right of the throne, triangular motifs

1 For earlier publications on Alakent Church, see Akyürek 2010, pp. 153–160; Akyürek 2015a.

embellished with stylized curled branches inside strips formed with reddish-brown bands on a white background and short, vertical bands parallel to one another could be seen. (Figure 2) On both sides of the scene, the two archangels are depicted standing frontally. There are fragments of paint belonging to the reddish-brown tunic and dark brown wings of the archangel on the left. (Figure 3) On the other side, the left wing of the angel on the right could be seen. The stripes and triangular motifs created with reddish-brown bands and the white pearls on the *tablion* and *loros* of the angel are barely visible. The background is blue, and the ground on which they stand that starts around the knees of the figures is green.

In the southern part of the soffit of the arch of the bema is the scene of the Baptism of Christ. (Drawing 1.II, Drawing 3, Figure 4) At the center of the scene, Christ is depicted standing in frontal view. The white garment he is wearing and his bare legs could hardly be seen. To the right of the blue stream in which Jesus is standing, three white fish depicted in profile could be noticed. (Figure 5) The figure on the left of Christ is probably John the Baptist. The majority of the section with John was destroyed, but it is possible to tell that he was portrayed standing, slightly turned towards Jesus. The dark brown animal-hide clothing of the figure is barely distinguishable. On the left of the scene, the light brown and yellow paint used in depicting the wing of the figure of an angel heading towards Jesus is visible.

In the northern part of the soffit of the arch of the bema are fragments that might belong to the *Anastasis* (?) scene. (Drawing 1.III, Drawing 4, Figure 6) The figure depicted standing slightly turned to the left in the center of the scene should be Jesus. (Figure 7) The figure with a red cloak was destroyed from the waist up. On the left side of the scene, there is another figure depicted standing slightly turned towards Jesus. The top part of this figure, with a brown cape and light blue tunic, did not survive from the waist up. There are noticeable dark reddish-brown bands and strokes on the right side of the scene. The light brown and white strokes in the lower left section should belong to the broken doors of Hades (?).

On the southern wall of the western vault is the scene of the Annunciation to the Virgin Mary. (Drawing 1.IV, Drawing 5, Figures 8–12) Mary is on the right side of the scene. The figure of Mary is completely destroyed below her shoulders. She is depicted with her body turned towards the left of the scene. The right hand of the figure with a reddish-brown *maphorion* is held around the height of her chest, and her open palm is facing the viewer. In the part to the lower right of Mary, a small fragment of a yellow throne, decorated with nesting squares drawn with dark bands and short horizontal strips, could be seen. Above the head of the figure, a round arch embellished with stylized curved branches could be barely distinguished. On the left of the scene the archangel Gabriel is depicted. The head, right hand, and wings of the archangel are partially visible. The figure, depicted standing and turned towards Mary, is performing the gesture of benediction with his right hand. The wrist of the right arm of the archangel is decorated with small circles inside horizontal strips. (Figure 10) In the upper middle part of the scene a semicircular motif was pictured, symbolizing the semi-circle of heaven. (Figure 11) Rays of light consisting of vertical bands parallel to one another extend from the vault of heaven towards the head of Mary. On top of these rays is a white dove portrayed in profile and flying towards the Virgin Mary. (Figure 12)

The scene in the southern part of the western vault is probably the Presentation of Christ to the Temple (?). (Drawing 1.V, Drawing 6, Figure 13) Only the lower section of the scene has survived partially, depicting the lower part of a standing figure, dressed in a light green cape and light reddish-brown tunic (Joseph?) to the left of the scene. In the middle of the scene next to this figure, depicted slightly turned to the right, is Virgin Mary (?) with a reddish-brown *maphorion*. To the right of the scene is a figure in a light reddish-brown cape and a light green tunic (a priest?), depicted standing and slightly turned to the left. The green background up to the height of the knees of the figures and the lower part of the red strip surrounding the scene have survived.

On the northern part of the western vault is the scene of Transfiguration of Christ (?). (Drawing 1.VI, Drawing 7, Figure 14) There is a large orange mandorla clearly visible in the middle of the scene that only has its lower part remaining. In the middle of the mandorla on a blue background, there is a standing figure (Christ?) depicted frontally. The lower part of the light reddish-brown cape and the light green tunic of this figure has survived. To the left of the scene, the tunic of a standing figure slightly turned to the right, defined with light green lines could be seen.

The scene depicted on the pediment of the western vault is probably the Crucifixion of Christ (?). (Drawing 1.VII, Figure 15) A large part of this scene with multiple figures was destroyed. The lower section of the brown cross and part of the legs of Christ could be seen in the middle of the scene. To the left of the scene are reddish-brown paint marks of the maphoria that Mary and the female figures behind her are wearing.

The scene with multiple figures on the pediment of the arch of the north wall should probably be the Nativity of Jesus (?) or the Dormition of the Virgin/Koimesis (?). (Drawing 1.VIII) The scene was almost entirely destroyed with only a very small fragment distinguishable. In the upper left part of the scene, the curving dark yellow strip on the dark blue background is noticeable. Below this strip are dark reddish-brown paint marks. On the upper right corner of this section are fragments of yellow and reddish-brown paint which might belong to the haloes and wings of angel figures. To the right of the scene are paint marks of a figure's garment.

At the narthex of the church, on the southern part of the east wall is the *Deesis* scene.[2] (Drawing 1.IX, Drawing 8, Figures 16–28) In the middle of this well-preserved scene is Christ, depicted frontally and standing. Christ is standing on a podium that has a reddish-brown top and decorated with white pearl motifs around the edges. The figure is depicted making a gesture of benediction with his right hand held up at the height of his chest; he holds the Gospel in his left hand at waist height. The white pearl motifs on top of the dark yellow-covered book with a reddish-brown border are eye-catching. Christ is wearing a dark, reddish-brown tunic with a thick, dark yellow strip on his right shoulder, and a white cape. The dark-haired and bearded figure has a dark yellow halo with a cross inside above his head. On the arms of the cross inside the halo are small rhombus and circle motifs formed with thin white lines and white pearls. His mother Mary is depicted to the right of Christ, slightly turned towards him in supplication. The left hand of the figure is at the height of her neck, and she has an open scroll in her right hand held at chest height. The figure has a dark, reddish-brown *maphorion*, and the cuff of her right sleeve and her tunic are white. A dark yellow halo surrounds the head of the figure. The seventeen-line inscription in her hand is a supplication dialogue between Christ and herself.[3] In the dialogue, the words of Christ are written in red, and the words of Mary in black letters.[4] (Figures 18, 19) The inscription reads:

2 Akyürek 2010, p. 157.
3 Akyürek 2010, p. 157.
4 Akyürek 2010, p. 157.

ΔΕ
ΞΕ ΔΕΗ
CΗΝ ΤΗC ΤΕ
ΚΟΥCΗC CΕ
ΛΟΓΕ·ΤΗ ΜΗΡ
ΕΤΗC·ΤΗΝ Β
ΡΟΤΩΝ CΡΝ
ΠΑΡΟΡΓΙCΑ[Ν]
ΜΕ·CΥΝΠΑ
ΘΗCΟΝ ΥΕ [ΜΟΥ]
ΑΛΛ ΟΥΚ Π[Ι]
CΤΡΕΦΟΥCΙΝ
Κ CΩCΟΝ Χ[Α]
ΡΗΝ·ΕΞΟΥC[ΙΝ]
ΛΙΤΡΟΝ Ε[Υ]
ΧΑΡΙCΤΩ C[ΟΙ]
ΛΟΓ[Ε]

Δέξαι δέησιν τῆς τεκούσης σε, Λόγε.
Τί, μῆτερ αἰτεῖς; τὴν βροτῶν σωτηρίαν.
Παρώργισάν με· συμπάθησον, υἱέ μου·
Ἀλλ' οὐκ ἐπιστρέφουσιν· καὶ σῶσον χάριν.
Ἕξουσιν λύτρον· εὐχαριστῶ σοι, Λόγε.]

The English translation follows:
Mary – O Word of the living God, fulfil the prayers of a mother.
Christ – What is your will, mother?
Mary – Remission of the mortals.
Christ – They made me angry!
Mary – Be thou merciful,
Christ – They do not feel regret,
Mary – Grant them redemption.
Christ – All will be saved.
Mary – I am grateful, O Word.[5]

To the left of Christ, John the Baptist is depicted slightly turned towards Christ. The left hand of the figure is pictured at chest height in supplication, and he has a white open scroll in his right hand. The bearded figure with dark hair down to his shoulders has a dark green cape and reddish-brown tunic. The background is blue. The head of the figure is surrounded by a dark yellow halo. The scroll that the figure holds has an eight-line inscription (Figure 21) taken from the Gospel of John:

5 Akyürek 2010, p. 157. I hereby extend my gratitude to Dr. Tolga Uyar and Dr. Maria Xenaki for translating these inscriptions.

ΗΔΕ Ο
ΑΜΝΟϹ
ΤΟΥ ΘΥ
Ο ΕΡΩΝ
ΤΗΝ
ΑΜΑΡΤΙΑΝ
ΤΟΥ ΚΟϹ
ΜΟΥ

ἤδε ὁ ἀμνὸς τοῦ Θ(εο)ῦ ὁ ἔρων τὴν ἀμαρτίαν τοῦ κόσμου,

"Behold! The Lamb of God who takes away the sin of the world!"[6]

1.2. Individual Figures

There are barely visible paint marks of two standing figures with haloes, depicted frontally, on the south wall of the bema. (Drawing 1.1–2, Figure 29) The thick, dark red vertical and horizontal strips between the two figures might belong to the trunk of a cross. Therefore, it could be presumed that the two figures depicted here are Constantine and Helena (?).

On the eastern part of the south wall in the lower section, Virgin Mary, who is depicted frontally and seated on a throne, could be just about distinguished. (Drawing 1.3, Drawing 9.3, Figure 30) The reddish-brown *maphorion* of the Virgin is moderately perceptible. The right side of the throne with a back has survived. There is a red motif of a circle defined with black lines on its circumference where the lower and upper dark yellow strips meet. On the yellow strips, emphasized with two thin black lines on their outlines, are stylized curved branches formed with black lines. On the throne on a white background, small rhombus motifs perpendicular to each other were created with twin black lines. There are also small black squares where these black lines intersect. Inside the rhombus motifs are four-petaled flowers. The background was depicted in blue.

In the middle of the lower part of the south wall, there is a bishop depicted standing frontally, down to the level of his knees. (Drawing 1.4, Drawing 9.4, Figure 31) The figure is almost entirely destroyed apart from the partially visible right shoulder and right hand. The figure with a red *phelenion* has a white *omophorion*. He holds a book with a yellow cover in his right hand held up to his chest. The background is blue.

In the lower part of the western section of the same wall there are fragments of reddish-brown paint that might belong to the skirt of a figure depicted frontally and standing. (Drawing 1.5, Drawing 9.5)

1.3. Ornamentations

Floral Ornamentations: The thick vertical strip located in the lower part of the south wall, separating the figure of the bishop in the middle from the representation of Mary in the east, contains floral ornamentations. The edges of the strip are red. Inside the strip are stylized curved

6 John 1:29.

branches formed with black lines on a white background. (Drawing 9.B1, Figure 32) On the north face of the eastern arch and the eastern face of the north arch are dark red curved branches on a white background. (Drawing 10, Figures 33, 34)

Floral and Geometrical Ornamentations: On the south side of the templon wall there are large nesting rhombus motifs formed with reddish-brown and green lines. (Drawing 11, Figure 35) These motifs were divided in the middle with a line into two triangles. Inside the triangles are stylized reddish-brown, curved branches on a white background. In the areas outside these rhombus motifs, there are stylized curved branches drawn with green lines on a white background.

On the western side of the soffit of the pointed arch of the window located approximately at the central axis of the south wall, there are rhombus motifs intersecting perpendicularly that are formed with black lines. (Drawing 12, Figure 36) At the small square areas on the lower corners of the rhombuses there are four-petaled flowers. The top section of these square motifs have red green stripes.

Geometrical Ornamentations: On the plastered side of the slab on the southern side of the templon on the east, there are vertical bands of red herringbone patterns and small triangular motifs on a white background, drawn especially around the edges. (Drawing 13, Figure 37)

2. Evaluation

2.1. The Painting Program

In the middle of the semi-dome of the apse, Virgin Mary was depicted on a throne with archangels on both sides. (Drawing 1.I, Figure 1) At several churches in Cyprus with a plan similar to Alakent Church, the semi-domes of the apses have depictions of the two archangels on either side of a central picture of the Virgin as *Platitera*, *Blacherniotissa*, or *Nicopoia*.[7] Considering the presence of paintings in Cyprus similar to those at Alakent, it could be thought that the Virgin depicted on the semi-dome of the apse of the church might have been one of these types.

On the southern part of the soffit of the arch of the bema, the scene of the Baptism of Christ was identified. (Drawing 1.II, Figure 4) Examples of a similar scene depicted on the soffit of the bema arch, as in Myra, are very limited in number. The 13th century St. Nicholas Church at Naxos is similar to Alakent Church in Myra in terms of architectural characteristics. It is the closest match with its scene of Baptism on the northern half of the bema vault.[8] In addition, Chapel No. 3, dated to the first half of the 10th century at Güllüdere in Cappadocia, is parallel to Alakent Church, due to having a similar scene in the northern part of the east wall.[9]

The iconographic data visible on the scene fragment of the northern section of the soffit of the bema arch suggests that the scene depicted here might be the *Anastasis*. (Drawing 1.III, Figure 6) That being the case, it is striking that the scenes of the Baptism of Christ and *Anastasis* are depicted facing each other on the northern and southern sides of the soffit of the arch. The location of the *Anastasis* scene in structures with similar plan-types in Anatolia generally varies. The Güzelöz Haç Church in Cappadocia is similar to Alakent Church in that the scene is located on the northern wall of the eastern wing of the cross. However, the depiction of two scenes with

7 For the depictions of the Virgin on the apses at Cyprus, see Megaw and Hawkins 1962, Fig. 15; Winfield 1971, Fig. 9 (Monagri , Panagia Amasgou); Hein, Jakovljevic, and Kleidt 1998, Fig. 51 (Lagoudera, Panagia Araka), Fig. 156 (Kalogrea, Christ Antiphonitis).

8 Chatzidakis et. al., 1989, pp. 82, 89, Fig. 13.

9 Restle 1969, III, Fig. 337.

opposite subject matter from the initial and final periods of the life of Jesus that faces one another is a practice of the late period. The painting scheme on the apse and the soffit of the bema arch emphasizes "the incarnation of Christ." In the painting scheme of the bema "the salvation and resurrection of mankind" was symbolically reflected with the scenes of the Baptism of Christ and the *Anastasis* (?) depicted facing each other.[10] On the vault of the bema at St. Nicholas Church in Naxos, with a plan similar to Alakent Church, the scenes of the Nativity and the Baptism of Christ were depicted facing each other in a corresponding practice.

In Alakent Church, on the apse and the bema, a "liturgical" program was pursued. The bishop figures, barely visible on the lower wall of the apse are there as "the authority that ensures and guards the Orthodox rites."[11] The bishops accompany the liturgy with the books in their hands. These figures, regarded as a sacred authority, emphasize that the liturgy practiced by the priests and deacons conforms to the Orthodox tradition.[12]

The scene depicted on the southern part of the western vault is probably the Presentation of Christ to the Temple (?) (Drawing 1.V, Figure 13). It is very likely that the scene on the northern part of the same vault is the Transfiguration of Christ (?). (Drawing 1.VI, Figure 14) Much like in the bema, in this part of the naos the practice of depicting two festival scenes from the infancy and ministry of Christ facing each other is deliberate for increased emphasis. Correlating scenes in a liturgical relationship to achieve new meanings, as in the case of Alakent Church, is usually a feature seen in the 11th century and later. The Crucifixion scenes at structures with a free-cross plan in Cappadocia are generally located in the west side.[13] At the Panagia Amasgou Monagri Church (12th century) in Cyprus, with a plan similar to Alakent Church, the scenes of the Nativity of Jesus and the Presentation of Christ to the Temple on the southern half of the western vault, and the Baptism and Transfiguration scenes in the northern half of the same vault were depicted together facing one another.[14] At the Panagia Kera (Kritsa) Church from the late period in Crete, with the same architectural characteristics, the Presentation of Christ to the Temple and the scene of the Baptism are also opposite one another on the northern and southern halves of the western vault.[15]

It is quite peculiar and noteworthy that the Annunciation scene on the southern wall of the western arch was depicted in the west side at a location close to the entrance. There are only a limited number of similar examples. (Drawing 1.IV, Figure 8) At Göreme Karanlık Church (12th–13th centuries) the scene was depicted on the two sides of the entrance on the eastern wall of the narthex that leads into the naos.[16] At the Panagia Amasgou Monagri Church in Cyprus, the

10 On the north wall of the western section and the north half of the vault of the Church of Panagia tou Arakou in Cyprus, the Baptism and *Anastasis* scenes were depicted together. See Stylianou 1958, Figs. 149–150.

11 The Orthodox Church offers a framework for "salvation" to the believers, and in this framework, it is necessary to enter into communion with Christ in line with the Orthodox faith. The ultimate goal is the communion with Christ, the "One who is offering and offered." For this liturgy, see Walter 1982; Meyendorf 1983; McGuckin 2008.

12 Gerstel 1993, pp. 75–120.

13 At Göreme's El Nazar,with a free-cross plan, the scene is located on the pediment of the western wing of the cross. In structures with a Greek cross-in-square plan like Göreme's Elmalı Church, it is at the southwest corner space. At Karanlık Church it is on the pediment of the western wing of the cross, while at Çarıklı Church on the vault of the western wing of the cross. For these examples, see Restle 1969, II, Fig. 13 (El Nazar), Fig. 175 (Elmalı), Fig. 204 (Çarıklı), Fig. 231 (Karanlık).

14 Boyd 1974, Fig. 19–25.

15 Spatharakis 1999, p. 105.

16 Restle 1969, II, Plan XXII.

Annunciation scene is on the north wall.[17] The scene of the Annunciation to the Virgin, one of the scenes often portrayed in the 11th century and later, is generally located in the east side close to the apse. The Annunciation scene is one of the two principal feasts related to Virgin Mary, and the beginning of the festival cycle as well as the cycle of Christ. Considering its location close to the entrance of the church at Myra, it could be argued that with this scene "the salvation of the soul or of mankind" was emphasized at the entrance.

The scene depicted on the pediment of the western arch is probably the Crucifixion of Christ (?). (Drawing 1.VII, Figure 15) The examples where this scene was depicted on the western wall generally belong to 12th century and later. The scene was depicted on the west wall of the single-naved structures at the island of Kythira in Greece; at the churches of St. Andreas Perleggianika (13th century), St. Basil Friliggianika (13th century), St. George Ntoyrianika (13th century), St. Demetrios Pourko (13th century) and St. George Perleggianika (15th century).[18] The scene was also depicted on the western walls of the churches of St. Stephan (12th century) and Panagia Mavriotissa (13th century) at Kastoria.[19]

It is understood that the fresco fragments on the pediment of the arch in the upper section of the north wall belong to a scene with multiple figures. Therefore, it is likely that the scene depicted here was either the Nativity of Jesus (?) or the Dormition of the Virgin (*Koimesis*). (Drawing 1.VIII) At churches in Cyprus, especially of the same size and similar type of plan, festival scenes such as the Annunciation to the Virgin, the Nativity, the Presentation of Christ to the Temple, the Baptism, the *Anastasis*, the Ascension, *Pentecost*, and *Koimesis* were depicted frequently. The location of the *Koimesis* scene in these churches is usually the north, south, or west wall. The scene was depicted on the pediment of the southern arch at Lagoudera Panagia tou Arakou Church with a similar plan type (12th century), and on the north wall at the Church of the Holy Apostles in Perachorio.[20]

At the narthex of the church, on the southern part of the east wall is the *Deesis* scene. (Drawing 1.IX, Figure 16) There are many examples where this scene, associated with the cult of death, is found on the narthexes of churches and at grave structures. The *Deesis* scene at the burial niche located on the northern wall of the western wing of the cross at the third southeast chapel of St. Nicholas Church at Myra is similar to the scene in Alakent Church in its positioning close to the entrance.[21] The scene was depicted in the narthex of Chora Curch (1321) in Istanbul,[22] and at St. Andreas Church (13th century) on the island of Kythira in Greece.[23] Additionally, in Anatolia the scene was also depicted in the narthex of the churches of Kokar (11th century); Pürenliseki (11th–12th centuries), and Yılanlı (11th century) in Ihlara; and at the St. Sophia in Trabzon (13th century).[24] The scene was extensively depicted in burial chapels generally from the end

17 Boyd 1974, Fig. 18.

18 Chatzidakis and Bitha 1997, p. 78, Fig. 8 (St. Andreas Perleggianika), p. 85, Fig. 18 (St. George Perleggianika), p. 125, Fig. 20 (St. Basil Friliggianika), p. 136, Fig. 4 (St. George Ntoyrianika), p. 173, Fig. 19 (St. Demetrios Pourko).

19 Chatzidakis et. al., 1989, p. 18 (St. Stephan), Fig. 12 (Panagia Mavriotissa).

20 Stylianou 1958, Fig. 153 (Lagoudera); Megaw and Hawkins 1962, p. 289, Fig. 42.

21 For the *Deesis* scene at Demre, see Çorağan Karakaya 2003, pp. 281–291.

22 Ousterhout 2002, p. 28.

23 Chatzidakis and Bitha 1997, p. 80, Fig. 12.

24 Rice 1968, Fig. 92 (Trabzon St. Sophia); Restle 1969, III, Plan LII (Kokar), Plan LIV (Pürenliseki), Plan LVII (Yılanlı).

of the 11th century onwards.[25] It was especially depicted in the crypt of the churches of St. Luke at Boiotia (first half of the 11th century) and Backova (1083–1100) on the apse.[26] At the churches of St. Sophia (10th century) in Vize and St. Barbara (1006–1021) in Soğanlı, the scene is located on the burial niches.[27]

The two figures depicted standing frontally on the southern inner surface of the jamb of the arch at the bema are thought to be Constantine and Helena (?). (Drawing 1.1–2, Figure 29) There are examples of both figures depicted in the apse or the bema from the 10th century onwards. At churches in Cappadocia such as the Çavuşin Güvercinlik (10th century), the Holy Apostles (10th century) in Sinasos (Mustafa Paşa) and the Belisırama, Bahattin Samanlığı (11th century), the figures are depicted on the apse.[28]

On the eastern part of the south wall in the lower section, the Virgin seated on a throne and depicted frontally is barely visible. (Drawing 1.3, Drawing 9.3, Figure 30) In Cyprus the Panagia tou Arakou Church in Lagoudera (12th century) was dedicated to the Virgin Mary and has her depiction together with the infant Jesus on the eastern part of the south wall.[29] The examples of depictions of Mary on the eastern part of the north and south walls of the naos, as in the case of Alakent Church, become concentrated in the 11th century in Anatolia.[30]

Taking into consideration churches of Middle Byzantine Period with similar architectural characteristics, it is probable that on the presently absent dome above the naos of Alakent Church, Christ Pantocrator was depicted.[31] (Drawing 1)

2.2. Iconography

Since the wall paintings of the church have been destroyed to a great extent, the iconographic data of the surviving scenes are limited. Therefore, our evaluations in this section are based on the depictions of Virgin Mary at the apse, the Annunciation to Virgin Mary, and the Baptism of Christ at the naos, as well as the *Deesis* scene at the narthex.

The depiction found on the semi-dome of the apse is thought to be the Virgin as *Platitera*, *Blacherniotissa*, or *Nicopoia*. (Drawing 2) On the semi-dome of the apse of the Church of Panagia Angeloktistos in Kiti (6th century), the earliest example in Cyprus, the Virgin *Hodegetria* is depicted in the middle with two archangels on either side.[32] Among the examples from the 12th century in Asinou, the Virgin *Blacherniotissa* is depicted between two archangels.[33] Both hands of the Virgin are in an orant pose. In another example from the 12th century at Panagia tou Arakou Church in Lagoudera, the Virgin *Nicopoia* is in the center with two archangels next to her.[34] Here,

25 Bogyay 1966, p. 1184.

26 Underwood 1975, p. 307.

27 For St. Sophia of Vize, see Ötüken and Ousterhout 1989, pp. 140–141, Fig. 6; for the Church of St. Barbara in Soğanlı, see Restle 1969, III, Plan XLVI, Fig. 433.

28 Restle 1969, III, Plan XXVI (Çavuşin), Plan XL (Sinasos), Plan LXI (Belisırama).

29 Stylianou 1958, Fig. 153.

30 For the examples of the representations of the Virgin in Anatolia, see Jerphanion 1925, I, pp. 171–176, Pl. 43.4 (Göreme, St. Daniel); Budde 1958, pp. 13–14 (Göreme, Eski Tokalı); Karakaya 2003, p. 20 (Erdemli, St. Nicholas).

31 For the Christ Pantocrator representations in Cyprus, see Megaw and Hawkins 1962, Fig. 3 (Perachorio Apostles); Hein, Jakovljevic and Kleidt 1998, Fig. 56 (Lagoudera Panagia Araka), Fig. 153 (Kalogrea Christ Antiphonitis).

32 Stylianou and Stylianou 1997, Fig. 17.

33 Winfield and Hawkins 1967, Fig. 15.

34 Nicolaïdès 1996, pp. 19–20, Fig. 6 (Lagoudera).

Virgin Mary holds the infant Jesus in her left hand and holds a white handkerchief. Her right hand is at the waist of Jesus. In examples from the late periods, it is usually the Virgin *Platitera* who is depicted between the angels. In the churches of Holy Cross of Agiasmati in Platonistasa (1494) and Panagia Amasgou in Monagri (1516), Virgin *Platitera* is depicted between the angels.[35] Virgin Mary has her both hands in an orant pose, and inside the medallion in the middle of her body is the infant Jesus.

It is not clear whether Mary depicted in the scene of the Annunciation at the naos is seated or standing. (Drawing 5, Figures 8, 9) But the ornamentations in the middle section of the scene indicate that Mary has a throne embellished with precious stones. Although the thrones in the Annunciation scenes in Anatolia during 10th–12th centuries mostly have cushions and ornamentations around the edges, towards the late period thrones with more detailed, rich ornamentations start to emerge. The depiction of Mary in a standing or seated posture in the Annunciation scenes is generally not a feature that might be related to a period.[36] In the depiction at Myra, Mary holds the palm of her right hand at about the height of her chest and faces the viewer. This gesture of Mary is seen often on scenes of the Annunciation after the 11th century.[37] The same gesture of Mary could also be seen on the scene at the third southeast chapel of the Church of St. Nicholas in Demre.[38]

Virgin Mary was portrayed with a reddish-brown *maphorion* on the wall paintings of the church. The reddish-brown or purple *maphorion* in the depictions of the Virgin is usually seen from the 10th century onwards in Anatolia and at other places.[39] Additionally, the reddish-brown or purple *maphorion*, thought to have originated in Anatolia, is also quite common in Cyprus.[40] On the 10th–12th century examples in Anatolia, the throne has a cushion and ornamentations around the edges but generally no back or sides.[41] In later periods, especially in some examples from the 13th–14th centuries, the throne is more detailed and elaborately ornamented.[42]

Behind Virgin Mary at Alakent Church, a round arch is clearly visible. (Drawing 5, Figure 11) This depiction of the Virgin in front of an architectural feature is a practice seen in Annun-

35 Winfield 1971, p. 260, Fig. 9 (Monagri); Stylianou 1985, Fig. 122 (Platonistasa).

36 For the Annunciation scenes, see Emminghaus 1972, pp. 422–437.

37 Muratoff 1935, Plate LXXIII. Hadermann-Misguich 1975, Fig. 8–39 (Cyprus, Panagia tou Arakou); Megaw and Hawkins 1977, Fig. 119 (Cyprus, Panagia Kanakaria).

38 For the Annunciation scene at the Church of St. Nicholas in Demre, see Doğan, Çorağan, Bulgurlu, Alas, Fındık and Apaydın 2014, pp. 82–83.

39 Mercangöz 1993, pp. 330, 333, drawing 14, 20. Based on an Armenian manuscript from the 11th century, its widespread use at churches in Cappadocia and appearance at the church of St. Sophia in Trabzon, this scholar believes that the blue tunic and purple *maphorion* originates in Anatolia; Karakaya 2005a, 336. The Virgin has a reddish-brown *maphorion* at the churches of Göreme Kılıçlar (10th century), Ihlara Sümbüllü (the beginning of 10th century), Niğde Eski Gümüş (11th century), and Göreme Saklı (1070). Furthermore, an Armenian manuscript from the mid-11th century notes that at Nerezi in Macedonia (1164) and at many rock churches in Cappadocia, the Virgin has a purple (reddish-brown ?) *maphorion* on top of her blue tunic. The clothing of the Virgin at Karanlık Church in Göreme (1200–1210), at Elmalı (1190–1200), at Yeni Tokalı (end of 10th century to 13th century), and at the Church of St. Sophia in Trabzon (1260) have these same colors.

40 Karakaya 2005a, p. 336.

41 Karakaya 2005a, p. 336. Additionally, for the examples of thrones in 10th–12th century scenes, see Restle 1969, II, Fig. 22, 24 (Göreme, Saklı), Fig. 60 (Göreme, Chapel 6a), Fig. 64 (Göreme, Eski Tokalı), Fig. 262, (Göreme, Kılıçlar); III, Fig. 304 (Çavuşin, Güvercinlik), Fig. 367 (Tagar, Trikonchos).

42 For the examples of thrones in the 13th–14th century scenes, see Schiller 1966, I, Fig. 96 (Rome, Sta. Maria Maggiore, 1290); Rice 1968, Fig. 108 (Trabzon, St. Sophia, 1260); Restle 1969, III, Fig. 415 (Söviş Şahinefendi, Forty Martyrs, 1216–1217).

ciation scenes since the early periods.[43] In Annunciation scenes, the angel was usually depicted reaching out towards Mary with one hand while holding a sceptre in the other. The Göreme Chapel 16 (mid-11th century), Tagar Trikonchos (1080), Göreme Chapel 11/St. Eustathios (12th century), and Martorana church in Palermo (1146–1150) all resemble the Alakent example as the angel depictions have the same features.[44] At Alakent Church, very important iconographic details include the semi-circular vault of heaven above and to the right of Mary's head, the rays of light that radiate from it, and the dove. (Figures 11, 12) In Annunciation scenes the dove is the Holy Spirit who gives life to Jesus. In Byzantine paintings, generally in 12th century and later examples, rays of light radiate from a semi-circular vault of heaven towards Mary and a dove in flight. In Cyprus, it is also possible to see these motifs in the depictions at the churches of Panagia Kanakaria in Lythrankomi (12th century) and Panagia tou Arakou in Lagoudera (1192).[45]

The iconographic data on the scene of the Baptism of Christ in the church is very limited. (Drawing 3, Figure 4) On the right side of the blue stream in which Jesus stands, there are three white fish depicted from the side. The figure to the right of the scene and on the left side of Jesus is probably John the Baptist. The Baptist was usually depicted on the left side of the scene, and from the 7th century onwards at a higher level than Jesus.[46] In the scene at Alakent Church, there are paint marks belonging to the brown and yellow wing of the figure of an angel turned towards and to the left of Christ. Although angel depictions are found in scenes of the Baptism since the early periods, the first examples were found in the East (Syria).[47] The number of angel figures in the examples of scenes in Anatolia and elsewhere varies as a feature pertaining to each period. In these scenes a single angelic figure is seen only rarely, and their numbers are two or three, increasing to four or six in the late periods.[48] At Myra, although only a fraction of the angel has survived, more than one angel is probably depicted here. Apart from the numerous fish in the river, it is not known whether a river god, as the personification of the Jordan River, a cross on a column, or a lit oil lamp were depicted in the scene at Alakent Church. In the examples of monumental painting from the late period, an increase in the numbers of figures and depictions in the Jordan River can be observed.[49] The fish, snake, and crab figures depicted in the Jordan River may represent the dragons whose heads Christ had crushed in the waters of Jordan.[50]

In the *Deesis* scene on the east wall of the narthex, Virgin Mary and John were depicted supplicating for forgiveness for all people, as Christ is judging each person according to their sins and good deeds on the day of the last judgment. (Drawing 8, Figure 16) In the *Deesis* scenes

---

43 For the Annunciation scenes from the 6th century, see Schiller 1966, I, Fig. 70 (Rabula Codex), Fig. 71 (Ivory, Maximianus cathedra), Fig. 72 (Mosaic, Parenzo Basilica).

44 Jerphanion 1942, Pl. 37, 2 (Göreme, St. Eustathios); Demus 1949, Fig. 49 a, b (Palermo, Martorana); Restle 1969, II, Fig. 66 (Göreme, Chapel 16); III, Fig. 367 (Tagar, Trikonchos).

45 Hadermann-Misguich 1975, Fig. 8–39 (Arakou); Megaw and Hawkins 1977, Fig. 119 (Kanakaria).

46 For the Baptism scenes, see Schiller 1971, I, pp. 128–142.

47 Schiller 1971, I, pp. 134–135. The scene with an angel at the catacomb at Ponziano in Rome has Eastern influences.

48 For the examples of scenes with a single angel, see Restle 1969, II, Fig. 62 (Göreme, Eski Tokalı Church, 10th century), Fig. 230 (Göreme, Karanlık, 12th century), III, Fig. 302 (Çavuşin, 10th century); for examples with two angels, see Restle 1969, III, Fig. 257 (Göreme, Kılıçlar, 9th century), II, Fig. 14 (Göreme, El Nazar, 10th century), Fig. 174 (Göreme, Elmalı, 12th century), Fig. 203 (Göreme, Çarıklı, 11th–12th centuries), Fig. 518 (Belisırma, Bahattin Samanlığı, first half of the 11th century).

49 The Baptism scenes at Gülşehir, Karşı Church (1212) and Ürgüp, Keşlik Monastery Archangelos Church (13th century) are similar to the scene at Myra due to figures such as the fish and snake depicted in the river.

50 Jolivet-Lévy 2002, p. 305.

representing the mediation of Mary and John the Baptist for the salvation of humanity, Mary is usually depicted to the right of Jesus and John the Baptist to the left, as in the scene at Alakent Church.[51] The depiction of Jesus seated or standing is not a feature related to the period in which the scene was executed.[52]

The posture of the Virgin's body depicted slightly from the profile and the position of her hands in the *Deesis* scene at Alakent Church conforms to the type of the Virgin *Hagiosoritissa*. The *Hagiosoritissa* type had emerged in the 6th century, but its widespread use started in the 10th and 11th centuries.[53] The Virgin of this type, the protector and bringer of goodness, is usually depicted in *Deesis* compositions.[54] The depictions of Virgin Mary where the Virgin *Hagiosoritissa* holds a scroll with an inscription of her dialogue with Jesus asking for forgiveness for humanity is called "the Virgin *Paraklesis*." This translates as the Virgin Intercessor.[55] The posture of Virgin Mary with her body slightly turned to the right, her head slightly tilted, and her hand positioned around her chest are similar to the figure of the Virgin at the Panagia Moutoullas Church (1280) in Cyprus.[56] The inscription on the open scroll held by Mary (Figure 18) could also be found in the examples of monumental painting in Cyprus. The open scroll in her hand in the *Deesis* scene at the Panagia Moutoullas Church in Cyprus bears the same inscription.[57] In Lagoudera at the Panagia Arakiotissa Church (1192) John the Baptist carries a scroll with the same inscription taken from the Gospel of John.[58] On all the paintings in the building Virgin Mary is depicted wearing a reddish-brown *maphorion*.

2.3. Style

The style of the wall paintings of Alakent Church could be followed, albeit partially, from the *Deesis* scene on the southern part of the east wall of the narthex, the scene fragment in the northern part of the soffit of the bema arch, and the Annunciation scene on the southern wall of the western arch.

The figures in the *Deesis* scene at the narthex of the church are mostly thin and long. (Figure 16) The shoulders of the figures are wide, and the legs depicted longer than the body are quite distinct. Their heads are usually smaller in comparison to the body. Generally, they have oval faces with almond-shaped eyes, a thin and long nose, and a small mouth, all pictured with reddish-brown contours. (Figures 20, 22, 26) Their curved eyebrows, close together, were accentuated with thick reddish-brown lines. The upper and lower contours of the eyes meet at the outer corner of the eye, and the upper and lower eyelids were made more prominent with curved reddish-brown lines. There are shadows in green around the eyes and on both sides of the nose. The representation becomes detailed through the use of line strokes on the hair and beards of the figures. The hands are proportional to the body and elegant with thin, long fingers. In addition, the fingers were distinguished from the palms with a reddish-brown line. (Figure 28) The contours of the hands and feet were also marked with reddish-brown lines. (Figures 25, 28)

The style of the paintings at the naos was slightly different from those at the narthex.

51 For the *Deesis* scenes, see Bogyay 1966, pp. 1178–1186; Bogyay 1968, pp. 494–499.

52 Çorağan Karakaya 2003, p. 283.

53 For the Virgin Hagiosoritissa, see Spitzing 1989, p. 230.

54 Spitzing 1989, p. 230.

55 Ševčenko 1991b, p. 2177.

56 Mouriki 1984, pp. 189–190; Hein, Jakovljevic and Kleidt 1998, Fig. 95.

57 Mouriki 1984, pp. 189–190; Hein, Jakovljevic and Kleidt 1998, Fig. 95.

58 John 1:29; Nicolaïdès 1996, pp. 107–110.

Just like Virgin Mary figure in the Annunciation scene, the thin and long nose, and the small mouth on oval faces were rendered with black contours. There are distinguishable light brown tones on the cheeks. In the scene on the northern side of the soffit of the bema arch, movement was conveyed with the extensive folds on the edges of the tunic and capes. (Figure 7) The curves on the clothes of the figures were rendered with lines. Light was depicted with patches of color or bands in white, and shadows with thick bands of dark color. The folds of the garments reflect the movement of their bodies as well as intensifying it, as seen on the fluttering ends of their capes.

Stylistically, the closest matching examples of the wall paintings at the church are the wall paintings at the Church of St. Nicholas in Demre, dated to the 12th century.[59] The number of wall paintings dated to the 12th century in Lycia are limited. The wall paintings in the east chapel of Church no. 3 at Gemiler Island –only a fraction of which have survived– have common features with the paintings at Alakent Church.[60]

The wall paintings in the narthex of Alakent Church and at the burial space at St. Nicholas Church have common stylistic features with the examples of monumental painting in Cyprus, dated to the 12th century.[61] Therefore, it is possible to imagine that the wall paintings at Alakent were made by local artists of the region. One example in Cyprus is the Panagia Church in Monagri.[62] The common stylistic features of these wall paintings from the early 12th century in Cyprus were originating from the school established in Cyprus in the first half of the 12th century.[63] The wall paintings of the northern church of St. Chrysostom in Koutsovendis, argued to be the work of artists from the capital, are dated to the beginning of the 12th century.[64] Another example from Cyprus with stylistic features similar to Alakent is the Panagia Phorbiotissa Church in Asinou (1105–1106).[65] The wall paintings at this church share common features seen in other examples in Cyprus from the early 12th century. With the arrival of artists from the capital, especially in the 11th–12th centuries, the art of monumental painting in Cyprus flourished.[66] Hence, in the paintings of Alakent Church, much like those at the Church of St. Nicholas in Demre, the influence of the capital is visible.

Like the examples from the early 12th century in Cyprus, the mosaics of Daphni (1080–1100), influenced by the capital, also have stylistic features similar to the wall paintings at Alakent Church and at the burial space in the Church of St. Nicholas.[67] Nea Moni of Chios, with a style succeeding the Komnenian painting, and the mosaics of Daphni display a new classical style

---

59 Ötüken 1998a, p. 555.

60 For the wall paintings in the east chapel of Church no. III at Gemiler Island in the Lycian region, see Asano 1995, p. 76, Lev. XI c.

61 Ötüken 1999, p. 491; Ötüken 2003, p. 39.

62 For the early wall paintings at the Panagia Church at Monagri in Cyprus, see Boyd 1974, pp. 286–291, Figs. 6–8, 10–17. The scholar has identified four different periods in the wall paintings of the church. Those dated to the beginning of the 12th century are located at the apse, the bema, and the diaconicon of the church. Boyd notes that the wall paintings of this period are distinguished from other wall paintings through the sharp brush strokes and the elaborate, skillfully rendered faces.

63 Boyd 1974, p. 289.

64 For the wall paintings of the Church of St. Chrysostom at Koutsovendis in Cyprus, see Papageorghiou 1965, pp. 17, 19; Mango 1990, pp. 63–94.

65 For the wall paintings of the Panagia Phorbiotissa Church at Asinou in Cyprus, see Papageorghiou 1965, pp. 15, 17, Figs. 10–13; Winfield and Hawkins 1967.

66 Papageorghiou 1965, p. 3.

67 For the mosaics of Daphni, see Diez and Demus 1931; Demus 1948, pp. 60–61; Grabar 1953, pp. 115–116; Lazarev 1967, pp. 194–196; Mouriki 1980, pp. 94–98; Kitzinger 1990, pp. 233–245.

emerging at the beginning of the same period.[68] The style of the mosaics of the St. Theodores Church (1081–1118) in Serres, with a similar style to Alakent Church, is usually considered to be comparable to the mosaics of Daphni and the wall paintings of the Church of St. Chrysostom in Cyprus.[69]

The white brush strokes on the faces of the figures and the deep shadows created by the earthy green background under the skin tone on the *Deesis* scene is similar in practice to the art of Comnenian monumental painting, as in Cyprus and Sicily in the 12th century.[70] Above the eyebrows, which continue down to the outer corner of the eyes, there are white, fine brush strokes worthy of attention at Alakent Church and on the figures in the northern and southern annexes of the Church of St. Nicholas in Demre. The dark triangular shading above the nose between the eyebrows, seen in the examples in Cyprus as well as at Alakent Church, creates a stern expression on the faces of the figures. The white brush strokes create an effect of light on the face, the forehead, under the eyes, as well as on top and at the sides of the nose. Such strokes were also utilized in the wall paintings at Panagia in Monagri, the Church of St. Chrysostom in Koutsovendis, at Daphni, and at the St. Theodores Church in Serres.[71]

The numerous vertical folds in garments seen at the narthex of Alakent Church, on the clothes of the solitary figure in the burial space at the Church of St. Nicholas in Demre, and on the outfits of the prophets on the dome at Daphni are indications of a development in late Komnenian painting.[72] Shadows were depicted with soft transitions in dark colors. The folds in the clothes at Panagia in Monagri and the Church of St. Chrysostom in Koutsovendis in Cyprus, are sharp, linear, hasty and schematic, just like on the figures at Myra. There are generally triangular folds at the skirts of the garments. In the examples in Sicily (Capella Palatina and Martorana church in Palermo), the folds were rendered in a linear fashion and geometrically.[73] The geometric folds emphasize motion: hanging, sticking, stretching, and fluttering, and at places terminate in the form of a V. In the miniatures of this period, the folds of the garments are also depicted in a linear fashion, just like in Alakent Church. While light and shadows were utilized to reveal the plasticity of the body, the linear folds provide an effect that emphasizes the movement of the body.

The manuscripts that display the same stylistic features as the wall paintings on the narthex also originated from the capital and were dated to the 12th century. In a Bible at the Vatican (Urb. gr.2), the outlines of the figures and the white light on the garments were depicted very starkly. The linear, geometric drapes of the clothes on the two-dimensional figures in a Bible at the Dionysiou Monastery in Athos (cod. 8) are especially prominent.[74] In addition, the Menologion (Add. cod. 11870) at the British Museum in London contains the first ten books of the life of Symeon Metaphrastes and written at the Bithynia Monastery at the beginning of the 12th century. It also originated from the capital, and has similar stylistic features.[75] The miniatures in Codex

68 Papageorghiou 1965, p. 3.

69 For the mosaics at the Church of St. Theodoroses (Metropolitan) in Serres, see Strati 1985–1986, pp. 88–104; Mathews 1997, pp. 47–49.

70 Ötüken 2004, p. 120.

71 Ötüken 2005, p. 276; Çorağan Karakaya 2003, p. 285.

72 Mouriki 1980, p. 95, Fig. 28.

73 Kitzinger 1990, p. 235, who states that the folds of the garments of the figures on the mosaics in Palermo are the enriched and enhanced versions of those seen in Daphni.

74 Demus 1949, p. 396.

75 For the Menologion (Add. cod. 11870) at the British Museum in London, see Lazarev 1967, p. 191; Beckwith 1968, pp. 124–125.

Ebnerianus of the New Testament from the early 12th century in the Bodleian Library in Oxford also have the same style as the paintings in Alakent Church.[76]

The hands were depicted more realistically in this period, indicating the renewed conventions in style. This also points to a later date. The powerful, workmanlike hands depicted in the Christ Pantocrator at Cefalù Cathedral in Sicily were similarly seen in in the *Deesis* at Alakent Church with Christ having distinctly knuckled fingers shown in a realistic manner. (Figures 24, 28) Additionally, the hands defined with outlines in dark contours in the examples found in Cyprus, could also be seen in Demre: at Alakent Church as well as the solitary figures at the burial space of the Church of St. Nicholas. The hands were depicted in a planar fashion with thin and long fingers and a horizontal line separating the palm from the fingers.

In Alakent's *Deesis* scene the humanistic expression of John the Baptist is noteworthy: his depiction with oblique eyebrows conveys his reclusive life and suffering. In other 12th century examples this expression was generally conveyed with posture and gestures in addition to the facial expression. The slightly tilted head and oblique eyebrows of the Virgin Mary and John in the *Deesis* scene at the third southeast chapel of the Church of St. Nicholas in Demre intensify the same expression.[77] However, the expression in the eyes of the figures in the mosaics at Daphni are more direct and lifelike.[78] The gestures and movements that reinforce the emotional, humane facial expressions are also seen in scenes at the Asinou Panagia Amasqou, the Church of St. Chrysostom in Koutsovendis, and other early 12th century examples in Cyprus. The serene faces of the figures at Cefalù Cathedral in Sicily, created with a humanist approach, have a spiritual quality like those in Myra.[79]

The style of the paintings at the naos of the church is different from the paintings at the narthex. It is possible to see this especially in the elaborate *modelé* created by the soft color transitions on the face of Virgin Mary in the Annunciation scene. (Figure 9) The creation of the *modelé* through the use of a multitude of colors and with free brush strokes is a 12th century feature.[80] The tightly packed, exaggerated, wavy folds that intensify the movement in the scene on the northern side of the soffit of the bema arch belong to the "new style" introduced in the second half of the 12th century. Small heads on top of long, thin bodies; linear, exaggerated, intricate folds of the garments; and exuberant figures making hasty moves are the defining features of this style. The geometric forms and the abstract arrangement created by linear folds, and light and shadow on the garments seen on the depiction of the bishop on the apse of the third southeast chapel of the Church of St. Nicholas in Demre and on the apostles on the Communion scene in the northeast corner space of the same church, became widespread in the 12th century. The linear, rhythmic folds reflecting the vibrant, moving quality of the figures and the flutter of the skirts of the capes amplifying the sense of motion in Palermo are reminiscent of the style of the scene in Alakent Church.[81] The important innovations in the art of this period can be seen in the wall paintings of the St. Panteleimon Church in Nerezi (1164). These bears the hallmark of the

76 For Codex Ebernianus of the New Testament (Auct. T. infra I.10) at Oxford's Bodleian Library, see Beckwith 1968, pp. 125–126; Patcht 1952, pp. 7–9, Figs. 3, 8, 9b, 11, 17.

77 Çorağan Karakaya 2003, p. 285.

78 Mouriki 1985, p. 218.

79 Rice 1986, p. 161.

80 Mouriki 1980, p. 93.

81 For Palermo, see Kitzinger 1990, Fig. XIV.

capital in its features.[82] One of the best examples of this "dynamic" style is the wall paintings at the Church of St. George (1191) in Kurbinovo. It features a variation of the style seen in Nerezi and is said to display provincial features.[83] A similar provincial style can also be seen in the wall paintings of Hagia Anargyroi (1170–1180) in Kastoria.[84] The earliest examples in Cyprus displaying the "dynamic" style are the St. Neophytos Monastery in Paphos (1183) and the Panagia tou Arakou Church (1192) in Lagoudera.[85] It has been suggested that the influence behind this style in Cyprus during the 12th century was the capital because of constant contact between them.[86] The wall paintings of the Chapel of the Virgin Mary at the John Theologos Monastery in Patmos were also made in the new style emerging in the late 12th century.[87] Additionally, in Crete, the wall paintings of the churches of St. George at Kournas and Myriokefala Panagia from the late 12th century are also examples displaying the same style.[88]

Furthermore, the miniatures painted by the abbot Ioannis of Kokkinobaphos Monastery included in several manuscripts (1120–1150) –the Homily of the Virgin Mary in the Bibliothèque Nationale in Paris (cod. gr. 1208) and the Homily in the Vatican Library (cod. gr. 1162)– show the capital's influence and also display stylistic characteristics parallel to the figures on the bema of Alakent Church and those in the northeast corner of the Church of St. Nicholas in Demre.[89] Another manuscript influenced by the capital, the Homily of Gregory of Nazianzus (cod. gr. 339) in Sinai, is dated to the middle of the 12th century.[90] Additionally, the 12th century Homily of Gregory Theologos (cod. 6) at the Panteleimon Monastery in Athos also originated from the capital and has a style similar to the wall paintings at the naos of Alakent Church.[91]

2.4. Ornamentation

The closest counterparts of the stylized curved branches (Drawing 9.B1, Figure 32, Drawing 10, Figures 33, 34) formed with black, reddish-brown lines on a white background on the south wall of the church and on the eastern and northern arches, can be found on the wall paintings of the southern annex of the Church of St. Nicholas in Demre (11th–12th centuries). Such motifs were also depicted extensively in the art of monumental painting of the same period.[92]

82 For the St. Panteleimon Church in Nerezi, see Hamann-Mac Lean and Hallensleben 1963, III, Figs. 29–45; Miljkovic-Pepek 1966.

83 For the wall paintings of the Church of St. George in Kurbinovo, see Haderman-Misguich 1975.

84 Malmquist 1979.

85 For the wall paintings of the St. Neophytos Monastery in Paphos, see Mango and Hawkins 1966; for the wall paintings of the Panagia tou Arakou Church in Lagoudera, see Stylianou 1958; Winfield 1971; Megaw 1972, pp. 196–202.

86 Mouriki 1980, p. 115.

87 For the wall paintings of the Chapel of the Virgin Mary at the Ioannes Theologos Monastery, see Orlandos 1962, pp. 285–302; Mouriki 1980, pp. 116–117. The influence of the capital on the wall paintings could be explained by the connection the priests at Patmo had with the capital.

88 Gallas, Wessel and Borboudakis 1983, pp. 93–94, 258–262, Fig. 52, 53, 103, 216, 218; Panayotidi 1986, p. 87, Fig. 17–18.

89 Ötüken 2002, p. 408. For the manuscripts depicted by Ioannis, see Anderson 1982, pp. 83–114; for the Homily in the Bibliothèque Nationale, see Grabar 1939, Fig. 47–49; Beckwith 1968, p. 127; for the Homily in the Vatican Library, see Lazarev 1967, pp. 192–193; Beckwith 1968, p. 116; Hutter and Canart 1991; Lafontaine-Dosogne 1992, pp. 196–201.

90 For the Homily of Gregory of Nazianzus (cod. gr. 339) at St. Catherine's Monastery, see Lazarev 1967, p. 193; Galavaris 1969, pp. 255–258, Fig. 377–397.

91 For the Homily at the Panteleimon Monastery (cod. 6) in Athos, see Lazarev 1967, p. 213; Galavaris 1969, pp. 209–212, Figs. 137–177, 179–180; Pelekanidis, Christou, Tsioumis and Kadas 1975, pp. 352–358, Fig. 296–322.

92 For this motif, see Restle 1969, II, Fig. 177 (Göreme Elmalı), Fig. 207 (Göreme Çarıklı); III, Fig. 385 (Susum-

On the inner surface of the eastern jamb of the arch on the south wall, the large rhombus motifs formed by green lines were divided in the middle by a reddish-brown line to create two triangle motifs. Stylized, curved branches were drawn with reddish-brown lines on a white background inside the triangles, and with green lines on a white background on the remaining space outside. (Drawing 11, Figures 35, 36) It is possible to find the same motif in the paintings of the burial space (12th century) at the Church of St. Nicholas in Demre. Additionally, the wall paintings of the Church of the Holy Apostles at Perachorio in Cyprus contain similar motifs.[93]

On the western side of the soffit of the pointed arched window approximately on the central axis of the south wall of the building, there are rhombus motifs perpendicularly intersecting one another. The spaces inside the rhombuses are divided into four square units formed with black lines. Inside each square, four-petaled flowers with reddish-brown and white petals were depicted. (Drawing 12, Figure 36) Similar ornamentations can be found in Cappadocia, especially in the wall paintings of the 12th–13th century churches of Elmalı and Çarıklı in Göreme and at the Söviş (Şahinefendi) Church of Forty Martyrs.[94]

2.5. Technique

The wall paintings at the naos and the narthex of the building were made by the fresco technique. Those at the naos have a thin plaster with a thickness of 2–3 mm. On the other hand, the wall-painting plaster layer of the *Deesis* scene at the narthex is quite thick, reaching 4–5 cm.

The lines marked with an engraving technique on the folds of the garments of the figures in the *Deesis* scene are especially striking. (Figures 23, 24, 27) On wall painting often the main outlines of the subject carved onto the plaster before being painted. Written sources state that the folds of the garments of figures were carved with a pointed piece of iron or a needle.[95] These engraved lines, seen in the Early, Middle, and Late Byzantine periods, were applied to make the brush drawings more pronounced and permanent.[96] It is worth noting that the same technique could be seen in the wall paintings at the Church of St. Nicholas in Demre. In these 12th century paintings the painter used a trowel to shape the plaster in order to form the painting.[97] These engraved lines are especially visible on the clothes of the solitary figures in the burial chamber on the south side of the Church of St. Nicholas in Demre. This same technique can also be seen in Cyprus on the wall paintings of the churches at Lagoudera and St. Philon at Aphentrika.[98]

The earthy colors used in the paintings of Alakent Church are black, white, reddish-brown (iron oxide), grayish-dark blue, dark yellow (ochre), and olive green. Black and white were used to produce darker and lighter tones of these colors. Lime white was used usually on the effects of light on clothes. The slightly bluish carbon-black was mixed with white to obtain the gray-blue. The extensively used reddish-brown was utilized on the stripes that mark a border around the subjects, on contours, and on clothes. On the paintings the gray-blue color has a matt finish, which was used extensively in the 11th–12th centuries. This blue, called azurite, was used in the background on a black underlay, and on garments. The dark yellow that appears on the ha-

bayırı St. Theodoros), Fig. 423 (Söviş Şahinefendi Forty Martrs); Rice 1968, Drw. 124 (Trabzon St. Sophia).

93 Megaw and Hawkins 1962, Figs. 53, 55.

94 Restle 1969, C. II, Fig. 194 (Çarıklı); C. III, Fig. 425 (Forty Martyrs).

95 Trowel, bone, and knife were used in marking the face and the folds of garments. See Winfield 1968, pp. 96–97.

96 Winfield 1968, p. 97.

97 Winfield 1968, p. 99.

98 Winfield 1968, p. 99.

loes of the figures, on the color of skin, and on clothing was obtained by mixing it with white. The natural earthy green (terre verte) usually forms the underlay under the color of skin in Byzantine monumental painting. This green, which has a matt finish at Alakent Church, can be seen quite regularly in the 12th–13th century examples in Cyprus.[99]

On the *Deesis* scene the faces of the figures were painted with a skin tone made by mixing dark yellow and white that was applied onto the green underlay below. The green underlay on the face was used for the shadows around the eyes, along the nose, and on the edges of the face. The same green, used for adding shadows, is also visible on the figures at the 12th century Cypriot churches of Panagia Amasgou in Monagri (beginning of century) and St. Chrysostom in Koutsovendis (1100).[100] The eyes and eyebrows, nose, mouth, and ears were rendered with reddish-brown lines. It is possible to see these reddish-brown lines on the faces used extensively from the 10th century onwards.[101]

As the face of Virgin Mary on the Annunciation scene in the naos so visibly demonstrates, a technique different than the one at the narthex was adopted here. In the naos the eyes, eyebrows, nose, mouth, and ears were emphasized with darker shades of the skin tone, just like on the faces of the figures in the Communion scene at the northeast corner space of the Church of St. Nicholas in Demre. On the figures at the third southeast chapel of the same church, the effect of light was rendered with paler tones on the faces. The use of white to render effects of light, with this degree of skill and diligence, is a characteristic of the 12th century and later.[102] The main color on the hands and feet is yellow. Contours were rendered with reddish-brown and black lines. The haloes of the figures are dark yellow. In general, the contours of the haloes are black on the inside, and white on the outside.

Painting the garments of the figures is usually started with the application of the main color. Then the darker shades of the main color are used in lines and patches of color to convey shadows. Finally, white color is applied in patches and lines in certain areas to create the effect of light. This technique, created with three tones of the same color, is seen in the garments. It became widespread in Byzantine monumental painting, especially after the 12th century.[103] It is possible to see the same technique used at Alakent Church and in various areas of the Church of St. Nicholas in Demre. In some examples, such as the Anatolian churches of Çavuşin (963–969) and Susam Bayırı St. Theodore (first half of 11th century) and the Cypriot churches of the Pantocrator cave (12th century) in Latmos and the Panagia Phorbiotissa in Asinou (1105–1106), the three-tone technique was utilized on the garments of the figures.[104] The technique consists of a main color and a darker and lighter shade of it. The darker shade is obtained by mixing black with the main color, and the lighter shade by mixing white. In this technique, on the main color of the garments patches of white were applied in parallel white lines, thick bands, or with brush strokes to render the effect of light.

99 Boyd 1974, p. 321.

100 Boyd 1974, Fig. C (Monagri, Panagia Amasgou); Mango 1990, Fig. 3, 7a–b (Koutsovendis, St. Chrysostom).

101 For the reddish-brown lines on the faces, see Restle 1969, II, Fig. 1 (Göreme, El Nazar, end of 10th century), Fig. 22 (Göreme, Saklı, 1070), Fig. 55 (Göreme, Chapel 6, second half of 10th century), Fig. 126 (Göreme, Chapel 9, end of 10th century), Fig. 166 (Göreme, Elmalı, 1190–1200), Fig. 197 (Göreme, Çarıklı, second half of 12th century), Fig. 283 (Göreme, Kılıçlar Kuşluk, first half of 11th century).

102 Winfield 1968, p. 127.

103 Cutler 1991, p. 482.

104 For the examples where the three-tone technique was used in painting garments, see Winfield 1968, Fig. 26a (Çavuşin); Restle 1969, pp. 136–137 (Çavuşin), p. 148 (Susam Bayırı, H. Theodore), p. 188 (Latmos, Pantocrator); Winfield and Hawkins 1967, p. 265 (Cyprus, Asinou Panagia Phorbiotissa).

As the cuff on the sleeve of the angel (Annunciation scene) and the halo of Christ and the book that he holds (*Deesis* scene) demonstrate, the details in the paintings were rendered with a fine brush and with lines in a mixture of reddish-brown and black. The embellishments on the garments, haloes, and books of the figures were rendered with black or reddish–brown lines made with a fine brush, and with brush strokes in the form of small dots in white and reddish-brown.

3. Conclusion and Dating

Alakent Church has significant features in terms of painting program, iconography, and style. These include a limited number of solitary figures and a total of nine scenes including the seven festival scenes and the two symbolic scenes. Its wall paintings have common features especially with the Church of St. Nicholas in Demre and 12th–13th century churches in Cyprus. As such, they bear the marks of regional characteristics.

The scenes that were depicted alongside the surviving scenes might possibly have been devoted to the incarnation, the sacrifice and resurrection of Christ, and to the salvation of mankind. The principal themes of the painting schemes of the 12th century and later were death and resurrection.[105] A total of seven festival scenes have survived at Alakent Church, albeit partially. Among the festival scenes of the Eastern Church, the ones most depicted in the late period were the Crucifixion of Christ, the Nativity of Christ, the Entry into Jerusalem, and the *Anastasis* and Ascension. The Baptism of Christ and Pentecost were depicted much more rarely.[106] Therefore, Alakent Church is one of the rare significant examples with the Baptism scene in the bema.

The proliferation of feast scenes in painting schemes in the 12th century and later was due to the changes in liturgy.[107] The scenes in the church formed a coherent liturgical unity, and the paintings at the naos, including the *Deesis* scene in the narthex, were arranged to revolve around the themes of incarnation, sacrifice, and salvation. Thus, it is possible to say that the painting scheme of the church is related to the rites celebrated at the church. The intercession for the "salvation of the mortals" with Christ expressed on the scroll held by the Virgin Mary in the *Deesis* scene confirms this thought. The inscription on the scroll is taken from a dialogue between the Virgin and Christ during the intercession (*paraklesis*). It is also known that the "Paraklesis" prayer was chanted during the Dormition Feast observed in honor of the Mother of God (*Theotokos*).[108] It is clearly seen that the Virgin Mary has a very special place in the painting scheme of the church. Several things makes one think that the church was very likely dedicated to the Virgin: a) her depiction in the *Deesis* scene at the narthex, b) her depiction in the Annunciation scene on the southern wall of the west wing of the cross, both seen upon entering the church, c) her depiction as a solitary figure on the eastern section of the south wall, and d) her depiction on the semi-dome of the apse as *Platitera*, *Blacherniotissa*, or *Nicopoia* emphasizing her as "the mediatrix of salvation." An increase in the number of churches dedicated to the Virgin and the Annunciation to the Virgin occurred in Macedonia and Cyprus, especially in the 12th century and later.

105 Ötüken, Bulgurlu, Yandım, and Peker 2007, p. 33.

106 Ötüken, Bulgurlu, Yandım, and Peker 2007, p. 33.

107 Ötüken, Bulgurlu, Yandım, and Peker 2007, p. 33.

108 The *Paraklesis* prayer is chanted every evening (1st-14th August) during the fast (*karem*) observed in honor of the Mother of God, except for the Feast of the Metamorphosis.

In the Church of St. Nicholas in Demre the wall paintings of the northeast corner chamber, the southern annexes of the burial space, and the third southeast chapel display common stylistic and technical features with Alakent Church. These are generally dated to the 12th century.[109] Due to their common characteristics with the examples in Cyprus from the early 12th century, the wall paintings of the burial space at the Church of St. Nicholas have been dated to same period. All were made by artists from the capital or by regional artists influenced by the capital.[110] On the other hand, the wall paintings at the naos of Alakent Church share similar stylistic features with wall paintings of the second half of the 12th century. These paintings have stylistic features parallel to the wall paintings of the third southeast chapel and the northeast corner chamber of the Church of St. Nicholas in Demre (second half of 12th century). Having similarities with contemporaneous wall paintings in Cyprus, they also influenced by the capital. However, the *Deesis* scene in the narthex of Alakent Church was made at a later period. Although a similar style could be observed in this wall painting, finding the same inscription present in this scene in 12th–13th century examples in Cyprus, as well as its position in the architectural schema, allows us rather to date this scene from the end of the 12th century to the 13th century.

109 Ötüken 1999, p. 491.

110 Çorağan 1999, p. 93; Ötüken 1999, p. 491; Ötüken 2004, p. 120; Karakaya 2005b, pp. 293–294; Karakaya 2005a, p. 335; Karakaya 2009, p. 98.

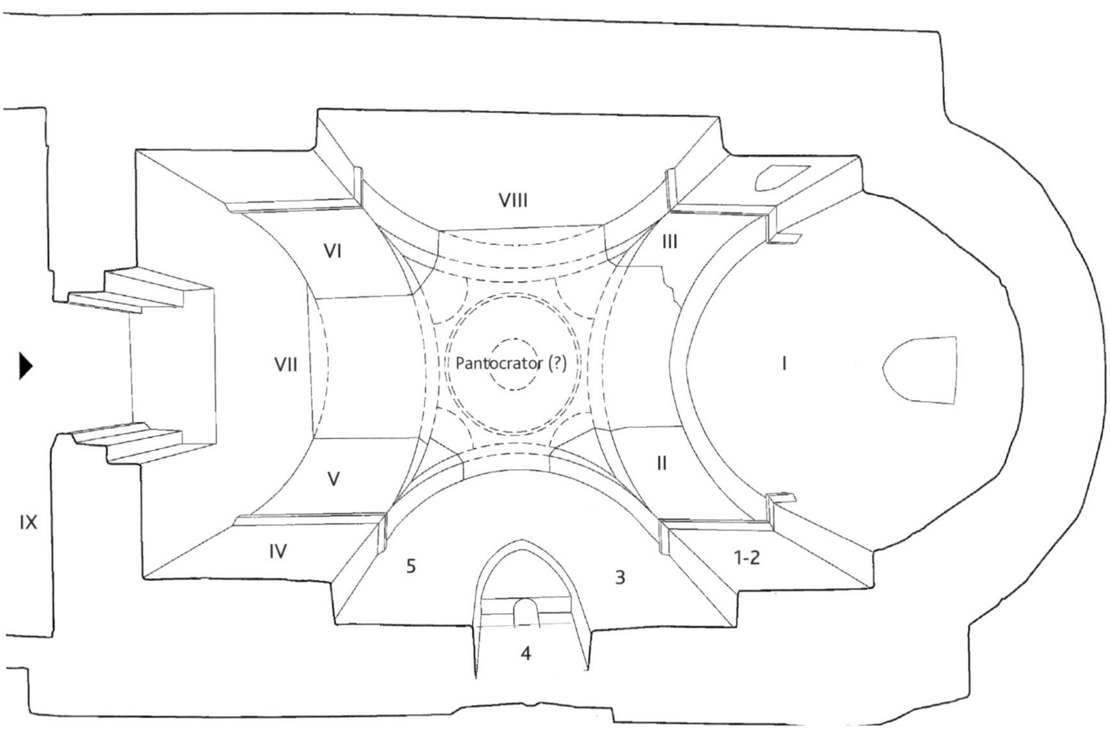

SCENES

I	Virgin Mary and the Archangels
II	Baptism of Christ
III	*Anastasis*
IV	Annunciation to Mary
V	Presentation of Christ to the Temple
VI	*Metamorphosis* (Transfiguration of Christ)
VII	Crucifixion of Christ
VIII	Nativity of Christ / Koimesis
IX	*Deesis*

INDIVIDUAL FIGURES

1-2	Constantine and Helena
3	Virgin Mary
4	A bishop
5	A saint

Drawing 1: Painting program of the church

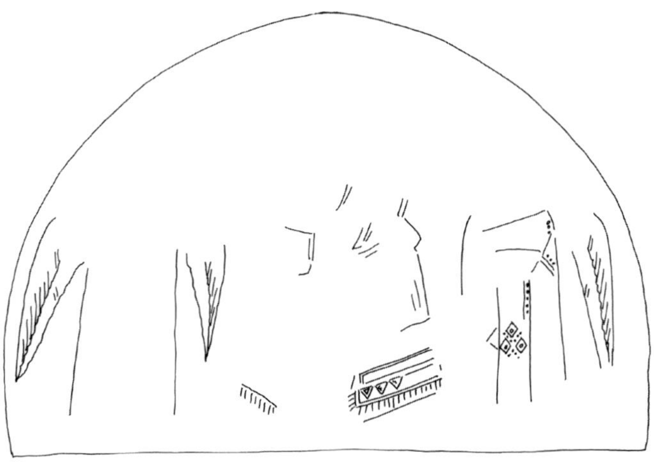

Drawing 2: Virgin Mary and angels on semi-dome of the apse

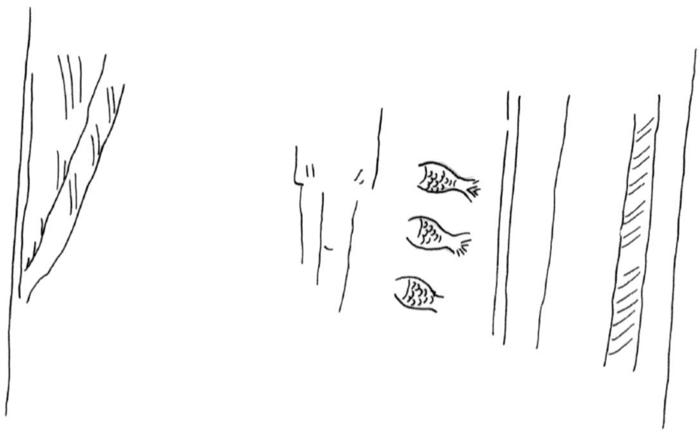

Drawing 3: Baptism of Christ

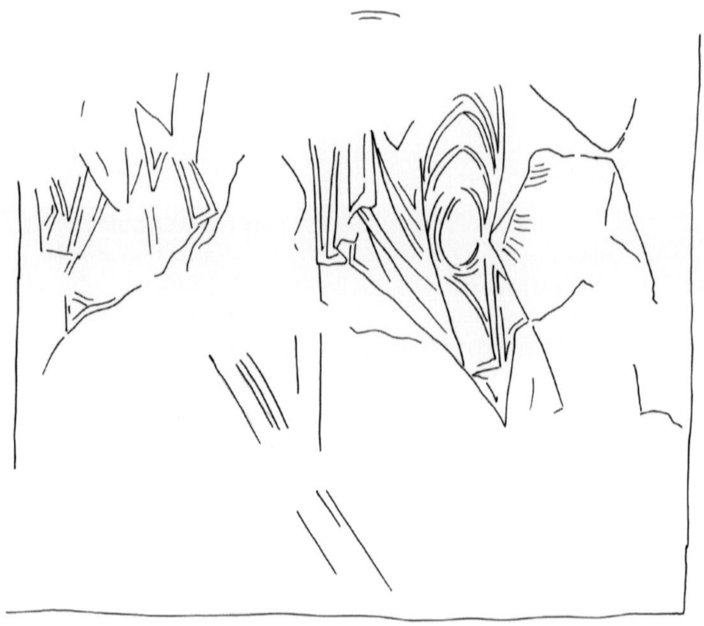

Drawing 4: *Anastasis*

Drawing 5: Annunciation to the Virgin

Drawing 6: Presentation of Christ to the Temple

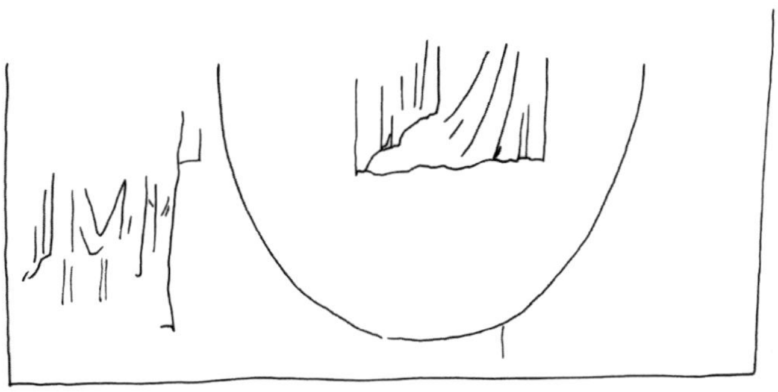

Drawing 7: Transfiguration of Christ

Drawing 8: *Deesis*

Drawing 9: Painting program on south wall

Drawing 10: Floral ornamentation

Drawing 11: Floral/ geometrical ornamentation 1

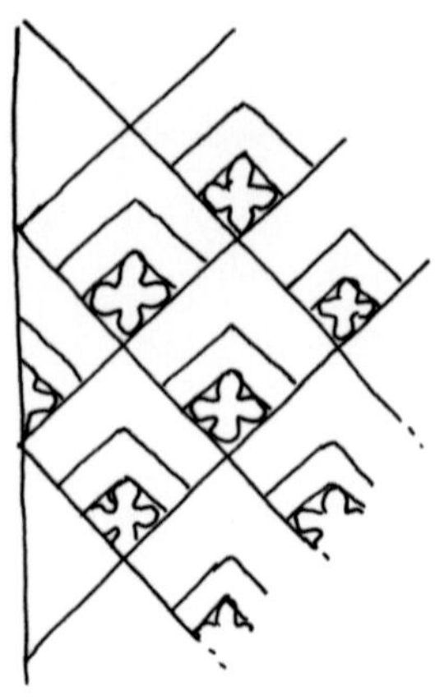

Drawing 12: Floral/ geometrical ornamentation 2

Drawing 13: Geometrical ornamentation

Figure 1: Virgin Mary and angels on semi-dome of the apse

Figure 2: Throne of the Virgin, detail from semi-dome of the apse

Figure 3: The Angel, detail from semi-dome of the apse

Figure 4: Baptism of Christ

Figure 5: The fish, detail from the Baptism of Christ

Figure 6: *Anastasis*

Figure 7: Christ, detail from the *Anastasis*

Figure 8: Southwest wall

Figure 9: Annunciation to the Virgin

Figure 10: Arm of the angel, detail from Annunciation to the Virgin

Figure 11: Semi-circle of heaven, detail from Annunciation to the Virgin

Figure 12: The dove, detail from Annunciation to the Virgin

Figure 13: Presentation of Christ to the Temple

Figure 14: Transfiguration of Christ

Figure 15: Crucifixion of Christ

Figure 16: *Deesis*

Figure 17: Virgin Mary, Christ, and John the Baptist, detail from the *Deesis*

Figure 18: Scroll of the Virgin, detail from the *Deesis*

Figure 19: Detail from the scroll of the Virgin

Figure 20: St. John the Baptist, detail from the *Deesis*

Figure 21: Scroll of St. John, detail from the *Deesis*

Figure 22: Christ, detail from the *Deesis*

Figure 23: Clothing of Christ, detail from the *Deesis*

Figure 24: Hand of Christ, detail from the *Deesis*

Figure 25: Feet of Christ, detail from the *Deesis*

Figure 26: Virgin Mary, detail from the *Deesis*

Figure 27: Clothing of Virgin Mary, detail from the *Deesis*

Figure 28: Hand of Virgin Mary, detail from the *Deesis*

Figure 29: Constantine and Helena

Figure 30: Virgin seated on a throne, detail from the throne

Figure 31: A bishop

Figure 32: Floral ornamentation, south wall

Figure 33: Floral ornamentation, north section of eastern arch

Figure 34: Floral ornamentation, east section of northern arch

Figure 35: Geometrical/floral ornamentation, southern side of templon wall

Figure 36: Geometrical/floral ornamentation, inside the arch of south window

Figure 37: Geometrical ornamentation, southern templon slab

VI.
Ceramic Finds

Özgü Çömezoğlu Uzbek
Istanbul University

During the excavations fragments of glazed and unglazed ceramic vessels were found both at the naos and the narthex of the church. It is known that in later periods a number of extensions were added to this church with 12th century features.[1] It was established that the threshold at the narthex of the building was raised in its final stages, and that a new arrangement using a simple dry stone wall was made to enter the naos from here. This stone wall also partially concealed the *Deesis* fresco on the western elevation of the naos, which is the southern part of the eastern wall of the narthex. This new arrangement also raises doubts as to whether the building still functioned as a church in its final stages. The ceramics found at the narthex were uncovered in alluvial deposits around the aforementioned wall and at levels above the threshold raised in later stages.[2] The ceramics found at the naos have common characteristics with those at the narthex, and were removed from various sections of the alluvium in the church. The stylistic similarities of the glazed ceramics indicate particularly that the ceramic artefacts found at the naos and the narthex were used during the same periods.

1. Catalogue

Glazed Ceramic Wares

Vessel No. 1

Illustrations Drawing 1, Figure 1

Dimensions d.r: 18.4 cm, d.b: 8.2 cm[3]

---

1 Akyürek 2010, p. 157.

2 The ground level of the threshold granting access from the narthex to the naos of the church is -4.00 m. Although excavations on the narthex were carried out up to -4.20 m, it was not possible to find a flat stone floor. The arrangement made at the entrance in the final period belongs to the phase above these levels. The ground level of the naos is -4.10 m, and the ground level of the apse is -4.00 m. However, the fact that the entrance from the narthex was made possible through an elevated threshold suggests that the ground level of the naos might also have been raised in the final stages.

3 d.r.: diameter of rim, d.b.: diameter of base.

Findspot Narthex east, at -3.60 m level.[4]

Description Sgraffito and paint were used together; it has a colorless glaze. It has abstract palmette motifs in a radial arrangement and a spiral infill between them. The radial composition is surrounded by an interlaced medallion. The colors of brown and green were applied alternately according to the composition of the decoration.

Vessel No. 2

Illustrations Drawing 2, Figure 2

Dimensions d.b: 8 cm

Findspot Naos, at -3.70 – -4.10 m level.

Description Sgraffito, and brown and green paint were used together. The remnants of the eyes of a mask are visible inside the medallion at the center. The rest of the composition is filled with a fish-scale pattern, and brown and green paint were applied alternately. It has two repair holes and a colorless glaze.

Vessel No. 3

Illustrations Drawing 3, Figure 3

Dimensions d.b: 7 cm

Findspot Naos, at -3.89 m level.

Description Sgraffito and brown paint were used. A fragment of a composition filled with fish-scale pattern is visible. It has a colorless glaze.

Vessel No. 4

Illustrations Drawing 4, Figure 4

Dimensions d.r: 18 cm

Findspot Narthex east, at -3.60 m level.

Description It has engraved strips on its body and on its rim, and has a dark yellow glaze. It has repair holes in two places.

Vessel No. 5

Illustrations Drawing 5, Figure 5

Dimensions d.r: 17.2 cm, d.b: 7.2 cm

Findspot Narthex east, at -3.43 m level.

Description There are engraved decorations on the medallion at the center and champlevé strips on the rim. It has a dark yellow glaze.

Vessel No. 6

Illustrations Drawing 6, Figure 6

Dimensions d.b: 7.5 cm

Findspot Naos, at -4.10 m ground level.

Description Sgraffito and green paint were used together. It has a light green glaze.

---

4 The depth of all levels were determined by setting the present ground level at '0'.

Vessel No. 7

Illustrations Figure 7
Dimensions d.b. could not be measured
Findspot Naos, at -3.20– -4.10 m level.
Description It has green spattered paint and a green glaze.

Vessel No. 8

Illustrations Drawing 7, Figure 8
Dimensions d.b: 7 cm
Findspot Apse, at -3.00 – -3.20 m.
Description Sgraffito and green paint were used together. Inside the medallion at the center is a four-leaf clover. It has a light green glaze.

Vessel No. 9

Illustrations Drawing 8, Figure 9
Dimensions d.b: 6 cm
Findspot Naos, at -3.70 – -4.10 m level.
Description At its center are marks of a tripod. The yellow glaze was transformed into green at certain places.

Unglazed Ceramic Wares

Cooking pot No. 1

Illustrations Drawing 9, Figure 10
Dimensions d.r: 10.05 cm, d.b: 7 cm
Findspot Narthex east, at -3.60 m level.
Description It has scorch marks.

Cooking pot No.2

Illustrations Figure 11
Dimensions d.r. could not be measured
Findspot Naos, at -1.60 – -2.20 m level.
Description It has a stripe of wave-like engraving on its body. It has scorch marks.

Cooking pot No. 3

Illustrations Drawing 10, Figure 12
Dimensions d.r: 14 cm
Findspot Apse, at -3.20 – -4.00 m level.
Description It has an interrupted comb decoration on the top of its rim. It has scorch marks.

Pitcher No. 1

Illustrations	Drawing 11, Figure 13
Dimensions	d.r: 5 cm
Findspot	Narthex east, at -3.60 – -4.00 m level.
Description:	It is made from pink fabric.

Pitcher No. 2

Illustrations	Drawing 12, Figure 14
Dimensions	d.r: 9 cm
Findspot	Naos, at -3.20 – -4.10 m level.
Description	It has grooves on its body. Its orange fabric has gray patches caused during firing.

Sphero-conical container sherd

Illustrations	Drawing 13, Figure 15
Dimensions	d: 7 cm
Findspot	Narthex, at -2.50 – -4.20 m level.
Description	It has a slightly porous brownish-red colored fabric, tempered with coarse sand and lime. It has patches of impressed decoration on its body.

2. Evaluation

Although few in numbers, the ceramic finds are important in terms of providing information about the stages of use of the church. The glazed ceramic finds consist of vessel parts. And among the unglazed finds are pitchers, cooking pots, and sherds of base, handle, and rims that we have not included in the catalogue.

The glazed ceramics display features of form and decoration common especially on eastern Mediterranean shores. The closest comparisons could be with the products of the Paphos and Enkomi workshops, active during the 13th-14th centuries in Cyprus. Among the finds are ceramic wares belonging to the Zeuxippus family, which were widely distributed around the Aegean and the Mediterranean. In addition, there are also common features with ceramics found in centers, such as Al-Mina, where the Crusaders were active.

Among the finds from Alakent Church, the decoration on the body of Vessel No. 1 is divided into eight sections. There are geometrical interlaced patterns within a horizontal strip on the upper part. The stylized palmette motifs in compositions divided into eight or four sections and the use of green and brown paint on this vessel are also seen in the products of the Paphos workshop in Cyprus. Although the form of the body of this vessel found in Alakent Church has similarities with the Paphos finds dated to the end of the 13th century to the 14th century, there are differences in the forms of the bases.[5] Another example decorated with an interlaced composition with a filling ornament found at Al-Mina was dated to the period when the Crusaders were in the region. This was produced by a local workshop thought to be active between 1200 and 1268.[6]

5 Papanikola-Bakirtzi 1996, pin. XVIII/91, pin. XXV/134.

6 Lane 1937, p. 46, Pl. XXIII.1.

On Vessel No. 2, inside the medallion at the center, partial traces of a mask could be seen. The surviving remnants of the vessel bear fish-scale filling patterns used together with paint. The closest matching counterparts of this vessel could be found among the products from Cyprus. Among the 13th century Paphos vessels there are examples of what was described as anthropomorphic rosettes or suns, utilizing a single color paint and sgraffito.[7] In another example from Cyprus dated to the 14th century, the mask at the center was described as an anthropomorphic sun. The space between the radial bands around this example also has a herringbone fill, and in accordance with this radial arrangement two different colors were used alternately.[8] There are also other examples dated to the same century where the central medallions were filled with different motifs.[9] Among the sherds of bases found at Alexandria, identified as 13th–15th century Cyprus ceramics, there are examples bearing a mask at the center described as a moon or a sun. Among the interlaced patterns herringbone was used as a filling ornament.[10] Depictions of sun similar to the one in Myra could be seen on products of the Port Saint Simeon workshop, active in Al-Mina during the first half of the 13th century. The presence of blank spaces on the surface of the plate and the borders filled with triangles are the main features that distinguish the products of this workshop from the products of Cyprus. The vessels from Cyprus are also separated from the works of this workshop through their concave rim forms and the characteristics of their glaze.[11] The vessel found at Alakent has similarities with the products of the Enkomi workshop in terms of its form.

Another example with a combination of sgraffito and paint is Vessel No. 3, which also has fish-scale filling ornaments. The ceramic wares found in Cyprus –with empty spaces between the motifs completely filled with fish scales and an additional green color used – were dated to the 14th century.[12] On the other hand, in terms of decoration, Vessel No. 4 carries similarities with vessels falling into the first group of the Zeuxippus family of wares produced at various centers around the Mediterranean between the end of the 12th and 13th centuries.[13] The 13th century examples of the Zeuxippus 1B group at the Benaki Museum in Athens display similarities of form and decoration to Vessel No. 4. Another example found in Dascylium –with similar features of color, decoration, and form– has a wave-like incised decoration on its neck that is different from our example. This example is also a vessel belonging to the first type of the Zeuxippus group and can be dated to the end of the 12th century to 13th century. Similar Zeuxippus vessels with inverted rims found at Kuşadası / Kadıkalesi (Anaia) also have common features in terms of form and decoration.[14] Vessel No. 5 also displays common features with vessels classified under the Zeuxippus family of wares. The examples found at Alanya Castle belonging to groups 1B and 1C have been dated to the first half of the 13th century with the help of stratigraphy.[15] Similar bases found at Carmel and

7 Papanikola-Bakirtzi 1996, p. 84, 218, pin. XII/65.

8 Papanikola-Bakirtzi 2004, no. 17.

9 Papanikola-Bakirtzi 2004, no. 60.

10 François 1999, pp. 212–213, no. 299–302.

11 Lane 1937, p. 49, Pl. 23/1B, 53, 54.

12 Papanikola-Bakirtzi 1989, pp. 78–79, no: 8.

13 Papanikola-Bakirtzi, Mavrikiu and Bakirtzis 1999, pp. 113–114; Böhlendorf-Arslan 2004, C. 1, pp. 128–129, C. 2–3 cat. nr. 625.

14 For the examples at Benaki Museum, see Papanikola-Bakirtzi, Mavrikiu and Bakirtzis 1999, no. 245 and 246; for Dascylium, see Doğer 2012, Table 14 / cat. no. 40; for the Anaia examples, see İnanan 2013, pp. 70–75, Tablo II/1, 2; İnanan 2010, pp. 120–122. These vessels found at Anaia are considered to be from the 13th century.

15 Like Myra, Alanya is also a settlement that had active trade relations with Cyprus in this century. At the same time, the finds were similarly found at the same level with Seljuk coins. Bilici 2010, pp. 106–107, 122; Megaw 1968, pp. 71–72. Megaw has stated that this rim form could also relate to Zeuxippus group Type II. However,

dated to the 13th century were considered as derivatives of the Zeuxippus family. This type of ware was also produced in the region around Cyprus, Syria, and Palestine, and the example here was a vessel of this style.[16] The closest matching counterparts of Vessel No. 5, in terms of the form of base and body, were found among the products of the Paphos workshop, active from the beginning of the 13th century until the end of the 14th century. The base sherds found in Alexandria, which have common features with the base of this vessel from Alakent, are also thought to be among the 13th century products of the Paphos workshop.[17] Vessel No. 5 also displays similarities in base and body form to the products of the Paphos workshop. Although the decoration on Vessel No. 6 with sgraffito and green paint could not be fully discerned since the vessel was recovered in fragments, the form of its base bears the characteristics of Paphos products.

Vessel No. 7 has a light green glaze and is decorated with spattered paint. There are examples of these types of vessels with white or red fabrics, and the pieces found at Alakent have a red fabric. The counterparts of these in Corinth had a red fabric and were determined to be produced locally and dated to the 12th century. There are also 13th century examples of these vessels produced at the Paphos workshop.[18]

The four-leaf clover motif at the center of Vessel No. 8 was a widely used motif throughout the 14th and 15th centuries. The base forms of the examples found in Cyprus and Northern Greece differ from the one from Myra. There are also examples where the perimeter or the inside of the central medallion is enhanced with motifs such as spirals.[19]

As mentioned earlier, some base, handle, and body fragments of unglazed ceramic ware unearthed during the excavations at the church were not included in the catalogue since it was not possible to determine their overall forms. During the work carried out around the building, fragments of *unguentaria* were also found. These unguentarium fragments were without context and had been carried with alluvium from undetermined locations.

The cooking pots in the catalogue have a porous fabric, tempered with coarse sand and limestone. There are scorch marks on their bodies. Example No. 1 is a thick-walled vessel with a globular body and a high-swung handle. There are examples similar to this vessel from around the 12th century. A similar example found in Stratonikaia was also evaluated to belong to the same century. There are also similar examples among the Saraçhane finds dated to the same period.[20] However, it can also be assumed that this form, favoring functionality, may have been in use for a long time.

We have no knowledge whether the cooking pots found at Alakent had a single or double handle. Cooking pots No. 1 and No. 3, and some others which were not included in the catalogue, were found with a single handle. There are a number of decorations on Cooking pots No. 2 and No. 3. There is a stripe of wave-like engraving corresponding to the middle part of the body on Cooking pot No. 2 and a group of interrupted comb decorations on top of the rim of Cooking

the example from Myra is different from the aforementioned type because it does not involve the use of paint (Megaw 1968, 7 p. 6, fig. 3/2004, pl. 16e).

16 Pringle 1984, 104, fig. 7/60–63.

17 For the Paphos finds, see. Papanikola-Bakirtzi 1996, p. 216, 218, pin. VIII/40; for the Alexandria finds, see François 1999, pp. 112–113, No. 296–298.

18 For the examples from Corinth, see Morgan 1942, pp. 84–85, fig. 64; for the examples from Paphos, see Papanikola-Bakirtzi 1996, pin. 28/156.

19 For the examples from Cyprus, see Papanikola-Bakirtzi 1989, pp. 150–151, no: 40–44; for the examples from Northern Greece, see Papanikola-Bakirtzi and Zikos 2007, no. 152.

20 For Stratonikaia, see Söğüt 2011, p. 202, res. 10b; for Saraçhane, see Hayes 1992, pp. 222–223, fig. 20/15.

pot No. 3. Straight and wavy linear stripes, elements of dashed lines, oblique/curved lines, and straight and wavy comb lines were also used as decorative elements on wares from Cyprus until the end of the 14th century. And Myra had close links with this center. Although there are similar examples of kitchenwares found at Nea Paphos from the 14th century and later, they could be also compared to examples from the 12th–13th centuries. Some of these vessels were also identified to have glaze on their rims and their inner sides.[21]

The pitchers have a porous fabric tempered with coarse lime. Pitcher No. 1 has a pink fabric, and Pitcher No. 2 has an orange fabric that has gray patches in some places. In terms of the context from which they were unearthed, these finds could be evaluated to belong to the same period as the other ceramic finds.

Only a single specimen of sphero-conical container was unearthed at the Alakent excavations. This vessel was tempered with coarse sand and lime, and has a slightly porous, brownish-red colored fabric. The functions of sphero-conical vessels are open to dispute. They are thought to be hand grenades filled with flammable materials such as naphtha. But it has also been suggested that they may have been containers for pharmaceuticals, alcoholic beverages, perfume, or mercury. They were widely used throughout the 10th–13th centuries; however, there are also examples dated to the 14th century.[22]

These vessels are thought to have originated in Central Asia and used in Silk Road trade to transport low density liquids. They were found between the 11th–13th centuries in a region including Western Anatolia, where Seljuk States and Beyliks also spread across. Examples found in Ani were also determined to belong to the same centuries. And among the examples found in Akşehir, there are specimens dated to the 13th–14th centuries.[23] Such vessels found in Anaia and described as bottles were associated with the 10th–13th century examples of the Turkish Islamic era. These examples, which also contain a turquoise glazed bottle, are thought to have contained some sort of liquid such as mercury or perfume.[24] The examples found in Samsat also have almond-shaped stamped reliefs similar to the ones in Demre. That the material used is ceramic, that they have decorations on their bodies, that there are examples with glaze, and that they have narrow mouths leads to the conclusion that they were used as containers for valuable liquids such as mercury, perfume, or body oils.[25]

Some of these vessels were found containing mercury, and it is known that mercury was used to make ointments. According to Ettinghousen, the fact that there are also glass bottles in this form and that the ceramic examples were glazed supports the hypothesis that these vessels were used for keeping small amounts of valuable liquids, such as perfumes or pharmaceuticals, which would be used by sprinkling.[26] It is thought that they were used in houses or pharmacies by being fixed on top of some sort of feet or placed into holes on top of a counter. They were also carried on a belt.[27]

Another thesis regarding the function of sphero-conical containers proposes that they

21 Gabrieli 2007, pp. 404–405; Gabrieli, McCall and Green, 2001, pp. 22, 28–29.

22 Mercangöz 2013, pp. 166–167; Çoruhlu 2010, p. 124; for the examples found in Iran and dated to the 9th-12th centuries, see François 1999, p. 32, nos. 140–142, especially no. 141.

23 Çoruhlu 2010, pp. 124–128, 130, Pl. VIIIa, Pl. VIIId.

24 Mercangöz 2013, pp. 166–167.

25 Bulut 1994, pp. 8–9.

26 Ettinghousen 1965, pp. 218–224.

27 Çoruhlu 2010, p. 123.

were used as explosives. That they were uncovered at locations related to the Byzantine castle in Rhodes has led to the idea that they were used as explosives/hand grenades. It has been suggested that these examples dated to the 10th–13th centuries were used in sieges between Arabs, Byzantines, and Crusaders.[28]

Compared to similar examples, the sphero-conical container from Alakent must have had an oval body that terminated in a rather narrow and short mouth on its shoulder. Although it is difficult to explain the function of this bottle –the only example of its kind found at the church– it is possible to understand that this was related to the presence of Turks around Myra from the 13th century onwards.

3. Conclusion and Dating

The church where the ceramics were found is dated to the 12th century due to its plan. It was determined that a number of extensions were added, especially to its narthex, during its use as a church. Both its architectural features, and the characteristics of the frescoes on the eastern wall of the narthex depicting a *Deesis* scene, display influences from Cyprus.[29] However, it is also understood that the building underwent a new arrangement at a later date, after being used as a church. This situation might have been a consequence of the newly forming social structure in the region. From the middle of 12th century onwards Turks began to settle in centers such as Khoma (Elmalı), Kibyra (Gölhisar), Podoliya (Avlan), Balbura (Dirmil), and Phaselis (Tekirova) in the area surrounding Myra.[30] While the presence of many groups of Turks in the Lycian hill country was known, the Byzantine Empire allowed the shores in the region to be used by Genoan and Pisan seafarers during this period. There are bays in Moron Hydor/Posidarisus (Adrasan) used by the Venetians and Genoese, and in Phoinix (Finike) used by Pisans. While the coasts were used extensively by the Crusaders in the second half of the 12th century, the Turkmens settled in the mountainous regions. In the 13th century, this situation evolved as the Turks expanded their borders towards the shoreline. Following the weakening of the Byzantines on the Mediterranean coast after the Fourth Crusade, the Seljuks began to establish their presence along the coast during the reign of Alaeddin Keykubat I (1221–1237).[31] From the end of 13th century onwards, the Turkmens began settling in villages. At the beginning of the 14th century, there were many Turkmen villages in the region. Although the activity of the Levantine merchants along the coast was in decline, trade continued to be carried on.[32] In 1362 Pierre de Lusignan, the reigning king of the Lusignan dynasty in the territory, launched an attack on Myra. The use of the ceramics found at the church should also be related to these commercial relations and the transformations that the building was subjected to in this environment. The fact that the glazed ceramics have similarities with the finds from centers under the rule of the Crusaders in the period could account for the influences of Cyprus and the Eastern Mediterranean on these wares.

Among these examples the find of a sphero-conical container –known from a number of places parallel to the spread of Turks in the region– is also noteworthy. The ceramics, almost all of which were found at the same level, are associated with the final phase of the building. The

28 Bonovas and Tzitzibassi 2011, pp. 62–63, no. 23.

29 Akyürek 2010, p. 157.

30 Çevik and Bulut, 2010, p. 29; Güçlü 2010, p. 306; Erdem 2006, p. 245.

31 Güçlü 2010, p. 306; Harrison 1963, pp. 122–124; Çevik and Bulut, 2010, p. 29; Erdem 2006, p. 246.

32 Erdem 2006, p. 248.

construction of a wall that partially covered the *Deesis* fresco on the outside of the building and the rearrangement of the entrance to the building suggest that at one point the building ceased functioning as a church. As mentioned earlier, the glazed and unglazed ceramics were unearthed together at the same levels at the naos but were more concentrated at the northeast corner of the narthex. The circumstances allow the evaluation of the unglazed ceramics together with the glazed artefacts, which could be dated in comparison to similar examples. The glazed ceramics bear similarities with ceramics found in the Aegean, and especially in the eastern Mediterranean, dated between the 12th and 14th centuries. The examples that have common features with the products of the Enkomi workshop known to be active in 13th–14th centuries and the Paphos workshop in Cyprus have a significant place among the finds. However, it is not possible to reach a conclusive decision about the production places of the unglazed ceramics. Although it is unknown whether ceramics were produced in Myra during the Middle Ages,[33] it could not be determined with certainty whether the ceramics found at the church were produced here or not. But the relation between the functions of the ceramics and the new arrangement of the building remains a question.

33 Çaylak Türker 2006, pp. 134–135.

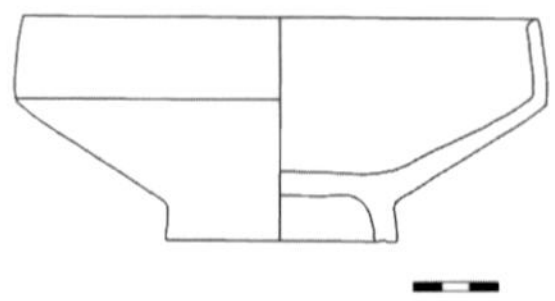

Drawing 1: Vessel No. 1

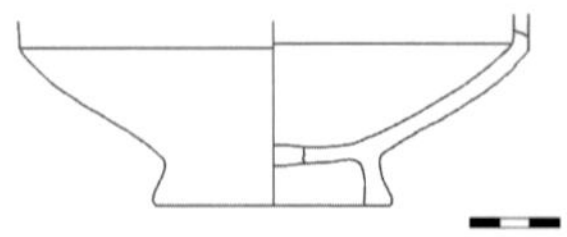

Drawing 2: Vessel No. 2

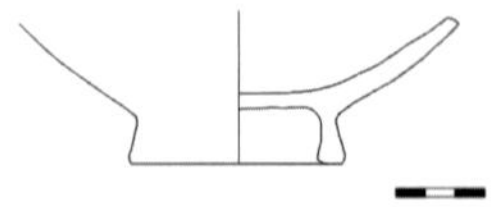

Drawing 3: Vessel No. 3

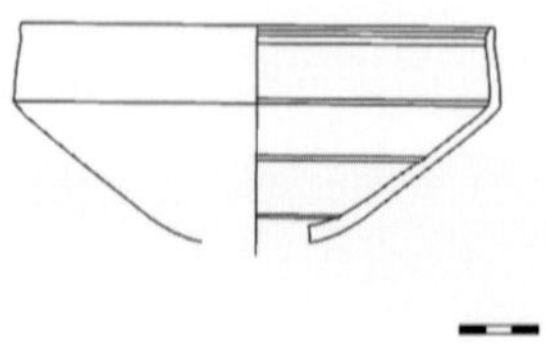

Drawing 4: Vessel No. 4

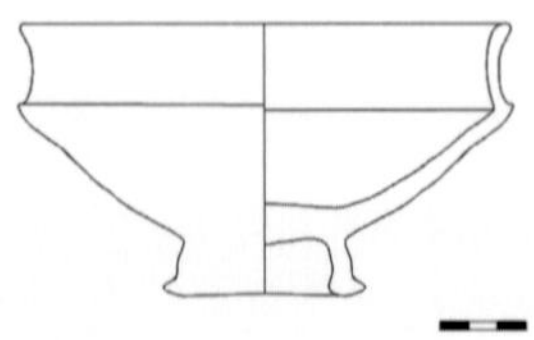

Drawing 5: Vessel No. 5

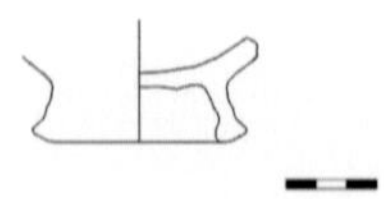

Drawing 6: Vessel No. 6

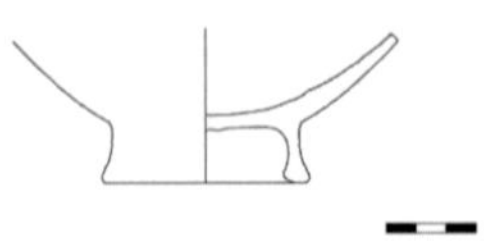

Drawing 7: Vessel No. 8

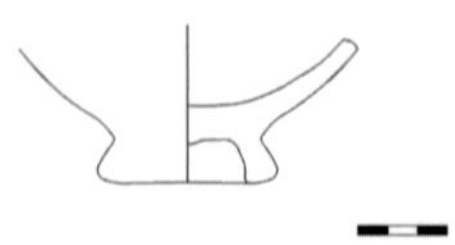

Drawing 8: Vessel No. 9

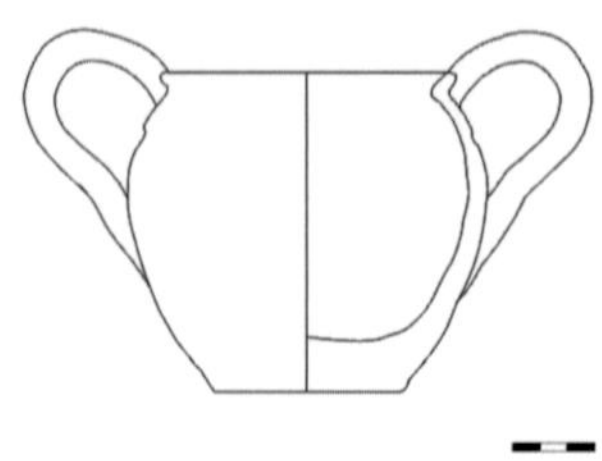

Drawing 9: Cooking pot No. 1

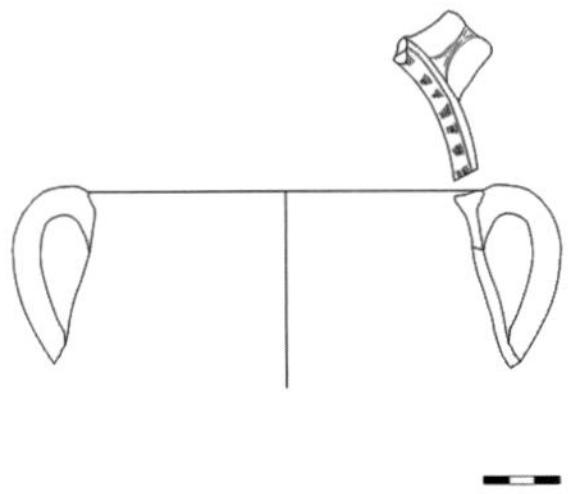

Drawing 10: Cooking pot No. 3

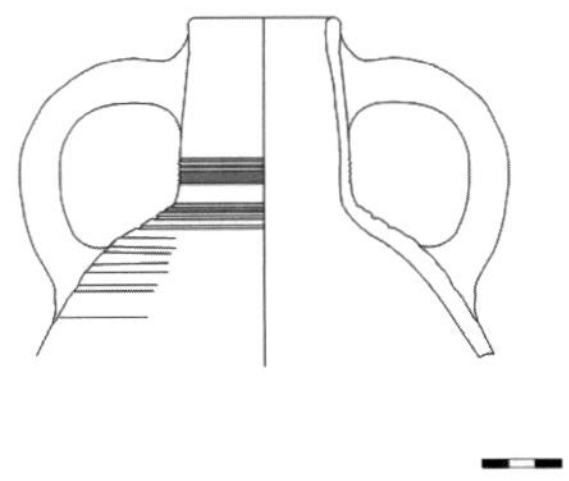

Drawing 11: Pitcher No. 1

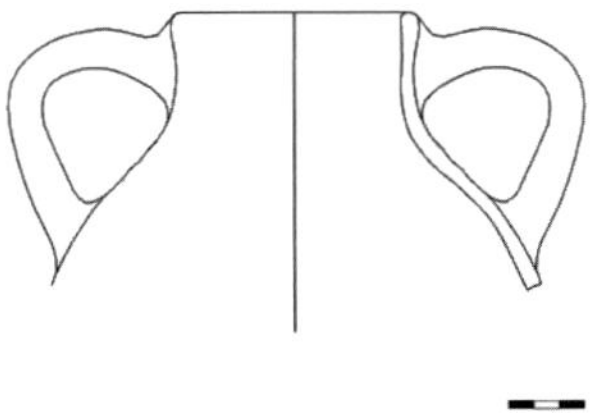

Drawing 12: Pitcher No. 2

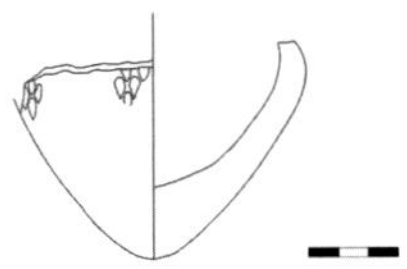

Drawing 13: Sphero-conical container

Figure 1: Vessel No. 1

Figure 2: Vessel No. 2

Figure 3: Vessel No. 3

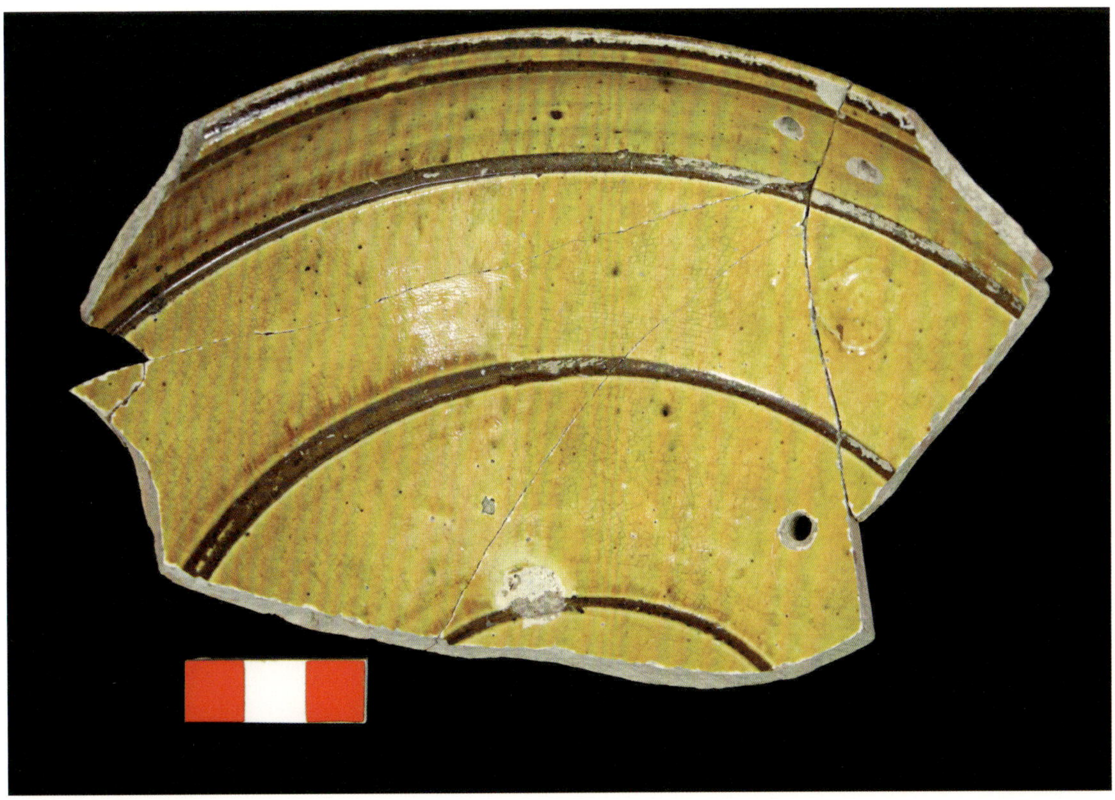

Figure 4: Vessel No. 4

Figure 5: Vessel No. 5

Figure 6: Vessel No. 6

Figure 7: Vessel No. 7

Figure 8: Vessel No. 8

Figure 9: Vessel No. 9

Figure 10: Cooking pot No. 1

Figure 11: Cooking pot No. 2

Figure 12: Cooking pot No. 3

Figure 13: Pitcher No. 1

Figure 14: Pitcher No. 2

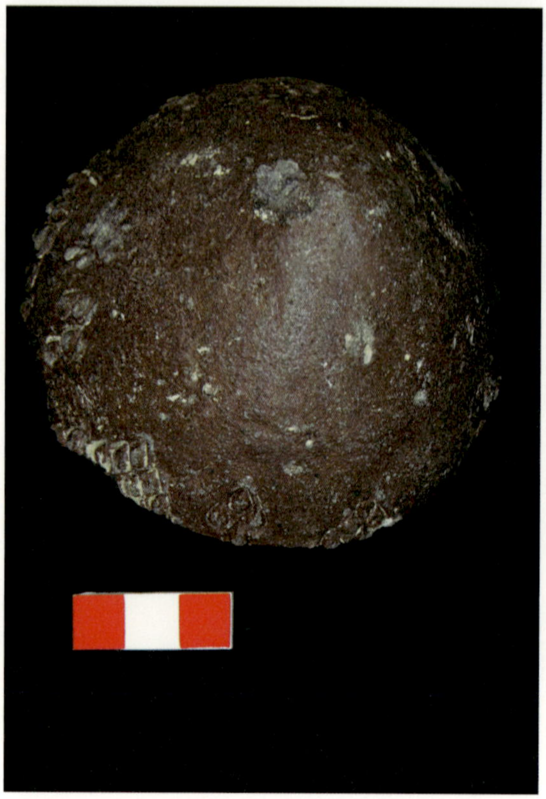

Figure 15: Sphero-conical container

VII. Inscriptions

Hüseyin Sami Öztürk

Marmara University

Christof Schuler

Kommission für Alte Geschichte und Epigraphik des Deutschen Archäologischen Instituts (DAI) in München

In 2010, within the scope of the "Myra – Andriake Excavations," an archaeological excavation was carried out at Alakent Church located in the vicinity of the Myra theater. Since it was buried under five-meter deep alluvium, the structure was well preserved. Excavation of the church, dated to the 12th century A.D., was completed to a great extent in 2010.[1]

During the excavations, five inscriptions used in the floor of the church were identified. Four of these inscriptions were seen and recorded by us, while the other inscription was evaluated through photographs and drawings. Four of these inscriptions were used as paving stones on the church floor. The remaining stone with an inscription had been transported to the excavation storehouse of the Myra – Andriake Excavation in 2010. These new inscriptions studied by the authors of this chapter are now discussed.[2]

1 For detailed information on Alakent Church, see Akyürek 2010, pp. 153–160; Akyürek and Çömezoğlu 2011, pp. 60–62; Akyürek 2015a, pp. 14–23; Akyürek 2015b, p. 30.

2 We would like to express our most sincere gratitude to Prof. Nevzat Çevik, who invited us to the Excavations at Myra and her harbor Andriake and allowed us to publish these inscriptions, and to Engin Akyürek, who invited us to write a chapter in this book.

1. The Tomb of So-and-So, the Son/Grandson of Apollonios (?), and his Family

Fragment of a white limestone sarcophagus, used as a paving stone in the church. The inscription is inside a *tabula ansata*; all of the corners are broken (Figure 1).

Date Found	2010
Inv. No.	25[3]
Dimensions	H: 50 cm; W: 65 cm; D: could not be measured; Lh: 3 cm / SBL:[4] 1 cm; *Tabula*: H: 36 cm; W: 37 cm.
Copy	Öztürk – Schuler 2010
Squeeze	—
Dated to	Due to the shape of the letter omega, 2nd century A.D.

[Τὸν τάφον κατεσκεύασεν - - - - - - - - - τ]ου̣ Ἀπ̣ο̣[λλω]-
[νίου - - - - - - - - - - - - - - - - ἐν ᾧ κηδε]υ̣θήσεται αὐτ[ὸς]
[καὶ -]Δ̣αμάρους κα̣ὶ *ν*
[- -]καὶ τούτ[ου γ]υνὴ̣
[- -καὶ ἔνγο]νοι αὐτοῦ Λικίν-
[νιος καὶ -]· ἄλλω δὲ μη-
[δενὶ ἐξέσται κηδευθῆναι ἢ ὁ κηδεύ]σας τινὰ *νν*
[ἐκτείσει - - - - - - - - - - - - - - - - - δη]ν̣άρια χει-
[λια -] *vac.*

Translation *So-and-so the son / grandson of Apollonios* (had this tomb built. In this tomb) *him and*... such-and-such *of Damares and*... *their spouse* so-and-so *and*... *their parents Licinnius and* so-and-so *will be buried. No one else is allowed to be buried. If anyone buries another person* ... (he will pay) *1,000 denarii.*

1 Here might be a short name of a person or the phrase β' τοῦ following this name.

1 Δαμάρης: This name is of Spartan origin and documented for the first time in Myra and Lycia. In Asia Minor, this name is known only from Amisos in Pontus.[5] Outside Asia Minor, it has been documented nineteen times including Arcadia and Laconia as well as in Crete and Delos.[6]

It is surprising that the name Damares, of Spartan origin, is seen for the first time in Myra and therefore in Lycia. However, recently a very interesting article about the influence of Sparta in Lycia and its neighboring regions was published.[7] The Spartan influence in the region

3 The inventory numbers seen next to the inscriptions are not excavation inventory numbers, but a separate number we have assigned to these inscriptions.

4 SBL = Space Between Lines.

5 See Corsten 2010, *s.v.* "Δαμάρης."

6 See Fraser and Matthews 1987; Fraser and Matthews 1997, *s.v.* "Δαμάρης." For this name, see also Pape and Benseler 1911, p. 266. For the examples of the name Δαμάρης, of Spartan origin, in Lakonia and Messenia, see also IG V.1, no. 38. 39. 66. 477. 541/44. 547/48. 1314.

7 İplikçioğlu and Schuler 2011, pp. 43-64 (= *SEG* LXI 1230).

was discussed through an inscription at a temple built for the Dioskouroi[8] found in Bozhüyük village (ancient Akarassos?) in the present-day Elmalı district of Antalya province. The site is located in the highland section of Lycia. The authors of the article view the worship of a Panhellenic God in Northern Lycia and Pisidia as a means of gaining prestige employed by cities since the Hellenistic Age.[9] And they provide examples in Pisidia from the cities of Selge, Sagalassos, Amblada, and Termessos. Selge has been associating its founders with Sparta since the Hellenistic Age; Sagalassos was using Spartan Heroes on coins of the Roman Imperial Period; the coins of Amblada had the legend of Ἀμβλαδέων Λακεδαιμονίων on them; and in Termessos there was mention of the worship of the cult of Helen.[10]

In addition to the mentioned cults of Doric origin in Termessos, in 2016 an interesting article about Pan, another god of Doric origin, was published.[11] With this new inscription, the god Pan, originating from the mountainous Arcadia region of the Peloponnesus peninsula, was also documented in Termessos after the specifically known locations of the Korykos Cave, Ephesus, Pergamon, Knidos, Apollonia and Lydai in Asia Minor. The earliest known evidence of this cult in Lycia is seen on the coinage of the dynast Pericles who reigned in Limyra in the 4th century B.C.[12] However, the known place of worship of this cult in Lycia, according to an inscription dated to the 1st or 2nd centuries A.D., was Lydai.[13]

The case mentioned above was a result of the process of Hellenization that started in the 4th century B.C. It is apparent that the Dorian influence in Lycia and the neighboring region of Pisidia is quite extensive, and the first example of this in Myra is documented by the use of the personal name of Damares.

2. The Tomb of Aurelia Euphrosyne and Family

Three corresponding fragments of a white limestone sarcophagus were used as spolia in the church. The basin fragment contains an unornamented *tabula ansata* in high relief, and the inscription is inside this *tabula*. The top and left sides are at a right angle, and the remaining corners are broken. The sarcophagus fragment in question is currently in the storehouse of the Myra – Andriake Excavations [Excavation Inv. No: MŞ10/4].

8 As is known, the word Dioskouroi is used to describe the Laconian twin brothers Kastor and Polydeuces in Hellenic mythology. The Dioskouroi, children of Zeus and Leda, were gods of Spartan origin and depicted as warriors bearing arms. (For sources on Dioskuoroi mythology, see Hermary 1986, p. 567). There are many iconographic similarities between the Dioskuoroi and Kakasbos-Herakles, who is worshipped quite widely in the area. These gods are depicted on horses and display the same characteristics in terms of form. For this reason, Robert 1983, p. 569, 573, thinks that the Dioskuoroi in the Pisidia-Kabalia-Lycia region are not Laconian gods, but "Guardian Gods" of Pisidia.

9 İplikçioğlu and Schuler 2011, p. 50.

10 For detailed information about the subject, see İplikçioğlu and Schuler 2011, p. 40. For the Dioskouroi Cult known from Termessos, see also Robert 1946, pp. 46-49, nos. 3-11. During the Beydağları Survey led by Prof. Nevzat Çevik, three new inscriptions dedicated to the Dioskuoroi, to Helena, and to the god Heracles were discovered in Kelbessos within the territory of Termessos, at a site called İnönü today. These inscriptions were prepared for publication by ourselves.

11 Çelgin and Kürkçü 2016, pp. 238-258.

12 Çelgin and Kürkçü 2016, p. 247.

13 *TAM* II (Kalinka), no. 130.

Date Found	2010
Inv. No.	29
Dimensions	H: 41 cm; W: 1.17 m; D: 14 cm; Lh: 2–3.4 cm.
Copy	Öztürk – FD 2010
Squeeze	—
Dated to	After 212 B.C.

Τὴν σωματοθήκην κατέστησεν
Αὐρηλία Εὐφροσύνη ἑαυτῇ καὶ τῷ ἀν-
δρί μου Ἐλπιδηφόρῳ καὶ τῷ υἱῷ μου
Αὐρηλίῳ Εἰρηναίῳ καὶ τῷ υἱῷ μου
Δημητρίῳ καὶ τοῖς θρεπταρίοις
μου Νείκῃ καὶ Ἐλπίδι· ἕτερον δὲ
μηδένα βληθῆναι εἰ .[1] . . . .ỌΥΝΔ̣
- -

Translation *Aurelia Euphrosyne built this sarcophagus for herself and for my husband Elpidephoros and his son Aurelius Eirenaios and to my son Demetrios and my foster children Neike and Elpis. No one else is* (allowed) *to be buried. If* ... (will pay).

6 The name Ἐλπίς is known in Myra from earlier times and fairly widespread in Lycia.[14]

3. The Tomb of Lysimachos

Two corresponding fragments of a white limestone sarcophagus basin used as spolia in the church. All of its corners are broken. In their second phase of use the edges were profiled. The inscription is inside a *tabula*. (Figure 2).

Date Found	2010
Inv. No.	—
Dimensions	—
Copy	From Photographs and Drawings (Excavation Archives).
Squeeze	—
Dated to	Due to the short left leg of the letter *Pi*, the Hellenistic Period

Λυσιμάχου τ-
ρὶς τοῦ Πρεπ-
vacat ελάο[υ *vacat*]

Translation (The tomb of) *Lysimachos III, the grandson of Prepelaos.*

14 For examples from Lycia, see Balzat, Catling, Chiricat, and Marchand. 2013, *s.v.* "Ἐλπίς". For this name, see also Zgusta 1964, § 358–6.

2 v.d. Πρεπέλαος is documented for the first time in Myra, and also known from one other instance in Lycia.[15] This name was documented in Macedonia on two occasions.[16]

The names Lysimachos and Prepelaos are evidence of the Macedonian influence in the city. The same could be said for another Lysimachos and the name of his father Alexander in inscription No. 4 below.

4. The Tomb of Lysimachos and Others Allowed by Him

Fragment of a white limestone sarcophagus, used as a paving stone in the church. This fragment belonging to the front of a sarcophagus basin has a simple and recessed *tabula ansata* with the inscription in it. The totality of the area around the *tabula* appear to have been scraped later. The upper edge of the basin fragment is at a right angle; the remaining corners are broken.

Date Found	2010
Inv. No.	26
Dimensions	H: 94 cm; W: 64 cm; D: could not be measured; Lh: 2–2.5 cm / SBL: 0.5–1 cm; *Tabula* H: 38 cm; W: ca. 42 cm.
Copy	Öztürk – Schuler 2010
Squeeze	—
Dated to	1st century B.C. / 1st century AD.

Τ̣ὸν τάφοṿ κα[τεσκευ-]
άσατο Λυσίμ[αχος]
Ἀλεξάνδρ̣ο[υ, Μυρεύς,]
ἑατῷ καὶ οἷς [ἂν συν-]
vac. χωρήσ̣[ω *vac.*

Translation	*This tomb was built by Lysimakhos* (of Myra) *the son of Alexander for himself and others allowed by him.*

5. The Tomb of Neikephoros

Fragment of a white limestone sarcophagus basin, broken on all sides and used as a paving stone in the church. To the left side of the basin is a fluted column, which indicates that the owner of the grave enjoyed a comfortable level of welfare. The inscription is inside a *tabula ansata*, and the *tabula* was rendered in high relief. However, the *tabula* was scraped off since it was used as paving on the floor. (Figure 3).

Date Found	2010
Inv. No.	24
Dimensions	H: 1.10 m; W: 75 cm; D: could not be measured; Lh: 2.5–3 cm. / SBL: 0.5–1 cm; *Tabula* H: 42 cm; W: 51 cm.
Copy	Öztürk – Schuler 2010

15 Balzat, Catling, Chiricat and Marchand. 2013, *s.v.* "Πρεπέλαος".

16 Fraser and Matthews. 2005, *s.v.* "Πρεπέλαος".

Squeeze —

Dated to Due to the features of the lettering in the inscription, 2nd century A.D.

Νεικ<η>φόρο[υ *vac.*(?)]
πραγματε[υτοῦ Φι-]
λοκράτου[ς τοῦ --]
4 σωνίδου̣ - -
vacat(?)

or

Νεικ<η>φόρο[ς *vac.*(?)]
πραγματε[υτὴς Φι-]
λοκράτου[ς τοῦ --]
4 σωνίδου̣ - - - - - - - -
vacat(?)

1 ΝΕΙΚΙΤΦΟΡΟ[(*sic!*).

Translation (The Tomb of) *Neikephoros the* pragmateutes *of Philokrates the son of –sonides.*
or
Neikephoros the pragmateutes *of Philokrates the son of –sonides* (had this tomb built for so–and–so).

1 The letter coming after the name, and before ΦΟΡΟ is pronounced as IT. This is probably a variation of letters. Here, the letter –η was used in place of the letter –ι.[17]

2 For the first time a πραγματευτής from Myra is documented. Four examples of a *pragmateutes* are known in Lycia: from Antiphellos,[18] Olympos,[19] Telmessos,[20] and Tlos.[21] The *pragmateutes* conducting business or trading on behalf of someone was managing this undertaking on behalf of Philokrates, as is understood from the rest of the inscription.[22]

2 v.d. Φιλοκράτης: This name, known only from Olympos and Telmessos until now, is documented for the first time in Myra and therefore in Central Lycia.[23]

4 | σωνιδου̣ - - - should be the genitive ending of a name. If this is the ending of a person's name, there are a lot of names that end with –σωνίδης.[24] Although it is apparently not possible

17 For examples on this subject, see Laminger-Pascher 1973, pp. 15–16; Gignac 1976, pp. 235–239.

18 *CIG*, no. 4299.

19 *TAM* II (Kalinka), no. 1020.

20 *TAM* II (Kalinka), no. 59.

21 *TAM* II (Kalinka), no. 603.

22 For the *pragmateutes* in Asia Minor, see also Robert 1937, p. 241.

23 For the examples of this name seen in Lycia, see Balzat, Catling, Chiricat and Marchand 2013, *s.v.* "Φιλοκράτης".

24 See Dornseiff and Hansen 1957, p. 153.

to complete the personal name that ends with –sonides due to its widespread use, the possibility that this name could be Θρασωνίδης should not be overlooked.

4 Further along this line, where the broken piece would have been located, one might expect to find the term Μυρέως.

Figure 1: Fragment of the sarcophagus of Apollonios

Figure 2: Fragment of the sarcophagus of Lysimachos

Figure 3: Fragment of the sarcophagus of Neikephorus

VIII.
Burials

Özgü Çömezoğlu Uzbek
Istanbul University

During the excavations around the church in 2011 and 2012, a number of graves in the area adjacent to the south and east facades were uncovered (Drawing 1, Figure 1). Five of the seven graves (G 1–5) were opened, and the work in this area was terminated after determining the characteristics of the burial ground. During the course of the work, it was observed that the skeletons in some of these graves were in a partially disintegrated state. The reason behind this must have been the floods in the region that swamped the area around the church. Two of these graves (G 2, 7) are in the form of arcosolia, adjoining the church from the southeast and northeast (Figure 2). The rest are simple graves dug in the ground, enclosed with stone blocks, and covered with stone slabs (Figure 3). No finds were unearthed in any of these graves. Five of these graves lie on an east–west axis, and two in a north–south axis. In only one of the opened graves (G 5) two burials were found, while the other graves (G 1–4) had the remains of only one individual.

The arcosolium tomb (G 2) adjacent to the southeast of the church is positioned on a north–south axis. (Figure 4) It has a pointed arch, and the front facade has survived with its original plaster. With colonettes on both sides it resembles an aedicula (Figure 5). It was built with irregular cut stone with the use of broken bricks as filling material between them. On its plastered eastern front facade, the plaster was engraved along the arch with courses imitating the rows of bricks, painted alternately in red and blue (Figure 6). Inside the tomb, red and blue paint from an unidentified wall painting was found on the north and south walls (Figure 7). Although a large portion of the plaster facing the burial place had fallen off, a red frame around the western wall could be identified (Figures 4, 7). The flood bank, constructed at a later date and extending from the east to the south side of the church, stretches across above this arcosolium. The surviving plastered surfaces indicate that the top of the arcosolium was plastered, but there was no information about whether the arcosolium was originally covered with tiles like the northeast arcosolium. The burial, which was covered with stone slabs, lies on a north–south axis like the arcosolium. The partial remains of a stone wall on the front facade of the arcosolium and the stones found fallen into the structure indicate that originally this facade was closed off. However, when it was uncovered, its interior was filled with alluvium and pebbles dragged by floods. The skeleton found inside the arcosolium was partially disintegrated. It is highly probable that the wall closing off the facade collapsed inwards because of the flood.

Another arcosolium (G 7) adjoining the northeast corner of the church and positioned on an east–west axis was built with irregular cut stone with the use of bricks among them (Figures 2, 8). This one was built in a simpler manner than arcosolium G 2. The square and rectangular tiles covering the eastern part of its pointed arch survived *in situ*. A burial place covered with stone slabs was found lying on an east–west axis (Figure 9).

In addition to the two arcosolium tombs mentioned above, other graves dug in the ground were also uncovered. One of these (G 4) is adjacent to the eastern facade of the apse. Just like G 2, it lies on a north–south axis, and the skeleton remains inside are in a disintegrated state (Figure 10).

The graves to the south of the church (G 1, G 3, G 5, G 6) remain within the dry stone wall built to enclose this area, referred to earlier as the flood bank (Drawing 1, Figure 1). These are all lying on an east–west axis with their heads toward the west. In a well-preserved example G 5, the arms were placed across the chest. As noted, two individuals were buried in this grave (Figure 11). G 6 was not opened.

To comprehend fully the location of the tombs and their relationship with the church, it would be helpful to consider the wall built around the southern facade that we have referred to as the flood bank. This belongs to the last phase of the church. Graves G 5 and G 6 were found under a floor covering made with mortar and small stones in the area enclosed by this wall. The aforementioned floor on top of G 5 and G 6 is at the same level as the original floor of the naos and its threshold from the first phase of the building. Additionally, the level of the top of the grave (G 4) lying on a north–south axis to the east of the apse and the levels of the top parts of the grave (G 2) inside the arcosolium are also in line with these. The wall that we have called the flood bank was built on top of this mortar–stone floor in the south, and contained part of the area where the graves were located. This also formed a boundary around the burial grounds. During the work carried out on G 5 and G 6, a coin dated to the period of John II Komnenos (1118–1143) was found on the level of the area to the south.[1] It is therefore possible to conclude that at least these three graves (G 4, G 5, and G 6) can be dated between the 12th century –the period considered to be the first construction phase of the church– and the period when the walls were added to the narthex and the southern area in the final phase of the church. So it can be proposed that these graves were built in the 12th and 13th centuries.

It is noteworthy that the arcosolium (G 2) located at the southeast corner of the church also contains a grave at the same level. At the same time, the red paint on the facade of this arcosolium and the engraved lines around the arch display common characteristics with the decorations on the plaster of the arch of the doorway on the western facade of the church. These similarities with the first phase of the church on the western facade, the grave's location adjoining the church, and the level of the grave all support the dating of this grave to the 12th century, the initial phase of the church. The other arcosolium (G 7), with a pointed arch and similar building materials, should also belong to the 12th or 13th century.

Also located in the area bounded by the wall in the south, graves G 1 and G 3 were unearthed at levels different than the others. These two graves, adjacent to the southern facade of

---

1 We would like to thank Mehmet Şengül from the excavation team who aided our work by dating this coin.

the church, were dug in the alluvium which had subsequently accumulated on top of the floor in this area. They indicate that the burial ground in the south was still used by Christians after the alterations of the church in its final phase. And this suggests that these graves were built during the final phase of the church while it was still in use between the end of 13th century and the beginning of the 14th century, or soon after it was no longer used.

The use of the area around churches as burial grounds is a common practice. There are also many examples of buildings built around churches as mortuary chapels. Also located in Myra and an important center of worship in the city, the Church of St. Nicholas similarly has a mortuary chapel, as well as an area to the northwest of the church used as a burial ground. There is also one arcosolium dated to the 12th–13th centuries in this burial ground, and one with the date 1118 in the western courtyard. On the eastern wall of the northwest arcosolium is a fresco depicting the Theotokos Hodegetria.[2] The similarities between these sites due to the presence of an arcosolium in each of these burial grounds, as well as both having fresco decorations, is noteworthy. The main difference between them is that the burials in the arcosolia at the Church of St. Nicholas in Demre lie on an east–west axis.

Churches with burial grounds and mortuary chapels in their vicinities at centers such as Kemerhisar, Yumuktepe, and Amorium in Anatolia could provide similar examples. In Christian graves burials were made on an east–west axis, and in many graves the head is located in the west. The arms of the body were placed diagonally across the chest or over the abdomen. There are also some cases where the arms were placed at the sides. In a number of graves more than one individual were buried in order to make better use of the space.[3]

On rare occasions, graves lying on a north–south axis were also found at Byzantine burial grounds. It is thought that the bodies were laid in this way to make the most of the burial space. The locations and directions of graves are thought to change from time to time depending on the area of the graveyard, its relation to other graves, or according to the topographical conditions. This practice is seen in Athens in the early period, and in Patras in the late period.[4] We have already mentioned that there were also burials on a north–south axis at Alakent Church in Myra. However, there is no definite data on why these graves were built in this direction.

All the other graves located to the south of the church, as we have mentioned earlier, lie on an east–west axis with the heads in the west. In the well-preserved G 5, the arms were placed across the chest, and no small finds were found in any grave.

2 These graves, dated to 11th and 12th centuries at the Church of St. Nicholas in Demre, lie on an east-west axis with their head ends to the west, and the arms of the body are placed diagonally across the chest. Of the two arcosolia found, the one in the western courtyard is dated to 1118, and the one in structure D to the northwest of the church is dated to the 12th-13th centuries. In both cases the burial lies on an east-west axis. See Ötüken 2006b, pp. 298–299; Ötüken 2008, pp. 139–140; Ötüken 2009, pp. 160–161, 168–169, dwg. 3.

3 At Köşkhöyük (Niğde) inside and around the mortuary chapel a number of graves with one or more individuals were found. They are dated to the 13th century; see Öztan and Açıkgöz 2011, pp. 136–137; Öztan, Açıkgöz and Arbuckle 2010, pp. 253–255. In the burials found at Yumuktepe some had arms folded diagonally across the chest, some over the abdomen, or with one arm over the abdomen and the other on the chest. The site has a church and a mortuary chapel; see Köroğlu 2005, pp. 275–277; Caneva and Köroğlu 2009, p. 154. The Lower City Church in Amorium also functioned as a mortuary church in the 10th-11th centuries. Graves were found both inside and outside the church. These graves lie on an east-west axis and have been used throughout a long period of time. Graves with multiple burials were found. See Ivison 2010, pp. 335–336, 338; Lightfoot, Tsivikis and Foley 2011, pp. 47–48.

4 Poulou-Papadimitriou, Tzavella, and Ott 2012, pp. 379-383, 407, 413.

The Coin of John II Komnenos

At the burial grounds to the south of the church, a coin was found. The catalogue information about this coin that belongs to the period of John II Komnenos (1118–1143) is as follows:

Obverse: Christ, with a beard and nimbus, wearing a tunic and colobion and seated on a backless throne. His right hand raised in benediction; his left hand holding the Gospel. Cover decoration: Five dots in a square shape. To the left and right of his head IC XC (Figure 12).

Reverse: Emperor on the left, St. George on the right is beardless and with nimbus, together holding a patriarchal cross on a three-stepped pedestal. Emperor wearing *stemma, divitision,* and *chlamys.* Saint wearing a short military tunic, cuirass, and *sagion,* holding a sword in his left hand (Figure 13).

On the left	On the right
IꞶ	[Θ
ΔEC	ΓE
ΠO	ꞶR
TH	ΓI]

Metal	EL
Weight	4.30 gr
Diameter	31.5 mm
Direction	6
Findspot	Alakent Church, area to the south
Level	Above ground
Mint	Constantinople
Denomination	Aspron Trachy
Reference	Tekin 1999, pp. 195, 295–296.

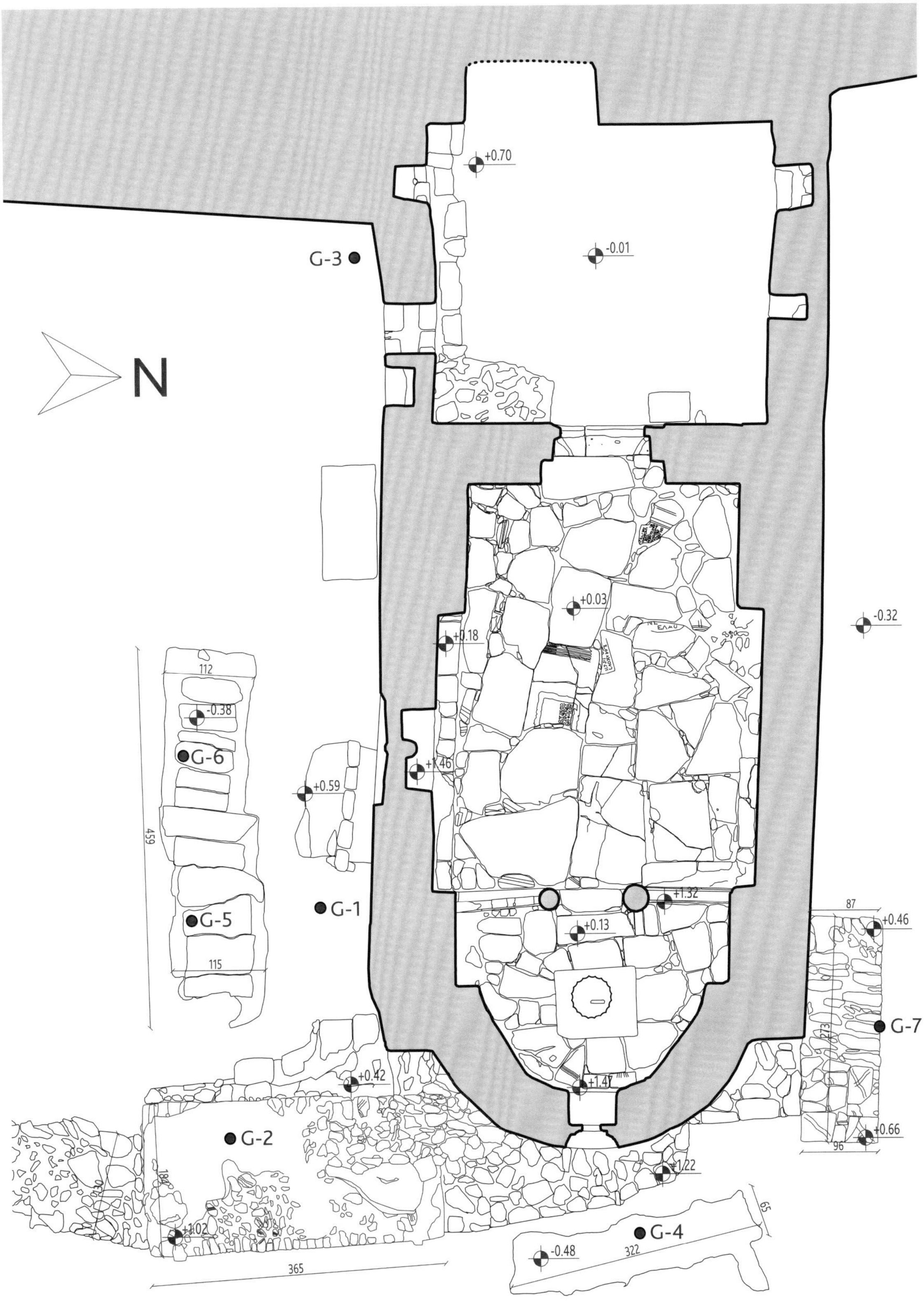

Drawing 1: Key to the burials

Figure 1: South facade and southern burial ground

Figure 2: North east and south east arcosolia (G 2, G 7)

Figure 3: G 5 south of the church

Figure 4: South east arcosolium, G 2

Figure 5: G 2, detail

Figure 6: G 2, detail

Figure 7: G 2, fresco fragments

Figure 8: North east arcosolium, G 7

Figure 9: Burial place in G 7

Figure 10: Grave in front of the apse, G 4

Figure 11: Skeletons inside G 5 south of the church

Figure 12: Coin of John II Komnenos, obverse

Figure 13: Coin of John II Komnenos, reverse

IX.
Conservation Treatments*

Sebahattin Küçük
Mimar Sinan Fine Arts University

Alakent Church, unearthed during the 2010 excavation season, provided important information concerning its period. At the church located southwest of the Roman theater, the dome above the present walking level was completely destroyed. However, the arches supporting the dome and the roof structure above the apse were preserved in a relatively good state.

The conservation and restoration process was programed to run concurrently with the excavation work. Protective precautions were implemented at excavated areas to prevent deterioration that could be caused by high temperatures. Moistened jute hessian was used, and a 1–3 cm thick alluvial fill was left in place on the surface of the walls. The restoration and conservation works begun parallel to the excavations helped determine the method of implementation in light of the data obtained through the process; the architectural documentation project, visual documentation, and material analysis were carried out.

The church was built using limestone, brick, lime mortar, and spolia materials. Spolia were reused especially on the floor and in the bema. The apse, pendentives, and arches on the north–south axis were built with stone and brick. The dome was completely destroyed, but the roof of the eastern part and the apse were preserved *in situ*. The bricks used in the pendentives and on some walls have a medium-baked red clay with a porous structure. The lime mortar, used as roof tile mortar and plaster as well as in wall masonry, contains stone shards, lime, and cream-colored sand.

Although the wall painting at the narthex was preserved in a good state under the alluvial fill, the wall paintings at the naos were not well preserved. The reason for this is that the wall paintings at the naos and arcosolium tombs had only a single layer of very thin (1–3 mm) lime plaster that was very fragile. In addition, plant roots had also caused serious damage to parts of the wall paintings that they extended across.

* The restoration and conservation work at Alakent Church was carried out by MSGSÜ (Mimar Sinan Fine Arts University) Traditional Turkish Arts Department faculty member and restoration expert Sebahattin Küçük and team members Berrak Küçük, Özgür Yıldırım, Can Özgeç, Cansu Can, and Selin Şahin.

Alakent Church has suffered structural losses and deterioration due to the damp environment in which it was buried for many years. It was buried under alluvium/clay up to five meters in height, brought by the floods of the Demre River. This new fill carried by the floods caused cracks and fissures at some places in the walls. Considering the extent of time that the building remained buried underground and the fissures and collapsed areas above the doorway on entrance the wall, we can state that the wooden door and window lintels have entirely decomposed. While being buried underground preserved the church, it also caused damage in various ways. Following the flood disaster, initially the effects of moisture, water, and microorganisms under the soil, and then the utilization of the area as a dumping ground along with the impact of the agricultural chemical wastes caused a continuous chain of destruction. The fact that a road passed over the site also added further to its physical destruction.

The purpose of the conservation and restoration works was to preserve the surviving remains without causing damage to the original structural features. The surface cleaning of the stone and marble elements of the structure and the removal of the alluvium layers left on for protection during the excavation were carried out mechanically. The unyielding layers of calcareous soil seen at certain places on the surface were cleaned in a controlled manner with distilled water and non-ionic detergent mixtures using cotton buds. Water vapor was utilized to clean stone and marble surfaces without plaster. Areas with fissures and cracks were cleaned to remove all alluvial deposits and prepared for injection with a mortar fill. Fissured stones were joined together using epoxy and fibre rods. The wall area located above the doorway, which was sagging down, was shored up with a support structure. The soil and debris filling the gap were cleaned, and the area was completed with lime mortar filling. The stones of the wall were stitched with epoxy fiber rods on both sides. The broken door lintel and jamb were removed, joined and put back in place. It was decided to leave the four arches supporting the dome of the church in their incomplete condition. For this purpose chrome nickel braces and plates for each arch were prepared and applied. For the missing parts of the *in situ* roof tiles, lime mortar filling and plastic repair were carried out, and the mortar was finished at grout level. The broken sections of the parapets at the bema were reconstructed, and plastic fill was applied to missing segments. No new replacements were utilized at any brick or stone section of the structure.

Local applications of fills were utilized in the missing parts of the lime mortar grouts of the masonry. The wall paintings inside the building and at the arcosolium tombs were damaged, and survived in sections. Precautions to regulate environmental conditions were taken during and after the implementation process. High temperatures and rapid temperature changes were stabilized by using jute hessian, protective shell systems, and the construction of a permanent roof over the structure. In the design of the modern roof system, sandwich panels were used to protect the building from the heat of the sun.

The alluvium layers left on the wall paintings during the excavation were removed mechanically. Surface supports were installed at places where there was a risk of breakage or separation from the wall. The surface areas between the plaster and the wall were cleaned, and injection fills were applied. Lime mortar was applied as border fill along the edges of the plaster sections where consolidation and filling were completed. In accordance with the results obtained from sample surface cleaning treatments, distilled water, and in some cases a mixture of distilled water with non-ionic detergent, was compressed onto the surfaces. Missing sections of plaster and frescoes in the apse were completed as a supporting measure, with a lime mortar fill rendered

1–2 mm below the existing surface level. The frescoes were not reconstructed or colored. The wall paintings remain with their original texture and colors, as they were preserved to the present day. Acrylic resin was applied to all surfaces for protective purposes. In the period following the treatments, the conditions, especially of the cracks, were continually examined, and it was observed that there was no structural movement. Continuing to carry out routine examinations of the structure is also advised.

The main objective of this work was to preserve Alakent Church in its original state. Only necessary treatments were carried out so as not to interfere with the original identity, condition, and testimony that the structure bears. Keeping a distance from the tradition of completing frescoes, which has been a dominant practice until quite recently, conservation treatments that preserve the existing elements in their natural state within an ongoing process were carried out.

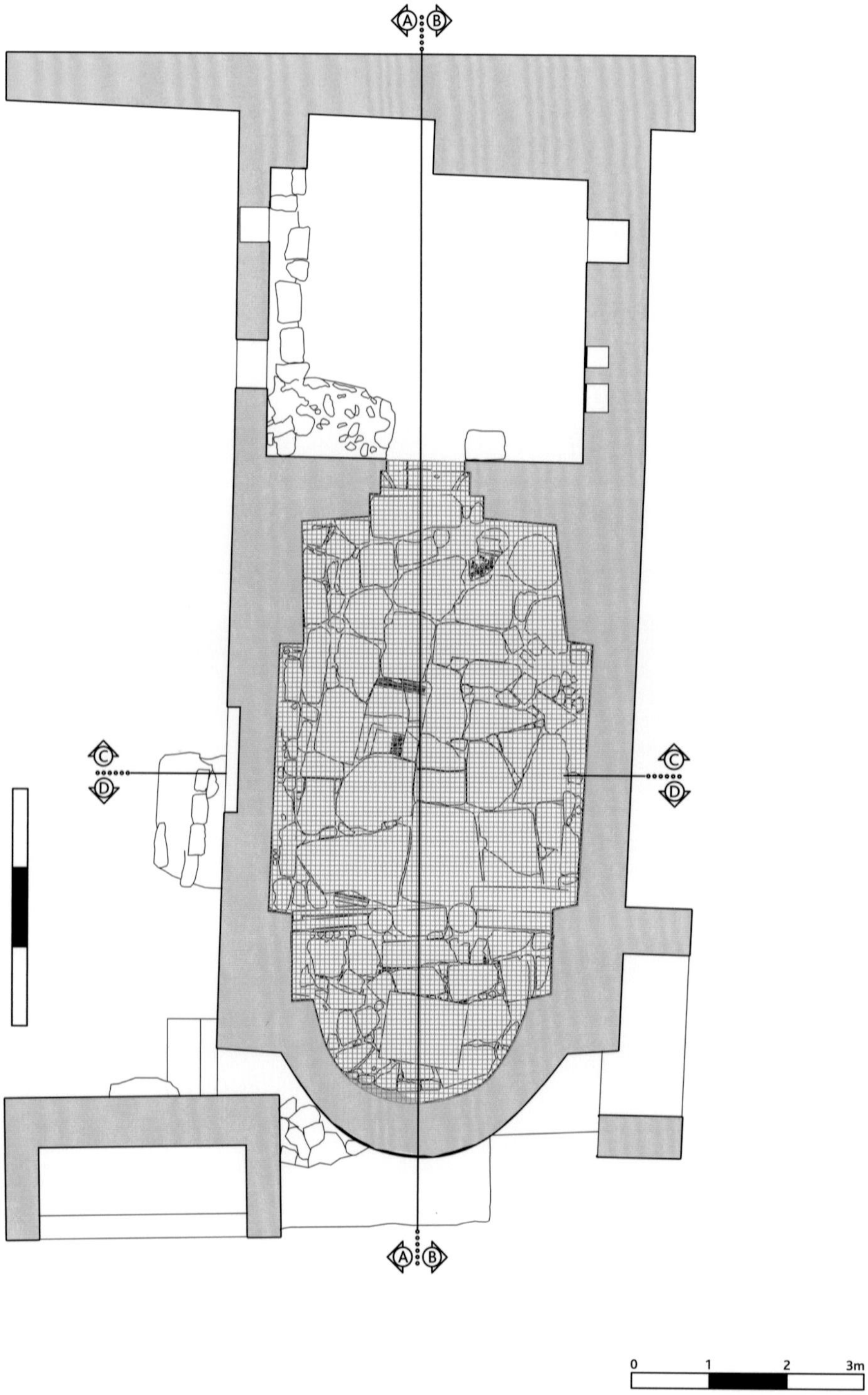

Mechanical cleaning

Drawing 1: Mechanical cleaning treatments, floor plan

Section A-A

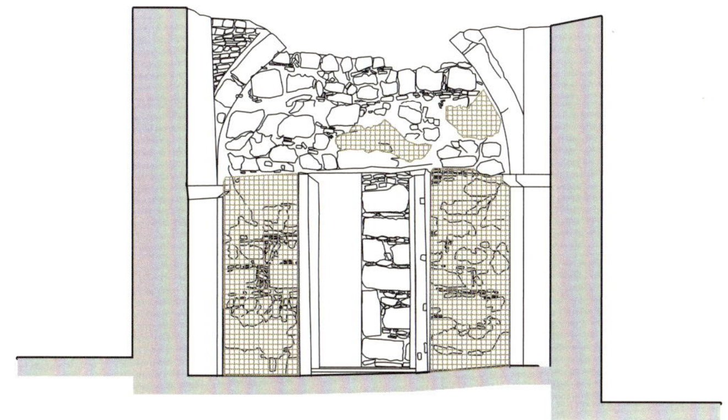

Section C-C

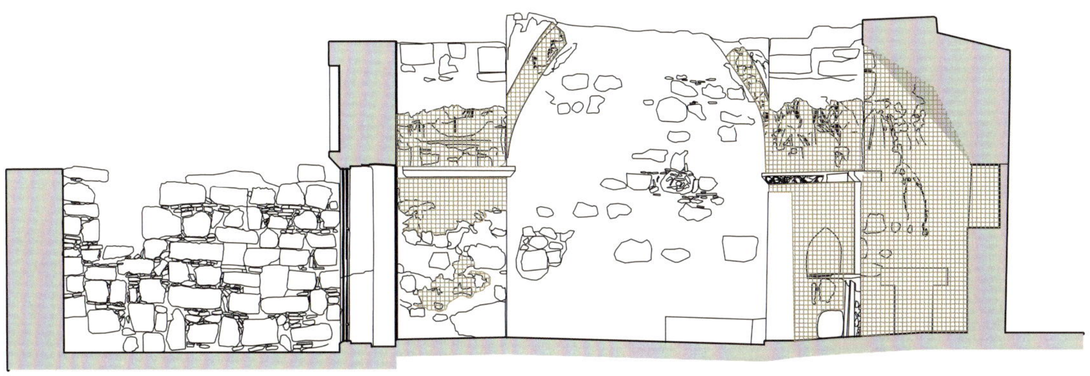

Section B-B

Section D-D

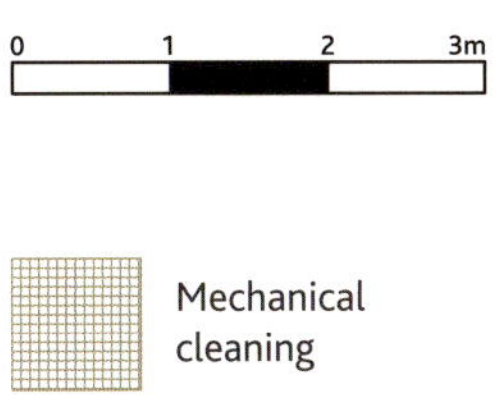

Drawing 2: Mechanical cleaning treatments, sections

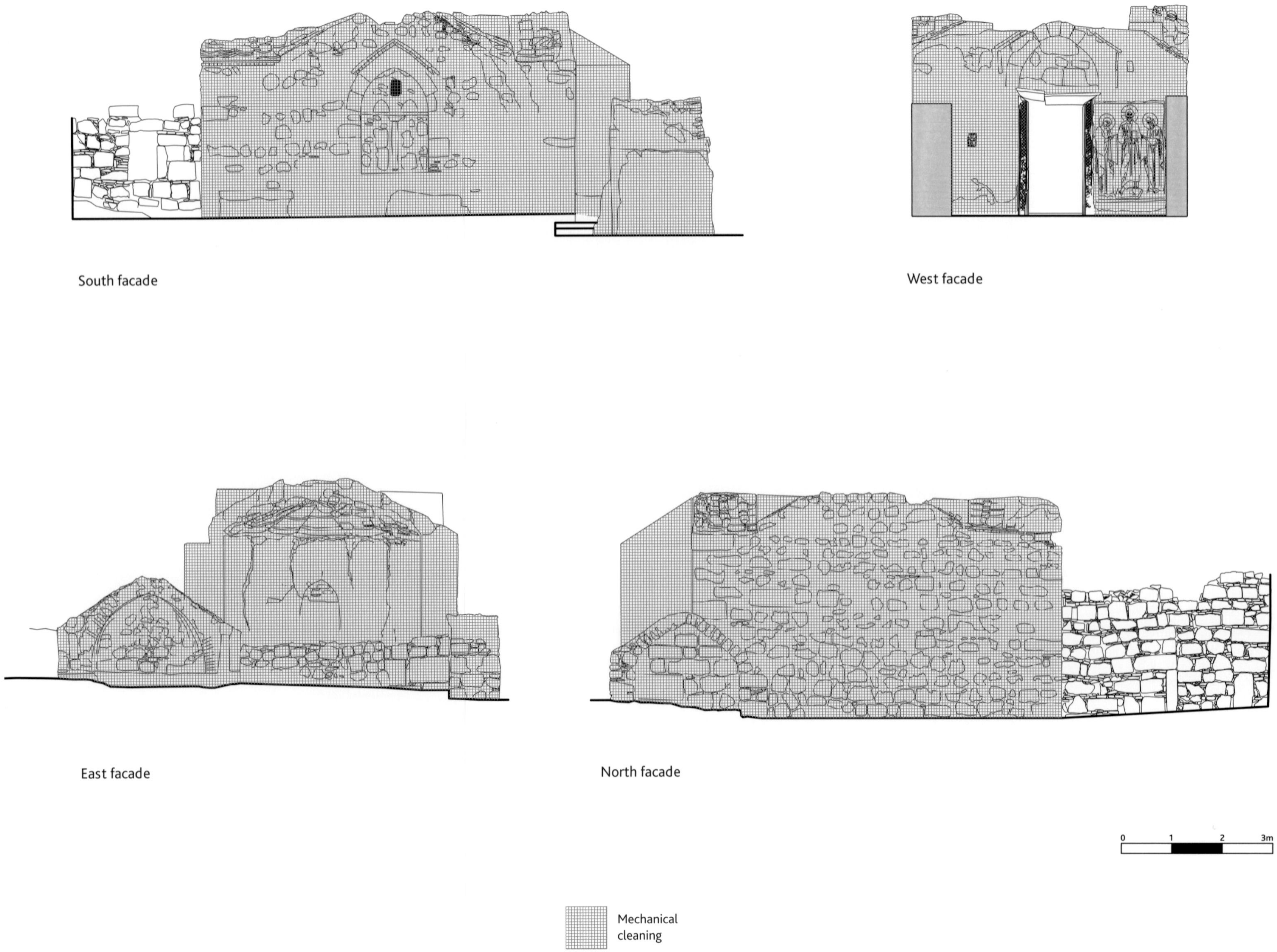

Drawing 3: Mechanical cleaning treatments, facades

Section A-A

Section C-C

Section B-B

Section D-D

Injection

Filling charges

Capping

Fresco edge filler

Drawing 4: Capping and plaster fill treatments, sections

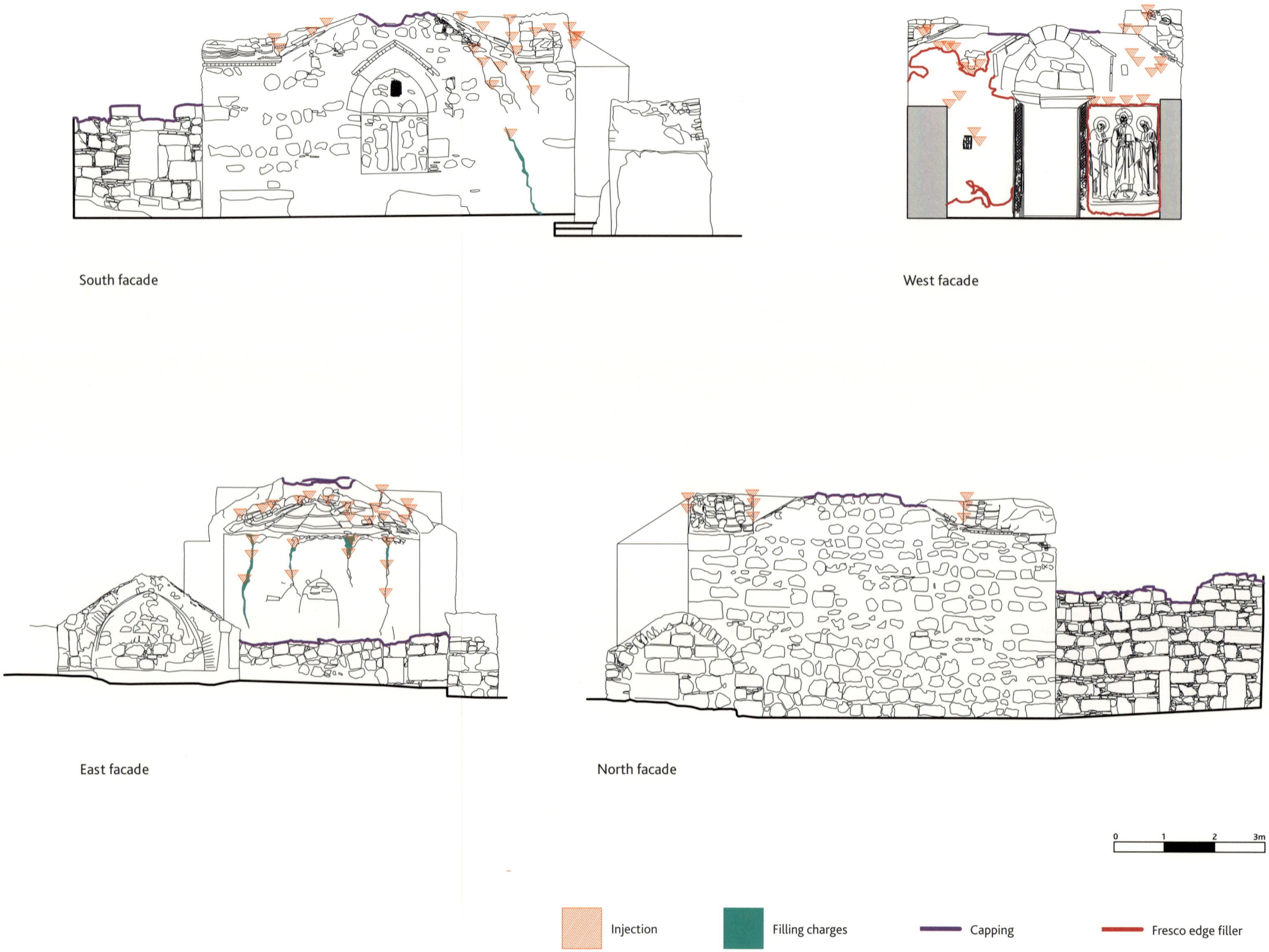

Drawing 5: Capping and plaster fill treatments, facades

Section A-A

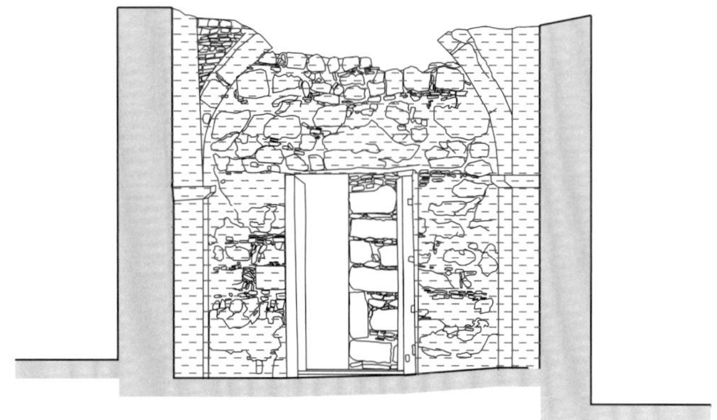

Section C-C

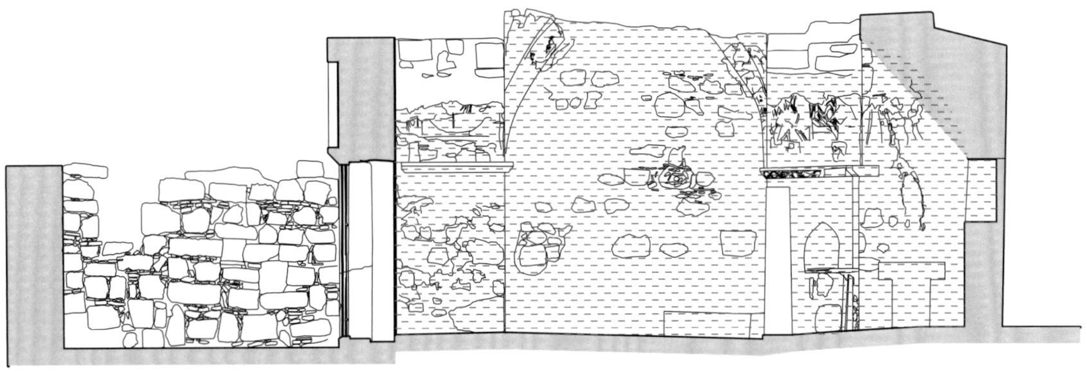

Section B-B

Section D-D

Protective

Drawing 6: Application of preserving agents, sections

South facade

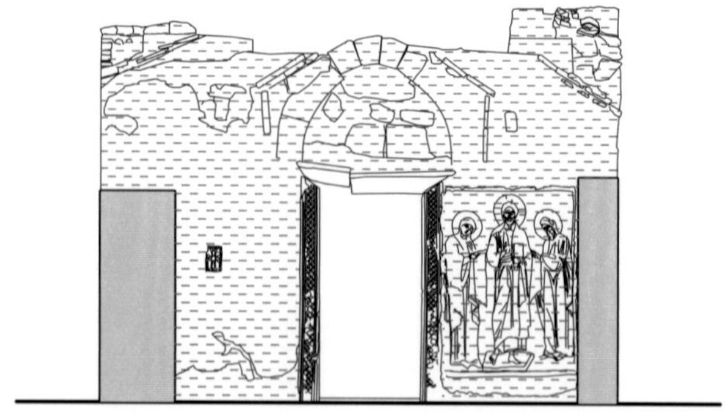

West facade

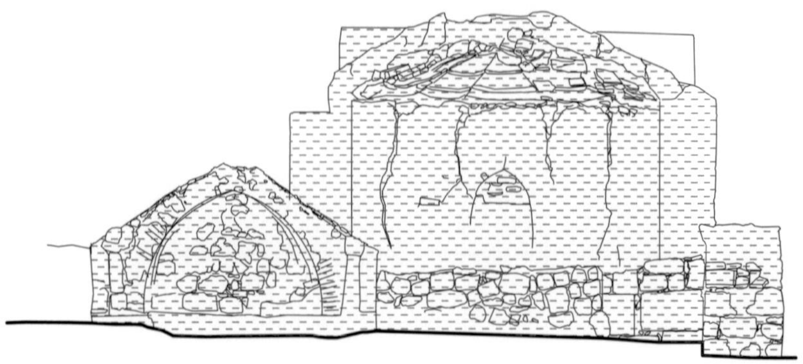

East facade

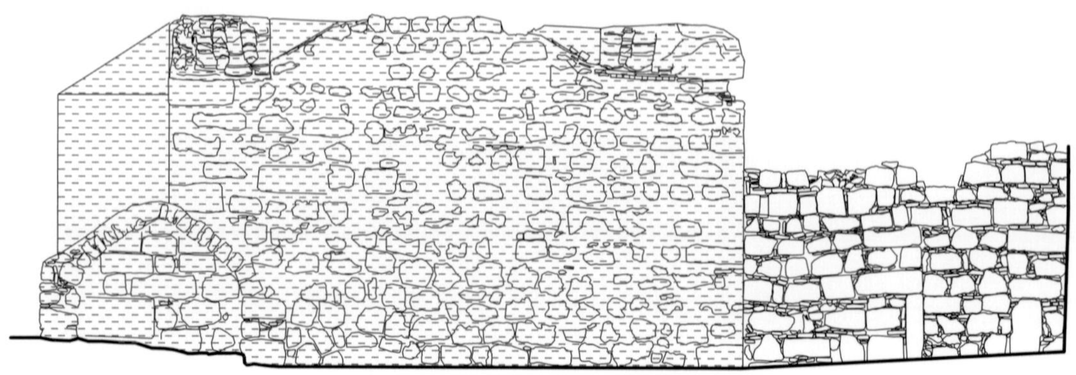

North facade

Protective

Drawing 7: Application of preserving agents, facades

Section A-A

Section C-C

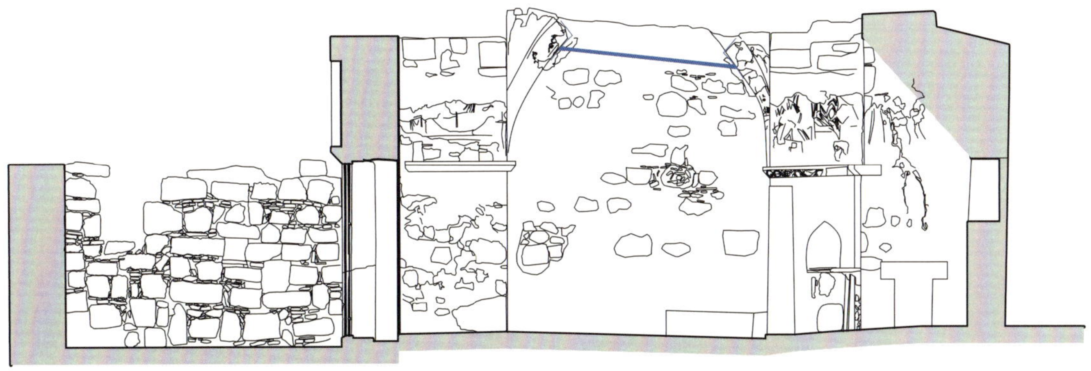

Section B-B

Section D-D

0 1 2 3m

Structural measures based on static concerns

Structural consolidation

Drawing 8: Structural precaution measures and completion work, sections

South facade

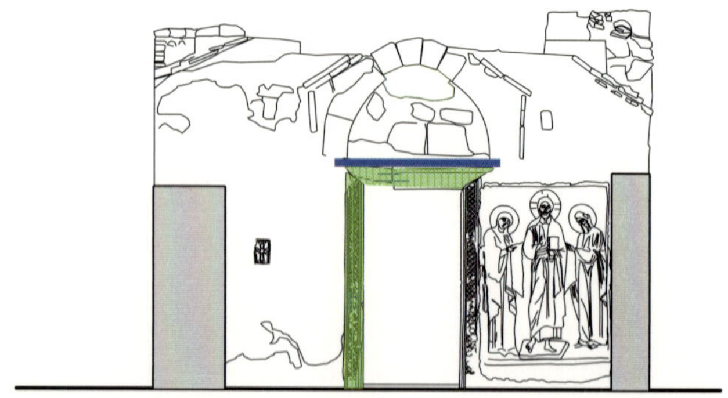

West facade

East facade

Structural measures based on static concerns

Structural consolidation

Drawing 9: Structural precaution measures and completion work, facades

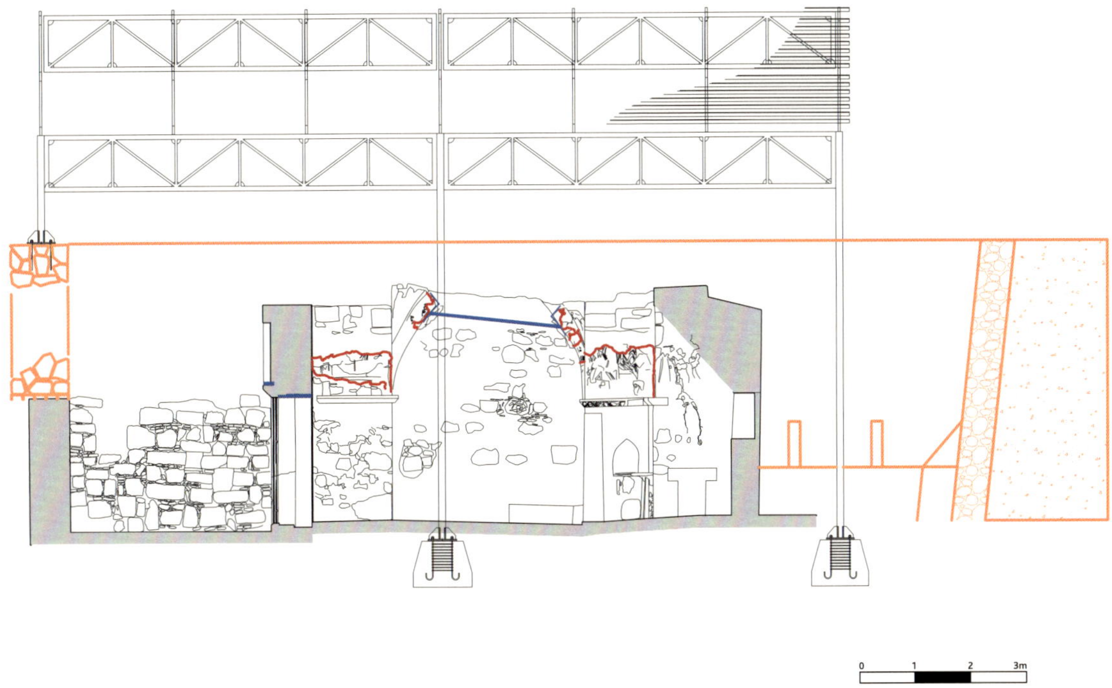

Retaining Wall

Protective Roof

Structural measures
based on static concerns

Drawing 10: Structural precaution measures and completion work

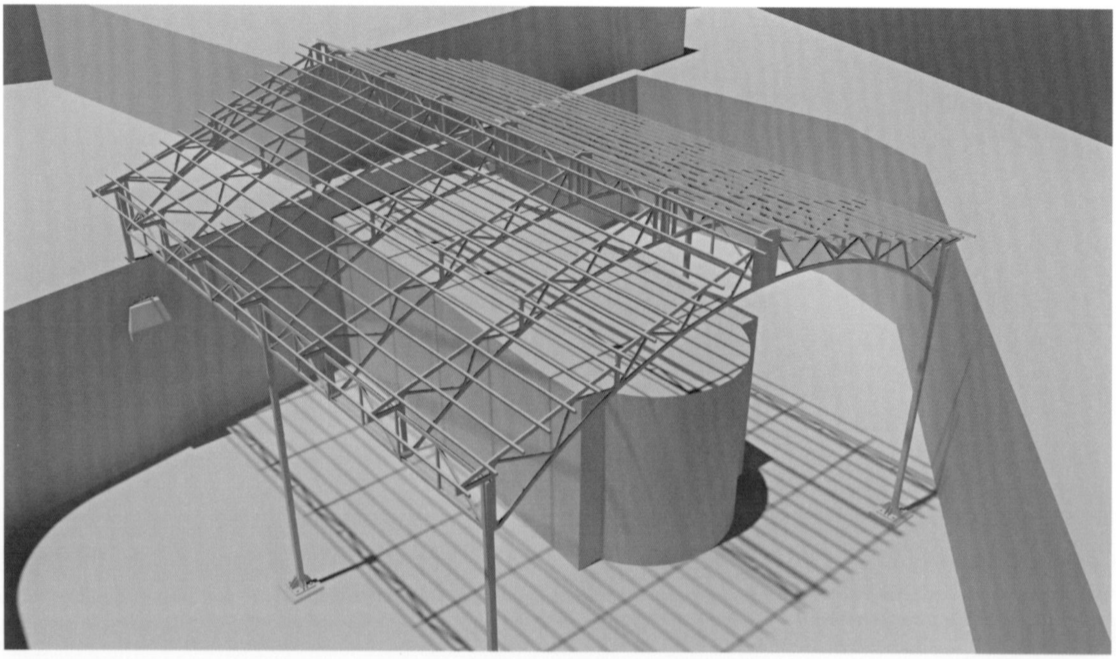

Drawing 11: Protective roof design 1

Drawing 12: Protective roof design 2

Figure 1: Conservation works running concurrently with the excavation

Figure 2: State of the wall at upper level of the apse

Figure 3: Door lintel at entrance of the naos

Figure 4: Precautionary measures on the arches

Figure 5: Preserved sections of frescoes on the naos walls

Figure 6: Injection treatment at cleaned cracks

Figure 7: Cracks and surface loss on wall of the apse

Figure 8: Mechanical surface cleaning on the *Deesis* scene

Figure 9: Surface cleaning on the *Deesis* scene

Figure 10: Partial areas of loss on the cleaned scene

Figure 11: Broken templon parapet

Figure 12: Templon parapet after treatment

Figure 13: Consolidation of the partially preserved frescoes above the entrance

Figure 14: Reconstruction of broken pieces of the door jamb

Figure 15: Clamping of rubble stone wall above the entrance

Figure 16: Work on western wall of the naos

Figure 17: Chrome nickel supporting braces on the arches

Figure 18: Contact points of supporting tie beams

Figure 19: Naos after treatment, southward view

Figure 20: Roofing over apse after implementation

Figure 21: Church after conservation treatments, viewed from southeast

X.
Conclusion

Engin Akyürek
Koç University

Alakent Church excavations have yielded important data both on the history of the city of Myra and on Byzantine architecture of the 12th–13th centuries in the region. During the excavation process –as in other excavation sites in Demre– after the modern cultural stratum no other cultural stratum was observed up to a depth of 5 m. A thick veil consisting entirely of silt had covered the Byzantine and earlier cultural strata. The first cultural stratum under the layer of alluvium was the level in which Alakent Church was located. This stratigraphy is consistent with the data of the excavations of the Church of St. Nicholas in Demre, which have been continuing since 1988. However, while there were late Ottoman finds on the top layer of the Church of St. Nicholas excavations, no such layer was encountered at the excavation of Alakent Church. The upper layers of the excavated area were completely destroyed, especially on the western part of the site, since it was relatively recently levelled by a grader during the building of a road.

The Myra plain was formed as a result of the alluvial deposits carried by the Myros creek from the Kasaba depression, filling the surface with flood sediments since the geologic eras.[1] The sediment covering the Byzantine cultural stratum represents the latest flood in history. We know that the ancient settlement of Myra was completely buried under silt probably in the early 14th century. Surprisingly, the surviving sources of the period report nothing about what happened to this important city of Byzantine Lycia. The facts about this matter have been revealed through archaeology. But one of the questions that remains unanswered is the time frame in which this disaster occurred. By what sort of a process was Myra completely buried under the silt? Was it a sudden disaster? Or was the city buried as a result of a process spread over a long period of time? Did the people do something to protect the city? Was the city evacuated in planned fashion or in a panic? Alakent Church excavations provide answers to a significant part of these questions.

First of all, it must be stated that the city was buried under silt not as a result of a sudden disaster, but due to a series of floods taking place over short intervals. Inspecting the cross sec-

1 Öner 2000, pp. 2, 7 passim.

tion of the silt deposit, it is possible to see that the accumulation was in 3–4 mm thick layers overlaid on each other over short intervals. This stratigraphy is best seen in the fill at the arcosolium tomb on the southeast, where the layers of silt filled the space with the deposits of the stream, and was sheltered from the continuous movement of water, which allowed the infill layers to remain intact throughout the process. The absence of any cultural stratum between the deposited fine silt layers suggests that the accumulation was slow, but almost uninterrupted. At least, there was not interruption long enough for a new cultural stratum to be formed.

How long might have it taken for the city to be completely buried? Of course, it would not seem rational to conclude that such a thick layer could accumulate in a couple of rainy seasons. There is also no data to confirm it. But the Alakent Church excavations proved that this process did not last for decades. The *Deesis* fresco that is about 2 m tall provides evidence supporting this. The alluvium that covered the church ensured that the building and the wall paintings were well preserved to this day, and the parts above the silt fill have disappeared. It is clear that the accumulated silt protected the areas it covered against the destruction of time to a great extent. When the *Deesis* scene is examined, it can be seen that the lower part and the upper part of the scene have survived with the same level of preservation. If the accumulation of 2 m of alluvium had lasted for, let us say, ten years, the upper parts of the scene would be more damaged and worn than the lower parts. The fresco was covered with silt in a relatively short period so has been preserved virtually without loss for over eight centuries.

In our opinion, the accumulation that buried the city happened neither in a short time like a year, nor in a time frame as long as decades. In all likelihood, the city must have been buried to a great extent at the end of a period of heavy rain that possibly lasted for three to four years. And this suggests that the inhabitants of the city might have combated the floods for some time, and then evacuated the city in a planned fashion. The Alakent Church excavation also provides evidence that would back this view. As mentioned in the chapter on architecture, the two windows located on the east and south walls of the church were gradually bricked up to be completely closed over two or three stages. Additionally, a sturdy but poor-quality wall, passing in front of the apse and extending southwards, was built to the east of the church. The excavations have shown that a stream passed in front of the apse of the church, followed the northern side of the building, and continued westward. Particularly in the northern part of the church, piles of gravel have been identified under the alluvial fill that might have been carried by a stream. Today, there is a stream that follows the same line, but has risen to the level of the semi–dome of the apse. This flows during wet seasons and causes floods in the neighborhood. Considering the dry rubble wall built as a barrier against this stream running from east of the church and the bricked up windows together, it can be deduced that the inhabitants of the church were combating the floods and the accompanying rush of mud for some time. This struggle probably lasted for a few years, but finally, at one point, they were unable to cope with a relatively large wave and abandoned the building. The church was not damaged, and it was evacuated without leaving behind any items and materials that could be transported. Then it slowly filled with the silt carried by the flood. This suggests that the building was evacuated in a planned fashion, and not in panic. Because the two columns of the iconostasis in the church were standing upright and without any deviation from the plumb line, this indicates that they were stabilized by being buried in silt without being subjected to the effects that would cause them to collapse. Our opinion is that the entire ancient city was buried under alluvium in a similar process.

Another outcome of Alakent Church excavations was the uncovering of the close relationship of Myra with the island of Cyprus between the 12th–14th centuries. The Lycian coast is located on the seaborne trade routes that connect the Eastern Mediterranean to the Aegean Sea and Constantinople via Cyprus and Rhodes. Exploring a map, it can be seen that the Lycian coast and the harbors on this coast are on the mentioned route. The wrecks of sunken ships would also confirm this. It is clear that the Lycian coast and Myra had a constant trade relationship with Cyprus. This relationship has continued throughout history. For Myra, which was not easily connected with the Anatolian mainland by land, the easiest Byzantine territory to reach was Cyprus by sea. Especially in the 13th century, when Constantinople was under the rule of Latins, Cyprus gained importance for Lycia and Myra. The data obtained from the Alakent Church excavations also reveal this interaction between Cyprus and Myra.

Although the ceramics found at the Alakent Church excavations were limited in numbers, they are significant examples providing valuable information. The closest matching examples of the glazed ceramics found at the excavation are the products of the Paphos and Enkomi workshops active in Cyprus during the 13th–14th centuries.[2] And this marks a close trading relationship with Cyprus.

Another evidence is provided by the wall paintings of the church. The *Deesis* scene, in which both the Virgin Mary and John the Baptist hold an inscription in their hands, has no counterpart in Turkey. The closest matching examples of such a wall painting are found in Cyprus.[3] Most of these examples are dated to the 12th century. Nevertheless, a later example at the Panagia Moutoulla Church, the inscription on the scroll held by the Virgin in the *Deesis* scene dated to 1280, is an exact match of the Alakent example.[4] Similar examples can also be found in places such as Rhodes, Crete, and Thessaloniki, but most are in Cyprus.[5]

Most of the closest examples architecturally similar to Alakent Church in terms of their plan, are also churches on Cyprus built since the 12th century. These examples are small-scale, single-naved churches with a central dome. Such single-naved churches had their domes supported by four arches and piers adjoining the walls. A rectangular plan was achieved by extending the nave to the east and the west by use of vaults.[6]

Some "Gothic" elements observed in the architecture of Alakent Church also provide important clues about the relationships with Cyprus. Gothic architecture started to emerge in the 12th century in Europe, and was later brought to the East by the Crusaders. Gothic influences in architecture also arrived in the Eastern Mediterranean, including Syria, Palestine, and Cyprus, from the end of the 12th century onwards, along with the Crusaders.[7]

The relationship between the Byzantines and Latins was always there, but the Crusades intensified this relationship. In the 13th century the Crusaders were active in a significant part of the Byzantine territory. These relationships led to the incorporation of some Gothic elements

2 See Chapter VI earlier in this volume.

3 For similar examples from Cyprus dated to the 12th century, see Chotzakoglou 2005: Panagia Phorbiotissa p. 599, fig. 406 (12th century fresco, renovated in the 14th century); Panagia Antiphonites pp. 629–630, fig. 513; Ioakhim and Anna (Kalliana) pp. 607–608, fig. 425; Panagia tou Arakou pp. 641–643. I am grateful to C. Chotzakoglou who brought these examples to my attention.

4 Rhoby 2009, Band 1, p. 334.

5 For other examples, see Rhoby 2009, pp. 334–341.

6 See Chapter III. 2.1 earlier in this volume.

7 Pringle 2015, p. 293 passim.

into Byzantine structures, especially those built in the 13th century. These elements influenced local architecture, especially in the form of pointed arches, pointed archivolts, double-pointed arch windows, colonettes and colonette capitals, and pronounced door frames. Charalambos Bouras has identified these influences in his examination of ten churches built in Greece in the 13th century.[8] These influences are particularly evident in Cyprus and some Aegean islands where the Latins settled more permanently and also built their own churches. Although Lycia was, for the most part, not as open to the influences of the Crusaders as the "Holy Land," the Aegean islands, and the Balkans, this region was in close contact with the Levant, and especially with Cyprus.

In Cyprus, especially in the 13th century, a Gothic style unique to the East had developed.[9] The emergence of this style was influenced by the Lusignans, a Frankish Catholic dynasty that came from the Levant and ruled Cyprus between 1192 and 1489. This influence did not originate directly from the European mainland, but was a hybrid style brought to the island by the Crusaders in the Levant.[10] Although Byzantine architecture in Cyprus maintained its own architectural style, it is also possible to see that some Gothic elements found their way into the architecture. These architectural elements were not dominant in the entirety of the buildings. They remained as singular, isolated elements such as pointed arches, archivolts, or colonette capitals. Bouras describes them as "isolated Gothic details" that were used mainly to create variety in ornamentation, and he indicates that they were not used widespread throughout the building.[11] Byzantine architecture remained largely indifferent to the core characteristic of Gothic, a vertical dynamism in the interior and the exterior, and the Gothic discoveries such as the ribbed cross vault and the clustered pier,[12] instead, in practice, integrated some of the Gothic architectural elements into its own design. For instance, there are a number of Byzantine churches in mainland Greece and on Cyprus where the pointed arch was used.[13] It should be noted here that the blunt-pointed arch was also used in Byzantine architecture –although not widespread– before the Crusaders.[14]

In Alakent Church, whose design completely conforms to Byzantine tradition, Gothic influence could be seen at two places. The first is the use of pointed arches. On the four large arches supporting the dome, on the windows of the apse, and on the south wall, blunt-pointed arches were used. Of course, the use of pointed arches on its own is not enough to be defined as Gothic. The pointed arch provides a structural advantage compared to the round arch since it transforms the lateral thrust to vertical and conveys it downwards. This might be the reason why it was preferred in Lycia, which is in an earthquake zone. However, it is possible to observe a Gothic aspect in the window on the south wall. The large window with a pointed arch was made narrower in the final phase of the church, and divided into two narrow and tall windows with pointed arches by the use of a mullion. On top of the two pointed arches in the section between the two, a spolia stone with two embossed rosettes was placed, as if imitating a Gothic trefoil or a rose window. Here it seems an attempt was made to emulate, or at least take as a source of inspiration, a typical Gothic window with twin pointed-arched windows placed inside a large pointed

8 Bouras 2001, p. 249 passim.

9 Pringle 2015, p. 304 passim.

10 Weyl Carr 1995, p. 243.

11 Bouras 2001, pp. 257–258.

12 Bouras 2001, pp. 259, 261.

13 Bouras 2001, pp. 252–253.

14 Bouras 2001, p. 258.

arch and a trefoil on top.[15] This had probably been seen in Cyprus, where they had the most interaction. The bricking up of the window was carried out in the final phase of the building, probably in the early 14th century. The windows must have been blocked as a last measure in combating floods before the church was abandoned. And this period is the time when Gothic architecture was becoming more fashionable in Cyprus.

Alakent Church was probably abandoned at the beginning of the 14th century and gradually completely buried under silt. So it remained very well preserved in the state at the time it was abandoned until the present day, and therefore provides very important information about 12th–13th century Byzantine architecture and painting. The most important data about the Byzantine architecture of the period is the decoration on the west wall of the church. The rubble stone wall, built with a neat workmanship, was plastered and painted with whitewash. On top of the white surface a pseudo-ashlar masonry pattern was drawn in red lines. The pseudo-ashlar masonry pattern was first incised on the entire facade using a pointed tool on the wet plaster, and then the red lines were applied over these incisions. The arch above the door, made of regularly shaped blocks of stone, was also first plastered, then a pseudo-brick arch was drawn on the plaster with a pointed tool. The "bricks" were painted white and red alternately. The same red and white brick arch decoration can be seen on the arch of the arcosolium tomb on the southeast side. The brick friezes on the dogtooth eaves were also plastered and painted with whitewash, and zigzag motifs were added in red lines on top of them. All this decoration is valuable because it has managed to survive from the end of the 13th century when the building was buried under alluvium, to the present day, untouched and without being renewed. It has the quality of a very important document about the exterior facade decorations of that period. The closest matching example of this kind of exterior decoration can be again found in Cyprus. At the Panagias Phorbiotissa Church in Niketari, a similar pseudo-ashlar masonry decoration made with a sharp tip and painted with red lines and zigzag motifs can be seen on small fragments of plaster preserved in their original condition.[16]

On the other hand, the roof tile covering unearthed *in situ*, especially in the north and northeastern parts of the roof, is important. For it displays the materials used in roofing and the way the vaults –and probably the dome that does not exist today– were covered. The arrangement of the bema that has survived in the state at the time the church was abandoned also contributes to our knowledge on this subject.

The church was probably used with a nonreligious function for a while after it was abandoned. This is indicated by the fact that the figure of the Virgin Mary was concealed behind a series of stones that were part of a wall. However, the absence of any finds apart from a few ceramic wares on this level, as well as no other strata on the alluvial deposits, indicates that this period of use was brief and possibly in the early 14th century.

Although there is no data to conclusively date Alakent Church, the finds unearthed in the excavation shows that the final use of the structure was in the beginning of the 14th century. Taking the architectural characteristics of the building into consideration, it can be argued that the

15 Jelena Trkulja argues that in Byzantine architecture the rose window motif exists independent of Gothic architecture. She provides examples from some Morava churches in Serbia and states that the origins of the fully developed rose window can be found in the decorative brick rosettes seen on Byzantine facades (Trkulja 2012, p. 143 et al.). However, considering the window in our case in its entirety, it seems more reasonable to interpret it as Gothic influence here.

16 Chotzakoglou 2005, see p. 522, Figs. 194–195.

date of the first construction was during the 12th century. Several of its close matching architectural counterparts were dated to the 12th century. Moreover, the coin of John II Komnenos dating to the 12th century,[17] found at the original floor level during the excavations at the burial grounds south of the church, provides an opportunity to establish a more precise dating of the building.

We have not found any information leading us to the original name of Alakent Church, but we have reason to believe that the church might have been dedicated to the Virgin Mary: Her prominence in the painting program of the church; her figure depicted in monumental dimension as seated on a throne between two angels on the apse's semi-dome; and the special importance attributed to her in the *Deesis* scene. We know that a number of churches built in Cyprus during the same period were dedicated to the Virgin. The cult of the Virgin has always had an important place in Byzantine culture, and its influence began to escalate from the end of the 5th century. From the 11th and 12th centuries onwards, it reached its peak throughout the empire.[18]

At the beginning of the 14th century, Myra was still primarily a Byzantine settlement with a considerable Christian population. While the great church of Nicholas was still in use, this church near the Roman theater was also being used. Alakent Church is different from the single-naved, barrel-vaulted, small and simple chapels constructed mostly during the 11th and 12th centuries.[19] Examples of these chapels are frequently encountered in the region. Its dimensions, its neat architectural design, its domed structure, its rich wall paintings – all these indicate that it was an important church of its time. In the region during the final years of Byzantine rule, the church of Nicholas was still the most important cult church of Myra, but it was not its only church. The presence of Alakent Church suggests that during the 12th–13th centuries the population in the area was concentrated here, possibly to the south of the ancient theater.

The fact that the church has remained very well preserved under the alluvium is evidence that the ancient city of Myra, buried under silt in the same way, might be equally well preserved. As a matter of fact, the archaeogeophysical studies carried out in the city, which have not yet been published, indicate that there are structures with high walls under the alluvium. The ruins start from the front of the ancient theater in the north and stretch approximately two kilometers to the south up to the Church of St. Nicholas, which now lies in the middle of the modern settlement. This data demonstrates that ancient Myra was a substantial urban settlement. The fact that only two churches, a Roman bath, and a theater from this expansive city are visible today suggests that Myra could be –borrowing the expression of Nevzat Çevik– "an Anatolian Pompeii."[20]

17 For this coin, see the earlier Chapter VIII.

18 Carroll 1992, p. 5.

19 For examples closest to Myra, the small chapels at Beymelek and in its lagoon can be considered. See Feld 1975, p. 419, Figs. 69–70, Table 140 A–E, Table 139 A, B.

20 Çevik 2013, p. 36.

ABBREVIATIONS

AA	*Archäologischer Anzeiger*
AJA	*American Journal of Archaeology*
ANMED	*Anadolu Akdenizi Arkeoloji Haberleri*
AnzWien	*Anzeiger der Philosophisch-Historischen Klasse. Österreichische Akademie der Wissenschaften*
ArkST	*Arkeometri Sonuçları Toplantısı*
AS	*Anatolian Studies*
AST	*Araştırma Sonuçları Toplantısı*
B.C.H	*Bulletin de Correspondance Hellénique*
BSA	*The Annual of the British School at Athens*
CahArch	*Cahiers archéologiques*
CIG	*Corpus Inscriptionum Graecorum, 4 vols., Berlin 1828–1877*
DChAE	*Deltion tes Christianikes Archaiologikes Hetaireias*
DOP	*Dumbarton Oaks Papers*
IstForsch	*Istanbuler Forschungen*
IstMitt	*Istanbuler Mitteilungen*
JNES	*Journal of Near Eastern Studies*
JÖB	*Jahrbuch der Österreichischen Byzantinischen Gesellschaft*
KST	*Kazı Sonuçları Toplantısı*
LCI	*Lexicon der christlichen Ikonographie, ed. E. Kirschbaum and W. Braunfels, 8 vols. (Rome – Freiburg – Basel – Vienna 1968–76)*
LGPN	*Lexicon of Greek Personal Names*
LIMC	*Lexicon iconographicum mythologiae classicae*, ed. H. C. Ackermann ve J. R. Gisler, I, 1 vdd, (Zürich–München 1981 vdd.)
MEFRM	*Mélanges de l'École française de Rome. Moyen Âge, Temps Modernes*
ODB	*The Oxford Dictionary of Byzantium, eds. A. P. Kazhdan et al., New York – Oxford 1991*
OrChrP	*Orientalia christiana periodica*
RA	*Revue Archéologique*
RBK	*Reallexikon zur Byzantinischen Kunst*
RDAC	*Report of the Department of Antiquities, Cyprus*
RE	*Paulys Real-Encyclopädie der classischen Altertumswissenschaft*
REB	*Revue des Études Byzantines*
TAM II	*Tituli Asiae Minoris, Tituli Lyciae: Lingua Lycia conscripti, E. Kalinka*
TIB	*Tabula Imperii Byzantini*

BIBLIOGRAPHY

Primary Sources

Dionysius of Fourna. *'The Painter's Manual' of Dionysius of Fourna*, transl. and commantery, P. Hetherington (London 1981).

Le Quien, M. *Oriens Christianus, In Quator Patriarchatus Digestus,* I (Graz 1958).

Malalas. *The Chronicle of John Malalas,* ed. E. Jeffreys, M. Jeffreys, and R. Scott (Melbourne 1986).

Nicholas of Sion. *The Life of St. Nicholas of Sion*, ed. N. P. Ševčenko, and I. Ševčenko (Brookline, Mass., 1984).

Strabon. *Antik Anadolu Coğrafyası, Geographika: XII–XIII–XIV*, çev. A. Pekmen (İstanbul 2000).

Theophanes. *The Chronicle of Theophanes Confessor, Byzantine and Near Eastern History, AD 284–813*, ed. C. Mango, and R. Scott (New York 1997).

Secondary Bibliography

Acara-Eser, M. 2010. "Hıristiyanlıkta Haç Kültü ve Ankara Anadolu Medeniyetleri Müzesi Koleksiyonunda Bulunan Bir Grup Haç," in *Bizans ve Çevre Kültürler. Prof. Dr. S. Yıldız Ötüken'e Armağan,* ed. S. Doğan, and M. Kadiroğlu, Ankara, pp. 27–43.

Akşit, İ. 1971. *Helenistik ve Roma Döneminde Likya*, İstanbul.

Akşit, İ. 1967. *Likya Tarihi*, İstanbul.

Akyürek, E. 2016. "Andriake: The Port of Myra in Late Antiquity," in *Trade in Byzantium, Papers From The Third International Sevgi Gönül Byzantine Studies Symposium*, ed. P. Magdalino, and N. Necipoğlu, İstanbul, pp. 465–487.

Akyürek, E. 2015a. "A Recently Discovered Thirteenth Century Church at Myra in Lycia," in *Proceedings of the 17th Symposium On Mediterranean Archaeology, SOMA 2013, Moscow, 25–27 April, 2013*, ed. S. Fazlullin, and M. M. Antika, Oxford, pp. 14–23.

Akyürek, E. 2015b. "Myra, The City of St. Nicholas," in *En Orient et en Occident le culte de Saint Nicolas en Europe: Xe–XXIe siècle. Actes du colloque de Lunéville et Saint-Nicolas-de-Port, 5–7 decémbre 2013*, ed. V. Gazeau, C. Guyon, and C. Vincent, Paris, pp. 21–37.

Akyürek, E. 2014 (June). "Andriake: Geç Antik Çağ'da Myra'nın Limanı," *Toplumsal Tarih*, pp. 22–27.

Akyürek, E. 2010. "Myra Şapeli Üzerine İlk Notlar," in *Arkeolojisinden Doğasına Myra / Demre ve Çevresi*, ed. N. Çevik, Antalya, pp. 153–160.

Akyürek, E. 2002. *Khalkedon'lu (Kadıköy) Azize Euphemia ve Sultanahmet'teki Kilisesi*, İstanbul.

Akyürek, E., and Ö. Çömezoğlu. 2011. "Myra Şapeli," in N. Çevik, and S. Bulut, "Myra ve Andriake Kazıları 2010", *ANMED* 9, pp. 59–70.

Alpaslan, S. 2003. "The Evaluation of the Motifs and styles of the Architectural Sculpture of the Byzantine Age in Antalya and Lycia," *Adalya* 6, pp. 252–264.

Alpaslan, S. 1996. "Antalya'nın Demre (Kale) İlçesindeki H. Nikolaos Kilisesi'nde Dini Ayinle İlgili Plastik Eserler" (diss., Hacettepe University, Ankara).

Alpaslan-Doğan, S. 2008. "La sculpture byzantine en Lycie et à Antalya: Sa place dans l'évolution de l'art byzantin," in *La sculpture byzantine VIIe – XIIe siécles. Actes du colloque international organisé par la 2e Éphorie des antiquités byzantines et l'École française d'Athènes (6–8 septembre 2000)*, ed. C. Pennas, and C. Vanderheyde, Athens, pp. 123–138.

Anderson, J. C. 1982."The Seraglio Octateuch and the Kokkinobaphos Master," *DOP* 36, pp. 83–114.

Androudis, P. 2007. "Ο ναός της Κοίμησης της Θεοτόκου στην Επισκοπή Άνω Βόλου και ο εντοιχισμένος γλυπτός του διάκοσμος", *DChAE*, 28, pp. 85-98.

Anrich, G. 1913–1917. *Hagios Nikolaos. Der Heilige Nikolaos in der griechischen Kirche, Texte und Untersuchungen*, 2 cilt, Leipzig – Berlin.

Armağan, M. E. 2010. "Kuşadası, Kadıkalesi'ndeki Bizans Dönemi Taş Eserleri" (diss., Ege University, İzmir).

Arslan, A. 2014. "Konya Çevresi Bizans Dönemi Mimari Plastiği" (disss., Anadolu University, Eskişehir).

Asano, K., ed. 2010. *The Island of St. Nicholas. Excavation and Survey of Gemiler Island Area, Lycia,Turkey,* Osaka.

Asano, K. 1995. "Church III on Gemiler Ada," in *The Survey, Osaka 1995,* ed. S. Tsuji, Osaka, pp. 72–78.

Aslan, E. 2010. "Myra Çevresinde Antik Denizcilik ve Sualtı Kültür Kalıntıları," in *Arkeolojisinden Doğasına Myra / Demre ve Çevresi,* ed. N. Çevik, Antalya, pp. 257–272.

Avramea, A. 2002. "Land and Sea Communications, Fourth – Fifteenth Centuries," in *The Economic History of Byzantium From the Seventh Through the Fifteenth Century*, ed. A. E. Laiou, Washington, D.C., pp. 58–90.

Balmelle, C., M. Blanchard-Lemée, J. Christophe, J.-P. Darmon, A. M. Guimier-Sorbets, H. Lavagne, R. Prudhomme, and H. Stern. 1985. *Le Décor géometrique de la mosaïque romaine I. Répertoire graphique et descriptif des compositions linéaires et isotropes*, Paris.

Balzat, J. S., R. W. V. Catling, É. Chiricat, and F. Marchand, eds. 2013. *Coastal Asia Minor: Caria to Cilicia* (*LGPN* VB), Oxford.

Bass, G. F. 1986. "A Bronze Age Shipwreck at Uluburun (Kaş):1984 Campaign," *AJA* 90.3, pp. 269–296.

Bass, G. F. 1961. "The Cape Gelidonya Wreck: Preliminary Report," *AJA* 65.3, pp. 267–276.

Beaufort, F. 1818. *Karamania or a Brief Description of the South Coast of Asia Minor and of the Remains of Antiquity. With Plans, Views etc. Collected During a Survey of the Coast, Under the Orders of the Lords Commissioners of the Admiralty in the years of 1811–1812,* London.

Beckwith, J. 1968. *The Art of Constantinople, An Introduction to Byzantine Art, 330–1453*, London.

Bennett, J. 2015. "Christianity in Lycia: From Its Beginnings to the 'Triumph of Orthodoxy," *Adalya* 18, pp. 260–287.

Bilici, S. 2010. "Alanya Kalesi Kazılarında Bulunan Bizans Sırlı Seramikleri," in *Bizans ve Çevre Kültürler: Prof. Dr. Yıldız Ötüken'e Armağan*, ed. S. Doğan, and M. Kadiroğlu, İstanbul, pp. 100–123.

Bloch, P. 1968. "Löwe," *LCI* 2, pp. 112–117.

Bogyay, T. 1968. "Deesis," *LCI* 1, pp. 494–499.

Bogyay, T. 1966. "Deesis," *RBK* 1, pp. 1178–1186.

Bonovas, N., and A. Tzitzibassi. 2011. Βυζάντιο & Άραβες / *Byzantium & the Arabs* (Exhibition catalogue), Thessaloniki.

Borchhardt, J., ed. 1975. *Myra, Eine Lykische Metropole,* Berlin.

Bouras, Ch. 2001. "The Impact of Frankish Architecture on Thirteenth – Century Byzantine Architecture," in *The Crusades from the Perspective of Byzantium and the Muslim World,* ed. A. E. Laiou, and R. P. Mottahedeh, Washington, D.C., pp. 247–262.

Bouras, Ch. 1981. "Το τέμπλο της Παναγίας Κρίνας και η χρονολόγησή της," *DchAE* 10, pp. 165–179.

Bouras, L. 1991. "Templon," *ODB* 3, pp. 2023–2024.

Bouras, L., and A. Cutler. 1991. "Cross, Processional," *ODB* 1, p. 553.

Boyd, S. 1974. "The Church of Panagia Amasgou, Monagri, Cyprus and Its Wall Paintings," *DOP* 28, pp. 277–334.

Böhlendorf-Arslan, B. 2004. *Glasierte Byzantinische Keramik aus der Turkei*, İstanbul.

Bryer, A., and J. Herrin, eds. 1977. *Iconoclasm,* Birmingham.

Budde, L. W. 1958. *Göreme, Höhlen Kirchen in Kappadokien,* Düsseldorf.

Bulgurlu, V. 2010. "Erken Gezginlerin Gözüyle Myra / Demre," in *Arkeolojisinden Doğasına Myra / Demre ve Çevresi,* ed. N. Çevik, Antalya, pp. 273–291.

Bulut, L. 1994. "Kabartma Desenli Samsat Ortaçağ Seramikleri," *Sanat Tarihi Dergisi* 7, pp. 1–18.

Büyükkolancı, M., and G. K. Öztaşkın 2010. "Selçuk-Efes 2010 Müzesi'nde Sergilenen St. Jean Kilisesi'ne Ait Korkuluk Levhaları ve Templon Arşitravları," *Pamukkale Üniversitesi Sosyal Bilimler Enstitüsü Dergisi* 7, pp. 39–49.

Campbell, S. 1988. *The Mosaics of Antioch,* (Pontificial Institute of Mediaeval Studies, Subsidia Mediaevalia 15), Toronto.

Caneva, I., and G. Köroğlu. 2009. "Excavations at Mersin Yumuktepe Höyüğü in 2007," *KST* 30.3, pp. 151–162.

Carroll, M. P. 1992. *The Cult of The Virgin Mary,* Princeton.

Chatzidakis, M., and I. Bitha. 1997. *Ευρετήριο Βυζαντινών Τοιχογραφιών Ελλάδος, Κύθηρα,* Athens.

Chatzidakis, M., N. Drandakis, N. Zias, M. Acheimastou-Potamianou, and A. Vasilaki-Karakatsani. 1989. *Νάξος. Βυζαντινή Τέχνη στην Ελλάδα. Ψηφιδωτά – Τοιχογραφίες,* Athens.

Childs, W. A. P. 1981. "Lycian Relations with Persians and Greeks in the Fifth and Fourth Centuries Re-Examined," *AS* 31, 55–80.

Chotzakoglou, Ch. 2005. "Byzantine Architecture and Art in Cyprus," in *History of Cyprus* III, ed. Th. Papadopoullos, Nicosia, pp. 465–787.

Clarke, G. 2008. "Third Century Christianity," in *The Cambridge Ancient History* XII: *The Crisis of Empire, A.D. 193–337,* ed. A. Bowman, A. Cameron, and P. Garnsey, Cambridge, pp. 589–671.

Corsten, T. ed. 2010. *Coastal Asia Minor: Pontos to Ionia* (*LGPN* VA), Oxford.

Cotsonis, J. A. 1994. *Byzantine Figural Processional Crosses,* Washington, D.C.

Cutler, A. 1991. "Color," *ODB* 1, p. 482.

Çaylak Türker, A. 2006. "Myra Seramik Hamur Gruplarının Kap Tipleri ile Değerlendirilmesi," *Adalya* 9, pp. 117–148.

Çelgin, A. V., and M. Kürkçü. 2016. "Termessos'ta Yeni Keşfedilen 'Pan Temenosu'", in *Vir Doctus Anatolicus: Studies in Memory of Sencer Şahin / Sencer Şahin Anısına Yazılar,* ed. B. Takmer, Ebru N. Akdoğu-Arca and N. Gökalp-Özdil, İstanbul, pp. 238–258.

Çevik, N. 2015. *Lycia Kitabı,* Antalya.

Çevik, N. 2013. "Myrrh – Breathing Myra – Andriake. Metropolis of Lycia, Sunken City of Saint Nicholas," *Actual Archaeology Magazine* 7, pp. 35–51.

Çevik, N. 2010a. "Myra. The Sunken Metropolis of St. Nicolas," *Current World Archaeology* 21, pp. 18–25.

Çevik, N. 2010b. "Myra ve Limanı Andriake: Kazıları Başlarken Ön-Düşünceler," *Arkeoloji ve Sanat Dergisi* 134, pp. 53–82.

Çevik, N., and S. Bulut. 2010. "İkinci Kazı Sezonunda Myra ve Limanı Andriake," in *Arkeolojisinden Doğasına Myra /Demre ve Çevresi,* ed. N. Çevik, Antalya, pp. 25–115.

Çevik, N., Ö. Çömezoğlu, H. S. Öztürk, and İ. Türkoğlu. 2010. "A Unique Discovery in Lycia: The Ancient Synagogue at Andriake, Port of Myra," *Adalya* 13, pp. 36–65.

Çorağan, N. 1999. "The Wall Paintings of St.Nicholas Church in Demre (Myra), Recent Discoveries," *Annali di Ca'Foscari* 38.3, pp. 87–94.

Çorağan Karakaya, N. 2003. "Antalya'nın Demre (Myra) İlçesi'ndeki H. Nikolaos Kilisesi'nde yer alan Deesis Sahnesi," *Adalya* 6, pp. 281–291.

Çoruhlu, Y. 2010. "Orta Asya'dan Anadolu'ya Kürevî – Konik Kaplar ve Yeni Dönem Kars / Ani Kazılarından Elde Edilen Örnekler," *Anadolu ve Çevresinde Ortaçağ* 4, pp. 123–158.

Ćurčić, S. 2010. *Architecture in the Balkans: From Diocletian to Süleyman the Magnificent,* New Haven.

Ćurčić, S. 2000. *Middle Byzantine Architecture on Cyprus: Provincial or Regional?,* Nicosia.

Ćurčić, S. 1999. "Byzantine Architecture on Cyprus: An Introduction to the Problem of the Genesis of a Regional Style," in *Medieval Cyprus, Studies in Art, Architecture and History in Memory of Doula Mouriki*, ed. N. P. Ševčenko, and C. Moss, Princeton, pp. 71–80.

Demus, O. 1949. *The Mosaics of Norman Sicily*, London.

Demus, O. 1948. *Byzantine Mosaic Decoration*, London.

Dennert, M. 1997. *Mittelbyzantinische Kapitelle. Studien zu Typologie und Chronologie* (*Asia Minor Studien* 25), Bonn.

Dennert, M. 1995. "Mittelbyzantinische Ambone in Kleinasien," *IstMitt* 45, pp. 137–149.

Diez, E., and O. Demus. 1931. *Byzantine Mosaics in Greece, Hosios Lukas and Daphni*, Cambridge, Mass.

Doğan, S. 2009. "Bizans Sanatında Yaşam Haçı Motifi ve Alanya Müzesi'ndeki Bir Bizans Sütun Başlığı," in *Ebru Parman'a Armağan. Sanat Tarihi ve Arkeoloji Yazıları*, ed. O. Alp, Ankara, pp. 139–154.

Doğan, S., N. Çorağan, V. Bulgurlu, Ç. Alas, E. Fındık, and E. Apaydın. 2014. *Demre–Myra Aziz Nikolaos Kilisesi*, İstanbul.

Doğer, L. 2012. *Daskyleion II: Hisartepe / Daskyleion Kazısı Bizans Seramikleri*, İstanbul.

Dornseiff, F., and B. Hansen. 1957. *Rücklaufiges Wrterbuch der griechischen Eigennamen: Im Auftrag der Sächsischen Akademie der Wissenschaften unter Leitung ihres ordentlichen Mitgliedes*, Berlin.

Drandakis, N. D. 1976. "Άγνωστα γλυπτά της Μάνης αποδιδόμενα στο μαρμαρά Νικήτα ή στο εργαστήρι του," *DChAE* 8, pp. 19–28.

Duggan, T. M. P. 2005. "Supplementary Data to be Added Chronology of Plague and Earthquakes in Antalya Province and in Adjacent and Related Areas," *Adalya* 8, pp. 357–398.

Duggan, T. M. P. 2004. "A Short Account of Recorded Calamities (Earthquakes and Plagues) in Antalya Province and Adjacent and Related Areas Over the Past 2,300 Years, an Incomplete List, Comments and Observations," *Adalya* 7, pp. 123–169.

Duggan, T. M. P., and Ç. A. Aygün. 2010. "Myra'nın Ortaçağ ve Sonrasındaki Limanı 'Taşdibi–Stamira'," in *Arkeolojisinden Doğasına Myra / Demre ve Çevresi*, ed. N. Çevik, Antalya, pp. 161–168.

Dvornik, F. 1956. *The Slavs, Their Early History and Civilization*, Boston.

Emminghaus, J. H. 1972. "Verkündigung an Maria," *LCI* 4, pp. 422–437.

Erdem, İ. 2006. "Ortaçağ Sonlarında Likya Levant Ticareti ve Türkmenler (12.–15. yy)," in *III. Uluslararası Likya Sempozyumu / III. International Lycia Symposium, 7–10 Kasım / November 2005 Antalya*, C. 1, ed. K. Dörtlük, B. Varkıvanç, T. Kahya, J. deCourtils, M. D. Alpaslan, and R. Boyraz, İstanbul, pp. 243–251.

Erel, A. C. 2010. "Kıbrıs'ta On İkinci ve On Üçüncü Yüzyıllarda Bizans Mimarisi ve Görülen Değişimler," in *I. Uluslararası Sevgi Gönül Bizans Araştırmaları Sempozyumu, Bildiriler / First International Sevgi Gönül Byzantine Studies Symposium, Proceedings*, ed. A. Ödekan, E. Akyürek, and N. Necipoğlu, İstanbul, pp. 380–389.

Ermiş, M. 2004. "İzmir ve Manisa Çevresindeki Orta Bizans Dönemi Templon Arşitravları," in *Sanat Tarihinde Gençler, Bilim Eşiği 1*, İstanbul, pp. 76–98.

Ettinghousen, R. 1965. "The Uses of Sphero-Conical Vessels in the Muslim East," *JNES* 24, pp. 218–229.

Eyice, S. 1980. *Son Devir Bizans Mimarisi, İstanbul'da Palaiologos'lar Devri Anıtları*, İstanbul.

Feld, O. 1975a, "Die Innenausstattung der Nikolaoskirche in Myra", in *Myra, Eine Lykische Metropole*, ed. J. Borchhardt, Berlin pp. 360–397.

Feld, O. 1975b. "Die Kirchen von Myra und Umgebung," in *Myra, Eine Lykische Metropole*, ed. J. Borchhardt, Berlin pp. 398–424.

Fellows, C. 1852. *Travels And Researches in Asia Minor, The Province of Lycia*, London.

Fıratlı, N. 1990. *La sculpture Byzantine figurée au Musée Archéologique d'Istanbul*, Paris.

Foss, C. 2002. "Pilgrimage in Medieval Asia Minor," *DOP* 56, pp. 129–151.

Foss, C. 1994. "The Lycian Coast in the Byzantine Age," *DOP* 48, pp. 1–52.

Foss, C. 1993. "Lycia in History," in *The Fort at Dereağzı and Other Material Remains in its Vicinity: From Antiquity to Middle Ages*, ed. J. Morgenstern, Tübingen, pp. 5–25.

Foss, C. 1991a. "Myra," *ODB* 2, p. 1428.

Foss, C. 1991b. "Kibyrrhaiotai," *ODB* 2, p. 1127.

Foss, C. 1991c. "Lycia," *ODB* 2, pp. 1257–1258.

Fowden, G. 1990. "Religious Developments in Late Roman Lycia: Topographical Preliminaries," *MELETHMATA* 10, pp. 343–370.

François, V. 1999. *Céramiques médiévales à Alexandrie: Contribution à l'histoire économique de la ville* (*Études alexandrines* 2), Cairo.

Fraser, P. M., and E. Matthews, ed. 2005. *Macedonia, Thrace, Northern Regions of the Black Sea,* (*LGPN* IV), Oxford.

Fraser, P. M., and E. Matthews, ed. 1997. *Peloponnese, Western Greece, Sicily, and Magna Graecia* (*LGPN* III A), Oxford.

Fraser, P. M., and E. Matthews, ed. 1987. *The Aegean Islands, Cyprus, Cyrenaica* (*LGPN* I), Oxford.

French, D. H. 1993. "The Road, Paths and Water Channel," in *The Fort at Dereağzı and Other Material Remains in its Vicinity: From Antiquity to Middle Ages*, ed. J. Morganstern, Tübingen.

Frend, W. H. C., and D. E. Johnston. 1962. "The Byzantine Basilica Church at Knossos," *BSA* 57, pp. 186–238.

Gabrieli, R. S. 2007. "A Region Apart: Coarse Ware of Medieval and Ottoman Cyprus," in *Çanak: Late Antique and Medieval Pottery and Tiles in Mediterranean Archaelolgical Context / Akdeniz Çevresindeki Arkeolojik Kazılarda Ele Geçen Geç Antik ve Ortaçağ Seramiği ve Mimari Seramiği* (*Byzas* 7), ed. B. Böhlendorf Arslan, A. O. Uysal, and J. Witte-Orr, İstanbul, pp. 399–410.

Gabrieli, R. S., B. McCall, and J. R. Green. 2001. "Medieval Kitchen Ware from the Theatre Site at Nae Pafos," *RDAC*, pp. 335–353.

Galavaris, G. P. 1969. *The Illustrations of the Liturgical Homilies of Gregory Nazianzenus*, Princeton.

Gallas, K., K. Vessel, and M. Borboudakis. 1983. *Byzantinisches Kreta,* Munich.

Gerstel, S. E. J. 1993. "Monumental Painting and Eucharistic Sacrifice in the Byzantine Sanctuary: The Example of Macedonia" (diss., New York University, New York).

Gignac, F. 1976. *A Grammar of the Greek Papyri of the Roman and Byzantine Periods,* C. I: *Phonology*, Milano.

Gombrich, E. H. 1994. *The Sense of Order: A Study in the Psychology of Decorative Art*, London.

Grabar, A. 1976. *Sculptures Byzantines du Moyen Age (XIe - XIVe siècle)*, Paris.

Grabar, A. 1953. *Byzantine Painting*, Geneva.

Grabar, A. 1939. *Miniatures Byzantines de la Bibliothèque Nationale*, Paris.

Güçlü, M. 2010. "Selçuklulardan Cumhuriyet'e Demre Bölgesi," in *Arkeolojisinden Doğasına Myra / Demre ve Çevresi*, ed. N. Çevik, Antalya, pp. 305–318.

Hadermann-Misguich, L. 1975. *Kurbinovo I–II, Les fresques de Saint Georges et la Peinture Byzantine du XIIe siècle*, Brussels.

Haldon, J. 2001. *Palgrave Atlas of Byzantine History*, Burlington.

Hamann-MacLean, R., and H. Hallensleben. 1963. *Die Monumentalmalerei in Serbien und Makedonien vom 11. bis zum frühen 14. Jahrhundert*, Giessen.

Harrison, R. M. 1972. "A Note on Architectural Sculpture in Central Lycia," *AS* 22, pp. 187–197.

Harrison, R. M. 1963. "Churches and Chapels in Central Lycia," *AS* 13, pp. 117–51.

Hayes, J. 1992. *Excavations at Saraçhane in Istanbul, vol. II: The Pottery*, Princeton.

Hein, E., A. Jakovljevic, and B. Kleidt. 1998. *Cyprus. Byzantine Churches and Monasteries: Mosaics and Frescoes*, Ratingen.

Hellenkemper, H., and F. Hild. 2004. *Lykien und Pamphylien* (*TIB* 8), Vienna.

Hermary, A. 1986. "Dioskouroi", *LIMC* 3, pp. 567–593.

Herrin, J. 1989. *The Formation of Christendom*, Princeton.

Hild, F. 2004. "Lykien in den Notitiae Episcopatuum," *JÖB* 54, pp. 1–18.

Hutter, I., and P. Canart. 1991. *Das Marian Homiliar des Mönchs Jakobos von Kokkinobaphos Codex, Vatikanus graecus 1162. Codices e Vaticanis Selecti 79*, Zurich.

Israeli, Y. 2000. "Christian Images and Symbols," in *Cradle of Christianity*, ed. Y. Israeli, and D. Mevorah, Jerusalem.

Ivison, E. 2010. "Kirche und Religöses Leben im Byzantinischen Amorium," in *Byzanz – das Römerreich im Mittelalter*, C. 2.1, ed. F. Daim, and J. Drauschke, Mainz, pp. 309–343.

Ivison, E. 2008. "Middle Byzantine Sculptors at Work: Evidence from a Church at Amorium," in *La sculpture byzantine VIIe-XIIe siécles. Actes du colloque international organisé par la 2e Éphorie des antiquités byzantines et l'École française d'Athènes (6–8 septembre 2000)*, ed. C. Pennas, and C. Vanderheyde, Athens, pp. 487–513.

İnanan, F. 2013. "Zeuksippus Tipi Seramikler ve Kuşadası, Kadıkalesi/Anaia Örnekleri," in *Bizanslı Ustalar – Latin Patronlar: Kuşadası Yakınında Kadıkalesi Kazısı Işığında Anaia Ticari Üretiminden Yansımalar / Byzantine Craftsmen – Latin Patrons: Reflections From the Anaian Commercial Production in the Light of the Excavations at Kadıkalesi nearby Kuşadası*, ed. Z. Mercangöz, İstanbul, pp. 59–76.

İnanan, F. 2010. "Kuşadası Kadıkalesi / Anaia Kazısı Zeuksippus Tipi Seramikleri," (diss., Ege University, İzmir).

İplikçioğlu, B., and C. Schuler. 2011. "Ein Tempel für die Dioskuren und Helena. Eine neue Bauinschrift aus Bozhüyük bei Elmalı im lykischen Hochland", *AnzWien* 146, pp. 39–59.

İşler, B. 2010. "Myra ve Çevresinde Bizans Dönemi," in *Arkeolojisinden Doğasına Myra / Demre ve Çevresi*, ed. N. Çevik, Antalya, pp. 233–255.

İşler, B. 2009. "Likya Bölgesinde Karabel Asarcık'taki Erken Bizans Dönemi Yerleşimi" (diss., tezi, Hacettepe University, Ankara).

Jacobek, R. 1999. "Bizans Piskoposluk Merkezi Limyra," in *Limyra. Zemuri Taşları*, ed. J. Borchardt, İstanbul, pp. 111– 115.

Jacoby, D. 2001. *Byzantium, Latin Romania and the Mediterranean*, Aldershot – Burlington.

Jerphanion, G. 1942. *Une nouvelle province de l'art byzantin, Les églises rupestres de Cappodoce*, Vol. 5, Paris.

Jerphanion, G. 1925. *Une nouvelle province de l'art byzantin, Les églises rupestres de Cappadoce,* Paris.

Jolivet-Lévy, C. 2002. *Etudes Cappadociennes,* London.

Kafalı Yılmaz, F. 2008. "Antalya'nın Günlük Yağış Özellikleri ve Şiddetli Yağışların Doğal Afetler Üzerine Etkisi," *Afyon Kocatepe Üniversitesi Sosyal Bilimler Dergisi* 10.1, pp. 19–65.

Kahraman, E., M. Softa, and G. Akan. 2010. "Demre (Antalya) ve Çevresinin Jeolojik Yapısı," in *Arkeolojisinden Doğasına Myra / Demre ve Çevresi*, ed. N. Çevik, Antalya, pp. 329–337.

Kalaycı, H. 2002. *Τά μυροβόλα Μύρα. Ἡ ἱστορία τῶν Μύρων ἀπό τόν 19ο αἰώνα ὥς τό 1922. Οἱ σχέσεις Ἑλληνικῆς Κοινότητας Μύρων καί Σταυροπηγιακῆς Μονῆς Ἁγίου Νικολάου* [Ἀνάλεκτα τοῦ Ἁγίου Νικολάου 1], Atina.

Karakaya, N. 2009. "Demre Aziz Nikolaos Kilisesi Duvar Resimlerinde Tek Figürler," *Anadolu ve Çevresinde Ortaçağ* 3, pp. 91–106.

Karakaya, N. 2005a. "Restorasyon Sonrası Demre-Aziz Nikolaos Kilisesi Duvar Resimleri," in *III. Uluslararası Likya Sempozyumu, Sempozyum Bildirileri Sempozyumu / III. International Lycia Symposium, 7–10 Kasım / November 2005 Antalya*, C. 1, ed. K. Dörtlük, B. Varkıvanç, T. Kahya, J. deCourtils, M. D. Alpaslan, and R. Boyraz, Antalya, pp. 331–344.

Karakaya, N. 2005b. "The Burial Chamber Wall Paintings of Saint Nicholas Church at Demre (Myra) Following their Restoration," *Adalya* 8, pp. 287–309.

Karakaya, N. 2003. "2002 Yılı, Kayseri Yeşilhisar İlçesi Erdemli Köyü'ndeki Kaya Kiliseleri Duvar Resimleri," *AST* 21.2, pp. 17–28.

Karpozilos, A., and A. Cutler. 1991. "Cross: The Cross in Everyday Life," *ODB* 1, pp. 550–551.

Karpozilos, A., A. P. Kazhdan ve A. Cutler. 1991. "Lions," *ODB* 2, pp. 1231–1232.

Katsioti, A., and H. K. Papavassiliou. 2002. "Μεσοβυζαντινή γλυπτική στη Λέρο και τη Νίσυρο," *DChAE* 23, pp. 121–148.

Kazhdan, A. P. 1991. "Theme," *ODB* 3, pp. 2034–2035.

Khalilieh, H. S. 2006. *Admiralty and Maritime Laws in the Mediterranean Sea (ca. 800–1050)*, Leiden – Boston.

Kingsley, S. 2009. "Mapping Trade by Shipwrecks," in *Byzantine Trade, 4th–12th Centuries*, ed. M. M. Mango, Farnham – Burlington, pp. 31–36.

Kitzinger, E. 2003. "Interlace and Icons: Form and Function in Early Insular Art," *Studies in Late Antique, Byzantine and Medieaval Western Art* 2, pp. 801–826.

Kitzinger, E. 1990. *The Mosaics of St.Marys of the Admiral in Palermo*, Washington, D.C.

Köroğlu, G. 2005. "2003 Yılı Yumuktepe Höyüğü Ortaçağ Kazıları," in *Ortaçağ ve Türk Dönemi Kazı ve Araştırmaları Sempozyumu* 8, pp. 273–288.

Krickl, E. 2005. *1892 Likya Günlüğü*, ed. N. Başgelen, İstanbul.

Küçükaşçı, M. S. 2006. "VII–XII. Yüzyıllarda Likya'ya Arap İlgisi," in *III. Uluslararası Likya Sempozyumu Sempozyumu / III. International Lycia Symposium, 7–10 Kasım / November 2005 Antalya*, ed. K. Dörtlük, B. Varkıvanç, T. Kahya, J. deCourtils, M. D. Alpaslan, and R. Boyraz, İstanbul, Vol. 1, pp. 376–383.

Lafontaine-Dosogne, J. 1992. *Iconographie de l'enfance de la Vierge dans l'empire Byzantine et en Occident*, Vol. 2, Brussels.

Laminger-Pascher, G. 1973. *Index Grammaticus zu den Griechischen Inschriften Kilikiens und Isauriens I (mit 3 Textabbildungen)*, Wien.

Lane, A. 1937. "Medieval Glass Finds at Al Mina in North Syria," *Archeologia* 87, pp. 19–78.

Lazarev, V. 1967. *Storia Della Pittura Bizantina*, Turin.

Lightfoot, C., N. Tsivikis, and J. Foley. 2011. "Amorium Kazıları, 2009," *KST* 32.1, pp. 47–68.

Loerke, W. 1991. "Roof," *ODB* 3, pp. 1812–1813.

Lovecchio, M. M. 1981. "La scultura bizantina dell'XI secolo nel museo di San Nicola di Bari," *MEFRM* 93/1, pp. 7–87.

Malmquist, T. 1979. *Byzantine 12th Century Frescoes in Kastoria, Agioi Anargyroi and Agios Nikolaos tou Kasnitzi,* Uppsala.

Mango, C. 1990. "The Monastery of St.Chrysostomos at Koutsovendis (Cyprus) and It's Wall Paintings, Part I; Description," *DOP* 44, pp. 63–94.

Mango, C. 1968. "The Monastery of St. Abercius at Kurşunlu (Elegmi) in Bithynia," *DOP* 22, pp. 169–176.

Mango, C., and E. J. W. Hawkins. 1966. "The Hermitage of St. Neophytos and It's Wall Paintings," *DOP* 20, pp. 121–206.

Mathews, T. F. 1997. "Religious Organisation and the Church Architecture," in *The Glory of Byzantium* (exhibition catalogue, Metropolitan Museum of Art, 1997), ed. H. C. Evans, and E. Wixom, New York, pp. 21–81.

Mathews, T. F. 1976. *The Byzantine Churches of Istanbul. A Photographic Survey,* London.

McGuckin, J. A. 2008. *The Orthodox Church an Introduction to its History, Doctrine and Spiritual Culture,* Massachusetts.

Megaw, A. H. S. 1972. "Background Architecture in the Lagoudera Frescoes," *JÖB* 21, pp. 196–202.

Megaw, A. H. S. 1968. "Zeuxippus Ware," *BSA* 63, pp. 67–88.

Megaw, A. H. S., and E. J. W. Hawkins. 1977. *The Church of Panagia Kanakaria at Lythrankomi in Cyprus, It's Mosaics and Frescoes,* Washington, D. C.

Megaw, A. H. S., and E. J. W. Hawkins. 1962. "The Church of Holy Apostles at Perachorio, Cyprus and It's Frescoes," *DOP* 16, pp. 279–348.

Mendel, G. 1914. *Catalogue des Sculptures Grecques, Romaines et Byzantines,* Tome 2, Constantinople.

Mercangöz, Z. 2013. "Kadıkalesi/Anaia Ticari Üretiminin Latin Patronları," in *Bizanslı Ustalar – Latin Patronlar: Kuşadası Yakınında Kadıkalesi Kazısı Işığında Anaia Ticari Üretiminden Yansımalar / Byzantine Craftsmen – Latin Patrons: Reflections From the Anaian Commercial Production in the Light of the Excavations at Kadıkalesi nearby Kuşadası,* ed. Z. Mercangöz, İstanbul, pp. 161–174.

Mercangöz, Z. 1993. "Orta Çağ Hıristiyan Tasvirlerinde Meryem'in Mavi Giysisi Üzerine," in *Sanat Tarihinde İkonografik Araştırmalar, Güner İnal'a Armağan,* Ankara, pp. 325–338.

Metzger, H. 1966. "Fouilles du Létoon de Xanthos (1962–1965)," *RA* 1, pp. 101–112.

Meyendorf, J. 1983. *Byzantine Theology Historical Trends and Doctrinal Themes,* New York.

Militsi, E. 2009. "Μεσοβυζαντινά γλυπτά από την ανασκαφή στο καθολικό της Παναγίας των Καστριανών στο Παλαιό Πυλί της Κω," *DChAE* 30, pp. 119–128.

Miljkovic-Pepek, P. 1966. *Nerezi,* Belgrade.

Morgan, C. H. 1942. *The Byzantine Pottery* (*Corinth* 11), Cambridge, Mass.

Morganstern, J. 1993. *The Fort at Dereağzı, and other material remains in its vicinity: From antiquity to the Middle Ages,* Tübingen.

Mouriki, D. 1985. *The Mosaics of Nea Moni on Chios,* Athens.

Mouriki, D. 1984. "The Wall Paintings of the Church of Panagia at Moutoullas," in *Byzanz und der Westen, Studien zur Kunst des europäischen Mittelalters,* ed. I. Hutter, Vienna, pp. 171–213.

Mouriki, D. 1980. "Stylistic Trends in Monumental Painting of Greece During the Eleventh and Twelfth Centuries," *DOP* 34, pp. 77–124.

Muratoff, P. 1935. *La Peinture Byzantine,* Paris.

Naumann, R., and H. Belting. 1966. *Die Euphemia – Kirche am Hippodrom zu İstanbul und ihre Fresken* (*IstForsch* 25), Berlin.

Nicolaïdès, A. 1996. "L'église de la Panagia Arakiotissa à Lagoudéra, Chypre: Étude iconographique des fresques de 1192," *DOP* 50, pp. 1–137.

Niewöhner, P. 2013. "Neue spät - und nachantike Monumente von Milet und der mittelbyzantinische Zerfall des anatolischen Städtewesens," *AA* 2013/2, pp. 165–233.

Niewöhner, P. 2008. "Mittelbyzantinische Templonanlagen aus Anatolien. Die Sammlung des archäologishen Museums Kütahya und ihr Kontext," *IstMitt* 58, pp. 285–345.

Orlandos, A. C. 1962. "Fresques byzantines du Monastère de Patmos," *CahArch* 12, pp. 285–302.

Osborne, J. 1997. "The Cross - Under - Arch Motif in Ninth Century Venetian Sculpture: An Imperial Reading," *Thesaurismata* 27, pp. 7–18.

Ostrogorsky, G. 1991. *Bizans Devleti Tarihi*, çev. F. Işıltan, Ankara.

Ousterhout, R. 2002. *The Art of the Kariye Camii*, İstanbul.

Ousterhout, R. G. 1999. *Master Builders of Byzantium*, Princeton.

Ousterhout, R. G. 1987. *The Architecture of the Kariye Camii in Istanbul*, Washington, D. C.

Ousterhout, R., Z. Ahunbay, and M. Ahunbay. 2009. "Study and Restoration of the Zeyrek Camii in Istanbul: Second Report 2001–2005," *DOP* 63, pp. 235–256.

Önal, M. 2008. "Euphrates Evinin Mozaikleri," in *IV. Uluslararası Türkiye Mozaik Korpusu Sempozyum Bildirileri. Geçmişten Günümüze Mozaik Köprüsü,* ed. M. Şahin, Bursa, pp. 79–92.

Öner, E. 2000. "Demre Çayı Deltası'nın Jeomorfolojik Gelişimi ve Myra Antik Kenti, Limanı ve St. Nikolaus Kilisesi," *ArkST* 16, pp. 1–18.

Ötüken, S. Y. 2009. "2007 Yılı Aziz Nikolaos Kilisesi Kazısı ve Duvar Resimlerini Koruma-Onarım-Belgeleme Çalışmaları," *KST* 30.4, pp. 159–176.

Ötüken, S. Y. 2008. "2006 Yılı Aziz Nikolaos Kilisesi Kazısı ve Duvar Resimlerini Koruma-Onarım Çalışmaları," *KST* 29.2, pp. 137–156.

Ötüken, S. Y. 2006a. "Myra-Demre Aziz Nikolaos Kilisesi Mimari Değerlendirmeler," in *III. Uluslararası Likya Sempozyumu / III. International Lycia Symposium, 7–10 Kasım / November 2005 Antalya,* ed. K. Dörtlük, B. Varkıvanç, T. Kahya, J. deCourtils, M. D. Alpaslan, and R. Boyraz, İstanbul, Vol. 2, pp. 523–531.

Ötüken, S. Y. 2006b. "2004 Yılı Aziz Nikolaos Kilisesi Kazısı ve Duvar Resimlerini Belgeleme, Koruma-Onarım Çalışmaları," *KST* 27.1, pp. 298–299.

Ötüken, S. Y. 2005. "2002 Yılı Demre-Myra Aziz Nikolaos Kilisesi Kazısı ve Duvar Resimlerini Koruma-Onarım ve Belgeleme Çalışmaları," *Adalya* 8, pp. 263–285.

Ötüken, S. Y. 2004. "2003 Yılı Demre-Myra Aziz Nikolaos Kilisesi Kazısı ve Duvar Resimlerini Koruma-Onarım-Belgeleme Çalışmaları," *KST* 26.1, pp. 111–126.

Ötüken, S. Y. 2003. "2001 Yılı Demre-Myra Aziz Nikolaos Kilisesi Kazısı ve Duvar Resimlerini Belgeleme, Koruma-Onarım Çalışmaları," *KST* 24.2, pp. 31–46.

Ötüken, S. Y. 2002. "2000 Yılı Demre Aziz Nikolaos Kilisesi Kazısı ve Duvar Resimlerini Belgeleme, Koruma-Onarım Çalışmaları," *KST* 23.2, pp. 401–414.

Ötüken, S. Y. 1999. "1997 Yılı Demre-Myra Aziz Nikolaos Kilisesi Kazısı," *KST* 20.2, pp. 481–503.

Ötüken, S. Y. 1998a. "1996 Yılı Demre-Aziz Nikolaos Kilisesi Kazısı," *KST* 19.2, pp. 541–565.

Ötüken, S. Y. 1998b. "Demre Aziz Nikolaos Kilisesi Kazısının Ortaçağ Araştırmalarına Katkıları," in *Sanat Tarihi Dergisi IX, I. Ortaçağ ve Türk Dönemi Kazıları Sempozyumu, 9–11 Nisan 1997,* İzmir, pp. 85–102.

Ötüken, S. Y., V. Bulgurlu, S. Yandım, and N. Peker. 2007. "Resim Sanatında İnancın İmgeleri," in *Kalanlar, 12. ve 13. Yüzyıllarda Türkiye'de Bizans,* ed. A. Ödekan, İstanbul, pp. 33–35.

Ötüken, S. Y., and R. Ousterhout. 1989. "Notes on the Monuments of Turkish Thrace," *AS* 39, pp. 121–149.

Öztan, A., F. Açıkgöz, and B. S. Arbuckle. 2010. "2008 Yılı Köşk Höyük Kazıları," *KST* 31.2, pp. 271–296.

Öztan, A., and F. Açıkgöz. 2011. "2009 Yılı Köşk Höyük Kazıları," *KST* 32.3, pp. 136–137.

Özügül, A. 2005. "İstanbul'daki Geç Antik ve Bizans Dönemi Kapı Çerçevesi Profilleri" (diss., İstanbul Technical University, İstanbul).

Panayotidi, M. 1986. "La Peinture monumentale en Grèce de la fin de l'iconoclasme jusqu'à l'avènement des Comnènes (843–1081)," *CahArch* 34, pp. 75–108.

Papageorghiou, A. 1965. *Masterpieces of Byzantine Art in Cyprus*, Nicosia.

Papadakis, A. 1991. "Synkellos", *ODB* 3, pp. 1993–1994.

Papanikola-Bakirtzi, D. 2004. *Colours of Medieval Cyprus, Through the Medieval Ceramic Collection of the Leventis Municipal Museum of Nicosia*, Nicosia.

Papanikola-Bakirtzi, D. 1996. *Μεσαιωνική Εφυαλωμένη Κεραμική της Κύπρου, Τα Εργαστήρια Πάφου και Λαπήθου*, Thessaloniki.

Papanikola-Bakirtzi, D. 1989. *Medieval Cypriot Pottery in the Pierides Foundation Museum*, Larnaca.

Papanikola-Bakirtzi, D., F. N. Mavrikiu, and Ch. Bakirtzis. 1999. *Byzantine Glazed Pottery in the Benaki Museum*, Athens.

Papanikola-Bakirtzi, D., and N. Zikos. 2007. *Εφυαλωμένη κεραμική Υστεροβυζαντινών χρόνων από τη Θράκη. Απόπειρα ανάγνωσης ανασκαφικών ευρημάτων*, Thessaloniki.

Pape, W., and G. Benseler. 1911. *Wörterbuch der Griechischen Eigennamen*, Graz.

Parman, E. 2002. *Ortaçağda Bizans Döneminde Frigya (Phrygia) ve Bölge Müzelerindeki Taş Eserleri*, Eskişehir.

Patcht, O. 1952. *Byzantine Illumination*, Oxford.

Pehlivaner, M. ed. 2004. *T. C. Antalya Valiliği, Antalya İli Envanteri, Kale İlçesi Kültür Envanteri*, Antalya.

Pelekanidis, S. M., P. C. Christou, C. Tsioumis, and S. N. Kadas. 1975. *The Treasures of Mounth Athos, Illuminated Manuscripts, II: The Monasteries of Iveron, St. Panteleimon, Esphigmenou and Chilandari*, Athens.

Peschlow, U. 1996. "Die Burg von Myra," in *Festschrift für Jürgen Borchardt zum sechzigsten Geburstag am 25. Februar dargebracht von Kollegen, Schülern und Freunden*, Vienna, Vol. 1, pp. 209–225.

Peschlow, U. 1990. "Materialen zur Kirche des H. Nikolaos in Myra im Mittelalter," *IstMitt* 40, pp. 207–258.

Peschlow, U. 1975a. "Byzantinische Plastik in Didyma," *IstMitt* 25, pp. 211–257.

Peschlow, U. 1975b. "A. Die Architectur der Nikolaoskirche in Myra," in *Myra, Eine Lykische Metropole in Antiker und Byzantinischer Zeit*, ed. J. Borchard, Berlin, pp. 303–359.

Pitarakis, B., and C. Merantzas. 2006. *Parıldayan Hatıralar. Sevgi Gönül Koleksiyonlarından Son Dönem Osmanlı İstanbuluna Ait Kilise Gümüşleri*, İstanbul.

Poulou-Papadimitriou, N., E. Tzavella, and J. Ott. 2012. "Burial Practises in Byzantine Greece: Archaeological Evidence and Methodogical Problems for Its Interpretation," in *Rome, Constantinople and Newly-Converted Europe. Archaeological and Historical Evidence*, ed. M. Salamon, M. Wołoszyn, A. Musin, and P. Špehar, Kraków – Leipzig, Vol. I, pp. 377–417.

Pringle, D. 2015. "Gothic architecture in the Holyland and Cyprus: From Acre to Famagusta", *Levant* 47/3 (2015), pp. 293-315

Pringle, D. 1984. "Thirteenth Century Pottery from the Monastery of St. Mary of Carmel," *Levant* 16, pp. 91–111.

Redford, S. 2000. *Landscape and the State in Medieval Anatolia: Seljuk Gardens and Pavilions of Alanya, Turkey*, Oxford.

Restle, M. 1969. *Byzantine Wall Painting in Asia Minor*, Recklinghausen.

Rhoby, A. 2009. *Byzantinische Epigramme aus Fresken und Mosaiken,* Vienna.

Rice, D. T. 1986. *Art of the Byzantine Era,* London.

Rice, D. T. 1950. "The Leaved Cross," *Byzantinoslavica* 11, pp. 71–81.

Rice, D. T. 1968. "Survey of Paintings," in *The Church of Hagia Sophia at Trebizond,* ed. D. T. Rice, Edinburg, pp. 88-163.

Robert, L. 1983. "Documents d'Asie Mineure", *BCH* 107, pp. 497–599.

Robert, L. 1946. *Hellenica: Recueil d'épigraphie, de numismatique et d'antiquités grecques,* III, Paris.

Robert, L. 1937. *Études Anatoliennes: Recherches sur les inscriptions grecques de l'Asie Mineure,* Paris.

Rott, H. 1908. *Kleinasiatische Denkmäler aus Pisidien, Pamphylien, Kappadokien und Lykien,* Leipzig.

Ruge, W. 1933. "Myrrha," *RE* 16.1, 1134 ff.

Ruggieri, V. 2005 "La scultura bizantina nel museo archeologico di Antiochia di Pisidia (Yalvaç), Rapporto preliminare: parte II," *OrChrP* 71, pp. 59–96.

Salvatore, M., and N. Lavermicocca. 1980. "Sculture altomedievali e bizantine nel museo di S. Nicola di Bari", *Rivista dell'Instituto nazionale d'archeologia e storia dell'arte* 3/3, pp. 93-135.

Sandin, K. A. 1992. "Middle Byzantine Bronze Crosses of Intermediate Size: Form, Use and Meaning" (diss., Rutgers State University, New Jersey).

Schiller, G. 1971. *Iconography of Christian Art,* London.

Schiller, G. 1966. *Ikonographie der Christlischen Kunst,* Gütersloh.

Scranton, R. L. 1957. *Medieval Architecture in the Central Area of Corinth* (*Corinth* 16), Princeton.

Sklavou-Mauroeidi, M. 1999. *Γλυπτά του Βυζαντινού Μουσείου Αθηνών: Κατάλογος,* Athens.

Sodini, J. P. 1980. "Une iconostase Byzantine à Xanthos," in *Actes du Colloque sur la Lycie Antique* 27, pp. 119–148.

Söğüt, B. 2011. "Stratonikeia 2009 Yılı Çalışmaları," *KST* 32.4, pp. 194–211.

Spatharakis, I. 1999. *Byzantine Wall Painting of Crete, I, Rethymnon Province,* London.

Spieser, J. M. 2001. "Doors, Boundaries and the Use of Space in Early Christian Churches", in *Urban and Religious Spaces in Late Antiquity and Early Byzantium,* Ashgate – Variorum, pp. 1–14 (XV).

Spitzing, G. 1989. *Lexikon byzantinisch christlisher Symbole,* Munich.

Spratt, T. A. B., and E. Forbes. 1847. *Travels in Lycia, Milyas and the Cibyratis,* I, London.

Strati, A. 1985–1986. "Το σωζόμενο ψηφιδωτό του Αποστόλου Ανδρέα από την Παλαιά Μητρόπολη Σερρών," *Μακεδονικά* 25, pp. 88–104.

Stylianou, A. 1958. "Αι τοιχογραφίαι του ναού της Παναγίας του Άρακου, Λαγουδερά, Κύπρος," in *Actes du IXe Congrès International des Études Byzantines, Thessaloniki, 1953,* Athens, Vol. I, pp. 459–467.

Stylianou, A., and J. A. Stylianou. [1985] 1997. *The Painted Churches of Cyprus, Treasures of Byzantine Art,* 2. ed., Nicosia.

Şahin, S., and M. Adak. 2007. *Stadiasmus Patarensis. Itinerta Romana Provincia Lyciae,* İstanbul.

Ševčenko, N. P. 1991a. "Christ: Types of Christ," *ODB* 1, pp. 437–439.

Ševčenko, N. P. 1991b. "Virgin Paraklesis," *ODB* 3, p. 2177.

Talbot, A. M. 2002. "Pilgrimage to healing Shrines: The Evidence of Miracle Accounts," *DOP* 56, pp. 153–173.

Tekin, O. 1999. *Yapı Kredi Koleksiyonu Bizans Sikkeleri / Byzantine Coins, The Yapı Kredi Collection,* İstanbul.

Tekinalp, V. M. 2006. "Arykanda Kenti Bizans Dönemi Mimari Plastik ve Litürjik Taş Eserleri," in *III. Uluslararası Likya Sempozyumu / III. International Lycia Symposium, 7–10 Kasım / November 2005 Antalya,* ed. K. Dörtlük, B. Varkıvanç, T. Kahya, J. deCourtils, M. D. Alpaslan, and R. Boyraz, İstanbul, C. 1, pp. 789–799.

Tekinalp, V. M. 2000. "Geç Antik Dönem Sonrasında ve Ortaçağ'da (M. S. 4.–14. yy.) Andriake Kenti" (diss., Hacettepe University, Ankara).

Temple, Ç. 2013. "Konya / İkonion ve Çevresinde Bulunan Bizans Dönemi Taş Eserleri" (diss., Hacettepe University, Ankara).

Temple, Ç. 2011. "Nevşehir Müzesi'nde Bulunan Bizans Dönemi Mimari ve Litürjik Taş Eserleri," in *Anadolu Kültürlerinde Süreklilik ve Değişim, Dr. A. Mine Kadiroğlu'na Armağan,* Ankara, pp. 537–552.

Trkulja, J. 2012. "The Rose Window: A Feature of Byzantine Architecture?", in *Approaches to Byzantine Architecture and Decoration: Studies in Honor of Slobodan Ćurčić,* ed. M. J. Johnson, R. Ousterhout, and A. Papalexandrou, Farnham, pp. 143–161.

Trkulja, J. 2004. "Asesthetics and Symbolism of Late Byzantine Church Facades, 1204–1453" (diss., Princeton University, Princeton).

Underwood, P. A. 1975. *The Kariye Djami, Vol. 4, Studies in the Art of the Kariye Djami and Its Intellectual Background,* Princeton.

Vryonis, S. Jr. 1975. "Nomadization and Islamization in Asia Minor," *DOP* 29, pp. 41–71.

Vryonis, S. Jr. 1971. *The Decline of Medieval Hellenism in Asia Minor And the Process of Islamization From the Eleventh Through the Fifteenth Century,* London.

Walter, C. 1997. "IC XC NI KA the Apotropaic Function of the Victorious Cross," *REB* 55, pp. 193–220.

Walter, C. 1982. *Art and Ritual of the Byzantine Church,* Aldershot-Burlington.

Walter, C. 1968. "Two Notes on the Deesis," *REB* 26, pp. 311–336.

Weitzmann, K. 1976. *The Monastery of St. Catherine at Mt. Sinai: The Icons,* Princeton.

Weyl Carr, A. 1995. "Art in the Court of the Lusignan Kings," in *Cyprus and the Crusades, Papers Given at the International Conference'Cyprus and the Crusades' Nicosia, 6–7 September, 1994,* ed. N. Coureas, and J. Roley-Smith, Nicosia, pp. 239–274.

Wickham, C. 2004. "The Mediterranean Around 800: On The Brink of the Second Trade Cycle," *DOP* 58, pp. 161–174.

Winfield, D. C. 1971. "Reports on Work at Monagri, Lagoudera and Hagios Neophytos, Cyprus, 1969/1970," *DOP* 25, pp. 259–264.

Winfield, D. C. 1968. "Middle and Later Byzantine Wall Painting Methods, A Comparative Study," *DOP* 22, pp. 63–139.

Winfield, D. C., and E. J. W. Hawkins. 1967. "The Church of Our Lady Asinou, Cyprus, A Report on the Seasons of 1965 and 1966," *DOP* 21, pp. 261–266.

Winfield, D., and J. Winfield. 2003. *The Church of the Panagia tou Arakos at Lagoudhera, Cyprus: The Paintings and Their Painterly Significance,* Washington, D.C.

Yıldırım, Ş. 2013. "Side Antik Kentinin Bizans Dönemi Dini Mimarisi" (diss., Anadolu University, Eskişehir).

Yıldırım, Ş. 2006. "Philomelion'daki (Akşehir) Bizans Dönemi Taş Eserler" (diss., Hacettepe University, Ankara).

Zgusta, L. 1964. *Kleinasiatische Personennamen,* Prague.

Zollt, T. 1994. *Kapitellplastik Konstantinopels vom 4. bis 6. Jahrhundert n. Chr.: mit einem Beitrag zur Untersuchung des ionischen Kämpferkapitells* (*Asia Minor Studien* 14), Bonn.

INDEX

T

U

V

X

Y

Z

PAINTING HISTORY

DELAROCHE AND LADY JANE GREY

PAINTING HISTORY

DELAROCHE AND LADY JANE GREY

STEPHEN BANN AND LINDA WHITELEY

WITH JOHN GUY, CHRISTOPHER RIOPELLE
AND ANNE ROBBINS

National Gallery Company, London

Distributed by Yale University Press

This catalogue is published to accompany
the exhibition *Painting History: Delaroche and Lady Jane Grey*
The National Gallery, London, 24 February to 23 May 2010

First published in Great Britain in 2010 by
National Gallery Company Limited
St Vincent House · 30 Orange Street
London WC2H 7HH
www.nationalgallery.co.uk

ISBN: 9 781857094794
525401

British Library Cataloguing-in-Publication Data.
A catalogue record is available from the British Library.

Library of Congress Control Number: 2009937847

Publisher Louise Rice
Project Editor Claire Young
Editor Rebecca McKie
Picture Researcher Suzanne Bosman
Production Jane Hyne and Penny Le Tissier

Designed and typeset in Brunel by Dalrymple
Reproduction by Altaimage, London
Printed in Italy by Conti Tipocolour

Cover, pages 8, 16, 24, 34 and 106–7 (details): Paul Delaroche (1797–1856), *The Execution of Lady Jane Grey*, 1833. Oil on canvas, double-lined, 251 × 302 cm. The National Gallery, London (NG53).

Opposite title page: Jules-Gabriel Levasseur (1823–about 1900), after Eugène Buttura (1812–1852), *Portrait of Paul Delaroche*, 1853. Engraving on paper, 28×21.5 cm. Private Collection

Contents

Director's Foreword

In the first 30 years of the National Gallery's existence, Paul Delaroche was the most successful artist in Europe. His reputation was established by critical and popular reception of his paintings – notably *The Execution of Lady Jane Grey* – at the Paris Salon, but it had an international dimension and the wealthiest collectors in London eagerly purchased his canvases. A minority of critics distrusted his success on the grounds that it was based on the superficial appeal of narrative suspense, sentiment and realism. However, gallery visitors were enchanted by the ability to travel so easily into another period, seduced by the compelling, if often spurious, detail of the set. The pulse races irresistibly at the impending fate of delicate innocence.

History painting, that is heroic narrative painting, had, at least since the establishment of academies of art in the late sixteenth century, seldom been associated with the skills of the painters of everyday life best exemplified by the Dutch artists who excelled in depicting straw on a tavern floor or satin worn by a lady. Modern painting of this kind could be seen as a threat to the appeal of a collection of Old Masters. In 1860 Charles Collins (son of the popular novelist, Wilkie Collins), writing anonymously in the mass-circulation journal *Household Words*, concluded his account of the National Gallery by invoking the far more accessible appeal of the photographic reproductions of history paintings by Delaroche's pupil Gérôme which could be seen in the windows of Bond Street.

Before long, the alliance of the theatrical and photographic would give birth to the cinema. But perhaps of no less significance in the history of the visual arts was the fact that an aversion to the historical narratives of Delaroche or Gérôme came to be an attitude expected from serious art lovers. To defend modern painting as well as Old Master painting entailed the dismissal of a painting like *The Execution of Lady Jane Grey*. This exhibition therefore explores a crucial episode in the history of art: the creation of a new type of picture which led to a re-definition of what serious art was, or should be, about. At the same time, it invites us to escape from the prejudices which this critical tradition has enforced, and to consider just how novel and exciting the work of Delaroche seemed to his original public. It is an honour for the National Gallery to have as external curators for this exhibition two of the foremost scholars in the reappraisal of French nineteenth-century art, Stephen Bann and Linda Whiteley. It is also a pleasure to acknowledge the expertise that has formed this accompanying publication, particularly that of John Guy, for his fascinating account of the real Lady Jane Grey, and of the Gallery's curators, Christopher Riopelle and Anne Robbins.

Perhaps the most telling aspect of the mixed modern attitude to this type of history painting is the extraordinary disappearance of *The Execution of Lady Jane Grey* from public display for several decades. We owe special thanks to Christopher Johnstone for the rediscovery of the rolled up but relatively undamaged painting in 1973. This has been the scenario played out again 35 years later, as the rediscovered masterpiece, *Charles I insulted by the Soldiers of Oliver Cromwell* was unrolled, having survived damage sustained during the London Blitz. We are indebted to Michael Clarke at the National Gallery of Scotland, Edinburgh, for his assistance with arranging this loan, and special thanks are extended to the National Gallery curatorial and conservation staff, whose meticulous care has enabled both of these paintings to be exhibited in public once again.

To mount such an exhibition would have been impossible without the collaboration of the Département des Peintures in the Musée du Louvre. We are deeply grateful to Henri Loyrette, Président-directeur, Christophe Leribault, Carel van Tuyll van Serooskerken at Département des arts graphiques, Vincent Pomarède, Directeur, Département des peintures and Sebastien Allard, curator of nineteenth-century paintings. The National Gallery is as ever indebted to all those who have generously loaned their pictures. I also thank the following for their assistance with mounting this exhibition: Timothy Wilson, Department of Western Art, the Ashmolean Museum, Oxford; Antony Griffiths and Sheila O'Connell at the Department of Prints and Drawings, the British Museum, London; Dame Rosalind Savill and Stephen Duffy at the Wallace Collection, London; Christopher Forbes at The Forbes Collection, New York; Bruno Racine, Président, Sylvie Aubenas and Marie-Hélène Petitfour, Directeur, Département des Estampes at the Bibliothèque nationale de France, Paris; Agathe Sanjuan, Bénédicte Rouvière and the Administrateur général Muriel Mayette at the Comédie-Française; Bertrand Gautier, Galerie Talabardon and Gautier; Sylvie Ramond, Director, and Stephane Paccoud of the Musée des Beaux-Arts, Lyon; Amaury Lefébure, Alain Pougetoux, Musée National des Châteaux de Malmaison et de Bois-Préau; Pascal Trarieux, Directeur, Musée des Beaux-Arts, Nîmes; and Antoine Cahen and Galerie Terrades.

NICHOLAS PENNY

Director, The National Gallery
December 2009

ACKNOWLEDGEMENTS

The authors wish to thank the following friends, associates and colleagues for their assistance with the exhibition *Painting History: Delaroche and Lady Jane Grey* and this, the accompanying catalogue: Sébastien Allard, the late Sir Jonathan Backhouse, Eric Bertin, Victoria Brown, Antoine Cahen, Christie's, Michael Clarke, Mhairi Doble, Stephen Duffy, Susan Foister, Dominique de Font-Réaulx, Christopher Forbes, Bertrand Gautier, Antony Griffiths, Colin Harrison, Rena Hoisington, Jan Howard, Amaury Lefébure, Georges Lenoir, Christophe Leribault, Muriel Mayette and her colleagues Agathe Sanjuan and Bénédicte Rouvière, Sheila McKinnon, Sheila O'Connell, Stéphane Paccoud, Alain Pougetoux, Sylvie Ramond, Francis Russell, Martin Spies, Emmanuel Starcky, Bertrand Talabardon, Pascal Trarieux, Michael and Dorothea Venator, Olivia Voisin, Norma Watt, Flora Whiteley, Jon Whiteley, Timothy Wilson, Helena Wright, and colleagues at the Sackler Library and the Department of the History of Art, University of Oxford, the Department of the History of Art and Institute of Advanced Studies at the University of Bristol.

The Story of Lady Jane Grey

John Guy

Jane Grey has always been enveloped in myth. Her date of birth is invariably wrongly stated, and allegations that her father verbally and physically abused her as a child have been invented over the centuries to turn her into a victim as well as a tragic heroine (fig. 1).[1] She was born at Bradgate in Leicestershire on the edge of the Charnwood Forest in the spring of 1537, the eldest surviving child of Frances Brandon, Henry VIII's niece, and her husband Henry Grey, Marquis of Dorset (later Duke of Suffolk).[2] Her father, unusually well educated for a nobleman, was a bibliophile. Both Jane's parents sympathised with the humanist and evangelical reformers, and she received a superb education based on the model that Sir Thomas More had devised for his eldest daughter, Margaret.

As a great-granddaughter of Henry VII, the founder of the Tudor dynasty, and a second cousin to Edward VI and his half-sisters Mary and Elizabeth, Jane was close to the court and its politics (see Jane's claim to the throne on p. 10). By the terms of Henry VIII's will, should his own children die without heirs, she was next in line of royal succession after any son that her parents might have.[3] And by the age of 11 she had caught the eye of Thomas, Lord Seymour of Sudeley, one of King Edward's uncles, who had married Henry VIII's sixth queen, Katherine Parr, shortly after Henry's death. Seymour had a scheme to marry Jane to Edward, and he bargained with the Greys for her wardship.[4] Jane was briefly installed at Seymour Place in London, but a serious scandal involving Seymour's ambitions and his relationship with the young Elizabeth, on whom he also had designs, led to his fall and execution on a charge of treason, and Jane returned to Bradgate to resume her studies.

In the summer of 1550, Roger Ascham, the most famous Tudor educationalist, visited Bradgate, where he found Jane reading Plato's *Phaedo* in Greek 'and that with as much delight as some gentlemen would read a merry tale in Boccaccio'. When he asked why she was not out hunting with her family in the park, she smiled and said smugly: 'All their sport in the park is but a shadow to that pleasure that I find in Plato.'[5] Afterwards, Ascham discreetly hinted that Jane was a better scholar than her cousin Elizabeth, whose tutor he briefly was.[6]

When Jane was 'just fourteen' in May 1551, her own tutor, John Aylmer, praised her in a letter to the leading Swiss reformer Heinrich Bullinger.[7] Jane was encouraged to write to Bullinger herself: an exiled German divine, John of Ulm, visiting Bradgate that spring, was shown a copy of one of these letters.[8] Although formal, sententious and awkward, her letters to Bullinger are in faultless Latin. 'In writing to you in this manner', she explains, 'I have exhibited more boldness than prudence: but so great has been your kindness towards me, in condescending to write to me, a stranger, and in supplying the necessary instruction for the adornment of my understanding and the improvement of my mind, that I should justly appear chargeable with neglect and forgetfulness of duty, were I not to show myself mindful of you and of your deservings in every possible way.'[9] She began to study Hebrew as well as Greek, so that she could read the Old and New Testaments in the original, and a year or so later, Mildred Cooke, a kinswoman and another brilliant intellectual, the wife of Sir William Cecil, Elizabeth I's future chief minister, sent her the Greek homilies of Saint Basil.[10]

As Jane matured, she became increasingly confident and assertive, determined to cultivate her status as an evangelical Protestant figurehead and not averse to one-upmanship. Although she had loved fine clothes and braided hair as a child, when urged by her father and tutor to imitate her cousin Elizabeth in dressing plainly, she quickly got the message, and when sent a costly dress of 'tinsel, cloth of gold, and velvet, laid on with parchment lace of gold' as a New Year's gift by Mary, a staunch Catholic, she asked curtly: ' "What shall I do with it?" "Marry," said a gentlewoman, "Wear it." "Nay," quoth she, "that were a shame to follow my Lady Mary against God's word, and leave my Lady Elizabeth, which followeth God's word." '[11]

Religion lay at the heart of the political crisis in Edward VI's reign. In the spring of 1553, when Jane was 16, the young king fell mortally ill and planned to exclude his sisters from the succession. He believed that neither could be trusted not to reverse or modify his new Protestant settlement. He was convinced that both were legally barred from inheriting the crown, for both had been declared illegitimate by his

The Tudor Succession

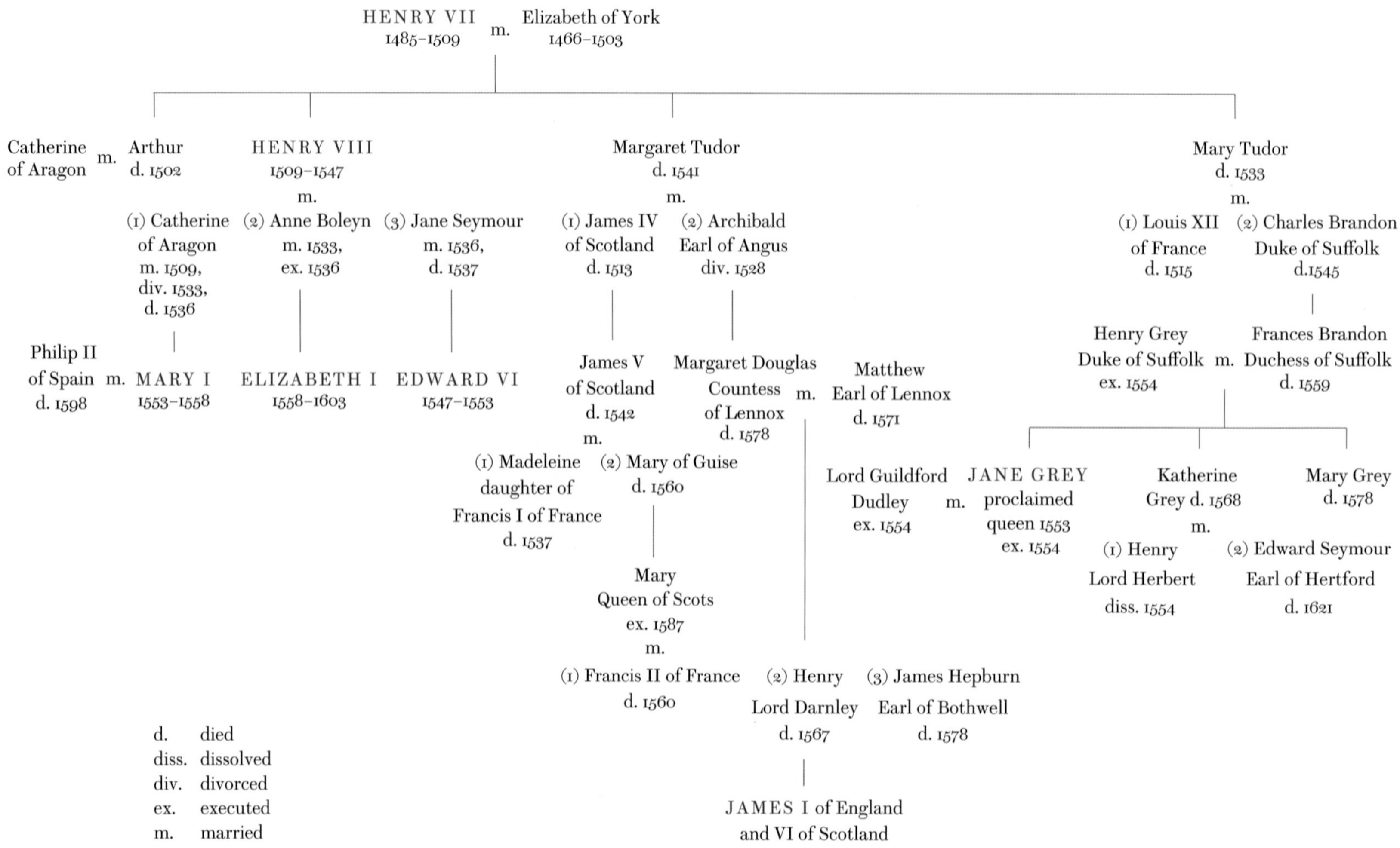

d. died
diss. dissolved
div. divorced
ex. executed
m. married

father's Parliaments.[12] At this stage the idea that any woman, including Jane Grey, might succeed him was anathema to Edward. When in April he first began to jot down his ideas to 'devise' the crown to a Protestant heir, his tuberculosis was in remission and he envisaged that before his death, Jane's mother, Frances, would have a son or that Jane herself would marry and that her son would be the rightful successor. To this end, a series of dynastic marriages was hastily arranged in late May by John Dudley, Duke of Northumberland, the effective regent: Northumberland's son, Guildford Dudley, was married to Jane and his allies betrothed to her sisters.

But in June 1553, it was clear that Edward was dying. With insufficient time to summon Parliament, he therefore 'devised' the crown 'to the L[ady] Jane and her heires masles', followed by her sisters Katherine and Mary, and by the eldest son of their cousin Margaret Clifford if they died without heirs.[13] How far Edward was Northumberland's puppet in making his 'device' is hotly contested, but the original document is in Edward's own handwriting throughout (fig. 2).

When Edward died on 6 July and Jane discovered she was queen, she wept, but prayed to God that: 'If what was given to me was rightly mine, His Divine Majesty would grant me such grace as to enable me to govern this Kingdom with his approbation and to his glory.'[14] Although not officially proclaimed queen at the Tower until the 10th, she saw herself as born to lead the Protestant cause. Many historians have depicted Jane as innocent and manipulated, but she had been aware of the contents of Edward's 'device' since at least the 7th, and despite her mother's anger on first learning that she herself had been passed over, the family was united behind her. What did genuinely shock Jane, and where she was naive, was in not realising that she would have to satisfy her new husband, Guildford, who demanded to be king. A furious row erupted between them at the Tower after Jane was handed the crown jewels. Married in haste to a man she barely knew, she was never in love, and told Guildford he could only be a duke.[15] Hearing this, he refused to sleep with her any longer until prevailed on to relent by the Earls of Arundel and Pembroke.[16]

Jane ruled until 19 July. Whether she was the Nine Days' Queen depends on whether her reign is said to have begun with her accession proclamation on the 10th or with Edward's death on the 6th, in which case she ruled for almost a fortnight. Her reign ended when the Catholic Mary, who considered herself to be the rightful heir, led a successful counter-coup. Warned of Edward's death, Mary had escaped to East Anglia to muster her forces. In any case, the Protestants were divided. Bishop Ridley of London preached vigorously for Jane, but John Bradford predicted civil war and suggested that Edward's 'device' had been the product of a deranged mind.[17] Although the young king had legally bound his privy councillors, nobles and judges to observe his 'device' in the final days of his life, their consent had been extracted by fear and threats, and most people, especially the citizens of London, continued to support Mary. The Duke of Northumberland was sent with an army to defeat her, but when a naval squadron off the Norfolk coast defected and handed over their artillery to her, his troops melted away.

As late as the 18th, Jane was still sending out letters signed 'Jane the Quene' to sheriffs and magistrates ordering them to rally and emphasising that her rule was founded on 'consent' to Edward's 'device'.[18] But even her kinsman William Cecil was among those preparing to slip away to Mary. 'And seeing great perils threatened upon us by the likeness of the time', he had scribbled in a note to Mildred, 'I do make choice to avoid the peril of God's displeasure.'[19]

By late July, Mary had recovered the capital and the Dudleys were imprisoned in the Tower. Jane, stripped of the crown jewels and her canopy of state, was escorted from the royal apartments and mocked by the guard. For the next six months she was lodged at the house of William Partridge, an officer in the royal ordnance within the Tower, where on 29 August the anonymous author of the *Chronicle of Queen Jane*, the most vivid and authentic account of the events of 1553–4, had dinner with her.[20] Sitting in the place of honour 'at the board's end', she made him welcome and asked for news of the outside world, before launching into a stinging attack on Northumberland, who had been executed a week before after a spectacular recantation and

[FIG. 1] Attributed to Levina Teerlinc (about 1520–1576), *Portrait of a Lady, possibly Lady Jane Grey*, possibly 1553. Body colour on thin card, 4.8 cm diameter, Yale Center for British Art. Paul Mellon Collection, New Haven (B1974.2.59). The jewel on her breast and the spray of foliage inserted behind it suggest that the sitter is Lady Jane Grey after her marriage to Guildford Dudley in May 1553. The 'ANO XVIII' (i.e. 'anno aetatis xviii') inscription presents a difficulty in that Jane was not quite seventeen when she was executed; however, such inscriptions are not always reliable.

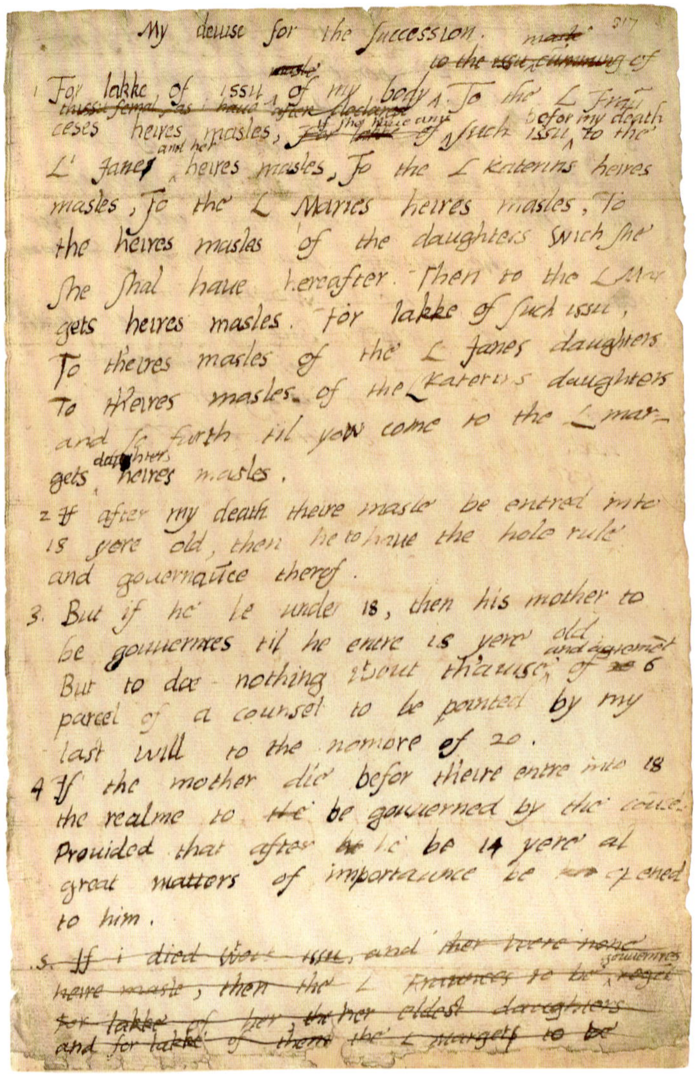
My deuise for the Succession.

1 For lakke of issu of my body to the L Fraunceses heires masles, for lakke of such issu befor my death to the L' Jane and her heires masles, To the L Katerins heires masles, To the L Maries heires masles, To the heires masles of the daughters wich she shal haue hereafter. Then to the L Margets heires masles. For lakke of such issu, To theires masles of the L Janes daughters To theires masles of the L Katerins daughters and so forth til yow come to the L Margets daughters heires masles.

2 If after my death theire masle be entred into 18 yere old, then he to haue the hole rule and gouernaunce therof.

3. But if he be under 18, then his mother to be gouuernres til he entre 18 yere old, But to doe nothing without thauise and agrement of 6 parcel of a counsel to be pointed by my last will to the nombre of 20.

4 If the mother die befor theire entre into 18 the realme to be gouuerned by the cownsel Provided that after he be 14 yere al great matters of importaunce be opened to him.

~~5. If i died wout issu, and ther were none heire masle, then the L Fraunces to be gouuernres regent for lakke of her, the her eldest daughters and for lakke of them the L Marget to be~~

[FIG. 2] Edward VI first began to draft 'My devise for the succession' in April 1553. Assuming Jane Grey's mother, Frances Duchess of Suffolk, had no sons, he left the Crown to 'the L[ady] Jane's heires masles'. Realising in early June that he would die before Jane even became pregnant, he altered this to 'Jane and her heires masles', making Jane his heir outright. If she too died without sons, the Crown was to pass to the 'heires masles' of her sisters, Katherine and Mary. In a final revision (not shown here), Edward 'devised' the Crown to Jane, Katherine and Mary in turn. Courtesy of The Honourable Society of the Inner Temple.

public reconversion to Catholicism in the hope of a pardon. 'I pray God', exclaimed Jane, 'I, nor no friend of mine, die so. Should I, who [am] young and in my few years, forsake my faith for the love of life? Nay, God forbid!' She vehemently denounced her father-in-law as the source of all her troubles. 'He hath brought me and our stock in most miserable calamity and misery by his exceeding ambition.'[21]

Jane, with her husband Guildford Dudley and two of his brothers, were tried for treason on 13 November at the London Guildhall. All pleaded guilty, and Jane, who stood before her judges wearing a plain black gown trimmed with black velvet, and reading from a prayer book, was sentenced to be burned at the stake or decapitated.[22] But the new queen, although determined to have her revenge on Northumberland and his co-conspirators, was inclined to pity Jane until stopped in her tracks by Sir Thomas Wyatt's rebellion in early 1554. Wyatt, whose forces reached the gates of London before they were defeated, aimed to overthrow Mary and replace her with Princess Elizabeth. Jane's father, who had been freed after a brief imprisonment, had promised to raise the Midlands for Wyatt. His action sealed his daughter's fate besides his own, although Jane had raised the stakes by writing a diatribe against Dr Thomas Harding. A former chaplain at Bradgate and Greek tutor to her sister, Katherine, Harding had reconverted to Catholicism. Jane was vitriolic in her denunciation, condemning him in language so scabrous that her Victorian admirers would refuse to accept it. She spoke of the relapsed Harding as 'sometime ... the lively member of Christ, but now the deformed imp of the devil, sometime the beautiful temple of God, but now the stinking kennel of Satan, sometime the unspotted spouse of Christ, but now the spotted paramour of Antichrist'.[23]

Jane's execution was fixed for 9 February,[24] but in a final bid to secure another propaganda victory, Mary sent John Feckenham, her own chaplain and confessor, to the Tower. Jane was obliged to hear him, but was unmoved. A record of their disputation survives, which ends with Feckenham saying, 'I am sure we two shall never meet [i.e. agree]', and Jane replying: 'Truth it is that we shall never meet, unless God turn your heart. For I am sure (unless you repent and turn to God) you are an evil case.'[25] She had resolved to become a Protestant martyr. In her last letter to her sister Katherine, she wrote: 'As touching my death, rejoice as I do, good sister, that I shall be delivered of this corruption, and put on uncorruption. For I am assured, that I shall for losing of a mortal life, win an immortal life.'[26]

On 12 February 1554, Jane and Guildford were executed. The manuscript of the *Chronicle*, an eyewitness report, says that Jane was 'nothing at all abashed, neither with fear of her own death ... neither with the sight of the dead carcass of her husband'.[27] She 'came forth, the lieutenant [of the Tower, Sir John Brydges] leading her, in the same gown wherein she was arraigned [i.e. tried at the Guildhall], her countenance nothing abashed, neither her eyes anything moisted with tears, although her two gentlewomen, Mistress Elizabeth Tilney and Mistress Ellen, wonderfully wept'. Jane 'carried a book in her hand, whereon she prayed all the way till she came to the said scaffold, whereon when she was mounted, etc'.[28]

In this account, which cuts away abruptly with the word 'etc.', there is no mention of a blindfold or of Jane groping for the block. Another equally well-informed source says that she 'conducted herself at her execution with the greatest fortitude and godliness'.[29] And yet very shortly, Jane would be reinvented not just as the steadfast martyr that she was, but as a victim. For the 'best' and most popular female martyrs throughout Christian history had always been innocent victims, virgins or ascetics.[30] And what better to counter Mary's propaganda triumph over Northumberland?

Soon a dossier of documents was circulating in London that included a fresh, more dramatic account of her execution, complete with the pathos of her groping for the block.[31] According to this apocryphal version, after making a short speech admitting her treason but claiming that 'touching the procurement and desire thereof by me or on my [be]half, I do wash my hands thereof in innocency before God', Jane protested her Protestant faith. Then, kneeling, she turned to Feckenham, standing nearby, saying:

> *'Shall I say this psalm?' And he said, 'Yea.' Then she said the psalm of Miserere mei Deus, in English, in most devout manner to the end. Then she stood up and gave her maid Mistress Tilney her gloves and handkerchief, and her book to Master Thomas Brydges, the lieutenant's brother: forthwith she untied her gown. The hangman went to her to have helped her of[f] therewith; then she desired him to let her alone, turning towards her two gentlewomen, who helped her of[f] therewith, and also [took] her frow's paste [i.e. head dress] and neckerchief, giving to her a fair handkerchief to knit about her eyes. Then the hangman kneeled down and asked her forgiveness; whom she forgave most willingly. Then he willed her to stand upon the straw, which doing, she saw the block. Then she said, 'I pray thee dispatch me quickly.' Then she kneeled down, saying, 'Will you take it off before I lay me down?' And the hangman answered her, 'No madam.' She tied the [hand]kerchief about her eyes; then feeling for the block, said, 'What shall I do? Where is it?' One of the standers-by guiding her thereunto, she laid her head down upon the block, and stretched forth her body and said: 'Lord, into thy hands I commend my spirit!' And so she ended.*[32]

An earlier, more authentic version of the dossier was in the possession of John Banks, the son of a London printer and a friend of James Haddon, one of Jane's father's chaplains at Bradgate. In March

[FIG. 3] Unknown artist, *Possibly Lady Jane Dudley (née Grey)*, 1590s? Oil on oak panel, 85.6 × 60.3 cm. National Portrait Gallery, London (NPG 6804). This recently rediscovered portrait, inscribed 'Lady Iayne', has been said to show Lady Jane Grey after her marriage. The panel on which it is painted was not cut down until around 1593, so the image could be a copy of a lost original or else based on a portrait of an unidentified sitter who was living, as the costume perhaps suggests, at around the same time as Jane.

1554 Banks sent his version to Bullinger with a suggestion that it be printed in Strasbourg.[33] But a London printer, John Day, obtained a copy, possibly clandestinely, and published it from a secret address near Stamford in Lincolnshire, where he had established a Protestant underground press under the pseudonym of 'Michael Wood'.[34] Then, obtaining the apocryphal material from an unknown source, a rival printer, probably Anthony Scoloker, issued a pirate tract including genuine and apocryphal material.[35] By doing so, he contradicted Day's earlier account of Jane's death and writings – in that earlier version there had been no trace of a vulnerable Jane. Meanwhile, Banks and Haddon had fled to Strasbourg, where Banks showed his own version of the dossier to Michelangelo Florio, the former pastor of a congregation of exiled Italian Protestants in London, who used it extensively in his *Historia de la Vita e de la Morte de l'illustrissima Signora Giovanna Graia*, written in 1561.[36]

A large portion of Banks's version of the dossier survives, from which it is clear that, even before Day comes into the story, documents once originally in Jane's own hand were being 'spun' to make her appear more innocent.[37] Haddon was aware of this doctoring. 'I am rather afraid,' he complained to Bullinger on 31 August 1554, 'that all the facts are not as described by him [i.e. Banks].'[38] He warned Bullinger against the likely damage to the Protestant cause that would be caused by this doctoring, but in vain.[39] The copies of Jane's writings and the account of her execution printed in John Foxe's *Actes and Monuments* (or *Book of Martyrs*) in 1563 include both doctored and apocryphal materials,[40] as do those of all the Elizabethan chroniclers apart from John Stow (who knew the true facts because he had obtained possession of the author's original of the *Chronicle of Queen Jane*).[41]

By the time of the 1570 edition of John Foxe's *Actes and Monuments*, the first blatant forgery – a supposed prison letter of Jane to her father – was added to the mix to make it appear that the teenage Jane had been forced to accept the crown against her will.[42] By the eighteenth century, 'Jane Grey' forgeries were rampant: a fake version of her last letter to Katherine was even inserted into the blank page of a manuscript in the British Library.[43] The only prison writings of Jane to survive in her own hand and in the form in which she wrote them are the brief notes she scribbled to her father and to Sir John Brydges in a prayer book in the hours before her death.[44] Her letter to Harding and her last letter to Katherine are both genuine, although both have come down to us in texts that were doctored for effect while in the possession of John Banks.[45]

The final twist is that the original eyewitness description of Jane's execution from the *Chronicle* was itself corrupted on first publication in 1850, when the text was expanded to incorporate the apocryphal material printed by Scoloker.[46] This occurred because the editor of the *Chronicle*, the antiquary John Gough Nichols, arbitrarily decided that the extraneous account must have been written by the same chronicler.[47] An admirer of Delaroche since 1833, when he exclaimed, 'We sigh for the time when our native painters of history shall display equal knowledge and equal accuracy!',[48] Nichols was heavily influenced by *The Execution of Lady Jane Grey*, which he knew from an engraving published in the *Art Journal* for 1849.[49] There, as in the painting itself, Jane's pathos and vulnerability are fully expressed: dressed in virgin white, she gropes blindly for the block assisted by Sir John Brydges and watched by the executioner, while her two gentlewomen swoon. She becomes the apotheosis of female innocence, and that a distinguished Victorian historian should have been so misled is a testimony to the power of art.

1. The best and most recent studies are de Lisle 2008 and Ives 2009. The myths about Jane are uncritically repeated in Davey 53. I am most grateful to de Lisle for discussing Jane with me on several occasions, but must take full responsibility for the arguments of this essay, which are my own.

2. Starkey and Grosvenor 2007, p. 83.

3. Levine 1973, pp. 163–4.

4. TNA (The National Archives, Kew), SP10/6, no.7; Haynes 1740, pp. 76–9, 83, 98.

5. Ascham 1570, p. 11; Vos 1989, pp. 144–7, 182–3, 192–3.

6. Vos 1989, p. 145.

7. Robinson 1846–7, I, p. 276.

8. Robinson 1846–7, II, pp. 429–30.

9. Robinson 1846–7, I, pp. 4–11, quotation from p. 10.

10. Robinson 1846–7, II, p. 432; TNA, SP10/15, no. 79.

11. Robinson 1846–7, I, pp. 278–9; Aylmer 1559, sig. n.1.

12. These events are extremely complex and must be interpreted in the light of often ambiguous evidence. Useful introductions may be found in Loach 1999, pp. 159–69; MacCulloch 1999, pp. 39–41; Alford 2008, pp. 51–7.

13. Inner Temple, London, Petyt MS 538, vol. 47, folio 317. Printed in Nichols 1850, pp. 89–90.

14. Malfatti 1956, p. 48.

15. Malfatti 1956, p. 48.

16. Malfatti 1956, p. 48.

17. MacCulloch 1996, p. 542.

18. BL (British Library), Harleian MS 416, folios 30-1v.

19. BL Lansdowne MS 104, folio 3.

20. Nichols 1850, pp. 24–6.

21. Nichols 1850, p. 25.

22. TNA, KB 8/23; Nichols 1850, p. 32.

23. BL, Harleian MS 416, folios 25–8. Although this is the earliest and most authentic manuscript, doctoring is already visible. Thus in the quoted passage, 'stinking' would be amended to 'stinking and filthy', and 'spotted' to 'unshamefast.' Overall, dozens of changes and interpolations were made for greater effect.

24. Nichols 1850, p. 55.

25. *An Epistle of the Ladye Iane a righte vertuous woman ... Wherunto is added the communication that she had with master Feckenham ... Also another Epistle whiche she wrote to her sister, with the words she spake upon the Scaffold befor she suffered* ([Barholm]: [John Day], 1554), sig. [B5v].

26. BL, Harleian MS 416, folio 28; *An Epistle of the Ladye Iane a righte vertuous woman*, sig. [B7].

27. BL, Harleian MS 194, folio 28r-v; Nichols 1850, pp. 55–6.

28. BL, Harleian MS 194, folio 28r-v; Nichols 1850, pp. 55–6.

29. This was Peter Martyr, a leading reformer and Oxford theologian with excellent political connections; Robinson 1846–7, II, p. 515.

30. Thomas S. Freeman in Freeman and Mayer 2007, p. 21.

31. *Here in this booke ye have a godly Epistle made by a Faithful Christian, A communicacion betwene Fecknam and the Lady Jane Dudley, A letter that she wrote to her Syster Lady Katherine, The ende of the Ladye Jane upon the Scaffolde* ... ([London?]: [Anthony Scoloker?], 1554).

32. *Here in this booke ye have a godly Epistle*, sig. [B3–B3v]. This version is the source for the Latin account of Jane's execution by Charles V's ambassadors now in the Library of the Escorial, printed in Malfatti 1956, pp. 72–3, 136. These ambassadors could not have witnessed Jane's death because in fear of Wyatt's revolt they had fled London to Flushing by 3 February 1554, not returning until after 18 February.

33. Robinson 1846–7, I, pp. 303–5; Fairfield 1972, pp. 226–7.

34. Day's original copy of the dossier is *An Epistle of the Ladye Iane a righte vertuous woman*. Fairfield 1972, pp. 220–32; Evenden 2004, pp. 383–94.

35. The pirate tract, with the apocryphal material, is *Here in this booke ye have a godly Epistle made by a Faithful Christian*. Evenden 2008, p. 31 and n.9.

36. Fairfield 1972, p. 227; Yates 1934, pp. 7–14; Garrett 1938, pp. 78–9; Wyatt 2005, pp. 100–1. Florio's book was not published until 1607: BL, 292.a.5.

37. The surviving portions of Banks's dossier are BL, Harleian MS 416, folios 25-8v; BL, Harleian MS 422, folios 41-3v.

38. Robinson 1846–7, I, pp. 293–4.

39. Robinson 1846–7, I, pp. 293–4.

40. Foxe 1563, pp. 917–23.

41. Stow 1592, p. 1054; Nichols 1850, pp. V–VI.

42. Foxe 1570, II, pp. 1581–2.

43. BL, Harleian MS 2370, folios 39v–41.

44. BL, Harleian MS 2342, folios 74v–7, 78–80; Nichols 1850, pp. 57–8.

45. BL, Harleian MS 416, folios 25-8 (where both letters are contained).

46. Nichols 1850, pp. 56–9.

47. Nichols 1850, p. 56 and note A.

48. Nichols made this remark in a short notice he wrote in the *Gentleman's Magazine*, 103: 1 (1833), p. 447. The subject was Delaroche's *Cromwell and Charles I*, exhibited at the Salon of 1831. For Nichols's authorship, see Emily Lorraine de Montluzin, 'Attributions of Authorship in the *Gentleman's Magazine*' at http://etext.lib.virginia.edu/bsuva/gm2.

49. *Art Journal*, vol XI, no. 2 (1849), p. 60. I owe this reference to Linda Whiteley and Stephen Bann. The engraving is by W.T. Green, and Nichols must have seen it, because as editor of the *Gentleman's Magazine* (a post he held from 1826 to 1856), he published four obituaries of artists or engravers that had appeared in that year's *Art Journal*, one of which, a memoir of Abraham Wivell, portrait painter, was extracted by himself. Cf. *Gentleman's Magazine*, New Series, 32 (1849), pp. 213–15 and *Art Journal*, vol XI, no. 2 (1849), p. 205. Further editorial cross-references appear in the *Gentleman's Magazine* to the *Art Journal*'s engravings from the Vernon Gallery, which were published from the beginning of 1849.

Lost and Found

CHRISTOPHER RIOPELLE

In the spring of 1973, a young curator at the Tate Gallery was at work on his first book, a monograph on the English Romantic painter John Martin. Christopher Johnstone, who would go on to direct the Auckland City Art Gallery in New Zealand, wanted to learn more about Martin's first major commission, *The Destruction of Pompeii and Herculaneum*. A monumental painting of 1822, it had entered the Tate in 1918, but according to reports had been lost there, along with several other works, when the Thames flooded the Gallery basement in the early hours of Saturday 7 January 1928. A report of 1930 stated that 18 oil paintings had been 'completely spoiled' in the flood, among them the Martin.[1] Decades later rumours circulated to the contrary. 'Someone had told me,' Johnstone recalled, 'that some of the paintings listed as lost or damaged beyond repair were not.'[2]

Acting on a hunch, Johnstone persuaded Tate conservators to double-check rolled canvases which had long been stored under large tables in the conservation studios. 'There were quite a few rolled works there. No one had looked at them for a very long time. ... No one had the faintest idea what was there – there were no labels attached.' Knowing the dimensions of the Martin, they looked for a large roll. Johnstone recalls the excitement as unfurling began, for it was then that they discovered the Martin largely intact, if battered. And there was an unexpected bonus. Bound up with it in the same roll was another monumental canvas that had been listed as lost in the flood, Paul Delaroche's *Execution of Lady Jane Grey* (cat. 53). 'My memory was that the Martin had a corner chopped out,' he recalled, 'but the Delaroche was pristine.' A photograph of the latter taken soon after the rediscovery confirms that the canvas was, by and large, in sound condition (fig. 4).

Lady Jane Grey had been bequeathed to the National Gallery by Lord Cheylesmore and accepted by the Board of Trustees on 16 December 1902. Two days later, on 18 December, it was transferred to the Tate Gallery, then known as the National Gallery Millbank, where paintings of the Modern Foreign Schools were displayed. Its subsequent exhibition history is complicated; by 1928, however, it was no longer on view but relegated to the basement. The flood put the Tate on an emergency footing. Nine ground-floor galleries were temporarily abandoned. Loan exhibitions were cancelled. Conservation work immediately began on endangered pieces, not least 14 paintings by Turner and thousands of works on paper.[3] In the commotion, Delaroche's canvas was not judged a priority. Listing it along with the Martin among the 18 spoiled paintings, the authors of the 1930 report added that in any event 'few of these ... would be regarded as of primary importance from an artistic point of view'.[4] *Lady Jane Grey* was rolled up, put away and, having been dismissed as aesthetically negligible, forgotten. In 1959 it was definitively listed as 'destroyed'.[5]

Strange fate for an artist whose reputation had once ranked with those of his acclaimed contemporaries Delacroix and Ingres! By common consent, *Lady Jane Grey* was among Delaroche's masterpieces. It had figured in one of the most significant collections of contemporary art of the day, that of the *richissime* Russian Count Anatole Demidoff, later Prince of San Donato. Prints after it were disseminated worldwide (cat. 78). Indeed, it had been an artistic *cause célèbre* of France's July Monarchy, famous from the moment it first went on display at the Paris Salon of 1834. Every day throughout the run of the exhibition, admiring crowds gathered in front of it. They found themselves inexorably drawn to the poignant image of the 17-year-old, blindfolded queen as she groped her way pitiably to the execution block. They were pulled in too by the intense realism of the scene, painted as if happening in our own space, and by the *extrême perfection* of its details, as one critic had it, including the rustling silk of the girl's dress and the strands of hay into which her severed head would soon fall. *Lady Jane Grey* secured the reputation Delaroche had begun to build in the 1820s for his depictions of scenes from English history. With it he again demonstrated his uncanny ability, as the critic Tardieu characterised it, to find 'subjects that attack the nervous system of the public'.[6] History seemed very real here, and utterly present. As another critic noted of the *Lady Jane Grey* phenomenon, Delaroche's 'name is repeated in every salon, in every shop, with the praises which accompanied that of M. Gérard fifteen years ago, that of David thirty years ago'.[7]

Not everyone was thrilled. The Salon of 1834 was meant to be Ingres's triumph. His supporters had been drumming up enthusiasm in advance for what they declared would be the master's greatest achievement, a large altarpiece, almost 10 years in preparation.[8] *The Martyrdom of Saint Symphorian* (fig. 5) is a crowded, complex and spatially ambiguous composition concerning an obscure early Christian sent to execution for his faith. Whereas it is limpidly clear what is to happen next to Lady Jane, and how she will die, the fate of Ingres's gesticulating martyr is far from obvious. Everyone in the picture seems to be frantically pointing here and there and shouting, but to what end? Some critics found the work very obscure indeed and the comparisons made with *Lady Jane Grey* were generally far from favourable. Others preferred the superior artistry of Ingres's painting, one describing it as 'a great and noble poem' as opposed to Delaroche's 'touching short story'.[9] But the public was united in its preference. Always thin-skinned, Ingres was appalled. Delaroche's work had a potent visceral impact, to be sure, but in its simple immediacy was it art to be compared with his own? Even years later, by then the eminent Director of the French Academy in Rome, Ingres continued to be assailed by nightmares of the 1834 Salon – 'the same vision everywhere, a horrible vision'[10] – where ignorant crowds flocked to *Lady Jane Grey* while shunning his own work hanging directly opposite. The famous rout of *Saint Symphorian* added to the legend of *Lady Jane Grey*; not only had it triumphed, but with its success Delaroche had vanquished the greatest artist of the age.

Soon after, Delaroche's painting disappeared from public view. Demidoff, 22 years old in 1834, sent his collection away from Paris to his sumptuous Villa San Donato outside Florence. *Lady Jane Grey* was installed there in grand style, the largest painting in a dazzling display. As far as contemporary art was concerned, however, nineteenth-century Florence was a provincial backwater, dismissed by Ingres as early as 1806 as 'thirty years behind the times'.[11] The impact the painting might have had, had it remained accessible to artists in Paris, was surely blunted by its aristocratic transalpine exile. It remained in Florence until, a few months before Demidoff's death in 1870, the collection was dispersed in a series of sales.[12] There, the Delaroche brought a handsome 110,000 francs from an English buyer. The high price mirrored the 90,000 francs achieved by a replica of his famous *The Artists of all Ages: Hémicycle des Beaux-Arts* (Walters Art Museum, Baltimore), acquired the following year by the American William

[FIG. 4] Paul Delaroche (1797–1856), *The Execution of Lady Jane Grey*, 1833. Oil on canvas, double-lined, 251 × 302 cm (cat. 53). These photographs from the National Gallery conservation dossier, taken in 1974–5, show *The Execution of Lady Jane Grey* before and during restoration.

Walters.[13] Delaroche remained very much to the taste of conservative British and American collectors.

The same was not true in France. His status there was not so much on the wane – he had died in 1856 and artists' reputations often decline after death – as spiralling into oblivion. Modern critical taste found little to appreciate in the high verisimilitude of Delaroche's art. Romantic vignettes from the lives of long-ago kings and queens, however poignant, were increasingly passé in the age of steam and telegraph. A more improvisatory sketch aesthetic was being championed by the young Impressionists and would soon triumph. The art of Delaroche's later years had turned increasingly sentimental and idealising, too, as he himself became more pious and mournful. If, as we will see in Stephen Bann's essay here, the model for Lady Jane had been a glamorous actress with a reputation to suppress, she was succeeded as artist's muse by a saintly wife, sanctified by early death, whom he would immortalise as the *Young Christian Martyr* (cat. 60). A posthumous retrospective exhibition at the Ecole des Beaux-Arts in 1857, prepared by dutiful friends, was to be Delaroche's last Parisian hurrah for a century or more.

Things were slowly beginning to change when *Lady Jane Grey* was rediscovered in 1973 and returned to the National Gallery soon after. An American scholar, Norman Ziff, was preparing a pioneering doctoral dissertation on the painter, completed in 1974 and published three years later.[14] The first slide Francis Haskell showed in 1973 when he delivered his lecture series on rediscoveries in art at New York University was a Delaroche self portrait.[15] Two Delaroche paintings would be included in the 1974–5 Paris exhibition *De David à Delacroix: la peinture française de 1774 à 1830*, a widely influential revisionist assessment of the era. Still, the decision to use National Gallery resources to restore the painting and, late in 1975, to put it on public display, was surprisingly forward thinking. Even then, as Bann has pointed out, *Lady Jane Grey* was presented 'primarily as a curiosity from a previous age'.[16] No attempt was made to promote the artist as a significant figure. On the contrary, an accompanying brochure reprinted an essentially negative assessment of him dating from 1857. The National Gallery's Keeper, Cecil Gould, faced with the task of making the painting 'palatable', penned a notably waspish essay, stating that, among the *cognoscenti*, the artist 'is regarded, when the twentieth century thinks of him at all, as something of a charlatan who merits his present obscurity'. Gould himself was not prepared to refute the opinion. 'The only question concerning him which is likely to interest the current generation,' he declared, 'is just why he was so successful in his lifetime ... [Such] huge, unsophisticated pictures ...

[FIG. 5] Jean-Auguste-Dominique Ingres (1780–1867), *The Martyrdom of Saint Symphorian*, 1834. Oil on canvas, 407×339 cm. Cathédrale Saint-Lazare, Autun

were manna to the Parisian public of the 1830s and 40s.'[17] By implication, it was unlikely London in the 1970s would be similarly taken in.

In 1834, the public had let its feelings for *Lady Jane Grey* be known. In 1975 it intervened in the matter again. Much to the surprise of the director, Michael Levey, the painting quickly established itself as one of the most popular in the National Gallery.[18] As they had at the Paris Salon, admiring crowds gathered in front of it, oblivious to the Gallery's tacit undertaking that they were not really supposed to like it. People wanted to know more about it, how it held such uncanny sway over them, why they found it so powerfully convincing, why, finally, it provoked such a *frisson* of sympathy and dread. That first reaction

[FIG. 6] H.H. Armstead (sculptor, 1828–1905), Albert Memorial frieze, detail showing the *Podium of the Painters*, London (constructed 1872). Paul Delaroche is shown seated in the centre. Positioned behind him from the left are Delacroix, Vernet, Ingres and Decamps.

has continued to this day. Such are the crowds which gather even now to study the canvas in rapt admiration that the polish on the wooden floor directly in front is repeatedly worn away and must be regularly renewed by caretaking staff. *Lady Jane Grey* has remained on view continuously for 35 years now; on the one occasion when it was loaned to a travelling exhibition in 2003, Gallery officials soon heard about visitors' displeasure. Parents are keen to show it to their children, and enraptured schoolchildren to show it to their parents. *Lady Jane Grey* is high on the list of reasons why people come to the National Gallery.

In the meantime, critics and art historians have caught up with the general public. Thanks to Delaroche exhibitions and monographs in recent decades, and surveys in which he figures with increasing prominence, he again plays a significant role in discussions of nineteenth-century art. Once more his achievement is assessed in relation to Delacroix and Ingres, and not dismissively. It is in this context of continued public fascination and growing scholarly appreciation that the present exhibition examines in depth the genesis of a remarkable painting which once survived a flood but had been written off nonetheless.

No less remarkable, a second major painting by Delaroche has recently emerged from obscurity. It too had been rolled up and stored away after suffering damage, in this case almost 70 years ago, and its reappearance now may well prove as significant for an evolving assessment of Delaroche's achievement as the rediscovery of *Lady Jane Grey* did in 1973.

Charles I insulted by the Soldiers of Cromwell (fig. 7) depicts the mockery and disdain to which the monarch was subjected by loutish guards in the days leading to his execution. The painting was commissioned by Lord Francis Egerton, the future Earl of Ellesmere, at the height of Delaroche's fame in the mid-1830s. His brother, the Duke of Sutherland, also acquired a painting on an English historical theme at the same time. On a visit to the artist's studio early in January 1836 Sutherland was able to study that work for the first time, pronouncing *Strafford on his Way to Execution* (cat. 54) 'one of the finest modern pictures I ever saw'. Egerton would be just as satisfied with his painting, the duke reassured their mother, as he had Delaroche's word that '*Charles I* will be as good'. [19] The two paintings were exhibited publicly for the first time at the Paris Salon of 1837. Perhaps because they were painted for scions of an august British family, they are sometimes described as pendants.[20] That the artist did not consider them so, and that he held *Charles I* in particular regard, is suggested by the request he made in the final days of the exhibition. Would the organisers be so kind as to move the painting into the prestigious Salon Carré of the Louvre – the room that gave the annual exhibition its name – and to hang it in the exact same place, 'and at the same height', where *Lady Jane Grey* had hung – and where it had enjoyed unprecedented public acclaim – three years earlier, at the Salon of '34? 'You see that I am not modest,' he wrote.[21]

The success of 1834 was not to be repeated. This time around, the public largely ignored the artist's paintings, and critics were divided. Perhaps that is why Delaroche sought to rehang his strongest submission in a more advantageous position before it was too late. It doesn't seem to have helped. Summing up his assessment of Delaroche's submissions that year – the third picture he showed was *Saint Cecilia* (cat. 58) – Théophile Gautier declared the 1837 Salon a 'fiasco' for the artist.[22] The frenzy that in the past had greeted his monumental depictions of moving moments from English history had begun to dissipate, in France at least. It was the last Paris Salon to which Delaroche would ever send his works. *Charles I* and *Strafford* were brought to Britain when the exhibition closed. The former canvas never returned to France. The death of the Earl of Ellesmere prevented it from

[FIG. 7] Paul Delaroche (1797–1856), *Charles I insulted by the Soldiers of Cromwell*, 1837 (detail). Oil on canvas, 284 × 392 cm. Private collection. This painting was badly damaged during the bombing of Bridgewater House, London, in 1941 (see fig. 8). This photograph was taken during treatment at the National Gallery Conservation Department in 2009. The photograph was taken from an acute angle.

travelling to Paris for the posthumous Delaroche retrospective exhibition of 1857 to which it had been promised. A reproductive engraving of 1842 by Achille Martinet (cat. 55) was largely responsible for keeping alive the memory, such as it was, of one of Delaroche's most ambitious multi-figure compositions.[23]

Both pictures enjoyed far greater success in Britain. Soon after arrival, in 1838, they were exhibited at the British Institution. This helped ensure that, in the words of Haskell, 'for at least two generations they remained by far the best-known French paintings in England'.[24] For decades, *Charles I* hung among the splendid collection of paintings at Bridgewater House, on Cleveland Row in Saint James's, the London home of the Ellesmere family. Other works there included masterpieces of the legendary Orléans collection, not least Titian's *Diana and Actaeon*, jointly acquired in 2009 by the National Gallery and the National Gallery of Scotland, Edinburgh, and its pendant, *Diana and Callisto*. A magnificent pile rebuilt to the plans of Charles Barry in 1847–50, in Victorian times respectable persons could gain admission to Bridgewater House and a view of the collection upon application; indeed, Barry's plans for the house were revised to include a separate staircase leading directly to the picture gallery so that visitors could gain access to the paintings without disrupting the household.[25] At nearby Stafford House they could see Sutherland's *Strafford* as well. The opening of the Wallace Collection in Manchester Square in 1900 brought an additional 12 paintings by Delaroche to public view.[26] With the bequest to the nation in 1902 of *Lady Jane Grey*, and the arrival at the Victoria & Albert Museum of *Saint Cecilia* the following year, in the early twentieth century London was, more so than Paris, the best place in the world to study the art of Delaroche in depth.[27] Moreover, the high esteem in which Britain held Delaroche among contemporary artists had already been memorialised in stone. Along with David, Delacroix, Géricault and Joseph Vernet, to name the Frenchmen of recent vintage, he sits among the sculpted artists on the *Podium of the Painters* of the Albert Memorial, directly opposite the Royal Albert Hall in London, completed in 1872 (fig. 6).

On the night of 11 May 1941, at the height of the Blitz, Bridgewater House was hit by a German bomb (fig. 8). The ground and first floors at the northwest corner of the building sustained structural damage, and a 10-foot-deep crater opened up in the street. *Charles I*, then hanging in the dining room, received extensive shrapnel damage in a pattern of 'wounds' that suggests the blast came from below. Indeed, the lower right side of the picture appears to have been slightly more affected by the blast than other areas of the canvas, suggesting that this edge was closest to the site of the detonation.[28] Conservators have counted more than 200 tears to the canvas, large and small, received that night. Significant traces of plaster dust from shattered walls have been found on the picture surface as well, blown there by the force of the explosion.

In the immediate aftermath of the attack, with rescue work to be undertaken as quickly as possible, remedial action began. The canvas was removed from its stretcher. Paper was laid down on the picture over the larger tears, those most vulnerable to flaking and paint loss, thus partially consolidating the surface. The canvas was rolled. Evacuated to a country house in the Scottish Borders, the painting remained there, safe and dry, until it was unrolled again – not without emotion on the part of the curators of the present exhibition – in June 2009. Its war wounds notwithstanding, the picture was discovered to be almost entirely legible. The indignities heaped upon a Christ-like king are as poignant now as ever they were. A conservation campaign is underway. Henceforth, a final, magisterial component of Delaroche's artistic achievement must be taken into account in any assessment of a painter who, today no less than at the height of his fame in the 1830s, deserves the rare and honourable epithet 'popular'.

[FIG. 8] Bridgewater House, St James's, London, following the bombing of 11 May 1941. Photograph *The Times*

NOTES & REFERENCES

1. London 1930, p. 8.

2. Johnstone's comments come in a letter of 25 January 1999 and an e-mail of 31 August 2009, copies of which are in the National Gallery dossier, Delaroche NG 53. Tate does not currently list the Martin in its collection.

3. London 1930, p. 8.

4. London 1930, p. 8.

5. Alley 1959, p. 298. Word reached the Louvre; the mount for a sheet of studies by Delaroche in the Cabinet des dessins, RF 35133, recto (cat. 66), which includes a compositional sketch for *Lady Jane Grey*, is annotated: *Jane Grey (Tate) détruit.*

6. '… des sujets propres à attaquer le système nerveux de son public.' A. Tardieu, *Le Courrier français*, cited in Lee 2007, p. 100.

7. '… dans tous les salons, dans toutes les boutiques, son nom est répété aujourd'hui avec les éloges qui accompagnaient, il y a quinze ans, celui de M. Gérard, et celui de David il y a trente ans.' Cited in Lee 2007, p. 101.

8. For an exhaustive study of the Ingres and its reception at the Salon, see Shelton 2005, pp. 15–53.

9. ' … l'un est un grand et noble poème, l'autre est une touchante nouvelle.' Lee 2007, p. 101.

10. '… la même vision, une horrible vision.' The story of Ingres's despair is told by a guest at the Villa Medici at that time, a Lady Charlemont of whom little is known. Bertin 1997, p. 55.

11. 'Malheureusement pour eux, ils sont en arrière de trente ans.' Ingres was writing to his prospective father-in-law, Pierre Forestier, from Florence on 1 October 1806. Cited in Riopelle 1999, p. 235.

12. On the prince and his collection, many works from which are now in the Wallace Collection, see London 1994.

13. Walters acted through the agent George Lucas to acquire the replica, which is the work of Delaroche and his student Charles Béranger. The complicated authorship of the work and its protracted acquisition history have been worked out by Stephen Bann in 'Reassessing Repetition in Nineteenth-Century Academic Painting: Delaroche, Gérôme, Ingres' in Kahng 2007, pp. 27–51.

14. Ziff 1977. For the revival of Delaroche's reputation, see Barringer 2001.

15. Haskell 1975. The lectures were published as *Rediscoveries in Art: Some Aspects of Taste, Fashion and Collecting in England and France*, London, 1976.

16. Bann 1997, p. 22.

17. Gould in London 1975, unpaginated.

18. Bann 1997, p. 22, cites a 1996 letter from Levey.

19. Letter of 8 January 1836, Sutherland Papers, National Library of Scotland. I thank Stephen Bann for furnishing this citation.

20. Nantes and Montpellier 1999, p. 297.

21. See Chronology, pp. 157–9.

22. *La Presse*, 10 March 1837, quoted in *Paul Delaroche*, see Nantes and Montpellier 1999, p. 297.

23. Better known in Britain was a mezzotint after the painting by Saunders, an impression of which is in the Ashmolean Museum, Oxford.

24. Haskell 1975, p. 66.

25. 'The Altered Plan of Bridgewater House, London', *The Builder*, 13 October 1849, p. 484.

26. On which see London 1997.

27. Three more Delaroche paintings figured in the Royal Collection, all of them depictions of the Emperor Napoleon, but they were not accessible to the public.

28. Information on the bombing of Bridgewater House in 1941 contained in the Westminster Civil Defence archive has been furnished by Rory Lalwan of the City of Westminster Archives Centre.

The Sense of the Past

LINDA WHITELEY

In 1823, Sir Walter Scott published his first novel on a French theme, a chronicle of the life and times of a real historical figure, Louis XI of France, seen through the eyes of an imaginary one: Quentin Durward, a Scottish archer. In contrast to his usual rapid pace of composition, *Quentin Durward* necessitated many hours of research, much of it in the Advocates Library in Edinburgh.[1] One of the initial sources of Scott's inspiration for the book, however, sprang from the visit of his friend, James Skene (a fellow advocate and amateur painter), newly back from a tour in France, with travel accounts, sketches and a collection of manuscripts, a resource to delight a novelist-antiquarian, eager to take a subject at some distance from his customary interests. Skene's architectural sketches must have been of special interest in this context, since the ancient castle of Plessis-les-Tours, west of Tours, was to play a central role in the narrative. While in Aix-en-Provence, where for some time he had a house, Skene had come to know the Marquis de Forbin, the descendant of an ancient Provençal family. The Marquis gave him a vivid account of the revolutionary years, and of the resulting devastation of his own chateau, La Barben (fig. 9), an account which Walter Scott was to adapt, in his introduction to *Quentin Durward*, as a fictional visit to a nobleman in whose 'curious Gothic library', he pored over ancient chronicles which, he claimed, formed the basis for the novel.[2] While living in Aix, where he had a number of friends, Skene may have come across a copy of one of the earliest volumes of the *Voyages pittoresques et romantiques en l'ancienne France*, a picturesque tour by Charles Nodier and Isidore Taylor, published from 1820, in which the link between medieval architecture and the history of 'l'ancienne France' was reinforced on almost every page (cat. 7). In Charles Nodier's words: 'As for ourselves, the last travellers among the ruins of old France, shortly to disappear, we choose to depict only those ruins whose secrets and whose history would otherwise be lost forever...'[3] Scott was already keenly aware of the power of buildings to evoke poetic and historic associations, and thus to stimulate literary creation; in *The Lay of the Last Minstrel*, published in 1805, the destiny of the St Clair family is embedded within the stones of Rosslyn Chapel (cat. 3):

Blaz'd battlement, and pinnet high,
Blaz'd every rose-carved buttress fair
So still they blaze, when fate is nigh,
The lowly line of high St Clair.[4]

Antiquarianism, the collection and study of historical remains, had been satirised since the seventeenth century as the pursuit of antique trivia by unworldly scholars. In early nineteenth-century France, however, it took a particularly popular and emotive form, in reaction to the destruction of antiquities during the Revolution. The Musée des monuments français, set up by Alexandre Lenoir in an abandoned monastery in Paris as a refuge for fragments of monuments and other works of art salvaged from destruction, became a place where what was lost could be reconstructed through the evocative power of relics.[5] Lenoir transformed the collection, set up originally as a simple repository, into a fashionable museum which was open to the public from 1795. It was divided into a series of rooms, each evoking a particular period of the French past. A number of artists, including Fleury Richard, Charles-Marie Bouton and Henriette Lorimier (cats. 1, 6), responded to the 'inspiration of the past' embodied in the museum, not only by incorporating the 'real' appearance of ancient artefacts into their work, but at times evoking by scenes from history which otherwise might have been left to the imagination of the visitor. When Bouton painted the *Fourteenth-Century Room* in the museum, he converted it, as it were, into a theatrical set, for the staging of the madness of Charles VI. This kind of evocation was to have a number of parallels with the pages of the *Voyages pittoresques*, to which Bouton himself (as well as a number of theatrical scene-painters) contributed.

The response of historians and artists to Lenoir's museum was echoed throughout France wherever there were ruins of ancient buildings destroyed by the Revolution. François-Marius Granet, one of the pioneers of 'historic genre', was first moved to paint a picture of this type by the sight of a moonlit Paris cloister which had been laid to waste during the Revolution,[6] while the haunting atmosphere of his *Choir of the Capuchin Church* (cat. 2), his most famous work, was inspired by the desolate interior of a chapel in the temporarily abandoned Capuchin monastery in Rome, which Granet, like Bouton, peopled with the ghosts of those who had once occupied the place.[7] The theme had an obvious appeal for painters like Pierre Revoil and Fleury Richard, who came from Lyon, a city devastated by a Revolutionary army in 1793, as it had for Auguste de Forbin, Granet's friend and fellow painter, and younger brother of Skene's informant, whose father and uncle had been killed in the sack of Lyon.[8] The emotion which affects their work is not only a romantic nostalgia for a distant past, but a political nostalgia for a world which had only recently been destroyed. Not all those who bought pictures of this type were royalists, nor all those who painted them, but it was, nevertheless, a kind of art which appealed strongly to those who were.

Revoil, Richard and their colleagues were known to contemporaries as the 'Troubadour painters', because of their liking for painting scenes set in the Middle Ages, with appropriate period detail. However, it is a slightly misleading term, since their subject matter covered several centuries, encompassing the scope of Lenoir's museum, including the Renaissance and the seventeenth century. The common thread in their work is a fascination with the history of the French monarchy and aristocracy, often in its more private aspects, and with its related artefacts. This was not conventional history painting in the manner of David (in whose studio several of the original Troubadours had been trained), but owed much to the finely painted, illusionistic art of seventeenth-century Dutch genre painters such as Gerrit Dou and Gabriel Metsu, a tendency still evident in certain works of Paul Delaroche.

THE DIORAMA

The *Voyages pittoresques* marked a transition between the antiquarian themes of the Troubadours and a new, often more lively and naturalistic, treatment of subject matter, accompanied by an emphasis on the sense of place. The atmospheric use of light which could be obtained through the use of lithography played its part in bringing the past to life, as it did in the works of the Troubadours, and as it was to do again in the Diorama, a spectacular entertainment which occupied a position somewhere between painting and theatre.[9] In one sense a forerunner of the cinema, it consisted of large scenic paintings on thin linen which was partially transparent, allowing its creators to simulate different light effects or weather conditions through the changing use of light and a revolving auditorium (see cat. 3).

Situated not far from the popular theatres of the Boulevard du Temple, the Diorama was devised by Louis-Jacques-Mandé Daguerre and Charles-Marie Bouton, two painters who had contributed to the *Voyages pittoresques*. Daguerre had begun his career as a scene painter, but shortly afterwards followed Bouton in painting atmospheric interiors in the manner of Granet and the Troubadours. Light itself, manipulated to create thrilling scene changes within a single picture, became a kind of silent narrator in the painted spectacles mounted by Bouton and Daguerre. It was also a keen interest in the power of light which was to lead Daguerre into his pioneering research into photography. The most striking achievement of the Diorama was the production of an irresistible illusion of reality, combined (and how unlike the still art of painting, in this respect), with an illusion of movement. Two early subjects, *The Ruins of Holyrood Chapel* and *Rosslyn Chapel* (both 1824), played to an audience already warmly receptive not only to the fascination of ruins, but to everything epitomised by the cult of Walter Scott. Delaroche had no known connection with the Diorama, but could not have failed to be aware of it. His own dramatic use of light in *The Princes in the Tower*, suddenly visible then partially obscured, announces their imminent fate; in *Lady Jane Grey*, like a swelling chord, it seems to mark her own brief progress from imprisonment to martyrdom.[10]

[FIG. 9] François-Marius Granet (1777–1849), *Vue du château de la Barben*, about 1797. Crayon and grey wash on paper, 15 × 19.2 cm. Musée Granet, Aix-en-Provence

PAINTING AND THE THEATRE

The impact of the new historicism of Granet and the Troubadours, and the example of the *Voyage pittoresques* on theatrical set design, were first visible in the popular theatre. The sets which Julien-Michel Gué designed in 1822 for a boulevard melodrama, based on Scott's *The Abbot*,[11] are in the manner of Nodier and Taylor's illustrations.[12] Some years later, Gué was to work again on an adaptation of Scott, collaborating with Eugène Delacroix on a production of Victor Hugo's *Amy Robsart*.[13] It was Baron Taylor himself, one of the editors of the *Voyages pittoresques*, who was to transpose the new manner to the classical theatre when, in 1825, he took up an appointment at the Comédie-Française, and immediately established a new kind of staging with his first production based on authentic detail and historical accuracy.[14] These innovations, as the great actor François-Joseph Talma acknowledged at the end of the first performance, marked the salvation of the French theatre.[15] In 1827, four years after the publication of *Quentin Durward*, Taylor produced a play on the subject of Louis XI (Scott's central character), in which he intended to evoke a vast tableau of France in the fifteenth century, based on a detailed documentation remarkably similar to Scott's preliminary work for *Quentin Durward*. Taylor could also draw upon his experience on the editorial board of the *Voyages pittoresques*. Pierre-Luc-Charles Cicéri, the designer of the sets for *Louis XI*, made use of sketches of the Château of Plessis-les-Tours made on the spot for the *Voyages pittoresques*,[16] while, as the critic of the theatre newspaper *La Pandore* noted, the staging itself recalled the work of the Troubadours: 'The production of *Louis XI* consists of a series of pictures in the manner of Richard and of Granet.'[17] He also observed, however, that while the new designs were based on the work of older artists, they were providing a model for imitation by a younger generation: 'At one time, our painting teachers forbade their pupils to copy actors' costumes; now, our art students are recommended to look to the theatre for models of truth and accuracy',[18] words which apply, with some aptness, to Delaroche's own work in these same years. The historicising poetics already established in the *Voyages*, together with a commitment to historical accuracy, were to give a new direction to French theatre and, in turn, a vivid source from which painters could draw inspiration. Delaroche's response to the particular theatricality of these productions goes some way to accounting for the peculiar force of his reconstitution of history.

If Delaroche's own direct debt to Fleury Richard and the other so-called Troubadours, visible in his *Filippo Lippi* (cat. 24), was short-lived (though his refined handling of paint, particularly evident in the gleaming satin of the dress of Lady Jane Grey, suggests a common debt to Northern art), the impact of a new kind of theatre was of extreme importance as a stimulus to his imagination. It is visible both in his small-scale pictures and in his large works on English themes, *The Execution of Lady Jane Grey*, *Cromwell and Charles I* and *Strafford on his Way to Execution*, in which he takes the potential of theatricality beyond the capacity of the stage itself, to the kind of narrative associated rather with the omniscience of the novel, or even the cinema.

The increasing tendency in the 1820s for French theatre to draw on pictorial forms is exemplified in the growing practice of dividing a play into so-called 'tableaux' rather than acts; thus, Alexandre Dumas's absurd *Catherine Howard*, produced in 1829, is described as a 'drame en cinq actes et huit tableaux'. On a number of occasions, paintings by Delaroche were recreated (or represented, on at least one occasion) in the theatre. The most famous instance of this is found in the staging of his friend Casimir Delavigne's play *Les Enfants d'Edouard*, which was closely based on Delaroche's painting, *The Princes in the Tower* (cat. 14), but his pictures of *Joan of Arc*, *Cromwell and Charles I* and *Lady Jane Grey* were also incorporated into theatre productions.[19]

CHARLES NODIER'S ROMANTIC COTERIE

Baron Taylor was not the only link between the *Voyages pittoresques* and the theatre of the 1820s; his co-editor, Charles Nodier, was also at the centre of the interacting worlds of painting, literature and the theatre. He too had written for the theatre, but in addition, he was host to a lively salon at the beautiful library of the Arsenal (of which he was the Keeper), and was also a frequent guest, together with Delaroche and Ary Scheffer, at the home of the sculptor Félicie de Fauveau (fig. 10), in the rue de la Rochefoucauld. There, the company would often entertain themselves by drawing in a range of experimental techniques, and by modelling in clay, possibly including small figures which, arranged on a miniature stage, could serve as models for painting.[20] We know that Delaroche used plaster models in preparation for *The Princes in the Tower*,[21] and one might easily imagine that he employed the practice of working from models in a little theatre from the careful *mise-en-scène* of *The Assassination of the Duc de Guise* (cat. 51).

Félicie de Fauveau was passionately interested in the Middle Ages and its artefacts: she collected manuscripts, and is said to have strongly encouraged Delaroche to take an interest in this period. It is also said that she intervened to obtain a commission for Delaroche to decorate a ceiling in the Musée Charles X, which was set up in the Cour Carrée of the Louvre in 1827.[22] She was, apparently, keenly interested in the question of usurpation, as was Delaroche himself, from the evidence of his paintings. However, while Delaroche's political sympathies are not clear, Félicie de Fauveau was an outspoken romantic monarchist, friend of the Duchesse de Berry and ally of the Comtesse de La Roche-Jacquelein, with whom she was later imprisoned for their part in a counter-revolutionary uprising in 1830. On her release from prison, she left Paris to spend the rest of her life in Florence, and there is no further evidence of what had been a productive, perhaps even an intense friendship. The original frame for *Lady Jane Grey*, however, by then hanging in the Demidoff collection in Florence, has been attributed to her design.[23]

FRENCH IMPRESSIONS OF ENGLAND

In 1821, Charles Nodier published his account of a journey from Normandy through England to Scotland, *Promenade de Dieppe aux montagnes d'Ecosse*, starting off, therefore, in a part of France with strong English connections, and ending in the country of Sir Walter Scott. In the course of his journey, like Théodore Géricault, at about the same time, he noted his impressions of English art. We now know, too, that Delaroche made this journey in early 1822, when he visited the collection of armour belonging to Samuel Rush Meyrick.[24] Like Richard Parkes Bonington and Delacroix, who visited the collection a few years later (cat. 12), he was probably drawn to it as a source of visual documentation. Delaroche did not work for Nodier's *Voyages pittoresques*, but in 1826, in company with his fellow students Eugène Lami and Bonington, he contributed two lithographs (cat. 9) to accompany texts from Walter Scott for a book of picturesque views of Scotland, brought out by Amédée Pichot, a translator of Scott and an ardent anglophile.[25]

A year earlier, Pichot had published his impressions of England,[26] adopting the fiction of a set of letters, in one of which, addressed to Delaroche, he discussed the most eminent English painters of the moment, reserving his warmest praise for the 'chaste' Sir Joshua Reynolds, and the illustrators Richard Westall and Thomas Stothard.[27] He also encouraged Delaroche to take a subject from Scott's 1816 novel, *Old Mortality*, a work in which he himself saw parallels with French history. This was a comparison which Delaroche seems to have taken up in the 1830s, when he turned to subjects from the English Civil War (though almost certainly not quite in the manner Pichot had imagined). The letters contain frequent references to Scott, and include extended accounts of visits to Scott's house at Abbotsford in the Scottish borders and to Rosslyn, outside Edinburgh.

[FIG. 10]
Ary Scheffer (1795–1858), *Portrait of Félicie de Fauveau*, 1829.
Oil on wood, 103.3 × 72 cm.
Musée du Louvre, Paris (RF1222)

[FIG. 11]
Paul Delaroche (1797–1856), *Joan of Arc*, 1824.
Oil on canvas, 277 × 217.5 cm.
Musée des Beaux-Arts de Rouen (982.6.1)

Three of the letters, in all, are addressed to Delaroche, and others to Charles Nodier, to Casimir Delavigne, and to Baron Taylor (chiefly about painting). Mary Stuart haunts several of the scenes Pichot describes, as does the family of St Clair, at Rosslyn, no doubt as a result of stimulating conversations with Sir Walter himself.

Through this gathering of correspondents, Pichot evokes the idea of a little circle with a shared interest in Britain, its history, politics, scenery, literature and art, at the centre of a world of anglophiles and antiquarians. It was, above all, English literature which excited interest in England in the years after Waterloo. A generation of young artists discovered sources of inspiration in the works of fashionable British writers: Shakespeare, Byron and (especially) Walter Scott. A number of these artists – Bonington, Lami, Delaroche and Camille Roqueplan – were pupils of Baron Gros, who, in his earlier years, had already made a careful study of English painting of the late eighteenth century.[28] Interest in British history, as well as literature, increased phenomenally in the studios of artists. This was a remarkable movement, particularly as few writers, other than Greek and Roman authors, had inspired artists before the 1820s.

Daguerre's brother-in-law, the dealer John Arrowsmith, best remembered for having introduced John Constable's work to France, was a powerful catalyst in the development of Anglo-French contacts (see cat. 11–13). It was a role for which he was well prepared by birth and upbringing. His mother was Irish, his father English, but he was brought up in France, where his father had been employed as an agent of the anglophile Duc d'Orléans, the notorious Philippe Egalité, on his estate at Monceau. His sister was god-daughter to the Princesse de Lamballe, who died in the Terror, like her close friend, Marie-Antoinette. We know little else about Arrowsmith's childhood, but, as Delaroche may have known, it must have been deeply marked by the events of the Revolution.[29]

According to his own account, Arrowsmith took Constable's pictures to France 'in order to give the French an idea of English painting', encouraged, perhaps, by the kind of (qualified) enthusiasm for English art expressed by Géricault, Nodier and Pichot. He also gave important support to a group of young French painters, several of whom, like Delacroix, were attracted in the 1820s to aspects of English art. At the Salon of 1824, where he showed Constable's *Hay Wain*, one of the most famous English paintings of the nineteenth century, he also exhibited Delaroche's *Joan of Arc* (fig. 11), one of the most talked-about French paintings of that year's exhibition.[30] Arrowsmith (together with two members of the royal family, the Duchesse d'Orléans and the Duchesse de Berry) was one of Delaroche's earliest patrons. They may have met in early 1822, and were in London together at the end of that year, when they visited the Meyrick collection of armour (cat. 11). It was Arrowsmith who first realised the commercial potential of making prints after Delaroche's work when he commissioned a mezzotint after his *Filippo Lippi enamoured of his Model*. This was the earliest of a number of paintings from which Arrowsmith commissioned reproductions in mezzotint, from the 'Engraver to the King', S.W. Reynolds, whom he brought over to Paris for that purpose. Thus Delaroche, almost from the first, was in contact with English circles, partly, at least, through the agency of Arrowsmith. On his return to England in 1827 to prepare for his work on *The Princes in the Tower*, Delaroche probably visited the Tower itself, and may have been sufficiently moved by its gloomy and forbidding atmosphere to continue the 'narrative of the Tower', in two further compositions, *The Execution of Lady Jane Grey* and *Strafford on his Way to Execution*.

THE SHAKESPEARE GALLERY

While Delaroche's illusionism, historicism and sense of place date his work to the period in which he worked, he also adopted elements from the work of a number of eighteenth-century British artists who had previously painted subjects from history in which a sense of spectacle and a feeling for theatrical effects were combined. Like David, and like his own master, Gros, he seems to have taken note of the heroic images of modern life painted by the Anglo-American artists Benjamin West and John Singleton Copley (notably when painting *The Taking of the Trocadéro*, which has been likened to Copley's giant *Siege of Gibraltar*),[31] and may also have known William Martin's extremely large *The Death of Lady Jane Gray* (if only from Francesco Bartolozzi's print, fig. 12).[32]

For his historical compositions, Delaroche turned to a group of British artists who had tackled medieval and later themes. He almost certainly did not know these works in their original form, but prints of them would have been easily available to him through his father, an eminent picture dealer, or through his mother's relations, who were Keepers of Prints at what is now the Bibliothèque nationale de France. The publication of these prints in England was initially due to the enterprising John Boydell, print-publisher and impresario of the Shakespeare Gallery (a series of large paintings on Shakespearean themes, commissioned by Boydell and exhibited in Pall Mall). It was Boydell's hope that he could turn the enterprise to profit by the sale of prints after the paintings, and though, in this respect, the Gallery was not ultimately successful, the prints themselves were widely distributed and became a source of imagery for artists throughout Europe.[33] The choice of Shakespeare as subject was an inspired one, allowing, as it did, the chance to represent scenes from English history from its earliest record, while the literary and theatrical character of the source offered a particular challenge to the artists, to rival or to transform the poetic text. A comparison with the theatre was, and is, inevitable, with such a programme, and it is clear that for Delaroche, certain of the Boydell images, enacted by apparently life-size figures, dominating their pictorial space, were of the greatest importance as elements in his own self-imposed task of reconstituting history. Among the most significant are those in which the dramatic action is suspended, and which thus have something of the character of a *tableau vivant*, as if, for the moment, the spectator steps out of a continuous narrative, to view a momentary synthesis of time, plot and character. The effect of the real, paradoxically, is heightened by the act staging of it, as a musical composition returns to life each time it is played. This is perhaps the aspect of the 'repetitive', in the sense of 'rehearsing', which seems to offer a clue to the nature of Delaroche's 'realism', for it is always a figured reality. This is particularly true in the case of those pictures of his which most evidently recall representation itself, whether within the actual theatre, or in its translation, as in Boydell's prints, or even

[FIG. 12] Francesco Bartolozzi (1727–1815), after William Martin (1753–1831), *The Death of Lady Jane Gray* [sic], 1790. Stipple engraving, 29.3 × 38.8 cm. Norwich Castle Museum and Art Gallery (NWHCM: 1978.20.2)

from the domain of painting itself, exemplified by Delaroche's common references to archetypal images of religious martyrdom. *Lady Jane Grey* clearly invites comparison with images such as Veronese's *Martyrdom of Santa Justina* (cat. 65), but, as contemporaries quickly noticed, Delaroche had also used a print after John Opie's *Execution of Mary Queen of Scots* as a source for his picture. This, presumably, is what Ingres had in mind when he described Delaroche's picture as a 'vignette anglaise'. Ingres was chagrined that *Lady Jane Grey* had enjoyed a critical triumph at the Salon of 1834 when his own ambitious *Martyrdom of Saint Symphorian* (fig. 5, p. 19) had been given a lukewarm reception. But the remark, although dismissive, points to a real difference between Ingres's grandiose but somewhat old-fashioned masterpiece and Delaroche's composition, which eliminates everything which is not central to the narrative.

The print after Opie was not published by Boydell, but by Robert Bowyer, in a series of illustrations to David Hume's *History of England*, commissioned by Bowyer in imitation of Boydell's enterprise. Bowyer's project, like Boydell's, demonstrates how closely, in fact, the genres of history, theatre and literature could co-exist in late eighteenth-century England. Hume's text is ostensibly historical, but has much in common with the novel, and for this reason it must have been a particularly potent source of inspiration to Delaroche. It was a combination which made it possible for him to create an imaginative reconstruction of historical figures, as important to him as it was to Sir Walter Scott. This explains, perhaps, why he never painted a picture directly after a work by Scott. Unlike Delacroix, who found much rich material for his imagination in fiction and poetry, Delaroche seems, almost invariably, to have turned to historians, such as Hume, Châteaubriand, Lamartine, Barante (fig. 19), or, in the case of Lady Jane Grey, significantly, to a Protestant martyrology, published by the Huguenot Jean Crespin in 1565.[34] A certain fidelity to his sources marks his work, and gives it what might be termed an 'imaginative impartiality'. In his paintings of the 1830s, in particular, he seems to stand back from his subject in the manner of a rigorous historian. This appearance of detachment, however, only adds to the dramatic impact of his themes. In the 1830s, for those with memories of the French Revolution, which of them would not have been reminded of the fates of Louis XVI, Marie-Antoinette and the Dauphin, before these images of earlier royal martyrs, Jane Grey, the Princes in the Tower and Charles I? Delaroche clearly made such associations in his own mind, as is suggested by a sheet of studies (cat. 66) in which thumbnail drawings for Lady Jane Grey appear alongside a composition of the Dauphin (by then Louis XVII) and his sister, in the prison of the Temple. As Delaroche read Jean Crespin's account, it may have been not only the pathos of the particular episode, but the parallel with recent events which led him to embark upon his own painted martyrology.

When preparing *Lady Jane Grey*, Delaroche must have drawn on a range of Boydell's images as a repertory or even, one is tempted to say, as a dressing-up box. The scene from *Othello, Act II, Scene I* (cat. 18) with its raised stage and tripartite arrangement of figures, the innocent victim in white, at the centre, the villainous Iago brooding in shadow to the left, his pose comparable with that of Delaroche's executioner, seems to offer a model. *Henry VIII leading Anne Boleyn to the Dance* (cat. 17) makes use of a similar, essentially frontal staging, typical of many of the Boydell prints; Henry's gesture may be compared with that of the Lieutenant of the Tower guiding Jane Grey to the block, and, whether or not Stothard intended it, Henry might be seen as leading his unhappy victim to a dance of death. Delaroche's interest in Henry VIII and his wives, at a period when he was beginning to plan *Lady Jane Grey*, is confirmed by the red chalk drawing in this exhibition which shows the seated king surrounded by several of his wives (cat. 49). The drawings on the verso of this sheet provide precise evidence of his interest in the contemporary French stage, with which he had several links. These drawings (which clearly anticipate the composition of *The Assassination of the Duc de Guise*), have recently been linked with Alexandre Dumas's *Henri III et sa cour*, a production with which, as the drawings prove, Delaroche must have been connected, though the suggestion that he designed the costumes has never been confirmed.[35] The kind of peepshow *mise-en-scène* employed in these drawings suggests the compositional methods which underpin several of his smaller pictures in the few years immediately before Jane Grey, notably *The Death of Mazarin* (Wallace Collection, London) and *The Assassination of the Duc de Guise*, and was not without enduring influence on later art, most obviously in the world of cinema. His return in *The Execution of Lady Jane Grey* to a large-scale composition illustrating English history, with its highly original and imaginative use of English prints allied to a resonant reference to archetypal religious imagery (and particularly to the theme of martyrdom), was to mark the beginning of a series of his most exemplary historical subjects.

NOTES & REFERENCES

1. Lockhart 1914, p. 253.

2. I am extremely grateful to Mrs Sheila McKinnon, who has prepared a biography of James Skene, and has very kindly provided me with a great deal of information about him.

3. De Cailleux, Nodier and Taylor 1820–1878 (1825 edn).

4. Maggi 1999, p. 262.

5. Haskell 1993, pp. 236–52.

6. Aix en Provence 2008, p. 51, n. 2, with a quotation from Granet's memoirs.

7. Bann 1999, p. 49.

8. For an account of Granet and the Forbin family, including Granet's painted decoration for what must have been the 'curious Gothic library' evoked by Scott, see Aix-en-Provence 2008, pp. 56–63, n. 5.

9. See Gernsheim 1956.

10. For a discussion of the importance of Daguerre and the Diorama in theatrical production, see Allévy 1938, pp. 41–50.

11. G. de Pixérécourt, *Le Château de Lochleven, ou la captivité de Marie Stuart*, staged at the Théâtre de la Gaité in Paris. Pixérécourt's name appears in the list of subscribers to the *Voyages pittoresques*.

12. Illustrated in Wright 1997, p. 87, fig. 30.

13. See Kemp 1973, pp. 214–27.

14. Michel Pichat's *Léonidas*.

15. Mirecourt 1854, p. 63, in Allévy 1938, p. 77, n. 1.

16. Allévy 1938, p. 78, n. 5.

17. 18 February 1827. Quoted in Allévy 1938, p. 79. Maurice Samuels draws attention to a similar comparison, this time with the new historiography of Prosper de Barante, which the critic Alfred de Nettement dismissed in 1836 'not in terms of politics, but in terms of vision… transforming the past into "une série de tableaux"'. Samuels 2003, p. 253.

18. *La Pandore*, 18 February 1827. Quoted in Allévy 1938, p. 78.

19. Ziff 1977, p. 39, for Alexandre Soumet's play *Joan of Arc* (1825); Meisel 1983, p. 239, discusses Cordellier-Delanoue's *Cromwell and Charles I*, in this light; for *Lady Jane Grey*, see the opening of the essay by Stephen Bann of this publication, p. 35.

20. For a recent discussion of Félicie de Fauveau, with bibliography, see Mascalchi 2005, pp. 50–9. I am grateful to Stephen Duffy for this reference, and for providing me with a copy of this article.

21. For a stimulating discussion of this aspect of Delaroche's work (and much else in this connection), see Doherty 2006, pp. 38–59.

22. This may explain why Delaroche made it a condition that his contribution should include a sculptural element.

23. Discussed in Mascalchi 2005, n. 20.

24. For this highly significant discovery, see Duffy 2009, pp. 284–92.

25. Pichot 1826.

26. Pichot 1825. Pichot had made the journey in 1822.

27. Bisson 1942, p. 182, n.1, suggests that Delaroche probably met Pichot through Charles Nodier.

28. For a searching article on this subject, see Joannides 1975, pp. 774–85.

29. The most vivid account of Arrowsmith's father is to be found in Birrell 1931. I owe this reference to Taylor 2001. An account of Arrowsmith's parentage, not altogether accurate, is given in Gernsheim 1956, pp. 7–8, n. 9.

30. For an extremely full discussion of this picture, see Paris 1983.

31. See Bann 2006, pp. 344–7.

32. I am grateful to Mhairi Doble (of Norwich City Hall), and Norma Watt (of the Norwich Castle Museum) for their very kind help in connection with this painting.

33. For a recent analysis of this, see Sillars 2006, pp. 254–99.

34. Crespin 1565. The account of Lady Jane Grey appears on pp. 454–60.

35. See the essay by Stephen Bann p. 35 of this publication for a discussion of these drawings and their possible significance.

The Victim as Spectacle: Paul Delaroche's 'Lady Jane Grey' and Mademoiselle Anaïs

STEPHEN BANN

On 30 March 1844, the first performance of Alexandre Soumet's play *Jane Grey* took place at the Odéon Theatre in Paris. After the execution scene, according to the stage directions: 'There appears in the distance the picture by M. Paul Delaroche'. This was not the very painting that the admiring Parisian public had seen a decade before at the 1834 Salon. That had passed into the collection of the wealthy Russian Count Anatole Demidoff, and would not be visible until the retrospective following the artist's death in 1856. But Soumet assumed that theatregoers would recall seeing the original picture in 1834, or at least be familiar with one of the engraved reproductions that appeared in illustrated magazines. Here is an episode where Delaroche's kinship with theatre is evident, and it leads to the following question. How may we understand the close link between *The Execution of Lady Jane Grey* and the practices of dramatic representation current in Paris over the period? I shall attempt to answer this question on two levels, first by underlining the relevance to his work of the concept of 'spectacle', and secondly by focusing on his relationship with one particular actress, Mademoiselle Anaïs, which helps us to understand the special appeal of his *Lady Jane Grey*.

In this debate about painting and theatre, it is not just a question of the painter copying dramatic effects. Even where Delaroche appears close to theatrical spectacle, the objective is to reinvigorate the art of picture-making. When the noted critic and novelist Stendhal appraised Delaroche's *Death of Elizabeth* at the 1827/8 Salon, he made the distinction clear by condemning the tendency of French painters to 'répétition'; by this he explicitly meant copying the manner of the classical actor François-Joseph Talma, which had 'ruined the pictures of the old adherents of David'. With reference to this aping of the conventional gestures of the stage, Stendhal claimed: 'The *Death of Queen Elizabeth*, by M. Delaroche, is free from this unfortunate fault. Thus the spectator believes himself to be taking part in this terrifying spectacle.'[1] For Stendhal, Delaroche's achievement was precisely to have broken with the clichés of Neoclassicism, and to have inaugurated a new, intense form of audience participation, giving the illusion of being a witness to the event portrayed. In 1850, Delaroche's pupil, the painter Ernest Hébert, reinforced this claim in a letter which pinpointed the achievement: 'you are the man who succeeded in moving people through the profound observation of concentrated drama, and through veiled terror (the gesture of Jane Gray [sic], the dog of the Princes in the Tower). The [Assassination of] the Duc de Guise is a masterpiece and perhaps even the masterpiece of present times.'[2]

Yet we get no further by endorsing contemporary judgements that credit the success of Delaroche's paintings to their kinship with spectacle. What must be explained is the variety of different levels through which this new direction may be understood, and especially its integral connection with Delaroche's representation of victimhood. The theme of the victim, or martyr, runs throughout his entire career, and is central to this exhibition. It is definitively expressed in his rendering of *Lady Jane Grey*. The previously unpublished material relating to Delaroche's personal life in the period when he was painting this work suggests a new dimension to his involvement in theatre. It does not in itself explain the dramatic effect of the work. But it shows that the emotional appeal of the historical victim was intensified, in this case, by Delaroche's passion for a luminary of the stage.

Before turning to biography, however, it is necessary to give an account of Delaroche's position as a rising young artist in post-Napoleonic France, which will demonstrate the differing facets of his engagement with 'spectacle'. The novelist Balzac, whose *Comédie humaine* is a barometer of the national scene, visualises two students living penuriously in a garret in the Latin Quarter in the early 1830s, and taking stock of the turbulent history of their times: 'We looked on all these things as a spectacle, and we complained about them without ourselves taking sides.'[3] In the mid-1820s Balzac inhabited the same building in the present rue Visconti as Delaroche and his friend from Baron Gros' studio, Eugène Lami. The situation of these rising young artists would not have been very different from the fictional case imagined by Balzac. Born in 1797 to the family of a cultivated but hardly wealthy picture dealer, Delaroche had just reached adulthood when Waterloo sealed Napoleon's defeat, and the exiled Bourbons returned to rule France through an untried system of constitutional monarchy on the English model. Destined early for an artistic career, he entered the studio taken over by Gros when his master Jacques-Louis David was exiled for signing the death sentence passed on Louis XVI.

Delaroche first exhibited at the 1822 Paris Salon, and made his mark at the 1824 Salon, when Stendhal predicted that his *Joan of Arc* (fig. 11) would 'make a name for its author'. This judgement followed on from Stendhal's denunciation of the conservative view that 'every painted figure should be the copy of a statue' and 'painting is all a matter of presenting a large quantity of fine muscles drawn very correctly'.[4] By contrast, Delaroche had excelled in creating a dramatic contrast between the crafty cardinal and a Joan who, 'chained upon her bed of grief, protests the truth of her answers with all the frankness and warmth of a heroic soul'.[5] In line with Stendhal's prediction, Delaroche steadily increased his reputation over the decade, with official state commissions and purchases featuring in his contribution to the 1827/8 Salon. Yet the July Revolution of 1830 brought about the replacement of the conservative government of the elder Bourbons by the liberal Duc d'Orléans, who reigned as Louis-Philippe. Delaroche and Lami spent the three heady days of revolution – Les Trois Glorieuses – roaming Paris, sketching the makeshift barricades, and documenting the mock-heroic progress of the wounded through the streets.[6]

Delaroche's rise to fame in the 1830s, and his election to the Académie des Beaux-Arts as its youngest member to date in 1832, should not obscure the point that the first phase of his career was spent in the Bohemian society of the Latin Quarter. In the early 1820s, he lived (with Lami and other Gros pupils) near the abbey of St Germain-des-Prés in a ramshackle building known as 'La Childeberte', whose indulgent landlady, Madame Chanfort, accepted pictures in lieu of rent. After her death in 1857, a painting by the young Delaroche was one of her possessions sold at auction.[7] A memoir recalling the lively role-playing of this community in the early 1830s is probably not far from the mark in respect of La Childeberte's denizens in the previous decade: 'They were minstrels, or corsairs, or proud valiant knights from the moment they got up till the moment they went to bed.'[8] This was the epoch when the exotic poems of Lord Byron and the romances of Walter Scott found fertile soil in a younger generation

[FIG. 13] Paul Delaroche (1797–1856), *Joas saved by Josabeth*, 1821. Oil on canvas, 355 × 259 cm. Musées des Beaux-Arts des Troyes (D.872.11)

[FIG. 14] Paul Delaroche (1797–1856), *Saint Sebastian*, about 1822. Oil on canvas, 117.2 × 95.1 cm. The Detroit Institute of Arts, Detroit, Michigan, Founders' Society Purchase, Acquisitions Fund (78.57).

that repudiated the values of the French classical tradition. Stendhal wrote *Racine et Shakespeare* (1823), to argue that the contrast between the French tragic dramatist and the English playwright who broke all rules was being replayed in the contemporary battle between Classics and Romantics. A large measure of national pride was invested in the French classical tradition, and the public character of dramatic representation made the Parisian theatre a cockpit for these antagonisms to be revealed. In advance of 1830, the production of lavishly staged plays like Alexandre Dumas's *Henri III et sa cour* and Victor Hugo's *Hernani* proved a rallying point for the Romantic generation. The 'fancy dress *conversazioni*' at La Childeberte were tremors registering a seismic shift in French culture.

Delaroche's involvement in these developments cannot be doubted. His first major Salon painting, *Joas saved by Josabeth* (1821), took its theme from Racine's quintessentially classical *Athalie* – yet its showing in 1822 was also the moment at which he gained the attention of the prince of Romantic painters, Théodore Géricault (fig. 13).[9] The direction taken by his work during his residence at La Childeberte became, increasingly, a rejection not just of the School of David, but of the studio disciplines derived from the French Academy. Auguste Massé's *Studio of Baron Gros* (1824 Salon), shows Delaroche as a bespectacled youth, who looks away from the nude model posed in the foreground. Though this is a fortuitous detail, Delaroche did rapidly relinquish compositions that depended on correct anatomical drawing. A commissioned *Saint Sebastian*, advertised as being exhibited in 1824, appears not to have reached its destination in a Paris church (fig. 14).[10] The extant Saint Sebastian, which might well be a fragment of the planned work, shows him using the male nude model for the last time. Another painting for the 1824 Salon, *Saint Vincent de Paul preaching* (1823), clearly features two residents of La Childeberte in period costume (cat. 10): the elderly painter Jean-Frédéric Schall and the Gros pupil Adolphe Roger (traditionally identified as the amorous painter in another 1824 exhibit, *Filippo Lippi enamoured of his Model*).[11] The most important work within this group was, however, *Joan of Arc* (1824). This ranks as Delaroche's first important 'victim' picture, and could hardly be more different from a traditionally conceived *Saint Sebastian*.

No doubt Delaroche's choice of models from his fellow residents can partly be explained by necessity. But it is of a piece with other features of his comprehensive revision of existing practice. Until recently, Delaroche's knowledge of English history painting was deemed a passing acquaintanceship, confined to one brief visit to England in 1827. His use of English print sources was played down since it was tainted with accusations of plagiarism.[12] The discovery of his signature in the Visitors' Book of the Meyrick collection of armour – dating from 1822 – shows that he could have seen English historical paintings at source, and undeniably had a more extensive knowledge of the English scene than previously supposed.[13] The critic Gustave Planche launched the accusation of plagiarism by claiming that John Opie's *Execution of Mary Stuart* (engraved by William Skelton for Hume's *History of England*) was the source for *Lady Jane Grey*. A less exclusive review of the visual evidence suggests that Delaroche did indeed view a range of English historical prints, together with paintings and prints after Old Masters depicting martyrdom that were themselves possible sources for the English artists. He must have been familiar with the representation of Jane Grey in Hume, although James Northcote's *Feckenham visiting Jane Grey in the Tower* (engraved by William Bromley) appears a convincing source for *Joan of Arc* rather than for Jane Grey's execution. The point is that Delaroche's study of visual sources formed part of a coherent compositional procedure. Having declined as a student to follow the conventional path that led to the Grand Prix de Rome in history painting (then the highest artistic honour that could be awarded to a young artist in France), he made an early decision to develop his subjects through sifting the extant visual materials – whether Ingres's *Paolo and Francesca* for *Filippo Lippi*, or English historical paintings for *Joan of Arc*. For *Death of Elizabeth*, there is an oil study revealing the intermediate stage between the monochrome English print and the splendidly coloured painting (fig. 23, see cat. 19). But such transpositions were not mere plagiarism. To reinforce the point, one has only to study Delaroche's drawings. These range from informal sketches to carefully constructed compositional studies. Proliferating in the late 1820s and 1830s, they are a remarkable demonstration of the way in which he conceived his major Salon works.

A sheet of drawings shown here (cat. 49) demonstrates this process at work. The three framed compositions, slightly different in their relative proportions, clearly depict the same subject, involving an entrance of armed men into a bedchamber, and a female figure who intercedes with one of them, while others attend to an opening on the left. All are dressed in period costume, and the compositions recall the two small cabinet paintings painted by Delaroche in the late 1820s: the pendants *Cardinal Richelieu* and *Cardinal Mazarin* (1831 Salon). Yet this sheet looks further ahead, to *The Assassination of the Duc de Guise* (1832). Delaroche is condensing in a sequence of compositions the lively dénouement of Alexandre Dumas's play, *Henri III et sa cour*, first performed on 10 February 1829. The King's favourite, Saint-Mégrin, has just escaped from the bedroom of his mistress, the Duchesse de Guise, through the window on the left, and the Duchess

[FIG. 15] Paul Delaroche (1797–1856), *The Assassination of the Duc de Guise*, 1832. Watercolour and body colour with gum varnish on paper, 14 × 25 cm. The Wallace Collection, London (P738)

[FIG. 16] Paul Delaroche (1797–1856), *Study after Alexandre Dumas's* Henri III et sa cour, about 1829 (cat. 50). Graphite on paper, 11.6 × 17.6 cm. Private collection

is restraining her furious husband by 'seizing him bodily' ('à bras de corps', as the stage directions stipulate)[14]. Together with a more finished drawing of the same scene (cat. 50), these sketches from about 1829 suggest that Delaroche was considering a pictorial rendering of Dumas's scene which could have been the first of two pendant pictures – the first study for the *Assassination* being dated 1830 and the version sold to Count Demidoff dated 1832 (fig. 15). There would have been a striking contrast between Guise's over-mighty behaviour in the first episode, and his death at the hands of the King whose authority he had flouted. In spatial terms, the draw of the open window that takes our attention in the first composition corresponds exactly to the device of the open door with the King arriving to enjoy his revenge.

A sketch at the top of the former sheet (cat. 49) depicts the space from above, with notations of entries, furnishings and the position of principal actors, as in the records of contemporary staging. Such sketches recur in Delaroche's drawings, and suggest prospective stage designs. But the crucial link is with his highly individual way of working. Having experimented with such possibilities on paper, he took them to a further stage by creating three-dimensional models in the form of miniature stage sets. The *Illustrated London News* later commented on this practice, with reference to the period properties of his *Princes in the Tower*: 'The costume of the Princes, the bedstead, and its draperies, were carved and made in England, from the best authorities, under the supervision of Delaroche who came expressly to London [in 1827] to visit the scene of his picture.'[15] Unfortunately nothing has survived of Delaroche's modelling, though there are records of two bronzes representing the head of Charles I. These derive from the small plaster model used in planning the composition of *Cromwell and Charles I*, and were cast after the work's success at the 1831 Salon.[16]

There are thus many ways in which the concept of 'spectacle' applies to Delaroche's early work: from the critical reception of his paintings by Stendhal to his practice of scenographic model-making, also reflected in his many drawings. The latter proclivity can also be identified with a desire to break away from academic studio practice, and the cultivation of the Bohemian milieu of La Childeberte, which provided models within a peer group also seeking to navigate the unruly currents of French Romanticism. However, the days spent observing the July Revolution of 1830 pinpoint a crucial stage in Delaroche's career. There was no Salon in that eventful year, and hence no chance to advertise the fact that his pendants of *Richelieu* and *Mazarin* would be entering the collection of the wealthy Swiss banker Pourtalès-Gorgier. Perhaps he was fearful for the loss of the patronage acquired to date in state purchases and commissions. Yet the accession of the former Duc d'Orléans to the throne must have offered reassurance, since Delaroche's first commission, when still a pupil of Gros, was for a *Deposition* to hang in the Duchesse's private chapel. Any doubts about the continuance of state and private patronage were, then, rapidly resolved. When the next Salon opened on 1 May 1831, Delaroche was poised to exhibit the fruit of several years' work. The event secured his reputation, placing him in the forefront of the tendency that cultivated the historical culture of Romanticism, and promoting his candidacy for the Academy. The German poet Heinrich Heine, covering the 1831 Salon, put it in a nutshell: Delaroche was the 'choir-leader' of a new school.[17]

This reference reminds us that the Salon was indeed the definitive 'spectacle', at which artists competed for attention. Held at the Louvre, it was a public forum where the fortunate placing of a work could well excite favourable comparisons. François-Joseph Heim's painting, *Charles X distributing Prizes after the Salon of 1824*, which shows the hierarchy of French artists lining up before their sovereign, also indicates that Delaroche's *Joan of Arc* hung directly to the right of Ingres's acclaimed *Vow of Louis XIII*.[18] Ingres's painting had arrived after the official opening of the Salon, and probably benefited from the shock effect of a late appearance. Delaroche may have learned from this example. He advertised four paintings in the original catalogue for the 1827/8 Salon, including the state-commissioned *Taking of the Trocadéro*. But his dramatic *Death of Elizabeth* (noted by Stendhal) arrived late, being listed only in the third supplement to the catalogue. At the 1831 Salon, the privilege of the latecomer was reserved for *Cromwell and Charles I* (cat. 23), which appeared in the second supplement. This created a new situation which some critics seized upon. Horace de Viel-Castel declared that Delaroche's early exhibit, *The Princes in the Tower* (cat. 14), was 'a fine miniature from an ancient chronicle whose touching simplicity moved us deeply', but gave special acclaim to *Cromwell*, where Delaroche had 'engraved his sublime subject with the broad burin of history'.[19] Viel-Castel also mentions that *Cromwell and Charles I* was hung next to Léopold Robert's *Harvesters in the Pontine Marshes*, one of the immediate successes of the Salon, and clearly demonstrated its superior interest.

The Salon thus played a major role in enabling reputations to be assessed within the public sphere. Delaroche sent no work to the 1833 Salon, provoking the poet and critic Théophile Gautier to assert that he was deliberately keeping back his much-touted *Jane Grey*. But this omission surely gave all the more impact to the unveiling of *The Execution of Lady Jane Grey* in 1834 (cat. 53).[20] Critical opinion then polarised around the respective merits of Delaroche and Ingres, who showed his long-awaited *Saint Symphorian*. A long-term result of the competitive nature of the Salon has been the retrospective construction of the history of French painting in the period as a duel between Ingres and Delacroix, with Delaroche uncomfortably poised between them, as the representative of the 'juste-milieu'.[21]

Undoubtedly the success of *Lady Jane Grey* at the 1834 Salon has contributed to pigeon-holing Delaroche's art in a fashion that has proved as long-lasting as it is misplaced. The Romantic avant-garde, in the person of Gautier, once again denounced him as a shrewd operator exploiting the 'rather foolish sensibility of the honest and good-natured public'.[22] The role that *Lady Jane Grey* the crowd-puller has continued to play in evaluating Delaroche's work has led to a disregard for the conditions in which this major work was conceived and developed. This is no matter of lacking preliminary drawings, since those that remain reveal much about his methods. The fact that one large sheet also features a pencilled reference to a sketch of 'La Dauphine et L.17', indicates that the broad lines of the composition were established before the July Revolution of 1830.[23] Delaroche thus had a period of at least three years to develop *Lady Jane Grey*, but little has been written to elucidate this phase in his career.

The essential point is that Delaroche's involvement with theatrical representation now acquires a human dimension. He exhibited one proof of his interest in the stage at the 1831 Salon: a portrait of the operatic diva, Mademoiselle Sontag, as Mozart's Donna Anna, from *Don Giovanni*. Doubtless he attached little importance to this picture, omitting it from the list of Salon exhibits that supported his candidacy for the Académie des Beaux-Arts in 1832.[24] Yet it is obvious that Delaroche's election as an academician did not immediately change his way of life. He still shared a studio in the heart of the Latin Quarter. His fellow artist and friend Eugène Lami was still immersed in the glamour of costume drama, causing Baudelaire to dub him later as the 'poet of official dandyism'.[25] It would be 1835, after his visit to Italy and his marriage to Louise Vernet, before Delaroche entered a new social sphere as a fond husband and family man. In the preceding years, he was more preoccupied with theatre than at any point in his life. In 1833, the very year that *Lady Jane Grey* was brought to completion, he was passionately involved with a woman who could claim to be a victim on several counts: the celebrated actress and *sociétaire* of the Comédie-Française, Mademoiselle Anaïs.

The evidence for Delaroche's closeness to this fascinating theatrical figure is secure, but the story has to be carefully reconstructed from the available documents. In 1832, Delaroche completed a delightful portrait of Mademoiselle Anaïs, which remains in the possession of her descendants, but has never been on public exhibition until now. In 1833, he despatched two rapidly penned messages to Anaïs protesting his passionate devotion. As these were notes conveyed by servants between residences, they are undated. But allusions to Anaïs's stage role confirm the approximate date. The play, *Les Enfants d'Édouard*, by Casimir Delavigne (dedicated to Delaroche and based on his *Princes in the Tower*) opened at the Théâtre National of the Odéon on 18 May 1833, with Anaïs playing a boy's role as Richard, Duke of York. It is also relevant that, in 1836, Anaïs presented a drawing by Delaroche to a fellow actress, Virginie Bourbier. This drawing is based on Lami's lithograph of the Duc de Richelieu costumed as the sixteenth-century Maréchal de St-Albon, for the The Mary Stuart Ball, hosted by the Duchesse de Berry in May 1829 (see cat. 36).

Taken in conjunction with manuscripts in Anaïs's dossier at the Library of the Comédie-Française, these documents provide the following conjectural narrative. Delaroche was introduced to Anaïs by Lami, who probably knew her as early as 1829. In 1832, Anaïs posed for her portrait, very probably in Delaroche's studio in the rue Visconti. In the early summer of 1833, while Anaïs was performing her role, Delaroche visited her frequently, though sometimes in mixed company, at her apartment in the rue des Beaux-Arts – a stone's throw from the studio and Delaroche's lodging at the Institut. What may be implied by the reference in one letter to visiting her, and 'working on [her] portrait'? Delaroche's tiny wash drawing of a young woman relaxing in a wing chair vividly evokes the scene suggested by this letter (fig. 17). But there is no known portrait of Anaïs by Delaroche, other than the studio portrait (though one exists by Henry Scheffer, dated 1833). Was Delaroche then working on a portrayal of Anaïs that would complete his characterisation of Jane Grey? The visual evidence supports this. A fine watercolour sketch for *Lady Jane Grey* (cat. 67, dated 1832) shows the principal model wearing a period dress that closely resembles the costume in the small wash drawing. The use of a famous actor as model would have been quite consistent with Delaroche's practice. He used the actor Edmond Geffroy as the model for the victim in his *Assassination of the Duc de Guise* (fig. 15).[26] But there would have been good reason for not drawing attention to the involvement of Anaïs when *Lady Jane Grey* was exhibited in 1834.The vehemence of Delaroche's letters, together with the biographical factors to be explored here, suggest that this was a tempestuous relationship that might not have survived. When Anaïs gave away her drawing in 1836, Delaroche was a happily married man, and the relationship was well and truly over.[27]

Up to now, virtually nothing has been written about Delaroche's private life before his marriage in 1835. The fascinating exception is a sentence by Alexandre Dumas, who comments (rightly) on the fact that he began his studies as a landscape painter, but adds: 'a woman, with whom he fell in love, and whose portrait he insisted on painting, changed his inclinations'.[28] It is hard to make sense of this assertion, which presumably relates to Delaroche's decision to move from the studio of the landscape painter Watelet to that of Gros. But the message that Delaroche was very susceptible to female charm can indeed be extrapolated from some of his earliest works: the 'Young Woman at the Harp' in his 1820 drawing, the court lady seen full face in the audience of *Saint Vincent de Paul*, and indeed the modest Lucrezia Buti in *Filippo Lippi*, might represent an individual model (or at least a type).[29] The more significant point is that Delaroche's portrayal of a girlfriend was the pivotal element in his decision to switch from one genre of painting to another. In this sense, there is an immediate relevance to the situation evoked here with regard to *Lady Jane Grey*, where the artist's attachment to the model does indeed accompany the conception of a work of unique intensity and originality. How Anaïs herself might have reciprocated the passion that permeates Delaroche's letters is impossible to assess. But in order to appreciate the professional (as well as the personal) factors involved in their relationship, it is necessary to retrace the career of this remarkable woman.

[FIG. 17] Paul Delaroche (1797–1856), *Mademoiselle Anaïs sleeping by the Fire*, about 1833. Brown wash heightened with white, 8 × 9.5 cm. The Peabody Collection. Collection of the Maryland State Archives (MSA SC 4680-13-0671)

Anaïs Aubert, known professionally as Mademoiselle Anaïs, was born in Paris on 22 June 1802. She was only a girl when, because of her family's impoverishment, she contacted the Duc de Duras (the official of the Bourbon court charged with supervising the theatre), and was authorised to take lessons with the veteran actor Paul-Eustache Baptiste (known as Baptiste *cadet*, as his father and brother were also actors). A letter dated October 1816 appointed her as a trial *pensionnaire* of the state theatre for a year, and she made her first stage appearances in 1817. Being slight of stature, she qualified only to perform the roles known as *ingenuités*: that is, parts for young, naïve women (immortalised in the French tradition by the comedies of Molière), and for adolescent boys (still reserved for female actors at that date). This was a professional limitation that began to rankle early in her career. After performing boy's roles in Racine's *Athalie* in 1820 and Alexandre Guiraud's *Les Machabées ou le martyre* in 1822, she wrote to the management committee claiming that she had made her début in tragedy, and so should be entitled to perform the major female roles of *amoureuses*. The reply was negative: no doubts were expressed about her 'intelligence' or her general appearance, but there were reservations about her 'stature which is not tall enough for the huge extent of the Théâtre français'. A print that shows her contemplating martyrdom as the youngest Macchabee brother – beside the Junoesque Mademoiselle George as her mother Semele – fairly proves the point. Nevertheless, being confined to *ingenuités* did not stop Anaïs shining as the most accomplished actress of the period in that domain. Reviewing her career in 1842, the critic J.T. Merle compared her favourably with the greatest actress of the day: 'if Mademoiselle Mars has been for thirty years *the diamond* of the Comédie-Française, we can say with equal justification that today Mademoiselle Anaïs is *its pearl*'.[30]

It is undeniable, however, that being the most celebrated *ingénue* of her times placed a burden on this talented young woman. Acceptance as a *sociétaire* of the Comédie-Française (a status which she achieved in 1832), ensured a regular income, and a degree of independence virtually unparalleled for a member of her sex. Yet being an *ingénue* meant maintaining a public façade that might well be at variance with her private inclinations. This is underlined in Théodore de Banville's satirical sketch of the social obligations of the *ingénue* – which explicitly cites Anaïs as the foremost representative from the previous generation:

> *The reputation for talent of an ingénue is in direct ratio to her reputation for ingenuity in public* [...] *If we meet her in the street giving her arm to a friend of her father (which happens to the most honest of our young girls) – Finally, if she is suspected of knowing more than Agnès [the Molière heroine], and having read something besides the fairy stories of Perrault* [...] *the ingénue no longer exists, the authors don't wish to hear of her, she has only to pack her bags, and go off and play duennas in the provinces.*[31]

Though Banville perhaps exaggerated the plight of *ingénuité*, there is little doubt that, in Anaïs's case, keeping a spotless reputation went somewhat against the grain. The story circulates that in 1826, after an unhappy love affair, she left Paris hurriedly, bade the coachman to drive due west until he reached the sea, and so launched a fashionable seaside resort in the Normandy village of Veules-les-Roses.[32] Anaïs appears also in the lengthy cavalcade of the mistresses of the playwright Alexandre Dumas. Though this connection is unproven, her presence was noted at the première of *Henri III et sa cour* in 1829, and she took a leading part in Dumas's light comedy, *Le Mari de la veuve* in April 1832. It is also true that her friend Virginie Bourbier, who received Delaroche's drawing in 1836, was temporarily 'the presiding nymph' in Dumas's household.[33]

All these sides of Anaïs's life, however, pale into insignificance beside the major personal factor that would have been dominant up to the times when Delaroche was close to her. The *ingénue* had a son. In 1818, she had joined a troop of French actors who played to great acclaim for an aristocratic audience in the private theatre of the Argyle Rooms in London. The visit was arranged through the Duke of Wellington, who had resided in Paris with the occupying British army in the years after the victory of Waterloo. Perhaps in Paris, or during her stay in London, Anaïs became acquainted with Major-General the Hon. Edward Stopford, an officer who fought under Wellington in the Peninsular Wars as the commander of the 1st brigade of the 1st Infantry division of the 3rd Regiment of Foot. In 1819, she gave birth in Paris to his son, who was christened at the British Embassy Chapel under the name of Edward. According to family tradition, General Stopford, who (being born in 1766) was considerably older, offered marriage, but she declined.[34] He provided financial assistance while the young Edward was being raised by his mother. After 1831, however, he arranged for their son to be boarded with an English couple in Paris, as a prelude to being naturalised British by Act of Parliament in 1836 under the name of Edward Stopford Claremont. After graduating from Oxford, Anaïs's son entered the British army as an officer in the Royal Canadian Rifles in 1840, and had a lengthy and distinguished career paralleling that of his father, reaching the rank of General before he died in 1890.

This personal history dovetails with Anaïs's position in the early 1830s, when she resolved to resume her acting career after an interval of several years. Engaged as a *pensionnaire* at the Comédie-Française for the year 1831/2, she became a full member of the company (*sociétaire*) from the 1832/3 season onwards, with an assured income that increased over the following years. The role that consolidated her reputation, and continued to be identified with her well into the future, was her appearance as the Duke of York in Casimir Delavigne's play, *Les Enfants d'Edouard*, which had its premiere on 18 May 1833, so concluding her first year in her new status. It was not surprising that Merle chose this role to illustrate his overview of her career (cat. 33). When Edmond Geffroy painted his group portrait of the *sociétaires* dressed in their favourite roles in 1840, Anaïs chose to appear in the colourful tunic of Richard, Duke of York – a costume that, according to regulation, she would herself have commissioned and paid for. In fact, there were two costumes: Octave Tassaert's lithograph of the production locates the showier outfit from the 1840 painting in Act II, but for the tragic denouement in Act III both princes wore black (cat. 30, fig. 27). Far from being a sentimental adjunct to the cast, the young York as conceived by Delavigne seems to have been regarded almost as the hero of the play. Building on hints from Shakespeare's *Richard III*, Delavigne had given him a precocious perception of the Duke of Gloucester's villainy that contrasted with his brother's passivity and his mother's credulity. Delaroche's earlier characterisation in the painting must have encouraged this portrayal of the prince as a pure child who could foresee, but not avert, the sad conclusion.[35]

A further detail is needed to complete the scene for the encounters revealed in Delaroche's two letters. Anaïs suffered from ill-health. In a letter of 1829 that mentions 'Eugène' (presumably Lami), she confessed to being plagued with headaches. A pathetic missive to the theatre management which could date from the run of Delavigne's play in the early summer of 1833 reads: 'I will appear on Saturday in [*Les Enfants d'Edouard*] despite the advice of my doctor who fears a relapse that would be caused by my tiredness but I am so bored by this long absence that I persist in my resolution.' In another letter, she admits to having 'a horrible cold', and is fearful of 'tiring my chest to the point of not being able to appear at all'. The show went on nonetheless: Anaïs writes to reserve seats for her adolescent son (himself an Edward, and a 'child of Edward'), with the request that he should not be placed 'too much to the side'. Another letter is sent on behalf of the artist whose painting was recreated in the staging of the final scenes: 'Monsieur Delaroche' wanted to reserve a box and four stalls in different parts of the house. This letter concludes playfully: 'You see I am not bothering you, but the Duke of York has the right to speak so.'

With this context in mind, we can get further in reconstituting the context for Delaroche's two letters. Scribbled on scrappy pieces of paper (for which Delaroche apologises), they were perhaps transmitted from what Lami termed 'the sombre and damp prison they call your lodging at the Institute'[36] to Anaïs's cosy apartment in the nearby rue des Beaux-Arts. The shorter, and possibly later, of the two also involves reserving a ticket for the play, in this case for Charles Guyot, probably a member of the family of print editors who published an album of theatrical designs in 1837.[37] But the intimate note is still sounded: 'Till this evening, my love, my excellent little actor! And [how is] your head?' The second, involving their mutual friend Lami as well as Guyot, is a more revealing indication that the lover is also an artist:

> *If you wish me to tell you my thoughts very frankly, my darling, I desire to pass the evening near to you, to tell you as much as I can that you are my angel, my happiness and my life! To work on your portrait and give you the occasion to exchange some spiteful little remarks with your friend Eugène if I can bring him along to you together with my good Charles Guyot. So then till this evening by your fireside and on my knees before your eyes that will cry no longer.*

The 'portrait' evoked here is not that of the fashionable actress, fan in hand, who had posed in 1832 (cat. 73). The latter belonged to the series of female studies that were Delaroche's speciality around 1830; it showcased the type of elaborate hairstyle 'in shining coils' that Balzac attributes to a *demi-mondaine* of the period.[38] The armchair in eighteenth-century 'Louis XV' style must be the same that supports the noble figure of the *Marquis de Pastoret* in Delaroche's 1829 painting (Museum of Fine Arts, Boston), and was a studio property which Delaroche later kept in his studio at the rue de la Tour aux Dames.[39] Yet the little Baltimore drawing, where Anaïs holds her head at the same angle but with her hair simply drawn back, suggests just such an intimate evening with Anaïs relaxing in a fireside chair, no longer competing with the wit of Eugène (see fig. 17).

What is striking about these letters is their mixture of devotion and detachment. Delaroche contemplates Anaïs as an artist while writing to her as a lover. The fact that she was taking the part of the young victim whose role was, at one remove, Delaroche's creation, must be added to the equation. He would have known, as did other close friends, that she was the victim of her early indiscretion, and a fond mother who had relinquished the care of her son. All these aspects, together with her state of health, must have aroused a complex blend of love and pity in Delaroche, all the more so as her status as an *ingénue* made her professionally untouchable. Though the earliest sketch for *Lady Jane Grey* dates from before July 1830, the process by which the composition acquired greater emotional depth was surely attributable to the way in which the central figure (crudely indicated in the first drawing) became the credible image of a slight young woman, whose 'gesture' (in Hébert's words) embodied 'concentrated drama'. Anaïs's early role as a martyr in *Les Macchabées* had long before acquainted her with the tragic eloquence of outstretched arms.

This series of sittings also involved giving substance to the protecting figure of the Lieutenant of the Tower. It is tempting to assume that the 'good Charles Guyot', whose presence Delaroche announced, was posing in that role. It is also interesting to note that the elderly Englishman who had fathered her son – whose ambiguous benevolence must have weighed heavily on Anaïs – was by then a Lieutenant-General. As for the executioner, he merited a separate study, turned this way and that in the studio. Delaroche characterised him in such a way that his involvement in the execution was marked by a degree of detachment, to be interpreted as a kind of moral recoil from the consequences of his action. We may suppose that all these different factors were involved in what Delaroche describes as 'work[ing] on your portrait'. Delaroche was certainly portraying Anaïs – obsessively so – at the period when *Lady Jane Grey* was finally taking shape. In no sense a conventional model, the actress before his eyes embodied so many aspects of the victim as spectacle.

A postscript is required to trace the new course that Delaroche's life and work was then about to take. On 15 October 1833 he became Professor at the Ecole des Beaux-Arts, and on 12 November he received the state commission to paint the inner walls of the Madeleine church, which was nearing completion. *The Execution of Lady Jane Grey* was applauded at the Salon from 1 March 1834 onwards, and on 20 June, conscious of the obligation to devise a major series of religious paintings, Delaroche left Paris for his first visit to Italy. Arriving in Rome in October, he announced his engagement to Louise Vernet, the daughter of the Director of the French Academy at Rome, in December, and married her on 28 January 1835. His reply to a friend's congratulations defined his mood at that time: 'It would doubtless be more humble, more appropriate to tell you that people exaggerate the qualities of Mlle Louise. I find that they are too right in judging her witty, good and attractive for me to make the effort to be modest, as good manners require; for the first time in my life, I am very proud.'[40] Eugène Lami rejoiced that 'this great event so influential on the second stage of life [has been] fixed in the happiest fashion for you – all Paris agrees about this and, with a few exceptions, everyone will congratulate you on your return'.[41]

It is hard to miss the underlying message that 'all Paris' was relieved to learn that Delaroche had extricated himself from an unfortunate relationship. And what might those 'few exceptions' imply if not a delicate reference to the different response of the former object of his friend's affections? Though Delaroche later rejected the Madeleine commission, his reputation would soon rest on a more durable basis than the fickle fortunes of the Salon. Between 1837 and 1841, he created the vast panorama of 'Artists of all ages' in the *Hémicycle* of the Ecole des Beaux-Arts. Images of joyful maternity appeared in his work in the early 1840s, when he became a father. Only in a series of small drawings, which must date from his second visit to Rome in 1843/4, would he return to the theme of the female martyr, sketching the Roman Saint Perpetua, cast into prison, and visited by her adolescent son (fig. 18). Yet after Louise's untimely death on 18 December 1845, Delaroche reverted to the record of female victimhood throughout history with *Marie-Antoinette* (1851) and two Roman subjects: *Béatrice Cenci* and *Young Christian Martyr* (both 1855). As for Mademoiselle Anaïs, she finally retired from the stage, and her benefit took place at the Théâtre français on 22 March 1849. The house was full, and Paul Delaroche took two seats in the Dress Circle.

actual size

[FIG. 18] Paul Delaroche (1797–1856), *Saint Perpetua visited in Prison by her Son*, about 1843. Pencil, 3.5 × 2.5 cm. Private collection

NOTES & REFERENCES

1. Stendhal 2002, p.152.

2. Letter from Ernest Hébert to Paul Delaroche, 11 March 1850. Bibliothèque nationale de France, Paris, Mss, N.F. 16800, ff.90-1.

3. Balzac 2008b, p. 417.

4. Stendhal 2002, p.59.

5. Stendhal 2002, p.60.

6. The sketches by Lami were published by Rittner in 1831 as a series of four lithographs under the title, *Croquis faits d'après nature dans Paris pendant les journées des 27, 28 et 29 juillet 1830*. See Lemoisne 1912, p.41. No record remains of any sketches made by Delaroche, though the lithograph titled 'Le Drapeau', attributed to Lami and Delaroche by their mutual friend Labouchère, and published by Rittner & Goupil, may also date from this period. See Bibliothèque municipale de Nantes, Collection Labouchère, Book I.

7. See Anon 1893, p.8.

8. Anon 1893, p.9.

9. For the circumstances of Delaroche's meeting with Géricault, and the relationship of the painting to an earlier performance of *Athalie* at the Théâtre français, see Bann 1997, pp.50–3.

10. See Ziff 1977, p.21.

11. For this choice of models, see Bann 2006, pp.353–5. The identification of Roger as the painter in *Filippo Lippi* dates back to Delaborde and Goddé 1858.

12. See Delaborde and Goddé 1858, pp.247–8.

13. See Duffy 2009.

14. Dumas 1974, vol. I, pp.68–9.

15. *Illustrated London News*, 4 February 1848.

16. See Ziff 1977, p.106 and fig. 46.

17. See Bann 1997, p.107.

18. For the Salons of the 1820s, see Chaudonneret 1999, p.80 ff.

19. See Bann 2007a, p.35.

20. The evidence suggests that Delaroche was indeed intending to submit the painting to the 1833 Salon, but ran out of time (see p. 132). The probability is that he did complete it in the summer months.

21. See Shelton 2000, p.80. As a result of this Salon, the critic Gustave Planche proclaimed that Ingres was the leader of the 'renovatory' wing of French painting, whereas Delaroche led the 'conciliatory' contingent. This idea was concretised in the notion of Delaroche as leader of the 'juste-milieu' (p. 89). The story of how the relative merits of *Lady Jane Grey* and *Saint Symphorian* became a lively point of debate at the 1834 Salon is recounted in Vigne 1998, pp.1–9.

22. Gautier 1994, p.187. This polemical article, very different in tone from Gautier's later writing on Delaroche, was translated and published by the National Gallery in 1975, when *Lady Jane Grey* was retrieved from storage and placed on view again.

23. 'Louis XVII' was the son and heir of the guillotined Louis XVI, and died after being imprisoned in the Temple prison in Paris. His sister, who initially shared his imprisonment, was later married to her cousin, the Duc d'Angoulême, and subsequently known as the Duchesse d'Angoulême, except for the period between 1824 and 1830, when her husband was the heir to his father, Charles X, and titled 'Dauphin'; hence her title as 'La Dauphine'.

24. See Ziff 1977, pp.97–8.

25. Baudelaire 1968, p.74.

26. See Bellier de la Chavignerie 1868, vol I, p.388.

27. It should also be noted that the two letters exhibited here have the singular feature in common that both mention 'Charles Guyot'. This possibly indicates that they were presented to Guyot by Anaïs, and may be unique in surviving her desire to be relieved of such reminders of her earlier life.

28. Dumas 1968, p.24.

29. The two former works are illustrated in Bann 2006, pp.351 and 354, the last in Bann 1997, p.130.

30. See Merle 1842, No. 61.

31. Banville 1859, vol. II, pp.23–4.

32. The story is dutifully recounted on the website of this Normandy resort, near Dieppe.

33. See Hemming 1979, pp.62–3, where Virginie Bourbier is described thus: 'A pert little piece with the French equivalent of a Cockney accent, she made an ideal girlfriend for the dissipated dramatist.'

34. I am greatly obliged to the following family connections of Mademoiselle Anaïs, through her son Edward Stopford Claremont, who have generously supplied me with information: the late Sir Jonathan Backhouse, Anne Stopford Claremont and Vyvyan Lord, and Michael Young.

35. See the critical essay by M. Duviquet in Delavigne 1846, vol. VI, p.20, where the Duke of York's innocent foresight is compared with that of Junie in Racine's *Britannicus*.

36. Lemoisne 1914, p.86.

37. Two volumes of the *Album des théâtres* were edited by Noël-J. Guyot and A. Debacq in 1837/8. The tone of Delaroche's letter suggests that 'Charles Guyot' might have been the elderly man who posed as the Lieutenant of the Tower. The person of that name recorded as associate and brother of the engraver Laurent Guyot might have been of the appropriate age in 1833.

38. Balzac 2008, vol 12, p.303.

39. It features prominently in the painting of Delaroche's studio done shortly after his death by his former pupil, Louis Roux, and photographed by Robert Bingham for Delaborde and Goddé 1858.

40. Letter to Labouchère, quoted in Nantes and Montpellier 1999, p.249.

41. Lemoisne 1914, p.86.

HENRIETTE LORIMIER (1775–1854)

[1] *Jeanne de Navarre and her Son at the Tomb of Jean V*, 1806

Oil on canvas, 199 × 168.5 cm
Musée National des Châteaux de Malmaison et Bois-Préau (MM88-5-1)

Provenance: bought for Empress Josephine, 1807; by descent to Queen Hortense; returned to the heirs of Napoleon III, 1881; Empress Eugènie's sale, 1881; Paris art market, 1988; acquired, Paris art market, 1994.

At first a mere depot for objects removed from churches and convents in the years following the Revolution, then picturesquely transformed by Alexandre Lenoir, who took charge of it in 1792, the Musée des monuments français (as it came to be known) opened on a permanent footing in 1795, in the abandoned convent of the Augustins. It survived there until 1816, the year following the Restoration of the Bourbon monarchy. Though this was not the original intention, this display of sculptural and architectural fragments, chiefly from France's medieval past, in a series of 'period' rooms, kept alive and stimulated an imaginative interest in the history of France and its associated artefacts. The many tombs, with their *gisants*, or recumbent figures, were among the relics which spoke most directly to the visitors to the museum, among whom were a number of artists. One was the painter Fleury Richard, a pupil of David, and one of the best-known of the little group known as the 'Troubadours' on account of their interest in subjects from medieval history, particularly in its more poetic and intimate aspects.

Richard's painting of Valentine de Milan, shown at the 1802 Salon (and now in St Petersburg), depicting a young widow mourning the death of her husband, the duc d'Orléans, was inspired by the contemplation of their tombs in Lenoir's museum. The painting itself became, in turn, a source for other artists. The present painting combines a debt to Richard's painting with details derived directly from Lenoir's museum: the tomb is a somewhat eclectic mix of identifiable sculpture, but the appearance and costume of this young widow recall, unmistakeably (as Alain Pougetoux has noted[1]), that of Valentine de Milan herself. Valentine's known concern for the education of her young son, the future poet Charles d'Orléans, must have made her seem a suitable model for the lesser-known figure of Jeanne de Navarre, who features in Henriette Lorimier's painting. Although the young widow was shortly to leave her children in the care of the duc de Bourgogne, when she herself became the second wife of Henry IV of England, her future destiny has, of course, no place in this work. Instead, the painter concentrates on a mother's grief at losing her husband, and on her devotion to his son, in a medieval variant on the theme of the widowed mother, famously represented in classical guise in David's *Andromache grieving over Hector*. It was Henriette Lorimier's only work of this kind. She may have intended a contemporary reference to the dynastic hopes at that time resting in the children of Napoleon's brother, Louis Bonaparte, whose wife, Hortense de Beauharnais, was the daughter (from her first marriage) of the picture's first owner, Empress Josephine.

The careful depiction of costume and setting (though the young Arthur's costume is an anachronism), the expression of mingled grief and devotion, and finely painted finish, as well as its large size – unusual for a picture of this kind – make clear, as François Pupil has emphasised, the link between this earlier generation of Troubadour artists and the work of Paul Delaroche. LW

1. Pougetoux 1994, p. 54. For further discussion, see also Chaudonneret 1980, p. 29; Pupil 1985, p. 490, Pougetoux 1995, pp. 47–51 and Denton 1998, pp. 219–46.

FRANÇOIS-MARIUS GRANET
(1775–1849)

[2] *Choir of the Capuchin Church, Rome*, 1817

Oil on canvas, 198 × 147.1 cm
Amgueddfa Cymru – National Museum of Wales, Cardiff (NMW A 481)

Provenance: one of at least 16 versions of this painting. This one commissioned by the Duchesse de Berry for the Chateau de Rosny in 1817; purchased by the 6th Duke of Devonshire at the Rosny sale in Paris, 22 February 1836 (Lugt 14225, no. 79), and remained at Chatsworth until 1975 when sold at Christie's; purchased by National Museum Wales 10 October 1979 from dealer Christopher Gibbs.

Born in Provence, Granet had close affinities with the School of Lyon, in personal and stylistic terms. Like Richard and Révoil, he was trained in David's studio. However, his lifelong friendship with another fellow student, the Provençal aristocrat Auguste de Forbin, enabled him to finance the pursuit of his studies in Rome, where he lived from 1802 to 1822. It was through his intimate experience of the architectural legacy of Rome, rather than among the medieval and Renaissance exhibits of the Musée des monuments français, that he was able to develop his powerful vision of a many-layered history.

Without doubt the most noteworthy of Granet's projects, and the one that confirmed his reputation in France, was the series of paintings devoted to the Choir of the Capuchin Church in the Piazza Barberini in Rome. It has been calculated that there are around 17 versions of this composition from the hand of Granet, all of which exhibit small but significant variations. There is no dispute that the first mention of the work comes in correspondence from the end of 1814, and that the Queen of Naples (Napoleon's sister Caroline) was his intended patron.[1] From that point onwards the record becomes confused. But another indisputable fact is that the first appearance in France of a painting bearing this title was at the Paris Salon of 1819. The illusionistic effect of the work gave rise to a celebrated remark by the French king, Louis XVIII: 'Monsieur Granet, someone tells me he has just heard one of your Capuchins sneeze.'

Isabelle Néto Daguerre has claimed that the present work is the version shown at the 1819 Salon, commissioned by the Duchesse de Berry and later passing through the collection of the 6th Duke of Devonshire.[2] Undoubtedly it is one of the largest and most impressive of the series. Although it represents the holding of the liturgy in the retro-choir of the Capuchin monks (the space behind the main altar of the church), the essential point is that Granet conceived it when the French occupation of Rome in 1810 had resulted in the suppression of the religious orders. In his words, 'the drum had silenced the sound of canticles'. It was essentially a remembered vision of the past that he sought to make concrete once again. 'My mind was so vividly taken over by all these thoughts that I resolved to make a larger picture out of them.'[3] Although indebted to the tradition of Netherlandish pictures of church interiors, Granet had effected a uniquely Romantic blend of nostalgia for the past and compelling illusion. SB

1. Rome 2003, p. 471.
2. Aix en Provence 1992, pp. 168–9.
3. Quoted in Bann 1999, p. 46.

LOUIS-JACQUES-MANDE DAGUERRE (1787–1851)

[3] *Interior of Rosslyn Chapel (Intérieur de Rosslyn Chapel)*, 1824

Oil on canvas, 113 × 97 cm
Musée des Beaux-Arts, Rouen (2004.3.1)

Provenance: Vicomte Vigier; Count A.P.; private collection; acquired 2004.

In company with Charles-Marie Bouton, whose painting (cat. 6) suggests the power of Lenoir's museum to transport the spectator, in imagination, to a period in remote history, Daguerre attempted a comparable conjuring-up of the past in a series of dramatic representations known as the Diorama (see page 26), which first opened in Paris in July 1822 with a view of Canterbury Cathedral (painted by Bouton), paired with a Swiss landscape. The chapel of Holyrood followed in 1823; a view of Rosslyn Chapel in 1824. The Diorama was not the first of such 'optical spectacles', but it was perhaps the most enduring and the most influential, in terms of its impact on certain theatrical figures with whom Delaroche was later associated. It exemplified a taste for the visual reconstitution of history which was evident in the art and the literature of the time. The images, painted on transparent linen, remained stationary, while the auditorium revolved, and could be transformed by means of changing light; by this means, too, figures could be made to appear and then to vanish, animating the scene with extraordinary realism.

Holyrood, the scene presented in 1823, was at that time particularly associated with Mary Queen of Scots. It was Walter Scott, however, at the height of his popularity in France, who lent a special interest to Rosslyn Chapel. He had evoked it at some length in *The Lay of the Last Minstrel*[1] (and also adapted aspects of it for his own Gothic interiors at Abbotsford).

Daguerre, from a family of Royalist sympathisers, may have been related to the famous eighteenth-century *marchand-mercier* Dominique Daguerre. Trained as a scene painter, he later worked with Pierre Prévost on his Panoramas, and is now chiefly remembered for his contribution to the development of photography, a development which Delaroche publicly endorsed. It has long been assumed that Daguerre never visited Scotland, but took his views of Holyrood and Rosslyn from existing prints, or from drawings. However, this painting, a 'record' of the gigantic work which he had shown at the Diorama, clearly shows holes in the columns which had never been recorded in previous images. This detail, as Angelo Maggi suggests, may therefore confirm, after all, a first-hand knowledge of the site.[2] LW

1. Maggi 1999, p. 263.
2. Maggi in Edinburgh 2002, p. 32.

RICHARD PARKES BONINGTON
(1802–1828)

[4] *Quentin Durward at Liège*, about 1823–8

Oil on canvas, 63.7 × 51.9 cm
Nottingham Castle Museum and Art Gallery
(NCM 1974–76)

Provenance: Possibly a commission from the duchesse de Berry, but never delivered; Bonington sale, London, 29–30 June 1829, lot 222; bought by Henry Bone for Joseph Neeld, MP; by descent to L.W. Neeld; London, Christie's, 13 July 1845, lot 120, bought Tooth; bought from Arthur Tooth & Son, 1974, with assistance of MLA/V&A purchase grant (NCM 1974–6).

Bonington, born in England, settled with his parents in France in 1817. Like Paul Delaroche, he became a pupil of Baron Gros, and was, like several of his contemporaries, an artist who cannot be classed as belonging entirely either to a French or to an English school. This was a milieu which in some respects Delaroche shared, in the early years of the Bourbon Restoration. Bonington's small-scale historical subjects, like Delaroche's *Filippo Lippi enamoured of his Model* (cat. 24), have much in common with the work of the earlier generation of Troubadour painters, but his rich and fluent handling of watercolour derives from contemporary English practice.

Quentin Durward, published in 1823, was Walter Scott's first novel on a French subject, and an immediate success in France. It became a source of inspiration to other writers, and inspired at least two plays on the subject of its main character, the perfidious and faintly sinister Louis XI. A year after the novel appeared, Camille Roqueplan, a fellow pupil of Delaroche and Bonington, sent a *Quentin Durward* subject to the Salon of 1824; Delacroix, shortly afterwards, painted two episodes from the novel, one of which was the highly dramatic *Murder of the Bishop of Liège*. Much later, Delacroix recorded that, towards the end of his short life, Bonington was haunted by the wish to complete a work on a more ambitious scale than the brilliant and charming watercolours which delighted collectors and fellow artists alike. This picture must owe something to this wish. One of the largest and most finished of his surviving works, it takes an incident from chapter XIX of the novel, in which Quentin Durward, a young Scottish archer in the bodyguard of Louis XI, travels to Liège on a secret mission from the king. The townspeople, in revolt against the duke of Burgundy and his kinsman, their bishop, assume that Durward has been sent as an envoy from the king in support of their rebellion, an uprising whose violent outcome is suggested by the powerful and ungainly figure of Nikkel Blok, the butcher, wielding an axe in the foreground. To the left is the armoured figure of Quentin Durward, marched between two prominent townsmen, one, clearly, the 'corpulent dignitary' of Scott's description. This representation of a reluctant hero, entirely faithful to Scott's narrative, involves the reconciling of disparate elements more easily conveyed in prose than in painting, and Bonington must have found the subject an awkward one.

The action is placed against a rapidly receding perspective, a little like that of Delaroche's setting for his *Caumont de La Force*, from about the same period. The source is probably to be found in the English topographical tradition: the 'lofty houses, the stately, though narrow and gloomy streets' of Scott's description echo some of Bonington's work on the *Voyages pittoresques*. As Patrick Noon has shown, one of the characters here derives from a figure depicted in relief on the rood-screen at Amiens, a reminder, more generally,[1] of Bonington's fondness for medieval architecture. Surviving studies after Northern artists, including Martin Schongauer, have also contributed something to the appearance of the crowd. The composition may have remained in Delaroche's memory when planning his vignette of Joan of Arc for Barante's *Histoire* (fig. 19). The figure of Durward himself, oddly motionless in the centre of the action, appears to be a self portrait; the armour must be an echo of the 'spirited sketches' he made when visiting the Meyrick collection (cat. 12), in 1825. LW

1. See P. Noon, *Richard Parkes Bonington, The Complete Paintings*, New Haven 2008, no. 414.

[FIG. 19] James Thompson (1788–1850) after Paul Delaroche (1797–1856), *The Capture of Joan of Arc*, engraving in *Histoire des Ducs de Bourgogne*, by Amable-Guillaume-Prosper Brugière de Barante, 1842 edn. Private Collection.

CLAUDIUS JACQUAND (1804–1878)

[5] *Thomas More, Lord Chancellor of England (Thomas Morus, grand chancelier d'Angleterre)*, 1827

Oil on canvas, 120.5 × 95.5 cm
Musée des Beaux-Arts, Lyon (A180)

Provenance: Bought from Paris Salon of 1827/8 by the City of Lyon.

Born in Lyon in 1804, Jacquand belonged to the second generation of the Lyon School, who had become known as the 'Troubadours' for their interest in historical subject matter from the medieval and Renaissance period. He studied at the Ecole des Beaux-Arts in Lyon under Fleury Richard, and his early work reflects Richard in the choice of historical anecdotes of a sentimental and emotive character, which he enlivened with vivid colour. Exhibited at the 1827 Salon, this portrayal of an incident from the Tudor period reflects the growing French interest in English history over the decade. Delaroche's vast *Death of Elizabeth*, shown at the same Salon, marks a radical change in scale, as well as a new audacity in the treatment of the subject matter.

Jacquand shows Henry VIII's Chancellor, Sir Thomas More, imprisoned in the Tower of London for his refusal to acknowledge the king's supremacy over the English Church. An extract from an unacknowledged source in the Salon catalogue explains: 'he refused the oath of supremacy required by Henry VIII and was condemned to death; his wife exhorting him in his prison to obey the sovereign, he replied: "How many years do you think I have left to live" – "Twenty years, at least" [she replied] – "What is twenty years, measured against eternity?" '[1] The use of the Latin form 'Morus' in the title could imply that Jacquand took the anecdote from a work of Catholic piety. But More's decision to follow his conscience held a broader appeal.[2] A play entitled *Thomas Morus, ou le divorce de Henri VIII* was published in Paris in 1827, and an earlier performance might also have prompted the subject.

Jacquand's figures owe little to historical research. The bearded figure of More bears no resemblance to known portraits, and it appears improbable that he might have had twenty more years to live! For the 57-year-old chancellor, Jacquand may have employed the veteran model featured in a previous painting of the Lyon studio by Jean-Marie Jacomin.[3] Yet he has taken some care over the furnishings of the Gothic chamber, both to reinforce the message of the work and to display his historical credentials. More's outstretched arm emphasises the vehemence of his reply, but it also draws our attention to a headless medieval statue on the far wall that anticipates his fate. The jug placed on a table in the left foreground plays no narrative role. But it reminds us that the Lyon painters were among the first French collectors of medieval domestic objects. SB

1. Sanchez and Seydoux 1999, p. 166.

2. The republican Paul-Louis Courier wrote in 1820 that he had 'always agreed with Chancellor Thomas Morus' on this point (*Courier*, 1820, vol. I, p. 148).

3. *L'Atelier de Révoil en 1817* (Musée des Beaux-Arts, Lyon, 2006–3).

CHARLES-MARIE BOUTON
(1781–1853)

[6] *The Fourteenth-Century Room in the Musée des Monuments Français*, 1817

Oil on canvas, 114 × 146 cm
Musée de Brou, Bourg-en-Bresse (982.156)

Provenance: Acquired from Galerie Didier Aaron & Cie, Paris, 1982.

Bouton, a pupil of David, first exhibited at the Salon in 1810 with a view of a subterranean chapel at St Denis, a picture now untraced, but no doubt inspired by the destruction of the early years of the Revolution, when numerous tombs were removed from that great church. In 1812, in a logical progression, he sent in a *Philosopher meditating beside the Tombs in the Thirteenth-Century Room at the Musée des Petits-Augustins* (this was Lenoir's Musée des monuments français). He continued to take the museum as subject, and to emphasise the force of its 'period' evocations, sending in 1814 a *View of the Fifteenth-Century Room*, and finally, in 1817, a year after the closure of the museum (and perhaps, as Marie-Claude Chaudonneret has suggested, as a final tribute to it [1]), the *Fourteenth-Century Room*. This is probably the second of two versions of this final view; the first (Musée Carnavalet, Paris) differs in representing only a single visitor taking notes.

The tombs of Charles V and Jeanne de Bourbon are visible to the right, placed on a base made up of wood panelling from the Sainte Chapelle; to the left, in a series of arches from Saint Denis, Lenoir had placed, upright, a set of formerly recumbent figures from tombs taken from Saint Denis and various Paris convents. In such a setting it is tempting to recall, with Marie-Claude Chaudonneret, the words of the historian Jules Michelet, remembering his childhood visits to the museum: 'What was I looking for? I hardly know – the life of the time, no doubt, and the spirit of the ages. I was not altogether certain that they were not alive, all those marble sleepers.' For Bouton, the 'life of the time' here takes form as the unhappy king Charles VI, subject to fits of madness, who broods at the tomb of his father, while his sister-in-law, Valentine de Milan, keeps curious onlookers at a distance.

This is anachronistic only if we do not interpret the scene as theatre: Charles VI was to appear and reappear as a subject, not only in historical accounts (notably in Prosper de Barante's *Histoire des ducs de Bourgogne*) but, in a period drawn to themes of madness, in the theatre and in opera too. Bouton himself shortly afterwards entered into partnership with Louis-Jacques-Mandé Daguerre, at this time still a theatre designer, to set up the Diorama, thus taking to its logical conclusion the power of light and architecture to reconstitute the past as dramatic experience. LW

1. Chaudonneret 1983, p. 413.

AUGUSTIN LEMAITRE (1797–1870)

[7] *The Gallery at the Hôtel de Bourgthéroulde, Rouen* (from *Voyages pittoresques et romantiques en l'ancienne France*, vol. 2, *Normandie*, plate 158), 1823

Lithograph on paper, 19 × 25.5 cm
Private collection

FREDERIC VILLENEUVE (1796–1842)

[8] *The Chapel of the Holy Sepulchre, St Jacques, Dieppe* (from *Voyages pittoresques et romantiques en l'ancienne France*, vol. 1, *Normandie*, plate 75), 1821

Lithograph, impression on tint stone, on India paper, laid down, 32 × 24 cm
Private collection

PAUL DELAROCHE (1797–1856) AND EUGENE LAMI (1800–1890)

[9] *Mary Stuart at Lochleven Castle* (from Amédée Pichot's *Vues pittoresques en Ecosse*, Paris, 1826, p. 51), 1826

Lithograph on India paper, laid down, 13 × 19 cm
Private collection

In 1821, Isidore Justin Séverin Taylor (1789–1879), shortly to receive the title of Baron, travelled to Scotland with Alphonse de Cailleux and the writer Charles Nodier, who was host to poets and painters at the library of the Arsenal in Paris. Nodier described the journey in his *Promenade de Dieppe aux montagnes d'Ecosse*. They both worked for the theatre, Taylor at the newly founded Panorama Dramatique, staging melodramas where scenery and effects were of the utmost importance. In 1825, Taylor moved to the Comédie-Française, where he later produced Hugo's *Hernani* and Dumas's *Henri III et sa Cour*, both associated with authentic costume and dramatic staging. He also contributed to the initial funding of the Diorama. As Eliane Vergnolle has noted, 'all these activities converged in the publication of the *Voyages pittoresques*', in which he collaborated with his two travelling companions, Nodier and Cailleux.[1] The *Voyages* continued, in a sense, the project of the now-closed Musée des monuments français, employing draughtsmen and lithographers to record the picturesque remains of the ancient buildings of France. Bouton, Daguerre and Bonington all collaborated on this enterprise.

The architectural remains, recorded in lithographs, and using the spectacular effects of light which lithography made possible, frequently included incidents and personages associated with their early history, in a manner comparable with the evocations of the Troubadour painters. Augustin Lemaître's view of the Hôtel de Bourgthéroulde presents it as a backdrop to just such a chivalric scene. The gallery, a slightly later addition of 1520, bears low-reliefs recording a major historic event of that very year, the meeting of Henry VIII and Francis I which became known, from the magnificence of tents and display, as the Field of the Cloth of Gold.

In the accompanying text, Nodier emphasises his commitment to continuing by other means the work of the Musée des monuments français, paying tribute to Alexandre Lenoir and also to the eighteenth-century antiquarian Bernard de Montfaucon, who had taken particular pains (without success) to interpret these relief sculptures.

7

Nodier commissioned one of the most gifted of his collaborators, Alexandre Evariste Fragonard, to make a set of lithographs recording for posterity the appearance of the crumbling sculptures, placing them in the book immediately after the present image. Though many of the plates make reference to events associated with the site depicted, some of the finest are merely evocative, with the simple placing of a contemplative spectator. Here, in Villeneuve's splendidly atmospheric Gothic chapel, a solitary figure in prayer acts as mediator for the viewer.

Paul Delaroche did not work on the *Voyages pittoresques*, but he knew Nodier, and probably through him met Amédée Pichot, a prominent anglophile translator of Scott and Byron, who took a particular interest in the young Delaroche. Pichot encouraged him (in 1825), to think of turning to Walter Scott for a subject, and in 1826 commissioned from him some illustrations for his own *Vues pittoresques de l'Ecosse*. This was a single volume offering a variation on the theme established by Nodier, and employing some of the same artists, including Bonington and Villeneuve. Pichot's descriptions, particularly in the early part of the book, feature frequent quotations from Scott, whom Pichot had met several times in 1822. *Mary Stuart at Lochleven* was to be Delaroche's second Scottish subject; a year or so earlier, he painted *Edward in Scotland* (cat. 25), an episode from the life of Charles Edward Stuart, whose history Pichot himself was in the course of writing. The image, in which Sir Robert Melville urges Mary Stuart's abdication, accompanies a long quotation from Scott's *The Abbot*. The history of Mary Stuart offered parallels with that of Lady Jane Grey (as indeed it did with the more recent fate of Marie-Antoinette), and had been the subject of a successful melodrama, *Le château de Lochleven*, by Pixérécourt in 1822. It was also the subject of a sculptural group which Delaroche's close friend Félicie de Fauveau sent to the Salon of 1827. The grieving women whom Delaroche shows here anticipate Lady Jane Grey's attendants, within a composition which, in its frontal and tripartite arrangement, resembles elements in the painting of Lady Jane Grey.

Pichot dedicated his book to the Duchesse de Berry, who felt a particular interest in the Queen of Scots. The duchess herself appeared as the Queen in the pentultimate year of the Restoration, and in a costume recorded by Delaroche's close friend Eugène Lami (who worked with Delaroche on his contributions to Pichot's book), seen in *The Procession up the Staircase* (cat. 36). LW

1. Paris 1979–80, pp. 105–119.

8

9

ZACHEE PREVOST (1797–1861), AFTER PAUL DELAROCHE (1797–1856)

[10] *Saint Vincent de Paul preaching before the Court of Louis XIII on Behalf of Abandoned Children (Saint Vincent de Paule prêchant devant la cour de Louis XIII pour les enfants abandonnés)*, 1834

Burin engraving on paper, 56 × 36.5 cm
Private collection

[FIG. 20] Paul Delaroche (1797–1856) *Study of a Child seen from Behind*, about 1823. Graphite, 23.9 × 19.2 cm. Musée des Beaux-Arts d'Orléans (598)

Several of the major paintings that marked the development of Delaroche's art have been lost or destroyed over the past two centuries. The artist himself recognised this danger, and took special pains to ensure that his work would be preserved in the form of reproductive engravings.[1] Exhibited at the Salon 10 years after the original had been shown at the Salon of 1824, this print reproduced the earliest of his paintings to be perpetuated in the traditional French manner.

Following upon his *Pietà* (1822 Salon), destined for the private chapel of the Duchesse d'Orléans, this commission from the elder branch of the Bourbon family marked a significant advance in the young Delaroche's career. Its first owner, the Duchesse de Berry, was the widow of the Duc de Berry (assassinated in 1820), and mother of the infant Duc de Bordeaux, who was in line to succeed to the French throne. Delaroche no doubt benefited from the fact that the duchess's extensive artistic patronage was exercised in competition with the Orléans family. He also made use of the painting to cement a connection with the ailing Théodore Géricault, who represented the most advanced and daring art of the day for the young students emerging from the studio of Baron Gros. He had overheard Géricault praising features of his *Joas* on a visit to the 1822 Salon, and seized the opportunity to visit him and gain his friendship. Around October 1823, when Géricault was mortally ill, Delaroche transported the *Saint Vincent de Paul* to Géricault's studio at the latter's request.[2] Given that the 'little dead children' featured in *Joas* had earned the senior painter's special praise, it is hardly surprising that Delaroche should have focused the right-hand section of the work on a picturesque grouping of 'abandoned children'.[3]

In other respects also, the painting testified to Delaroche's evolving studio practice. The way the light falls on the soaring Gothic columns of Notre-Dame implies an interest in the medieval interiors of the Lyon School, and perhaps in the lithographic renderings of Norman churches already being published in the *Voyages pittoresques*. Prominent members of the court audience seem to have been modelled by Delaroche's fellow lodgers at La Childeberte, beside the Abbey of St Germain des Prés. The elderly man on the left (for whose pose there exists a study) is probably the painter Jean-Frédéric Schall, and his seated neighbour is Adolphe Roger, the Gros student who modelled as the amorous painter in *Filippo Lippi enamoured of his Model* (also 1824 Salon). There is an especially charming pencil study for the small child closest to the saint (fig. 20).[4]

The engraver of the painting, Zachée Prévost, was a former pupil of the renowned engraver Bervic, and a close friend of Louis Henriquel-Dupont, who had exhibited an acclaimed aquatint of Delaroche's *Cromwell and Charles I* at the 1833 Salon.[5] At Prévost's death in 1861, this engraving was held to rank among his finest. SB

1. See Bann 2001, pp. 39–40.
2. Halévy 1861, p. 250.
3. See Paris 1991, pp. 300 and 305, for the chronology of Delaroche's contacts with Géricault.
4. See Bann 2006, pp. 354–5.
5. See Bann 2008, p. 61.

[11] Meyrick Visitors' Book, 1820–30

The Wallace Collection, London. Hertford House Historic Collection (HHHC 2007.395)
Ink on paper, object size 23.8 × 19.7 × 1.2 cm

Provenance: Bought (with unknown provenance) at a books and manuscripts sale, Phillips, Son and Neale, London, 1 October 1981, lot 294. Gift of Mrs Daphne Lucas, 2003.

EUGENE DELACROIX (1798–1863)

[12] *Studies of armour from the Meyrick Collection*, 1825

Lead on paper, 19.1 × 27.9 cm
The Wallace Collection, London. Hertford House Historic Collection (PA2 / HHHC 2006.2)

Provenance: Delacroix sale, Paris, 17–29 February 1864, no. 655 or 656; Sotheby's, London, 15 February 1950; presented to the Library of Hertford House, 1954.

ROBERT BELL (1806–1872?), AFTER SIR JOHN WATSON GORDON (ABOUT 1788–1864)

[13] *Portrait of Sir Walter Scott in his Study*, 1871

Engraving on paper, printed by McGlashon, 68 × 42 cm
Private collection

Samuel Rush Meyrick, a barrister, was the first to make a systematic study of arms and armour. He rearranged the armouries of Windsor and the Tower of London in order of historical development, and formed a collection of his own, displayed, until 1830, at his London house, and later at his newly built castle in Herefordshire. His romantic view of the Middle Ages invites comparison, inevitably, with Sir Walter Scott, one of the first visitors to sign this book. During the 1820s, as Stephen Duffy notes, more than fifty British artists visited the collection.[1] As Meyrick had hoped, the collection was clearly of great interest and value for those contemplating the treatment of historical themes. Duffy mentions 'a dozen or so French painters', a particularly interesting aspect of the book which throws new light on friendships and encounters otherwise only occasionally glimpsed through correspondence. Géricault was the first major French painter to sign the book, apparently in 1820. We know of his strong interest in British art, and his powers to transform the work of minor English artists, including Henry Alken and Ben Marshall, into unforgettable images of his own, particularly in his series of London lithographs. It is possible that Géricault's known encouragement of the young Paul Delaroche shortly before his own death may help to account for Delaroche's engagement with British art early in his career.

Barely two years after Géricault's visit (and this is one of the surprising revelations of the book), Delaroche visited the collection, in company with his fellow pupils Hippolyte Bellangé and Eugène Lami. The evidence for this visit overturns the earlier assumption – based on later accounts – that Delaroche paid his first brief visit to London in 1827, to collect material for *The Princes*

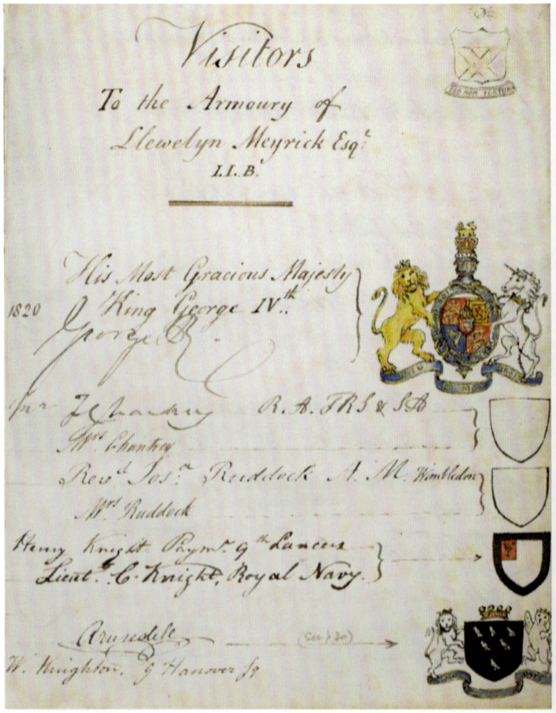

11

in the Tower. As Stephen Duffy points out, Charles Clément's claim that Géricault visited the Tower armoury cannot be proved by any surviving drawings;[2] there is no evidence, either, that Delaroche did so on this early visit. However, since the Tower armoury was, at that time, in the course of Meyrick's own rearrangement, it is at least possible that Meyrick may have talked about it to him, perhaps kindling the fascination with the Tower which was to underpin three of Delaroche's English subjects during the coming decade.

An additional interest attaches to the appearance of the name of John Arrowsmith (see page 30), the Anglo-French picture dealer, almost immediately above the names of the three young French painters. It is possible that he was already beginning to

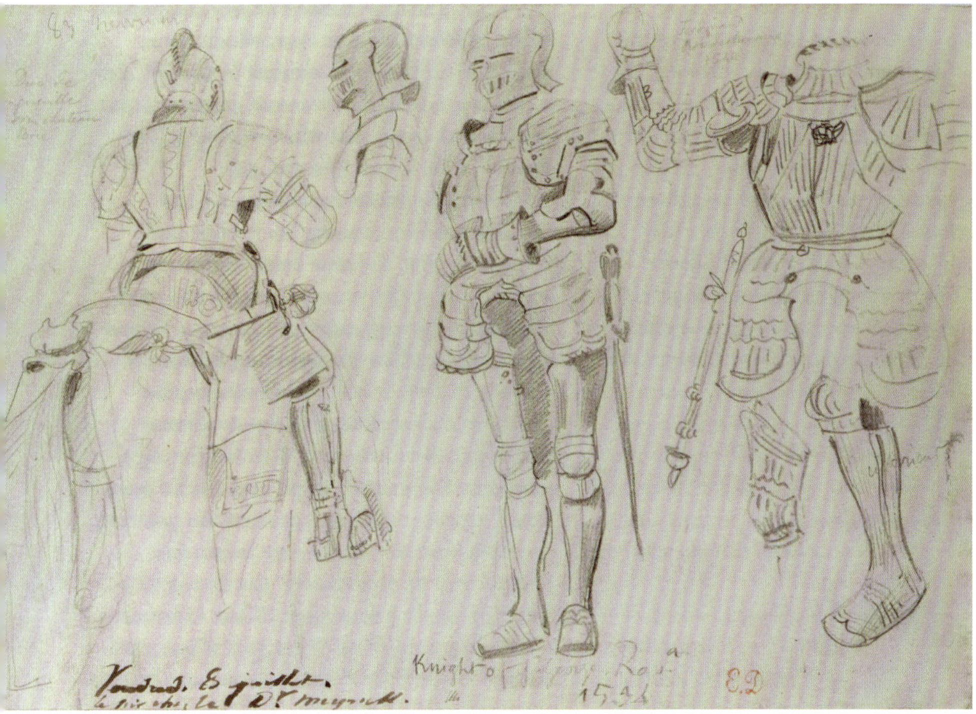

12 13

form his plan to take a professional interest in the work of Delaroche, and perhaps he too encouraged an interest in English subjects, as Stephen Duffy suggests.

There are no known surviving drawings recording Delaroche's visit to the Meyrick collection, though there are several by Bonington. Delacroix's visit, on 8 July 1825 (he also visited on the next day), is documented and dated by this sheet of studies of sixteenth-century armour (cat. 12). It shows, from left to right, the 'Buckhurst' armour, now in the Wallace Collection; a suit of German armour (Warwick Castle), and a suit of late sixteenth-century armour, also in the Wallace Collection. Thus Delaroche, Bonington, Delacroix, Alexandre Colin, and the now little-known Gillot Saint-Evre, all artists who turned to English subjects in the 1820s, were no doubt stimulated and inspired by the visits which this absorbing book records.

Robert Bell's print reproduces a posthumous portrait of Sir Walter Scott (cat. 13), showing him in his study at 39 Castle Street, his Edinburgh house until it was sold in 1826.[3] The map of Scotland on the wall, the suit of armour to one side, and Scott's absorption in, presumably, some of the many documentary sources for his own work, provide a characteristic image of Sir Walter Scott of the kind probably in the thoughts of Bonington and Delacroix when they visited the Meyrick collection, taking from it (at least in the case of Delacroix, and quite possibly of Bonington too) a plan to think about *Quentin Durward* as a subject for painting. LW

1. See Duffy 2009, pp. 284–92 for a very full discussion of the book and its significance. The Wallace Collection website, www. wallacecollection.org/ learning/research provides a transcription of the book.

2. Duffy 2009, p. 287.

3. Russell 1987, p. 43.

PAUL DELAROCHE (1797–1856)

[14] *The Princes in the Tower (Les Enfants d'Édouard)*, 1830

Oil on canvas, 181 × 215 cm
Musée du Louvre, Paris (Inv.3834)

Provenance: acquired by the French state from the Salon of 1831 for 6,000 francs and exhibited at the Musée du Luxembourg; transferred to the Louvre in 1874.

In the catalogue of Delaroche's work published after his death it was noted: 'In general [...] Paul Delaroche began his pictures in proportions or in forms that were different from their definitive forms and proportions.'[1] This observation, made with regard to his *Death of Elizabeth*, applies in particular to the studies leading up to *The Princes in the Tower*, and the two versions of the picture that were painted. Delaroche was certainly familiar with the scene from Shakespeare's *Richard III* that had been strikingly portrayed by Sir Joshua Reynolds' pupil, James Northcote, in 1790, and was reproduced in Francis Legat's engraving for the Shakespeare Gallery. The recent revelation of his visit to England in 1822 makes it possible that he saw the original work, and may have met its author, who specially prized this evocation of 'the murder of two innocent children'.[2] On his subsequent visit of 1827, one of Delaroche's priorities was to discover the historical context of this episode from English history. As was later explained in the *Illustrated London News*: 'The costume of the Princes, the bedstead, and its draperies, were carved and made in England, from the best authorities, under the supervision of Delaroche who came expressly to London to visit the scene of his picture.'[3]

In contrast to Northcote, who conveyed little of the context, Delaroche was determined to give some authenticity to the chamber in the Tower of London where the two sons of Edward IV were imprisoned. He consulted visual documents from the period, such as the *Annunciation* by Rogier van der Weyden in the Louvre, from which he borrowed the detail of the hanging medallion on the back wall.[4] In 1828, he plotted his composition with the aid of small plaster figures of the two princes, which remained in the possession of his family 30 years later.[5] Throughout these preparations, however, he was committed to a composition 'en hauteur' – that is to say, taller than it was broad – as in Northcote. At what must have been a late stage in the creation of the work, he decided to make a radical change in its proportions, and 'had about 65 centimetres of canvas sewn on at each side'.[6]

The additional flanking pieces, which remain visible today, enabled him to transform the composition. The left-hand strip enabled him to introduce the dramatic detail of the barred door, with candle-light penetrating through a crack, and the small dog who detects the approach of the assassins. There is, however, a dearth of preliminary studies that might trace this change of plan. Two drawings in the Fogg Art Museum that have now rightly been attributed to Delaroche do not help. As Louis-Antoine Prat has argued, they appear to relate more closely to the second version of *The Princes in the Tower*, painted for the English collector John Naylor in 1852.[7] Yet Delaroche was clearly contemplating a version akin to Naylor's work as early as 1831, when he produced the unique lithograph of the two princes on their knees beside the bed.[8] The Fogg drawings confirm that possible variants were occurring to Delaroche at an early stage. But they do not indicate the transformation of the work by the addition of the little dog and the door. Here the drawings derived from Delaroche's study of *Henri III et sa cour*, which focus attention on the open window to the left, are a better guide to the dynamic interpretation of pictorial space that was revealed in *The Princes in the Tower* (see cat. 50).

Delaroche chose the models for the two princes from among his friends and acquaintances. Reliable later testimony indicates that the younger prince was modelled by the young sister of the artist Félicie de Fauveau, while the brooding Edward V was Henri Delaborde, future biographer of Ingres and secretary of the Académie des Beaux-Arts, who was then beginning a period as Delaroche's pupil and studio assistant.[9] Among those who praised the painting on its appearance at the 1831 Salon was Delaroche's former master, the Baron Gros, who reportedly exclaimed: 'What expression in these two children! What wit! What intelligence in the little dog who looks and listens so well!'[10] SB

1. Delaborde and Goddé 1858, opp. plate 6.
2. Bann 2006, pp. 362–4.
3. Quoted in Bann 1997, p. 94.
4. His intermediary drawing is reproduced in Bann 1997, p. 101.
5. Delaborde and Goddé 1858, opp. plate 14.
6. Delaborde and Goddé 1858.
7. Prat 1997, p. 70. See Bann 2005, p. 30 for Naylor's commission.
8. Reproduced in Bann 1997, p. 95.
9. See Benoist 1994, p. 143, and Larroumet 1904, p. 125.
10. Quoted in Bann 1997, p. 100.

FRANCIS LEGAT (1761–1809), AFTER JAMES NORTHCOTE (1746–1831)

[15] Shakespeare Gallery: *King Richard III, Act IV, Scene III: The Murder of the Princes*, 1790

Etching and engraving on paper, 56.5 × 41 cm
The British Museum, London (Dd.6.26*)

WILLIAM SKELTON (1763–1848), AFTER JAMES NORTHCOTE (1746–1831)

[16] Shakespeare Gallery: *King Richard the Third, Act IV, Scene III: The Burial of the Princes*, 1795

Etching and engraving on paper, 56.5 × 41.4 cm
The British Museum, London (Ee.2.151)

ISAAC TAYLOR (1730–1807), AFTER THOMAS STOTHARD (1755–1834)

[17] Shakespeare Gallery: *Henry VIII, Act I, Scene IV: Henry VIII leading Anne Boleyn to the Dance*, 1798

Etching and engraving on paper, 50.4 × 63.5 cm
The British Museum, London (Dd.6.27)

THOMAS RYDER (1746–1810), AFTER THOMAS STOTHARD (1755–1834)

[18] Shakespeare Gallery: *Othello, Act II, Scene I: The Meeting of Othello and Desdemona*, 1799

Stipple engraving on paper, 49.8 × 63 cm
The British Museum, London (1977.U.739)

John Boydell opened his Shakespeare Gallery in Pall Mall in 1786, having commissioned from Thomas Banks a sculptural group representing Shakespeare between the Dramatic Muse and the Genius of Painting – exactly representing his own ambition for the Gallery. He was able to meet the great expense of his scheme from the proceeds of some thirty years of commercial success, during which he had also succeeded in establishing a British school of engravers to rival the perfection of the French. It was a success based largely on commissioning and selling reproductive prints; the most famously successful was William Woollett's engraving after Benjamin West's *Death of Wolfe*, published in 1776. Not only did Boydell receive £15,000 for it, over 15 years, but he also established, with this celebrated print, a precedent for the representation in the grand manner of a recent historical event.[1]

Preliminary discussions for the Shakespeare Gallery began at a dinner party in Hampstead, at the home of his nephew, Josiah Boydell, who was later to become a business partner. At home in Cheapside, among Boydell's own pictures, hung James Northcote's *The Murder of the Princes in the Tower*, from *Richard III*. Northcote later claimed this as the origin of the scheme, though other artists, including Romney and Fuseli, also claimed to have thought of the idea (Fuseli while lying on his back looking at the Sistine Chapel ceiling).

The essence of the scheme was the publication of a series of large plates illustrating the plays of Shakespeare, and a smaller series planned to accompany an edition of the plays; some two hundred prints in all. Boydell commissioned the paintings from which these were made; they hung in the Shakespeare Gallery, together with other contemporary works from his own collection, but the engravings themselves were at the heart of it. The engravers, indeed, were often paid more than the painters, who included Sir Joshua Reynolds, Benjamin West and James Barry, as well as a number of artists better known as illustrators. The whole enterprise invited both keen interest and criticism; Charles Lamb famously complained: 'What injury did not Boydell's Shakespeare Gallery do me with Shakespeare. To have Opie's Shakespeare, Northcote's Shakespeare, light-headed Fuseli's Shakespeare, wooden-headed West's Shakespeare, deaf-headed Reynolds's Shakespeare, instead of my and everybody's Shakespeare' – perhaps not unlike the response to the film of a favourite book. However, it was not criticism of this kind, but the war with France which led to the ultimate failure of the gallery, ending in Boydell's near-bankruptcy in 1804.

The last quarter of the eighteenth century saw the rise of a marked enthusiasm for Shakespeare, stemming in part from the acting of Mrs Siddons and David Garrick, and stimulated by Garrick's Shakespeare Jubilee at Stratford in 1769. Various illustrated editions appeared, as well as books of plates. Boydell's, however, was on a different scale, as he describes it in his *Preface*: it was for artists 'to carry into execution an undertaking, where the national honour, the advancement of the Arts, and their own advantage, are equally concerned'.

Though some of the artists involved occasionally used actors to model the principal parts, the compositions themselves were not based on theatrical performance; many, indeed, are set in landscapes of a kind almost impossible to present in a theatre. Not surprisingly, perhaps, for a scheme aiming at 'the advancement of the Arts', and

Engraved by Francis Legat.
SHAKSPEARE.
King Richard the Third.
ACT IV SCENE III.
15

SHAKSPEARE.
ACT IV. SCENE III.
16

[FIG. 21] Caroline Watson (1760–1814), after Sir Joshua Reynolds (1723–1792) *Death of Cardinal Beaufort*, from 'Henry VI part II, Act III, scene III', 1792. Engraving, 60 × 37 cm
Private collection

opening only 20 years after the founding of the Royal Academy, it was the example of Sir Joshua Reynolds, and particularly the advice repeatedly given in his Discourses, which underpinned much of the imagery. In his 12th Discourse, he advised young artists that 'hints may be taken and employed in a situation totally different from that in which they were originally employed'. For Reynolds, as for Fuseli, the example of Michelangelo was the most compelling. Reynolds's *Death of Cardinal Beaufort* (fig. 21), itself indebted both to Poussin and to Michelangelo, must certainly have been a 'hint' to which Delaroche responded, as well as the very much milder Westall, in his *Wolsey resigns the Seals*, since he incorporated elements of both into his image of Joan of Arc (figs 11, 26).

Of the present examples, Northcote's *Murder of the Princes*, though very different from Delaroche's version, takes up the theme of innocent victimhood (and, by extension, of usurpation), central to so much of Delaroche's future work. *The Burial of the Princes*, resembling, as it does, Caravaggio's *Deposition* (about 1600–4, Pinacoteca Vaticana, Rome), thereby draws some of its force from this structural reference to a sacred subject, in a manner which anticipates Delaroche's own methods. *Lady Jane Grey*, *Charles I insulted*, and *Marie-Antoinette* are among those works whose compositions recall specific types of sacred imagery. We may think again of Reynolds's advice to 'take hints'; the hands, so strangely and alarmingly emerging at the foot of the stairs here, provide a motif which Delaroche uses, with equal dramatic effect, for the blessing bestowed by Archbishop Laud as Strafford makes his way to execution (cat. 54). The portcullis, too, reappears in that work. The structures of *Henry VIII leading Anne Boleyn to the Dance*, and *The Meeting of Othello and Desdemona* are certainly more reminiscent of the theatre itself than are Northcote's differently dramatic works, but, typically, they represent a posed moment, tableau-like; a singular pause within the diffuse action of a play. The central, innocent figure, not yet a victim, raised, as if on a stage, in the case of *Othello*, and the silent brooding figure to the right, may have suggested to Delaroche some elements of his *Lady Jane Grey*, which has a similar effect of suspended motion.

Paul Delaroche was not alone in responding to these prints. They were widely known on the Continent; the Venetian painter Benvenuti made drawings after several of them, and an album of drawings in the Louvre, attributed to the engraver Charles Pierre Joseph Normand, reproduces a number of them, including Smirke's *First Age* (RF 41744, recto) from *As You Like It*, another composition (fig. 22) from which Delaroche may have taken some hints, for works which were certainly unrelated to its own subject. The notion of entrances and exits, an essential element of theatrical performance, may also have played its part in suggesting the central dramatic idea of Delaroche's *Princes in the Tower*. LW

[FIG. 22] Peltro William Tomkins (1759–1840), after Robert Smirke (1752–1845) *The First Age*, from 'As You Like It, Act II, Scene VII', 1799
Engraving, 45.6 × 54 cm. Private collection

1. See Sillars 2006, pp. 254–99 for the recent account, and a full bibliography.

SHAKSPEARE.
King Henry the Eighth.
ACT I. SCENE II.

17

SHAKSPEARE.
Othello.
ACT II. SCENE I.

18

JEAN-PIERRE JAZET (1788–1871), AFTER PAUL DELAROCHE (1797–1856)

[19] *The Death of Elizabeth (Derniers Moments de la Reine Elisabeth 1603)*, 1844

Mezzotint on paper, 74 × 61 cm
Published by Goupil and Vibert, Paris, 1844
Bibliothèque Nationale de France, Paris (AA6)

[FIG. 23] Paul Delaroche (1797-1856), Oil sketch for *Death of Elizabeth*, about 1827. Oil on canvas, 43.2 × 35.6 cm. Private collection.

When *The Execution of Lady Jane Grey* (cat. 53) appeared at the Salon of 1834, the critic Gustave Planche complained that Delaroche had plagiarised a work by the English painter John Opie, taking his composition from Opie's *Execution of Mary Stuart* (cat. 62). This was only partially true; Delaroche's composition, as the present exhibition makes clear, is much richer and more complex in its allusive references. However, in his review Planche also referred to an earlier work, *The Death of Elizabeth* (Musée du Louvre, Paris), from the Salon of 1827, in which, undeniably, the debt to another English picture was clear. Like the Opie, it had been engraved for Robert Bowyer's Historic Gallery. Bowyer's scheme resembled Boydell's, and employed a number of the same artists, but illustrated David Hume's *The History of England* rather than the works of Shakespeare. In this case, Delaroche's source was Robert Smirke's *Queen Elizabeth appointing her Successor* (1796, untraced), engraved for Bowyer by James Neagle. In the entry he supplied for the Salon catalogue, Delaroche gives Hume as his source, with no attempt to conceal his borrowing. Perhaps Smirke's image, as an 'enactment', offered itself as a credible representation, and had the merit of following closely Hume's text, an instance of Delaroche's habit of depending on what he took to be an authentic historical account. It may have been for this reason, too, that Delaroche, rather uncharacteristically, as far as we can judge from his known work, made a painted copy of Smirke's composition, though his final version differs from it. The Salon picture's immense size was probably, as Stephen Bann suggests, an attempt at a spectacular *grande machine*, comparable with Achille Devéria's *Birth of Henry IV*.[1] It was not as widely admired as other works by Delaroche; its unrelieved hot colouring, and the pitiless representation of the dying queen, struck critics as somewhat disagreeable, but it was nonetheless bought by the state for 6,000 francs, the same price as Devéria received for his picture.

Jazet, nephew of the late-eighteenth-century engraver Louis-Philibert Debucourt, made this print very much later, when Delaroche's most famous Salon pictures were being translated into the medium of large and elaborate engraving, published by the firm of Goupil in partnership with Jazet's own son-in-law, Théodore Vibert. Here, Jazet is taking a composition belonging to an earlier period in Delaroche's work, and for this has used the *manière noire* popularised, in Arrowsmith's time, by S.W. Reynolds and his French followers, of whom he was one.[2]

The print bears a dedication to the Duke of Sutherland, the first owner of *Strafford on his Way to Execution* (cat. 54), and marks the Duke's continuing interest in Delaroche's historical subjects. LW

1. Bann, in London, Minneapolis, New York, 2003, pp. 35–6.

2. As Patrick Noon has pointed out, in 1829 Jazet made an aquatint after Bonington's *Amy Robsart and the Earl of Leicester* (cat. 39). The term *manière noire* was used in French for both mezzotint and aquatint. See P. Noon, *Richard Parkes Bonington, The Complete Paintings*, New Haven 2008, p. 438.

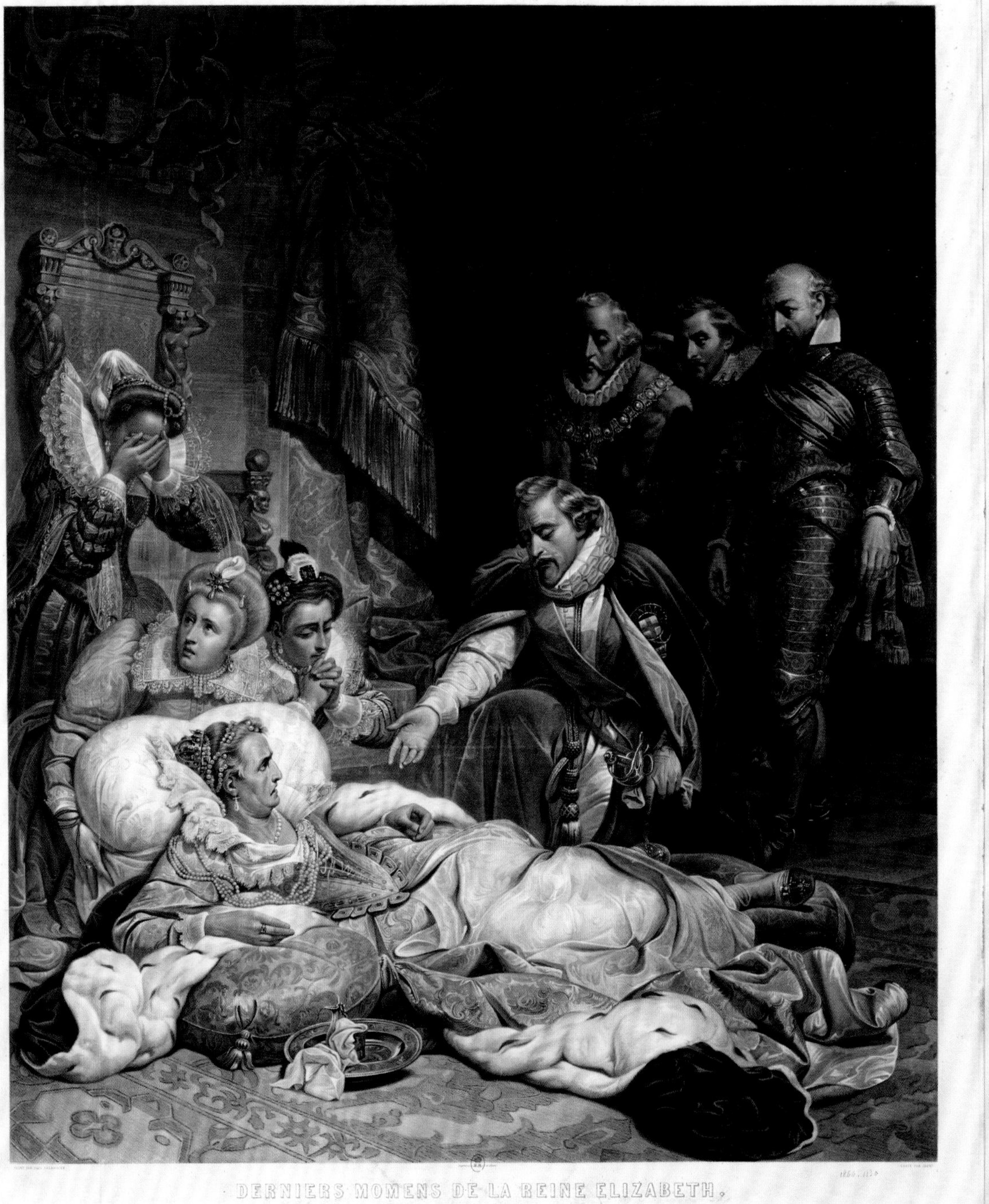

DERNIERS MOMENS DE LA REINE ELIZABETH.

1603.

Dédié à Monsieur le Duc de Sutherland

Paris _ Goupil & Vibert, Rittner, Bulla & Delarue, Jeannin _ Éditeurs.

JULES FRANÇOIS (1809–1861) AFTER PAUL DELAROCHE (1797–1856)

[20] *Louis-Antoine d'Artois, Duc d'Angoulême, at the Fort of the Trocadéro, 31 August 1823*, about 1850

Engraving on paper, 34 × 24 cm
Private collection

FRANCESCO BARTOLOZZI (1727–1815)

[21] *Mr Copley's Picture of the Siege of Gibraltar as Exhibited in the Green Park near St James's Palace*, about 1800

Photomechanical print on paper, 9.9 × 12.8 cm
The British Museum, London (1894.0102.67)

ACHILLE LEFEVRE (1798–1864) AFTER PAUL DELAROCHE (1797–1856)

[22] *Taking of the Trocadéro (Prise du Trocadéro)*, about 1845

Engraving on paper, 18 × 20 cm
Private collection

[FIG. 24] Paul Delaroche (1797–1856), detail from *Eight Studies of Fighting Soldiers*, around 1827. Graphite, 34.3 × 25 cm. Museum of Art, Rhode Island School of Design (57.107)

The Bourbon regime of the Restoration had witnessed the occupation of France by foreign troops following the Battle of Waterloo in 1815. In 1823, the opportunity finally arose for the dynasty to prove itself in a military campaign. French troops under the command of the Duc d'Angoulême, the nephew of Louis XVIII and prospective heir to the throne, intervened on behalf of the duc's Bourbon cousin, Ferdinand VII of Spain, who was suppressing a liberal uprising. This action culminated in the successful capture of the Trocadéro, a fortified position near Cadiz.[1] A year later, in 1824, Angoulême's father ascended the throne as Charles X, making his elder son the Dauphin of France. Moves were made to commemorate the campaign with a commissioned painting, in the tradition of the great battle pictures of the Empire. Baron Gros, Delaroche's master, originally accepted the task, but withdrew after a disagreement with the government over engraving rights. Eventually, in February 1827, the decision was taken to commission Delaroche. He demanded a fee of 10,000 francs, which he later received.

It was made clear to Delaroche that he would have no subsidy for a visit to the battle's location in southern Spain. In fact, he chose the spring of 1827 to make a visit to England. It is already on record that, during this excursion, he researched the costumes and furniture for his *Princes in the Tower*.[2] The likelihood that he also seized the opportunity to view contemporary battle paintings while on the other side of the Channel must be strong. Étienne Delécluze, the critic and former student of David, reflected on the kinship of the first work with David's less than heroic later paintings, such as *The Coronation of Napoleon* (1806–7, Musée du Louvre, Paris). However, the broad concept

20

21

of the composition, with the commanding officer and his staff aligned to the right, while witnessing the successful attack that proceeds the one below (22), evokes a well-known previous painting of a successful British engagement in southern Spain: John Singleton Copley's *Defeat of the Floating Batteries at Gibraltar, September 1782* (1791, Guildhall Art Gallery, London). Delaroche could have seen this work in London, and might have been familiar with William Sharp's engraving of 1810.[3] Bartolozzi's print shows that it was a popular painting on regular display (21).

There exists a fine ink drawing for the first painting in a private collection.[4] Delaroche was later commissioned to paint a second version of the event, with Angoulême playing a more active role (20). A drawing for this composition demonstrates that he made numerous new studies from the life, one of which served for the officer shading his eyes to the right (fig. 24). Both the engravings on exhibition are taken from the *Galeries historiques de Versailles*, which illustrated the paintings of famous French battles over the ages. The works themselves were not included in Delaroche's retrospective exhibition of 1857, and remain in store at Versailles. SB

1. See Ziff 1977, pp. 57–61.
2. See Bann 1997, p. 94.
3. See Bann 2006, pp. 346–7.
4. Illustrated in Bann 1997, p. 162.

PAUL DELAROCHE (1797–1856)

[23] *Cromwell and Charles I (Cromwell découvrant le cercueil de Charles Ier)*, 1831

Oil on canvas, 230 × 300 cm
Fonds national d'art contemporain (Cnap), Ministère de la culture et de la communication, Paris, Fnac PFH – 2803. On long-term loan to the Musée des Beaux-Arts, Nîmes.

Provenance: 1830, state commission (5,000 francs), allocated to the Nîmes museum in 1834.

Delaroche's *Cromwell and Charles I* arrived late at the 1831 Salon, where his *Princes in the Tower* was already on exhibition. As the critic Horace de Viel-Castel observed, the work 'took the attention of the public straight away, [and they] were silent for hours on end, astonished by the deep and melancholy ideas that this painting awakened in them'.[1] The scene showed Oliver Cromwell viewing the body of Charles I, King of England, after his execution by order of the Parliament on 30 January 1649. But it struck home in France as providing a directly contemporary lesson. French writers like Châteaubriand and the historian François Guizot accustomed the French public to thinking of the English Civil War as a forerunner of their own Revolution. Here was a powerful visual symbol that exposed the historical predicament in which the French nation was still involved, less than a year after the July Revolution of 1830 had forced the exile of the elder branch of the Bourbon dynasty. As Viel-Castel exclaimed: 'It is at a period like our own, in a century when the destinies of kings have been found to weigh little in the scales of the great interests of the people that the picture of Cromwell arrives, and strikes us with all its high morality.'

Yet the fact that the work was commissioned by the state before the July Revolution indicates that Delaroche could not have anticipated this fortuitous timing. It was later claimed that the decision to send the painting to Nîmes could be traced to the Duchesse de Berry, mother of the Bourbon heir to the throne, who had earlier acquired his *Saint Vincent de Paul* (cat. 10).[2] But by 1831 the Duchesse de Berry was in exile, and it is more likely that the destination of the work was secured by Guizot, who held high office in the new government of Louis-Philippe.[3] Guizot was born in Nîmes, and would have been mindful of the extreme suffering of the city during the Revolution. Once it was hung in the city museum (then lodged in the Roman temple known as the Maison Carrée), the citizens of Nîmes became deeply attached to the work. They refused to permit it to make the journey to Paris for the Delaroche retrospective in 1857.

If *Cromwell* held a special message for the French and for the Nîmois in particular, it was also the painting that established Delaroche's reputation in Europe as a whole. The German poet Heinrich Heine wrote a lengthy criticism in which he hailed the artist as the 'choir-leader' of the new French school of historical painting, and memorably characterised the depiction of Cromwell: 'There he stands, a form as firm as earth, "brutal as fact", powerful without pathos, naturally supernatural, marvellously commonplace, outlawed and yet famous, beholding his work almost like a woodman who has just felled an oak.'[4] Delaroche responded to this general acclaim by arranging for the young printmaker Louis Henriquel-Dupont to engrave an aquatint, which was shown at the 1833 Salon. Even the reduced version of the work which Delaroche painted as an aid to Henriquel's reproduction found an honoured place in the nascent collection of the city of Hamburg. *Cromwell* was also recreated as an authorised full-scale replica by Delaroche's favoured ex-pupil Charles Jalabert, which was exhibited at the Royal Academy in London in 1850.

Towards the end of his life, Delaroche looked back on the work as a touchstone of the new approach that he had brought to the rendering of historical subjects. 'At the time of my *Cromwell*,' he claimed, 'people reproached me for making it too true, and now this figure has become the type for anyone wishing to represent him, either in the theatre, or in sculpture, even in England, where they are proud of this *big hypocrite*.'[5] By this time, the painterly qualities of *Cromwell* were also appreciated. Charles Blanc wrote that 'to find a costume drawn with more facility, better modelled in its surfaces, better detailed in its folds, in fact rendered with a brush that is freer, more flexible and at the same time firmer, one must go back as far as Van Dyck'.[6] SB

1. Viel-Castel 1831, p. 269.
2. Gillet 1934, p. 257.
3. Guizot owned a drawing for *Cromwell*, with a personal dedication by Delaroche, which is now in the Musée Tavet-Delacour, Pontoise.
4. Heine (no date), p. 81.
5. Quoted in Bann 1997, pp. 106–7.
6. Quoted in Nantes and Montpellier 1999, p. 289.

SAMUEL WILLIAM REYNOLDS (1773–1835), AFTER PAUL DELAROCHE (1797–1856)

[24] *Filippo Lippi enamoured of his Model whilst painting in a Convent*, 1828

Mezzotint on paper, 27.9 × 22.6 cm
The British Museum, London (1868.0612.364)

SAMUEL WILLIAM REYNOLDS (1773–1835), FINISHED BY ALEXANDRE SIXDENIERS (1795–1846), AFTER PAUL DELAROCHE (1797–1856)

[25] *Edward in Scotland* (*Edouard en Ecosse*), 1833

Mezzotint and etching on paper, 50.8 × 40.5 cm
The British Museum, London (1902.1011.7980)

GEORGE MAILE (ACTIVE 1800–1842), AFTER PAUL DELAROCHE (1797–1856)

[26] *The Children of the Storm* (*Les Enfants Surpris par l'Orage*), about 1827

Mezzotint on paper, 54 × 42 cm
Private collection

SAMUEL WILLIAM REYNOLDS (1773–1835), AFTER PAUL DELAROCHE (1797–1856)

[27] *Joan of Arc*, 1829

Mezzotint on paper, 48.5 × 37. 5 cm
Bibliothèque Nationale de France, Paris (AA-4)

When John Arrowsmith bought John Constable's *Hay Wain* and *View on the Stour* in 1823, he was confident that he would be able to show both pictures at the Salon of 1824. As Constable observed, it was part of an ambitious scheme to give the French some notion of English art. Arrowsmith must have known that certain painters and writers in France had already developed a taste for English art, and this probably helps to account for his confident speculation in the work of Constable. However, his plan was an elaborate one, and was in part dependent on S.W. Reynolds, whom he brought over to Paris for the purpose of making prints after Constable's work. This was to involve not only the Salon pictures, but also an additional set of twelve views of Brighton subjects. Arrowsmith's finances were not sound, and the scheme, which might have extended Constable's reputation in France far beyond the circle of his immediate admirers there, came to nothing. In the interim, however, Arrowsmith and his associate Claude Schroth, picture dealer to the Duchesse de Berry, managed to commission a series of prints after the work of a number of young artists, both English and French, in whose work they took an interest.

As a result of his own part in this, Reynolds (already admired in France as a landscape painter) was at the centre of a group of painters, some French and some English, linked by ties of friendship and esteem. These included Bonington, his friend Frederick Tayler (a particular protégé of Reynolds, who studied a little with Delaroche, and sat to him for his portrait in 1825), Paul Huet, Delacroix, and Delaroche himself, one of the most frequently reproduced of all the artists associated with the two dealers during the 1820s. Schroth and Arrowsmith commissioned Reynolds to make prints after works by all of these, and after works by a slightly older generation: Charlet, Léon Cogniet, Forbin, Géricault, Granet and Prud'hon. These were all artists who offered, in one way or another, a challenge to the Davidian tradition, exactly as Arrowsmith had intended.[1]

Reynolds, an intimate friend of the great Shakespearean actor Edmund Kean, and a fierce radical in politics, was an outstanding engraver in mezzotint, training a younger generation including Samuel Cousins and David Lucas in England, as well as several printmakers in France. George Maile, long settled in France, and Alexandre Vincent Sixdeniers both occasionally worked with him, and are likely to have learned something of his technique. Mezzotint was at that time known in France as the *manière noire*, and, as Auguste de Forbin remarked, appeared peculiarly suited to reproducing the qualities of the English School.[2] In 1819, Reynolds had contributed plates to J.M.W. Turner's *Liber Studiorum*; during the period of his frequent stays in France, working for Schroth and Arrowsmith, he was also engaged in engraving a large part of the *oeuvre* of Sir Joshua Reynolds. As a warm admirer of John Constable, no doubt he discussed his admiration for these and other painters with his young French colleagues. *Filippo Lippi enamoured of his Model*, the earliest of Delaroche's pictures to be engraved by Reynolds, shows the influence of the Troubadour artists as well as that of Ingres's *Paolo and Francesca* (1819, Musée Condé, Chantilly), but might also be compared with Bonington's small-scale watercolours on historical subjects. The *Children of the Storm* shown here in the version engraved by Maile, and published by Arrowsmith, must owe something to Henry Thomson's *Distress by Land* (fig. 25) at Stourhead, and is

PHILIPPO LIPPI
chargé de peindre un tableau dans un couvent, devient amoureux de la religieuse qui lui servait de modèle
Gravé par S. W. Reynolds, Graveur du Roi d'Angleterre, d'après le Tableau Original de P. DelaRoche, à Paris, chez Arrowsmith
Déposé
24

EDOUARD EN ECOSSE.
25

[FIG. 25] Henry Thomson (1773–1843?) *Distress by Land*, 1811.
Oil on canvas, 237.5 × 145.4 cm
Stourhead/The National Trust

more English than French in appearance.[3] The original painting belonged to Claude Schroth, as did *Edward in Scotland* (originally called *Miss Macdonald*). Delaroche painted this scene at about the time he was contributing to Pichot's *Vues pittoresques en Ecosse*. It represents Flora Macdonald bringing food to the cave in which Charles Edward Stuart, the Young Pretender, is hiding. Uncharacteristically for Delaroche, at least in later years, it probably comes from a literary source, Alexandre Duval's play *Edouard en Ecosse*; first produced in 1802, when it was immediately withdrawn, for political reasons; it was briefly revived in 1814, and then again, successfully, in 1819.[4] The original painting, at present untraced,[5] is an early example of Delaroche's interest in Stuart history and, more generally, in the question of legitimate monarchy. *Joan of Arc*, the largest and most dramatic of these works, introduces the theme of martyrdom which runs through so much of Delaroche's later work. It too may have a play as its source: Loeillard d'Avrighi's *Jeanne d'Arc à Rouen*, first performed in 1819.[6]

All the paintings, except *The Children of the Storm*, appeared, with success, at the Salons of the Restoration. Arrowsmith's plan to produce prints after popular Salon successes was short-lived, owing to his lack of capital. However, the eventual successor to his print-publishing business, and thus the subsequent owner of these early plates, was Adolphe Goupil, with whom the name and international reputation of Paul Delaroche was later so closely associated. LW

1. Whitman 1903, p. 172.
2. Vauthier 1918, p. 172.
3. Paul Joannides originally suggested this to Stephen Bann, who kindly passed it on to me.
4. Oddly, Alexandre Duval chooses to call Miss Macdonald 'Malvina'; presumably because the play first appeared in a period of particular enthusiasm for Ossian.
5. A version appeared as lot 200 in a Christie's sale held in Glasgow on 12 June 1996. I am extremely grateful to Mr Francis Russell and to his colleagues for their kind assistance in trying to establish its present whereabouts. At present, however, it is once again untraced.
6. See Rouen 1983, p. 17 and n. 44–5.

Gravé par Maile, d'après P. DelaRoche, chez Arrowsmith.
deposé

26

JEANNE D'ARC.

27

PAUL DELAROCHE (1797–1856)

[28] *Joan of Arc interrogated in Prison by Henry Beaufort, Cardinal Bishop of Winchester*, about 1824

Pen and brown ink over graphite on paper with grey, brown and blue wash, squared in graphite, 22.7 × 17.5 cm
Ashmolean Museum, Oxford (WA 2001.165)

Provenance: Yvonne Tan Bunzl, 2001.

[FIG. 26] Paul Delaroche (1797–1856) *Joan of Arc in Prison*, 1823–4. Oil on canvas, 21 × 17.6 cm The Wallace Collection, London (P604)

When Delaroche's immense painting of *Joan of Arc*, now at Rouen, appeared (to great acclaim) at the Salon of 1824, it belonged, like John Constable's *Hay Wain*, to the dealer John Arrowsmith, who had known the young artist for several years (cat. 11). In his review of that year's Salon, the critic Auguste Jal mentioned that the owner was proposing to have the picture engraved in England, by Samuel William Reynolds. In fact, Arrowsmith was planning a very much more ambitious scheme, which involved bringing Reynolds to France, and was, arguably, to determine the course of Delaroche's later career and reputation (cats. 24–7).

The present watercolour, obviously a preparatory work, since it is squared for transfer, may have been a stage in the making of Reynolds's mezzotint after the painting. It resembles a smaller version, in oil, in the Wallace Collection (P.604), in which the slight differences from the Salon version correspond with some elements in this watercolour: the light hair of the secretary standing behind the bishop; his own jutting chin and sharper features, and the construction of his pectoral cross. The watercolour may thus be based on the Wallace Collection picture, and made in order to transfer the composition to the mezzotinter's copper plate. The monochrome character of the colouring seems to confirm this; had it been intended simply as a record of the painting, Delaroche would surely have chosen to give it some of the intensity of colour with which he dramatised the confrontation between Joan and the Bishop of Winchester. The fitfully lit staircase, curving out of sight to the rear, occupies rather more space than in the Rouen picture, giving a more 'gothic' character to the subject, in keeping with the fashionable taste for dimly lit interiors of the kind associated with Granet and Bouton, and in which Reynolds himself specialised while in France. The figure of the Cardinal Bishop is of a type which derives, in the 'borrowing' vein of Sir Joshua Reynolds and from Michelangelo's *Prophet Ezekiel*, in the Sistine Chapel and Reynolds's own *Death of Beaufort*, but Delaroche drew on a large number of sources,[1] including a similar figure in James Northcote's print, *Feckenham and Lady Jane Grey*, from Bowyer's Gallery (cat. 63). Clearly, then, already at some point while working on his *Joan of Arc*, Delaroche would have been prompted to think about the history of Lady Jane Grey.

If we can rely on the inscription on the reverse, 'anc. coll. Coutan', this watercolour (together with what seems to have been the earliest version of the subject [fig. 26]), was one of a large number of preparatory works by Paul Delaroche in the collection of Louis-Augustin Coutan, a keen admirer of the kind of painting Arrowsmith was hoping to encourage; he also collected works by Bonington, Constable and Delacroix, from whom, in 1823, he commissioned a scene from *Ivanhoe*, Delacroix's first subject taken from Walter Scott. To judge from the number of preparatory drawings formerly in his collection, Coutan was particularly interested in Delaroche's working processes. LW

1. M.-P. Foissy-Aufrère discusses many of these, and other sources, literary and historical, in Rouen 1983.

PAUL DELAROCHE (1797–1856)

[29] *Study after François Clouet (about 1516–1572), Portrait of Charles IX*, 1830s

Graphite on paper, 11 × 8.5 cm
Private collection

Provenance: formerly Delaroche-Vernet Collection.

[30] *Boy in Costume relating to Younger Prince in the play Les Enfants d'Edouard*, about 1832

Graphite with body colour on paper, 28.6 × 23 cm
Collections de la Comédie-Française, Paris (MC. ENF.1833 [H1 Bis])

Provenance: design for a Comédie-Française production

Of Delaroche's interest in the theatre, especially in the period from 1829 onwards, there can be no doubt. It is often asserted that he designed costumes for the theatre and the opera during this period. But Alexandre Dumas fails to confirm the tradition that Delaroche was involved in the costumes for Dumas's play *Henri III et sa cour* (1829), although there is clear evidence that he drew upon the last act for his own compositional studies (cat. 50). Dumas does, however, assert that Delaroche was the designer for Casimir Delavigne's *Marino Faliero* later in the same year, and pokes fun at the rumour that he tried to 'get the movement of the wind' into his costumes.[1] Though there is every possibility that Delaroche did collaborate with his friend Delavigne, the prints depicting the costumes do not disclose whether he realised this ambition!

Delaroche did undoubtedly make autograph sketches after historic portraits, and these might have served for costume designs. His rapid study after François Clouet's full-length portrait of the French king Charles IX (Musée du Louvre, Paris) could have been made in the process of collecting details of period dress for the first production of Meyerbeer's opera *Les Huguenots* in 1836. Charles IX was the monarch in whose reign the slaughter of the Huguenots known as the Massacre of Saint Bartholomew's Day took place in 1572. Delaroche's interest in being associated with this opera is easy to understand, given his view that post-revolutionary France was still suffering from the long-term effects of that divisive outbreak of religious intolerance. But once again there appears to be no convincing visual evidence of his involvement.

This is partly a consequence of the types of visual documentation that have survived. Theatre costumes were put on record after the event in print collections such as the *Galerie dramatique* of Martinet (cat. 55). In the case of the Comédie-Française, there are also surviving sets of the actual designs used for the production of costumes. Indeed Delavigne's *Les Enfants d'Edouard* is one of the first plays for which such an extensive visual record – accompanied by a contemporary inventory of the costumes – remains extant. But the set of costume studies in question is not from Delaroche's own hand. By this time, he was delegating duties to pupils. Gustave Larroumet explicitly states: 'In Delaroche's studio, the pupil most fond of the theatre and the most knowledgeable about history [was] Henri Delaborde. It [was] he who, under the master's direction, designed the costumes for [Delavigne's] *Louis XI* and the *Enfants d'Edouard*.'[2]

In this context, Olivia Voisin's discovery of a drawing in the dossier of *Les Enfants d'Édouard* is significant. It relates broadly to the costume that Richard, Duke of York wears in the early acts of the play, not omitting the dagger that he half-draws impulsively in Act I, Scene 9 (see cat. 33). A version of the striking plumed hat, which does not feature in Alexandre Lacauchie's later costume prints of the Duke of York (cats. 33, 34), does, in fact, make its appearance in Maleuvre's contemporary print of the costume for Martinet's *Galerie théâtrale*. Though debatable as an authentic period feature, this can be related to the fashion for plumed hats that developed after their spectacular display on the heralds assisting at the Coronation of Charles X in 1827.[3] This drawing is clearly not a conventional costume design, but a posed portrait in costume, possibly involving the young Delaborde, who had already modelled the elder prince for Delaroche's painting. The quality and style of the drawing suggest that it was sketched by Delaroche himself. Presumably it was passed on to the theatre for reference in the devising of Anaïs's first costume. SB

1. Dumas 1966, pp. 107–8.
2. Larroumet 1904, p. 126.
3. See the reference to the fashion in Hugo 2009, vol. 2, p. 89. Such plumed hats can be seen in Lami's lithographs of several of the participants in the Duchesse de Berry's Ball (1829). A portrait of an unnamed woman, signed and dated by Delaroche in 1829, features another fine example.

29

30

LOUIS MARIN-LAVIGNE (1797–1860)

[31] *Mademoiselle Anaïs, in the role of Misaël in 'The Macchabees'*, about 1824

Coloured lithograph on paper, 27 × 20 cm
Private collection

ATTRIBUTED TO PIERRE MALEUVRE (1740–AFTER 1803)

[32] *Mademoiselle Georges and Mademoiselle Anaïs: Roles of Salome and Misaël in 'The Macchabees'*, about 1824

Engraving on paper, 23 × 16 cm
Private collection

CHARLIER, AFTER DRAWING BY ALEXANDRE LACAUCHIE (ACTIVE 1833–1846)

[33] *Mademoiselle Anaïs Aubert: Role of Duke of York in 'The Princes in the Tower'*, about 1840

Coloured engraving on paper, 29.5 × 20 cm
Collections de la Comédie-Française, Paris

ALEXANDRE LACAUCHIE (ACTIVE 1833–1846)

[34] *Mademoiselle Anaïs Aubert*, about 1840

Lithograph on India paper, 32 × 25.1 cm
Private collection

Anaïs Aubert (1802–1871), known professionally as Mademoiselle Anaïs, was one of the most famous French actresses of her day. Because of her small stature, she was obliged to specialise in the roles of boys and naïve young women, known as 'ingenuités'. Her first important engagements were at the Théâtre de l'Odéon, in the Latin Quarter of Paris. She played the part of Misaël, the youngest of the Macchabee brothers, in Alexandre Guiraud's five-act tragedy, *Les macchabées ou le martyre*, which opened on 14 June 1822. From 1832 onwards, she was a *sociétaire* of the Comédie-Française, that is to say, a full salaried member of the illustrious national company. In this capacity, she played the role of Richard, Duke of York in Casimir Delavigne's three-act tragedy, *Les Enfants d'Edouard*, which opened at the Théâtre National (the present Comédie-Française) on 18 May 1833.

The prints that display her in these two roles indicate the attempt to preserve expressions and gestures in such mementoes of the live performance. The charming lithograph by Marin (a pupil of Delaroche's future father-in-law Horace Vernet) appears not to represent a specific moment in the play. However, the print from Martinet's *Galerie dramatique*, which shows her beside the celebrated Mlle Georges, has a brief text that refers it to the final act of *Les macchabées*. The boy Misaël (clothed in a blue robe in the coloured version of the print) is being warned by his mother, Salome, that he is due to rejoin his elder brothers as a martyr in heaven. The engraving after *Les Enfants d'Edouard* by Charlier, from Martinet's second series, also refers to a dramatic climax: in Act I, Scene 9, young Richard threatens to draw a dagger on his uncle, the scheming Duke of Gloucester. The draughtsman for this print, Alexandre Lacauchie, has retained all the details of the elaborate costume in his contemporary lithograph, where Anaïs is posed beside a wooden chest with Gothic carving. This lithograph, published around 1840 to accompany an account of Anaïs's notable career, is intended to represent the actress in her favourite role. She chose to wear the same costume for her appearance in Edmond Geffroy's group painting, *Les Sociétaires de la Comédie-Française* (1840).

Most revealing of the close connections between the staging of Delavigne's play in 1833, and Delaroche's 1830 painting, are the two lithographs after drawings by Octave Tassaert that must be records of the live performance (fig. 27). These portray significant moments in the drama. The episode from Act II, Scene 9 focuses on the gesture of defiance by the elder prince, when he demands that Gloucester remove his cap in the presence of their mother, the widowed queen. The episode from Act III, Scene 14 demonstrates how closely the staging followed Delaroche's composition at this final stage of the tragedy. Between these two episodes, Anaïs has changed her costume from (to quote the theatre inventory) an outfit of 'gold-imprinted sky-blue silk' to one of black silk, more in harmony with Delaroche's original colouring.[1] SB

1. See the costume inventory dated June 1833, 3AP Costumes XIXe, Bibliothèque de la Comédie-Française.

L. Marin.
Mlle ANAÏS
Artiste du Théâtre Royal de l'Odéon
Rôle de Misaël dans les Macchabées.
No. 45
A Paris, chez NOEL ainé et Cie Editeurs Rue de Vaugirard N° 34.

31

.... Mon fils, voilà tes frères.
Melle GEORGES ET Melle ANAÏS.
Rôles de Salomé et de Misaël dans les Machabées.

32

33

34

[FIG. 27] Hippolyte Garnier (1802–1855), after Octave Tassaert (1800–1874), *Les Enfants d'Edouard*, 1833. Lithographs, 35.5 × 37 cm, Smithsonian: National Museum of American Art.

PAUL DELAROCHE (1797–1856)

[35] *Portrait of Casimir Delavigne*, 1826

Charcoal and coloured chalks on white paper, 27.9 × 21.9 cm
Galerie Talabardon & Gautier, Paris

Delaroche's early friendship with the writer Casimir Delavigne (1793–1843) may have encouraged his own interest in historical and literary subject matter, and certainly led to his early involvement with the theatre. At the Lycée Napoléon (now Henri IV) in Paris, Casimir was a schoolfellow of the playwright and opera librettist Eugène Scribe, who sometimes collaborated with Casimir's older brother Germain. Delaroche may have met Scribe through his friendship with the Delavigne brothers, and thus obtained his commission to design the costumes for Meyerbeer's *Les Huguenots* (1836), for which Scribe provided the libretto.[1]

Casimir Delavigne began his literary career as a poet: after Napoleon's defeat at Waterloo he began a series of poems known as the *Messéniennes*; the third and fourth of these, which Delaroche must have known, dealt with the life and death of Joan of Arc. Delavigne devoted a later poem in the series to Byron and the cause of Greek independence; his first play, *The Sicilian Vespers*, performed at the Odéon in 1819, enjoyed considerable success, particularly among liberals, who found in it analogies with the contemporary situation in France.

In 1829 he put on *Marino Faliero*, based on a Byron subject which had recently been painted by Delacroix (Wallace Collection, London). The production was extraordinarily lavish, with music by Rossini. Delaroche is said to have designed the costumes.[2] At this point Delavigne was one of a young generation of writers who were open to the latest developments in the world of literature and theatre. However, the interest and protection of the Duc d'Orléans, soon to become King Louis-Philippe, tended, after 1830, to place him in the position of a semi 'official' writer; a position not unlike that of his friend Paul Delaroche, with whom he was often compared. The comparison of the two became inevitable after the production of Delavigne's play *Les Enfants d'Edouard*, in 1833, with its unmistakeable references to Delaroche's painting (cat. 14).

In 1826, the date of this portrait, Delaroche had not yet painted any of the formal portraits in oils at which he later excelled. In the small-scale drawings of these early years, which were often informal studies of friends, he frequently used coloured chalks. This may have been in response to a vogue within the little circle of the painter and collector Jules Auguste, a fellow pupil in Gros's studio, who worked in pastel. The circle included Bonington, Delacroix, Paul Huet and another pastellist, Baron Schwiter (whose portrait by Delacroix hangs in the National Gallery). Charles Lenormant, without making a sharp distinction between coloured chalks and pastel (a distinction which by the nineteenth century was not always clear), wrote of Delaroche's work in this charming vein reminiscent of the intimate portraiture of the eighteenth century: 'This is a new direction, in which no doubt we shall see many come to grief, before anyone succeeds in it half as well as M. Delaroche.'[3] LW

1. There is no known documentary evidence for this, though it is commonly stated, and Alexandre Dumas mentions it in his *Memoirs*.
2. Sechan 1883, p. 118.
3. Lenormant 1833, p. 152.

EUGENE LAMI (1800–1890)

[36] *The Procession up the Staircase (La montée dans le grand escalier)*, 1829

From the *Quadrille de Marie Stuart* (*Mary Stuart Ball*), published by Fonrouge, 1829
Coloured lithograph on paper, 52 × 35 cm
Private collection

Marie-Caroline Ferdinande of Bourbon-Two Sicilies, Duchesse de Berry, the early widowed daughter-in-law of Charles X, was at the centre of a society considered to be exceptionally agreeable and brilliant. She collected pictures, admired the work of the Troubadour painters, commissioned *Quentin Durward* subjects from Bonington (cat. 4) and Delacroix, and in 1822 gave Delaroche one of his first commissions. Her dealer was Arrowsmith's associate Claude Schroth; her keeper of paintings Ferréol Bonnemaison, who shared her interest in contemporary art, and bought Delaroche's *Joan of Arc* (now in Rouen) from Arrowsmith.

She took a particular interest in Mary Stuart, an interest no doubt stimulated by the French royal family's temporary exile at Holyrood, and perhaps also by her own position as a young foreign consort at the French court. For the Monday of Carnival week, 2 March 1829, she arranged a fancy-dress ball which came to be known as the *Quadrille de Marie Stuart* (*The Mary Stuart Ball*). Alexandre Dumas claimed for it something more substantial than a mere frivolity; he placed it among current attempts to resurrect earlier periods of history (to which, he added, he was himself no stranger, as his own *Henri III et sa cour* (cat. 50), whose first performance had taken place the month before, would confirm).[1] The ball was intended to recall the arrival of Mary Stuart at the French court as wife of the Dauphin, the future (and short-lived) Francis II. The English ambassadress, Lady Stuart de Rothesay, took the role of the Scots Queen Mother, while several guests came dressed as their own sixteenth-century ancestors. The Duchess took the part of Mary Stuart. Henri Duponchel, who was director of the Opéra, and whose name has also been associated with part of the planning of the ball, described crowds flocking, in the weeks before, to the Print Room of the Bibliothèque royale in pursuit of the degree of authenticity to which Dumas had also aspired in his play. Dumas tells us that Lord Drummond (played by a Captain Drummond) was the most magnificent (though this distinction was claimed for several guests, and most frequently refers to the Duc de Richelieu, cat. 38).[2] It was Richelieu, according to Duponchel,[3] who wore a costume based on Clouet's portrait of Charles IX; in that case, one similar to the Earl of Leicester's costume in Bonington's picture (cat. 39).

There is some uncertainty about the authorship of the costume designs; Dumas's remarks, echoing Duponchel,[4] suggest that the guests each made their own arrangements, but some artists' names have been mentioned, including Alexandre-Evariste Fragonard, the finest artist associated with the *Voyages pittoresques*. The duchess herself said later that Lami, Isabey and Duponchel were the designers. The ball was commemorated in a set of coloured lithographs based on watercolours by Lami. The two had collaborated three years earlier on the *Vues pittoresques d'Ecosse*, in which there were several references to Scott's novel *The Abbot*, and thus to Mary Stuart, whose imprisonment and flight to England are integral to the novel. The Marquis de Pastoret, whose portrait Delaroche painted in the same year, made the arrangements with Lami on behalf of the duchess. A bound copy of the book, bearing the name of one or other noble guest written on the flyleaf, was presented to each. The present image (which comes from a copy originally belonging to one of the *dames d'honneur*, the Comtesse de Montcalm), represents one of the three key moments of the ball – the procession up the grand staircase of the Pavillon de Marsan – and is one of the finest. The great green looped curtain to the side heightens the effect of theatricality, though in retrospect it might seem, like the looming trees in Jean-Honoré Fragonard's *Fête de St Cloud* (Banque de France, Paris), to be about to fall upon the final *fête galante* of the Restoration. LW

1. Dumas 1866, vol. I, p. 4.
2. In fact Dumas may have been thinking of the costume of the Duc de Richelieu (cat. 38).
3. Duponchel 1829, p. 250. I am grateful to Michael Venator for this reference and for much kind help with contemporary theatrical memoirs.
4. Duponchel 1829, p. 244.

PAUL DELAROCHE (1797–1856)

[37] *Study of a Man in Sixteenth-Century Costume (possibly Eugène Lami)*, about 1834

Graphite and coloured chalks on paper, 25 × 20 cm
Private collection

Provenance: Anaïs Aubert; given to Virginie Bourbier 1836; James Mackinnon, 1995.

EUGENE LAMI (1800–1890)

[38] *Jacques d'Albon, Maréchal de St André, represented by the Duc de Richelieu*, 1829

Costume print from the *Quadrille de Marie Stuart (Mary Stuart Ball)*, published by Fonrouge, 1829
Coloured lithograph, 52 × 35 cm
Private collection

This figure drawing by Delaroche suggests a complex relationship between his art and the other contemporary modes of representation, both private and public. It was presented by him to the actress Mademoiselle Anaïs, perhaps early in 1834, and given away to another actress, her friend Virginie Bourbier, in 1836.[1] Previously it was suggested that the study portrayed the actor Firmin (Alexandre Ferré) in the role of Saint-Mégrin in Dumas's *Henri III et sa cour*.[2] However it has recently been shown that the clothing exactly copies the print of the dashing young Duc de Richelieu in period costume at the Duchesse de Berry's Ball in 1829. This opens up several possibilities, some of which may be dismissed without ado.

There is the possibility that the study is a costume design. Yet the emphasis rests undoubtedly on the face of the subject, and not on the detail of the costume, which is lightly sketched. In no way could this delicate and understated drawing be seen as a study for the costume worn at the ball, or indeed for the lithograph deriving from it. Rather, the kinship with the lithograph suggests that the latter is only being used as a point of reference. The vivid characterisation of the face depicted in coloured chalks is unmistakeable. Does this imply that Delaroche has attempted, for some reason, to depict the Duc de Richelieu more vividly than he appears in the lithograph? There is some similarity between the two faces. But the differences are also evident. The coiffure of the subject of the drawing is more unruly, his eyes more deep-set and, unlike with Richelieu, there is a patch of hair below his lip that matches his moustache. Besides, there is no particular reason why a portrait of Richelieu should have been presented by Delaroche to Anaïs, who had no obvious connection with the aristocratic young officer.

A further interesting possibility remains. Eugène Lami was Delaroche's closest friend and fellow lodger throughout the period. It was probably Lami who introduced Delaroche to Anaïs, and a letter exhibited here (cat. 75) indicates that he was privy to their intimate meetings. Jules Boilly's *The Students of Baron Gros in 1820* shows him tousle-headed, with thick dark eyebrows.[3] The portrait of Lami by Delaroche exhibited in 1857, which has the same dimensions as this drawing and indeed dates from April 1834, cannot be traced.[4] But a small self portrait, featuring his elegant moustache, appears in Lami's group study *The Salon of Countess Samoïloff* (cat. 80), where Delaroche is also included in the company.[5] This tiny self portrait does indeed recall the lively face represented in the drawing. The latter might thus represent Eugène Lami *in the guise* of the Duc de Richelieu as the Maréchal de Saint-André – as an actor miming his own lithograph, so to speak. Such a playful tribute by Delaroche to an artist and mutual friend – with whom he was not in competition for the actress's favours – would have been a witty present for Anaïs. SB

1. The ink inscription at the base of the sheet, still just visible, records the gift to Bourbier: 'Offert à Virginie Bourbier par son amie Anaïs le 18 octobre 1836' (Given to Virginie Bourbier by her friend Anaïs 18 October 1836). The pencil inscription '34' on the verso may indicate the date of composition.

2. Bann 1997, pp. 182–3.

3. Reproduced in Bann 1997, p. 42.

4. See Paris 1857b, p. 69.

5. Listed in Lemoisne 1914, p. 172: a later version of the study is reproduced in Lemoisne 1912, opp. p. 100.

37

Jacques d'Albon, Ml. de St André,
Représenté par
Mr le Duc de Richelieu.
Engl Lami 1829.

38

RICHARD PARKES BONINGTON
(1802–1828)

[39] *Amy Robsart and the Earl of Leicester*, about 1827

Oil on canvas, 35 × 27 cm
Ashmolean Museum, Oxford (WA 1933.3)

Provenance: Alexander Hamilton Douglas, 10th Duke of Hamilton, and by descent to the Beckford collection; sold Christie's, London, 6 November 1919, lot 109 (as *The Declaration*); bought by Colnaghi; sold Christie's, London, 31 July 1925, lot 31; bought by Gooden & Fox (for Mrs W.F.R. Weldon); presented by Mrs W.F.R. Weldon in 1933.

The picture received its present title only in 1937, but may represent, as then suggested, the scene from Sir Walter Scott's novel *Kenilworth* in which Amy Robsart urges her husband Robert Dudley, Earl of Leicester, to end the secrecy surrounding their marriage, a secrecy which he, as a favourite of Queen Elizabeth, wishes to maintain. The scene may relate to a moment at the beginning of Chapter 7 describing the arrival of Leicester on one of his occasional visits to Amy Robsart at Cumnor:

Meanwhile the Earl, for he was of no inferior rank, returned his lady's caresses with the most affectionate ardour but affected to resist when she strove to take his cloak from him.

"Nay", she said "but I will unmantle you. I must see if you have kept your word to me, and come as the great Earl men call thee, and not as heretofore like a private cavalier."

Scott lays particular emphasis, in the course of the novel, on the richness of Amy's dress and the dazzling brilliance of her apartments at Cumnor; the kind of brilliance Bonington took particular delight in evoking in paint, as he does here. For Amy Robsart, however, it served only to heighten the irony of her permanent isolation from the court.

There is a lithograph with a similar composition in Bonington's album *Cahier de six sujets*, published in 1826. Like the composition of *Quentin Durward*, therefore, this work has some affinities with the picturesque imagery circulating within print albums in the 1820s; Nodier's publication, the *Voyages pittoresques* (see cats. 7–9) was a magisterial version of such an enterprise. The costumes here look French rather than English; Bonington, like Delaroche (cat. 4), made sketches after Clouet's *Henri II*, and his *Charles IX*, both in the Louvre,[1] and apparently made use of *Charles* IX for the figure of Leicester. In 1827 Delacroix began to design the costumes for Victor Hugo's *Amy Robsart* (it opened in 1828, but ran for only one night). The present painting is not dated, but since Bonington and Delacroix were close friends, and as it is probable that it dates from the same period, we may suppose that they discussed together the scenes of the play. As Patrick Noon has observed, Bonington has drawn on several antiquarian sources for details of costume, in addition to his studies after Clouet, showing the same concern for authentic period costume which characterised theatrical productions in the late 1820s[2] and, indeed, the preparation of costumes for the *Quadrille de Marie Stuart* (cat. 38). As Henri Duponchel commented, the most historically accurate of all the costumes at the Duchesse de Berry's ball was that worn by the Duc de Richelieu; describing the sumptuous details, he wrote 'comme on en peut voir dans le portrait de Charles IX par Clouet'.[3] Though Bonington's picture recalls certain features of 'Troubadour' painting, and shows a concern for the details of period costume, it also derives much from the artists he and Delacroix both admired – Rubens, Titian and Watteau – and from what Delacroix called 'the afternoon light of Veronese'. LW

1. Illustrated in Nottingham 2002, p.69, no. III. Both are reduced versions, painted in the studio of François Clouet. The original life-size portrait of Henry II is in the Palazzo Pitti, in Florence, and that of Charles IX in Vienna.

2. Mr Michael Venator has brought two related images to my attention: a lithograph by Fontenay from this period, showing an actor in a costume which exactly recalls the Clouet portrait, as sketched by both Delaroche and Bonington,and a figure in a watercolour by Delacroix in the Louvre (RF 10639), which closely resembles the others, and may represent a character from Meyerbeer's *Les Huguenots*, for which Delaroche may have designed costumes.

3. Duponchel 1829, pp.249–50.

PAUL DELAROCHE (1797–1856)

[40] *Study for 'The Madness of Charles VI'*, about 1829

Graphite on green paper, 41 × 35 cm
Private collection
Provenance: Delaroche-Vernet Collection. Shepherd DeRom Gallery, New York 2005.

[41] *Study for 'The Madness of Charles VI'*, about 1830

[42] *Study for 'The Madness of Charles VI'*, about 1830

[43] *Person in Medieval Costume with a Throne*

[44] *Empty Throne with Pensive Man nearby, Arms Crossed*

[45] *Study of the Interior of a Medieval Throne Room*

[46] *Figure bending towards a Man seated on a Throne*

[47] *Person standing near a Window, in a Throne Room*

[48] *Two Figures, One seated in a Chimney Hearth*

41. Graphite on beige paper, 7.1 × 5.5 cm (RF 34971)
42. Graphite on beige paper, 6.5 × 6 cm (RF 34973)
43. Graphite and stump on paper, 8.4 × 6.7 cm (RF 34974)
44. Graphite and stump on paper, 15 × 26.5 cm (RF 34970)
45. Graphite on paper, 11.4 × 13.3 cm (RF 34972)
46. Graphite on paper, 5.6 × 8.5 cm (RF 34975)
47. Graphite on paper, 4.9 × 9.4 cm (RF 34976)
48. Graphite on paper, 11.1 × 8.5 cm (RF 34977)

44–8 are undated (mid-nineteenth century)
Musée du Louvre, Département des Arts Graphiques, Paris

Provenance: Delaroche-Vernet-Henraux donation

40

In this group of drawings by Delaroche, all but the first are mounted together, bearing the collection stamp of Delaroche's son Horace, and entered the Louvre in the family donation. The links within the whole group are evident; almost all involve a medieval interior with a throne, with at least one robed figure. The first drawing, which also features the stamp, stands alone in being on green paper, and is larger and more finished than the others. This drawing can also be tentatively dated. There exists a counterproof of the main figure (repeating the motif in reverse), on the verso of one of Delaroche's drawings after Dumas's *Henri* III *et sa cour*. It is argued elsewhere (cat. 50) that the latter drawing should be dated around 1829. Yet if this date is also accepted for cat. 40, it does not necessarily apply to all the Louvre drawings. Delaroche's compositional studies were often spread over several years.

Though it is difficult to date the remaining drawings, it is easy to identify the subject matter of several of them. Cats. 40, 41 and 42 all appear to relate to historical accounts in circulation concerning the 'madness' of the fourteenth-century French king Charles VI. This theme was not unusual in French art of the period. Daguerre's future collaborator Charles-Marie Bouton portrayed the mad king visiting his father's tomb in his painting of the fourteenth-century room in the Musée des monuments français (see cat. 6). But Delaroche probably consulted a more accurate historical source. Prosper de Barante's *Histoire des Ducs de Bourgogne*, first published in 1824–6, ranked as one of the most popular histories of the period, yet also drew critical praise for its fidelity to the style of the medieval chronicles. In condensing contemporary accounts of the bout of madness that overtook Charles VI in 1396, Barante wrote: 'He broke all the windows where he saw the fleur-de-lis. The sight of the queen roused him to fury, and he could not recognise his children.'[1] Charles's aversion to the royal lilies on the throne hangings must be the subject of 41, while his blank attitude to his own family is depicted in 41.

This connection with Barante's text prompts a further suggestion about cats. 41 and 41. Both are small drawings, whose internal framing suggests the form of a vignette. The first fully illustrated edition of the *Ducs de Bourgogne* (1837) published in its third volume a wood engraving by J. Thompson after Delaroche's specially commissioned *Joan of Arc* (p. 52).[2] The first volume had already featured the onset of Charles VI's madness, which occurred while he was riding in the Forêt du Mans, with a vignette designed by the painter Ary Scheffer.[3] Maybe Delaroche originally thought of tackling the subject himself, together with his Joan of Arc assignment. If so, it would be appropriate to date these two drawings to the early or mid-1830s.

Yet it would be implausible to associate all these drawings with such a project. The most striking of them, cats. 40 and 43, are also among the least specific, featuring little

41

42

43

44

more than a distraught figure in medieval dress and a throne. Cat. 40, with its intimation of a female presence on the extreme left, and shadowy onlookers wearing domed headdresses to the right, is especially atmospheric, and evokes a theatrical setting. The mood of Hamlet's soliloquy, 'To be or not to be' comes to mind – though this is not the extrovert Hamlet whom Delacroix would import from English stage productions for his sequence of lithographs (1834–43). Once again, Barante may be relevant. In his preface to the French translation of *Hamlet* (1824; republished 1835), he wrote: 'We do not see him regretting power, aspiring to glory, or burning with warlike ardour. He falls into melancholy even more than into grief.'[4] SB

1. Barante 1842, vol. 1, p. 319.
2. Barante 1842, vol. 3, opp. p. 395.
3. Barante 1842, vol. 1, opp. p. 255. The French sculptor, Antoine-Louis Barye, exhibited a work on this subject at the 1833 Salon.
4. Barante 1835, p. 3, p. 260.

45

46

47

48

PAUL DELAROCHE (1797–1856)

[49] *Henry VIII and his Wives* (recto) and *Three Studies in a Scenographic Manner, with a Stage Plan* (verso), about 1829

Red chalk (recto) and graphite (verso) on near-white wove paper, 10.5 × 16.6 cm
Private collection

[50] *Study after Alexandre Dumas's 'Henri III et sa cour'*, about 1829

Graphite on paper, 11.6 × 17.6 cm
Private collection

Provenance for cats. 49 and 50: formerly Delaroche-Vernet Collection

[51] *Study for The Assassination of the Duc de Guise*, 1830

Watercolour and graphite on white paper, 21 × 31.6 cm
Musée Fabre, Montpellier Agglomération (inv. 876.3.10)

Provenance: J. Claye collection; Bruyas legacy, 1876.

49 RECTO

49 VERSO

Taken together, these studies provide a unique insight into Delaroche's working procedures in the years shortly before his success at the 1831 Salon. They demonstrate conclusively the impact of Romantic dramatic productions upon his distinctive manipulation of pictorial space. They also show how what would prove one of his most celebrated paintings, *The Assassination of the Duc de Guise* (1834, Musée Condé, Chantilly), had its origin, both thematically and in visual terms, in the experiments of these years.

The striking drawing of Henry VIII and his wives testifies to Delaroche's lengthy engagement with English historical themes, which was confirmed by his visit of 1827 and the subsequent appearance of *The Death of Elizabeth* at the 1827/8 Salon. The name of 'Cath[erine] How[ard]', one of Henry's beheaded queens, is visible in the top right-hand corner of the study, while one decapitated lady extends out her dripping head on the left. The caricatural aspect of this composition is underlined by the fact that it is somewhat reminiscent of the solemn ordering of Ingres's *Apotheosis of Homer*, the installation of which at the Louvre in November 1827 was a highlight of the 1827/8 Salon. Ingres also created flanking figures who hold out their arms towards an enthroned central figure. But he did not feature the axe and block in the foreground which anticipates a prominent feature of *The Execution of Lady Jane Grey*.

It is the verso of this sheet that suggests a more precise dating for both drawings. On 10 February 1829, the eagerly awaited premiere of *Henri III et sa cour* by the young Romantic author Alexandre Dumas took place at the Comédie-Française. The cream of Parisian society (including Dumas's employer, the Duc d'Orléans) packed the theatre to witness the intrigues of the sixteenth-century royal court of France, with high romance and violence featured in equal measure. It is in the last scene of the final act that the Duc de Guise bursts into his wife's bedroom, accompanied by armed guards, in his attempt to surprise her in a guilty tryst with the king's favourite, Saint-Mégrin. The agile courtier has jumped out of the window, only to be cut down by Guise's men in the street below. This is the denouement that Delaroche conveys in these three related drawings on a single page. On the related sheet with only one drawing (cat. 50), there is a direct response to the stage direction that the Duchess, 'bending at the knee, grasps hold of her husband to restrain his fury'; meanwhile, his henchman stands at the window, interpreting the violence outside.[1]

Although the first sheet also features a plan of the 'stage' seen from above, it must be stressed that Delaroche was not just reproducing a theatrical spectacle. The often-repeated statement that he was involved in the design of the costumes worn in this production has no clear factual basis. But, in any event, it is irrelevant to the central issue. This is the point that Delaroche evidently recognised the potential for utilising the 'lost space' belonging to the wings of the proscenium stage in a dynamic pictorial composition. Maybe this was the reason why he decided to add the outer bands of canvas to his *Princes in the Tower* around this time (see cat. 14). Probably these drawings were at the beginning of the train of experiments that culminated in the daring use of space in his *Assassination of the Duc de Guise*.

Indeed, the precedent impels us to see the genesis of that important painting in a new light. In Dumas's play, the duke is an overweening subject who directly challenges the king's authority. The final line of the last scene reads: 'Now that we have finished with the valet, let us look after the master.' If Delaroche had painted this picture with the *Assassination* as its pendant, the comparison would have hinted that the rebel was getting nothing but his just deserts. Yet after the young Duc d'Orléans (elder son of King Louis-Philippe, and a descendant of the Guise family) acquired the *Assassination* in 1834, it came to be regarded as a document of martyrdom.

Though the dating of these drawings to around 1829 helps to corroborate the ascription of the date 1830 to cat. 51, questions have been raised about the authenticity of the latter. It is true that this fine study has some features that recur in the 1834 painting, though they do not appear in

50

the intermediate watercolour study for *The Assassination of the Duc de Guise*, bought by Count Anatole Demidoff in 1832 (see p. 39). For instance, the rightmost assassin has a cloak flung over his right shoulder, both in the 1830 study and in the 1834 painting, while in the Demidoff watercolour – and the related drawing in the Victoria and Albert collection – the cape covers both shoulders.[2] But this need not imply that the Montpellier drawing should be dated closer to the final painting (let alone dismissed as a forgery). A curious note in Goddé's catalogue acknowledges that, 'some years before' 1834, Delaroche had completed a watercolour which was stolen from him, and thereupon decided to abandon the painting; yet 'one night the scene appeared to him afresh in a dream, and he set to work straight away'.[3] If this remark in fact refers to the Demidoff watercolour – which had surely not been stolen, but might well have been inaccessible to him – it is no wonder that certain details emerged differently in the Duc d'Orléans's final painting. If it refers to the Montpellier study, then Delaroche certainly achieved a startling clarity of recall. Notwithstanding this issue, it is evident that the Montpellier study anticipates all the most original features of the Orléans painting. SB

1. Dumas 1974, p. 68.
2. For further illustrations of these related works, see Bann 1997, pp. 138, 191 and 193.
3. Delaborde and Goddé 1858, opp. plate 17.

ALEXIS FRANÇOIS GIRARD (1787–1870) AFTER PAUL DELAROCHE (1797–1856)

[52] *Portrait of Henriette Sontag*, 1832

Mezzotint on paper, 32 × 25 cm
Bibliothèque Nationale de France, Paris (Ef 242-a)

Henriette Sontag (1806–1854), a lyric soprano, was much admired in her earliest years both by Beethoven and by Goethe. She was engaged at the Paris Opera in 1827, and in the following year married, in secret, the Sardinian ambassador to the Hague, Count Carlo Rossi. Delaroche represented her in her role as Dona Anna in Mozart's *Don Giovanni*, in the dramatic moment at the end of Act I when she, Don Ottavio and Dona Elvira remove their masks and sing together, confronting Don Giovanni with his crime. The original portrait (formerly in Dresden) appeared at the Salon of 1831, but according to Charles Lenormant was already well known in the society world and in the studios.[1] In deference to her husband's wishes, Henriette Sontag withdrew from professional life after the public acknowledgement of their marriage in 1830 (though she returned, in 1849, with *Linda di Chamounix*, in London).[2] On seeing the picture at the Salon,[3] Charles Lenormant found a 'touching melancholy' in her expression, which, together with the mask which she has removed, and holds in her hand, may carry some suggestion of a valedictory appearance.

Girard's print, which was published by Rittner and Goupil, marks the resumption of the firm's interest in Delaroche's career, after the earlier commitment of John Arrowsmith and Henry Rittner (with whom Goupil had by then entered into partnership).[4] In the following year, they published a print after Delaroche's portrait of the actress Marie Dorval, suggesting that the renewed interest in Delaroche's work arose first in connection with portraits of currently fashionable performers. The painting of Henriette Sontag belonged to a brief but highly significant period in Delaroche's own life, when the theatrical world was indeed one with which he was particularly, and in one respect intimately, familiar. LW

1. Lenormant 1833, pp. 151–2.
2. Her husband lost his diplomatic post when Charles Albert, king of Sardinia, abdicated in favour of his son, Victor Emmanuel, in 1849.
3. The original painting disappeared in 1945. There is a half-length version in the State Hermitage Museum in St Petersburg.
4. Goupil joined Rittner in 1827. By then Arrowsmith had ceased to have any direct connection with the firm, though he may have continued an informal association.

PAUL DELAROCHE (1797–1856)

[53] *The Execution of Lady Jane Grey*, 1833

Oil on canvas, double-lined, 251 × 302 cm
The National Gallery, London (NG1909)
Signed and dated lower right: Paul DelaRoche / 1833.
Frame inscription: *L'EXECVTION DE / LADY JANE GREY / EN LA TOVR DE / LONDRES L'AN 1554'*

Provenance: 1833, bought by Count Anatole Demidoff (1812/13–1870) for FF 8,000; 4 March 1870, sold at Demidoff sale to John Heugh; 24 April 1874, Christie's, bought by Agnew's; 11 July 1874, bought by A.G. Kurz; Kurz sale, 9–11 May 1891, Christie's, bought Agnew's; sold to the 1st Lord Cheylesmore, 7 May 1892, No. 78; bequeathed to the National Gallery, 16 December 1902, by the 2nd Lord Cheylesmore; transferred to the Tate Gallery (then National Gallery, Millbank), 18 December 1902; 1928, damaged in the Thames flood; 1958, declared a total loss[1]; 1973, rediscovered at Tate and transferred to the National Gallery, London.

This huge but finely wrought painting is one of the best examples of the historical dramas that made Delaroche more popular in his lifetime than his contemporaries Ingres or Delacroix. *The Execution of Lady Jane Grey* shows the young great-granddaughter of Henry VII, who, following the death of Edward VI in 1553, reigned for nine days as queen. Deposed by the supporters of the Catholic Queen Mary, she was tried for treason and beheaded at Tower Hill on 12 February 1554.

Delaroche shows the instant when the victim, blindfolded and stripped to her petticoat, is guided to the block by Sir John Brydges, Lieutenant of the Tower. Overcome with emotion, two of her ladies-in-waiting lean against a pillar to the left. The executioner stands aside with rope and dagger, resting on the handle of his axe; at the back, the tips of guards' halberds can just be seen beyond the black scaffold.

With its echoes of the death of Queen Marie-Antoinette 40 years earlier, the story of Lady Jane Grey's fate carried real historical significance. A preparatory drawing for the painting (cat. 66) includes a vignette for a different, subsequently abandoned composition clearly annotated 'La Dauphine et L[ouis] 17 au temple'. The juxtaposition of the two scenes on the same sheet supports the parallel between the fate of Lady Jane Grey and that of the French royal family condemned to the guillotine. An often-drawn analogy between the French and English revolutions had revived an interest in lesser-known English historical figures. The burgeoning Anglomania of the time resulted in an appetite for paintings of ill-fated English royalty. Louis XVII of France and Edward V of England were innocent child victims who died because of political circumstances; so was Lady Jane Grey.

As Stephen Bann suggests (cat. 66), Delaroche may not have initially planned to represent Lady Jane Grey, but probably toyed with the idea of depicting another doomed English royal. Jane Grey was hardly a newcomer to the Salon; there were at least four occurrences of the subject in the two decades preceding Delaroche's showing in 1834.[2] Yet her story, arguably still little-known in France, was only familiar to the *cognoscenti*, and the subject may not have been popular with the public. To allow viewers a full grasp of the painting, Delaroche ensured the facts were set out in the Salon *livret* with a few lines of explanation: 'Jane Grey, whom Edward VI had, through his will, appointed heir to the English throne, was, after a nine-days long reign, imprisoned by order of her cousin Mary, who, six months later, had her beheaded. Jane Grey was executed deep in the Tower of London, aged seventeen, on 12 February 1554.' This background information precedes a vivid description of the scene taken from the *Martyrologe des Protestans*, dated 1588.

The story of Lady Jane Grey had been recounted in historical literature, with accounts of her life in all histories of England. In France, Madame de Staël had turned the Nine Days' Queen's life into drama with her eponymous play,[3] and N.H. Nicholas's *Literary Remains of Lady Jane Grey* had just been translated into French.[4] Delaroche's factual sources for the painting may have been influenced by such literary reminiscences, but historical accuracy was his main goal. He could have opted for a romanticised version of Lady Jane Grey's last moments as the foundation for his painting, but instead, for the sake of accuracy, favoured a sixteenth-century account of the execution, then believed as historically reliable, however dry and obscure.[5]

Delaroche's historical reconstitutions had to be plausible, and the making of his paintings was preceded by extensive research. Endowed with a curious mind and an awareness of visual culture, he had amassed a lot of material which he was able to form and synthesise. The study of *Lady Jane Grey* reveals that Delaroche's visual repertoire for the painting was varied; a compromise between various English sources, Troubadour formulae (see p. 26), and motifs from both religious art and Davidian painting. These were acquired through visiting galleries and exhibitions or sifting through publications or print portfolios. Delaroche came to London in 1827 'expressly to visit the scene of his picture'[6] of the young princes, and researched details of the Tower which could have been used for cat. 53.[7] He probably would have encountered Charles Robert Leslie's *Lady Jane Grey prevailed on to Accept the Crown*, then on display;[8] the young queen's dazzling white dress and delicate hand gesture may have stayed in his memory.

L'EXECVTION·DE
LADY JANE GREY
EN·LA·TOVR·DE·
LONDRES·L'AN·1554

Prints were easily accessible to Delaroche; the son of print collectors and nephew and cousin of print curators,[9] he was able to immerse himself in the tradition of both Old Master and English prints, and frequently used these as a basis of compositions for his historical scenes. His knowledge of James Northcote's *Lady Jane Grey at Prayer*, or *Feckenham, by order of the Queen, visits Lady Jane Grey in the Tower* (cat. 63)[10] is obvious in the finished painting, where the figures are placed on a similar platform, with the Lieutenant of the Tower in the place of Feckenham.

During the eighteenth century, as evident in Northcote's print, Lady Jane Grey was usually depicted on her way to the scaffold during,[11] rather than at the moment of execution. With the exception of a seventeenth-century woodcut,[12] Delaroche had no obvious model for the representation of the young queen kneeling at the block. Instead, he adapted the iconography – richer and more varied – of the execution of Mary, Queen of Scots. The most immediately identifiable source for Delaroche's picture is John Opie's *Execution of Mary Queen of Scots*, engraved by Skelton (cat. 62), produced in 1795 for Bowyer's *Historic Gallery*. The queens' virginal dresses and blindfolds are strikingly alike. In both images, two ladies-in-waiting collapse in distress; Opie's soldier, blindfolding the queen and bending down to guide her, finds an arresting counterpart in Delaroche's Lieutenant of the Tower. Finally the static pose of the executioner – head tilted and eyes lowered to his victim – reinforces the parallels. So obvious were Delaroche's borrowings from the well-known English model that it attracted harsh criticism, culminating with the accusation of plagiarism.[13] 'This is not the first time [...] Mr. Delaroche has stolen from the English', noted Gautier in his Salon review,[14] alluding to his basing of his earlier painting of Elizabeth on one of Smirke's compositions.[15] The Skelton engraving was not his sole source either; his own composition of *Mary Queen of Scots* dismissing Melville (cat. 9), lithographed by Eugène Lami and published in the *Vues pittoresques de l'Ecosse* in 1826, was another obvious precedent.

Delaroche drew inspiration from a wide cultural repertoire accumulated over the years, which included religious imagery. Like David and Géricault before him, he 'alluded to some of the most hallowed pictorial structures of religious art in his secular pictures ... [He] transcended their value in infusing his paintings with the unique authority of religious art'.[16] The compositions of *Joan of Arc* and *The Princes in the Tower* are derived from early Annunciation scenes, while *The Death of Elizabeth* carries clear reminiscences of typical depictions of the Deposition of Christ.

Other pictorial types also influenced the painting's structure and style. Its box-like spatial construction recalls David's paintings, in particular *The Oath of the Horatii* (fig. 28), where the grieving women are similarly relegated to one side of the composition.[17] The weeping ladies in *Lady Jane Grey* also owe a clear – if anachronistic[18] – debt to Hans Holbein's female portraits such as *Anne of Cleves* (1539, then as now in the Louvre), an inspiration noted by Gautier in 1858.[19] Finally, the artist's very reliance on accurate sources likens his picture to the genre of Troubadour painting, as practised by Revoil and Fleury Richard, who exerted much influence on the young Delaroche with their predilection for medieval historical subjects. Yet, for all these borrowings, Delaroche's interpretation of this historical event is strikingly original.

By the time *Lady Jane Grey* was completed in 1833, it was widely anticipated. Théophile Gautier commented: 'how they beat the drums and sounded the trumpets for the Jane Grey painting, two years in advance! Jane Grey who was already expected in the previous Salon...' (see p. 40).[20]

In line with early nineteenth-century academic studio practices which he had been taught and was himself to propagate in his own atelier, Delaroche's large-scale paintings took a long time to complete. Their production followed a painstaking sequence of stages reflecting as well as structuring the artist's creative process. The first step was to define the composition broadly in vignettes – small, unresolved drawings. Then an *esquisse* (coloured compositional sketch) established the composition. After this stage, he made detailed drawings filling in the main elements, often after the live model.

In fact, the formation of this picture seems to have been relatively straightforward, described by Stephen Bann as the painting by Delaroche 'whose genesis is most easy to trace'.[21] Technical examination has revealed no major alterations on the canvas, and despite its large size, there is no evidence that the artist had assistance. The surviving preparatory studies attest to a sequence of steps. Cat. 66 (p. 130) shows the painter experimenting at an early stage with variations for Lady Jane Grey's pose – from standing to kneeling – and with that of the executioner. Delaroche's proposals for these two figures perhaps reveal his study of John Opie's composition (cat. 62), obvious in the central vignette.

The date '1832' inscribed on the Whitworth sketch for Lady Jane Grey (cat. 67) is a gauge of his progress.[22] The main elements of the scheme are now in place. Although more freely executed and less elaborate – particularly in the architecture and some significant differences in both the overall colour and the executioner's figure – this small but inspired watercolour was probably intended as a fully resolved plan for the canvas. It is clearly stated in the *Martyrologe des Protestans*, quoted in the Salon catalogue, '... le bourreau, ayant pris sa hache, luy coupa la teste' (see footnote 5), that the executioner performed his task with an axe. Delaroche was probably unaware of this text while working on this sketch, as a sword can be seen here. This new historical detail may have led him to revise not only the weapon itself, but also the executioner's general attitude and character – turning him from a steady profile view to a more attractive semi-frontal pose in the finished painting. Delaroche also later alters his facial features, differentiating them further from the governor's; for both these figures new models are used. Enlargement on the canvas meant that the costumes of Lady Jane Grey and her ladies-in-waiting had to be simplified and, as a consequence, become more dramatic, and the figures, rather short and squat in the watercolour, are now more refined and elegantly proportioned.

Once his composition was set, Delaroche continued to try out some variants, probably using models, looking for new formal solutions to unresolved problems. *A Study for Two Hands* (cat. 70) shows Lady Jane Grey's hands as she tentatively approaches the block, wearing the long-sleeved dress which appears in the watercolour, as well as in the first stages of the painting (infrared reflectography reveals traces of her sleeves' edges across both her wrists).[23] This study attests to the importance of rendering the young victim's hesitant gesture; it was probably drawn from the model, presumably Mademoiselle Anaïs (on whom, see p. 41), who would have conveyed the queen's reticence effectively.

Two pencil drawings (cats. 68[24] and 69) focus on the figures' positions, with the kneeling queen being helped by the cloaked Lieutenant of the Tower. Both appear in the final painting with little modification. The squarish, detailed study in lead point and red chalk complements the drawings just described in finalising the poses and costumes of the executioner and maids. Praying while facing the central group, the seated lady-in-waiting bears strong echoes of the figure of Margaret Roper (1505–1544), Thomas More's eldest daughter, in Holbein's famous drawing of the *Family of Sir Thomas More*, which Delaroche may have known (Kupferstichkabinett, Öffentliche Kunstsammlung, Basel); Rowland Lockey's *Family of Sir Thomas More* (fig. 29) is adapted from Holbein's completed painting (now lost, destroyed by fire in the eighteenth century). In cat. 53, the figure is flipped, slumped against the large column in a state of collapse. The standing lady-in-waiting hiding her face is only slightly altered – her dress is reworked to incorporate spectacular black velvet sleeves deployed like wings. On the left of the sketch, there is a detailed study of the executioner, adopting the pose of the final version, but attired differently – hatless and with short boots.

Despite its size, the canvas used by Delaroche is a single piece of linen, prestretched (probably to order) and preprimed, onto which the artist applied – as was then the custom – a second layer of priming.[25] He could then transfer the drawings, starting by drawing vertical and horizontal lines on the canvas. These squaring lines, of various scales are still faintly visible with the naked eye but clear in infrared reflectography: at some stage, the artist decided to lower the area of the execution

[FIG. 28]
Jacques Louis David (1748–1825) *The Oath of the Horatii*, 1784. Oil on canvas, 326 × 420 cm Musée du Louvre, Paris (3692)

[FIG. 29]
Rowland Lockey (active about 1593–1616), adapted from a lost painting by Hans Holbein the Younger (1497/8–1543) *Family of Sir Thomas More*, 1593. Oil on wood, 227.4 × 330.2 cm The National Portrait Gallery, London (NPG 2765)

block. More *pentimenti* can be observed in the costume of the executioner (who was originally wearing a sash around his hips), with a gathering of fabric on the side – perhaps a bag – as well as boots, as seen in cat. 72. The position of the pike behind the balustrade and the angle of the banisters may have been altered as well.

After transferring his composition to the canvas, Delaroche started to paint the figures, in brown or grey shades of paint with various depths of tone. This stage of the painting – the *ébauche* – defined the areas of light and dark. The painting was then coloured in, with some components, such as the architecture, the seated lady-in-waiting's sleeves and Brydges's fur coat, very thinly painted – and brought to completion.

The smooth surface of the finished work belies the considerable labour involved in its execution. Delaroche's technique is notable for its high finish, and a slickness of touch reminiscent of the meticulous manner of Northern artists. His treatment of Lady Jane Grey's sleek, luminous satin dress brings to mind Gerrit Dou's *Femme Hydropique* (1663, then as now in the Louvre).[26] Delaroche certainly knew the Louvre's collection of fifteenth-century Northern painters: a few years earlier, while at work on his *Princes in the Tower*, he did a pencil sketch of Rogier van der Weyden's *Annunciation* which is itself now in the museum. [27] A quote from Rogier's painting can be seen in Lady Jane's dress, spreading out on the left just like the Virgin's, with the same heavy gathered folds spilling into the floor. Delaroche not only borrowed Rogier's design, but also mimics the crisp smoothness of his fastidious finish.

However, Delaroche's avoidance of 'touch', his suppression of any visible brush mark on the canvas, went well beyond a simple tribute to the skills and technqiues of Northern Renaissance artists. As a painter, Delaroche was above all motivated by the desire to move the public. With their impersonal technique and clear legibility, his paintings gave the viewer the greatest opportunity to project their own feelings into the picture. The same can be said of their spatial construction, which 'maximises the potential for emotional identification with the actors'.[28]

This, Delaroche's second painting set in the Tower of London, is staged in a dark but architecturally detailed Romanesque hall, where a narrow scaffold has been erected. As indicated by the halberds below, there is no way out. Although historically inaccurate – real executions would be held outdoors[29] – this suggestion of a deliberately oppressive space immediately engages the viewer.

For maximum impact, only five well-individualised life-size figures occupy the whole width of the canvas. The ladies-in-waiting, distressed, cannot bear to watch the execution, and the men's half-turned faces, means that none of the figures' eyes are actually visible – 'There are five figures and you can't see anyone's eyes', as Gautier commented, both intrigued and irritated by Delaroche's clever trick;[30] yet the viewer is irresistibly drawn to the scene. This magnetism relies on a carefully choreographed arrangement of the figures on the scaffold. The strict symmetry of the composition is softened by an ingenious juxtaposition of the protagonists. Delaroche has skilfully alternated frontal, half- and fully turned figures. Similar variety is introduced in each figure's height – seated, standing, kneeling, bent, standing again – and they are all placed within the space to create an impression of depth. This controlled diversity gives the composition its arresting rhythm. In addition, recurrent motifs help us to establish a narrative. The lacing of Lady Jane Grey's corset finds an echo in both the cushion and the executioner's waistcoat. A knot in the blindfold responds to a tied ribbon in her bodice, and to the loops in the executioner's rope. From left to right the story unfolds, starting from the royal garments of which the young queen has been stripped, and, via her dazzling wedding ring and the executioner's axe, ending in the centre with the straw spreading around the block, as yet unstained. Catching the light with its golden hues, blindingly bright, Delaroche's straw looks strangely appealing despite its prickliness and grisly purpose. Gautier commented: 'the straw whose object is to mop up the victim's blood is so realistic that more than one spectator has been tempted to pluck a blade of it.'[31] The illusionism of the painting is such that the viewer is made to feel that 'Jane's head will fall from the block and drop at our feet, so that in a flash, for a moment, we might sympathise with her plight [...].'[32]

The moment Delaroche chooses to depict – the short, tense instant between life and death – carries indeed the greatest dramatic tension. A coffin awaiting on the right, just visible, shows that her fate is unavoidable.

With its raised platform, stage props and small cast, all bound with psychological ties, Delaroche's painting has often prompted comments about its theatricality. Treating an historical event as if it were as a stage performance was certainly a modern way of dealing with the 'grand genre' of history painting, which Delaroche had reinvigorated. Having witnessed Napoleon's fall in his youth, the artist was drawn to paint the decline of historical figures rather than their moments of glory. Executions, exiles, abdications invaded his repertoire; the caption of a caricature of the artist stated with humour:

'Paul Delaroche with his funereal expression takes pleasure in surrounding himself with corpses and bones. With him, everything dies ... apart from his painting' (fig. 30).[33]

This was a new type of history painting; with its glorification of the hero, David's epic style no longer suited the new era of the Bourbons and Louis-Philippe.[34] Instead, Delaroche's paintings demystified neoclassical idealism by conveying a powerful sense of disillusion, prompting a meditation on power and vanity. Delaroche's strategy, the opposite of David's, also diverged from Delacroix's or Géricault's in the sense that it remained true to the tradition of depicting an historical figure, rather than representing the new forces of society. Focusing on his heroes' despair, Delaroche revealed their human side. He emphasised Lady Jane Grey's ordinariness, conveyed by her simple, poignant gesture of grasping for the block.

[FIG. 30] Anon *Paul Delaroche à la mine funèbre s'entoure avec plaisir de cadavres et d'os. Jane Gray [sic], Mazarin, héros et héroïne. Chez lui, tout meurt ... excepté ses tableaux*, date unknown. Lithograph, 44.6 × 33.5cm. Ecole nationale supérieure des beaux-arts, Paris (5632)

With such a subject, and such a treatment, on such a grand scale, the painting was bound to cause a stir at the Salon. When it opened on 1 March 1834, the long-awaited *Lady Jane Grey* had been given the best location in the exhibition: 'hung in a place of honour, to the detriment of Delacroix, Ingres and Decamps, [...] in the place reserved for the masters'.[35] There, with its stunning immediacy and dramatic intensity, the large canvas caused a sensation among the public. The excitement it provoked led reviewers to remark: 'not for many years has a work of art achieved a greater popular success than the *Jane Grey*'.[37] Enthusiastic crowds gathered around the painting. Amaury-Duval, Ingres's pupil, remembered: 'we could not struggle against the painting's vast number of admirers. The entrance next to which it was exhibited in the Salon carré was filled by the crowd attracted to the work of Delaroche.'[37] Indeed it eclipsed Ingres's ambitious if impenetrable *Martyrdom of Saint Symphorian* (see p. 31). Delaroche's canvas was naturalistic enough to fascinate the crowds without shocking them; in a Salon still dominated by the division between the classical current and the 'nouvelle Ecole', its success had no undertones of polemic or scandal.

Unsurprisingly, the painting lingered long in the memories of both public and critics. On seeing *Lady Jane Grey* again in 1857, Gautier recalled the impact of the picture two decades' earlier: 'Lady Jane's small hands, waxen in colour and stretched out as though searching for the block, made a profound impression at the time on the sensibility of the philistines and may even do so again now.' But he remained dubious about the painting's grounds for success: '... Such a scene, so moving in itself, does not constitute fine painting ...'[38]

Gautier was to remain the painting's most virulent detractor. His criticism was directed against Delaroche in general, whom he regarded as a shallow, untalented populariser. In fact, the painting's most notable qualities attracted Gautier's most acerbic comments. Its realism, refined brushwork and attention to detail were viciously mocked. With sharp irony, he notes: 'Mr Delaroche [...] has to such a degree washed, soaped, waxed and brushed away the horror that he has given it a certain prettiness: the most horrible scenes become agreeable to the eye, by means of the way he arranges the stage props of death in a coquettish manner.'[39]

The artist's borrowings from Opie's *Mary Queen of Scots* had not escaped Gautier's attention either.[40] Others joined him in this accusation of plagiarism, which was probably the most damaging to Delaroche's reputation. Max Raoul speculated: 'Rumbling has been heard from artists that M. Delaroche has stolen again',[41] while Gustave Planche wondered: 'I ask, is there not a striking analogy between the work of Opie and that of M. Paul Delaroche?'[42]

Theatricality was another common line of criticism: if the relationship between the picture and stage performance was noted, it was not always in Delaroche's favour. When cat. 53 was exhibited again as part of Delaroche's retrospective at the Ecole des Beaux-Arts, Gautier cynically commented: '*The Execution of Lady Jane Grey* is a romantic canvas in the manner of Casimir Delavigne, a writer with whom Paul Delaroche had much in common. The painter and the poet were even able to exchange subjects for tragedies and pictures, to such an extent was their view of art identical. In addition, both of them enjoyed in their life- time the sort of popular success which does not always come to serious art.'[43]

Whether or not a 'serious' work of art, *The Execution of Lady Jane Grey* achieved – even by Delaroche's standards – an exceptional popularity, and marked the apogee of the artist's fame, which culminated in his being awarded the title of Officier de la Légion d'Honneur on 1 May 1834. At that point the artist may have considered producing a sequel for the painting, a project he appeared to have abandoned. [44]

Purchased by Count Demidoff, the painting was withdrawn from public display after the Salon, not to be exhibited until the 1857 retrospective exhibition. The new critical attention it generated then shows that its impact was largely undiminished. After that date, the painting's reputation developed mainly through the medium of prints. Usually, the most successful Salon paintings were popularised through poor-quality, cheaply produced lithographs. Instead Delaroche, who was to become the most extensively reproduced artist of his time, was intent on ensuring public awareness of his paintings, and paid careful attention to the quality of reproductions of them. In 1835 a contract signed with the print publisher Adolphe Goupil guaranteed the production of high-quality engravings after his paintings. In view of the picture's success, Goupil's firm commissioned the engraver Paolo Mercuri to produce an engraving after *Lady Jane Grey*.[45] With its stylistic restraint and perfect legibility, the painting was the ideal candidate for reproduction – it has been argued that Delaroche may have conceived it with mass-reproduction in mind – but the Mercuri engraving was not completed until 1858. Soon after that, a profusion of images were produced in various media, including photography, a discipline in which Delaroche showed a pioneering interest.[46]

Astoundingly successful as a composition, *The Execution of Lady Jane Grey* inspired countless painted replicas, copies and variations.[47] However, its impact resonated in areas well beyond the realm of the visual arts, inspiring playwrights as well. Having been inspired by the stage, it made sense that Delaroche's painting – just like his earlier *Death of Elizabeth*, [48] should, in turn, be recreated on the stage. Indeed Delaroche's famous compositions provided ongoing popular entertainment in the form of *tableaux vivants*, which prolonged their impact on the public. In a nostalgic evocation of the atmosphere of the Paris opera in the 1830s, Jules Janin recalls the staging of these 'abominable *tableaux vivants* [...] during the opera ball'. Following a stage display based on Delaroche's *Cromwell and Charles I* (cat 23), 'the curtain [...] suddenly was raised again! This time the scaffold was all set!' There follows a description very close in detail to Delaroche's painting of *Lady Jane Grey*: 'what a strange *tableau vivant*! At the end the curtain fell.'

The Execution of Lady Jane Grey had permeated the French stage, the painting in its own right was the inspiration for at least three plays: [49] Alexandre Leblanc de Ferrière's *Jeanne Gray* in 1834; Alexandre and Gabrielle Soumet's *Jane Grey* in 1844,[50] and, in 1856, *Jane Grey*, co-written by the team of playwrights Eugène Nus and Alphonse Brot.[51]

The 1834 and 1856 plays culminate with the staging of Delaroche's painting as a theatrical tableau. In the last scene of the former, the painting progressively unfurls, with the actors gradually positioning themselves on the scaffold-like stage, slowly giving flesh, three-dimensionally, to Delaroche's canvas. Twenty years after the 1834 Salon and before the retrospective show had any chance to revive interest in the painting, Nus and Brot's play *Jane Grey* culminates in a similar staging of the 'beau tableau', with the following stage directions: 'The two ladies-in-waiting are going to take their positions as in Delaroche's painting, against the side columns. Jane Grey supported by the officer searches with her hands the place where she needs to put her head on the executioner's block. Drum roll as the curtain begins to fall.' [52]

It is tempting to think that Théophile Gautier had seen the *tableau vivant* described by Janin, or attended a performance of Nus and Brot's play, and that he may have had its final tableau still in mind when writing of Delaroche two years later: 'Each of his pictures is the fifth act of a melodrama or tragedy, at the base of which one could write as a final instruction: "La toile tombe".' [53]

Indeed, the curtain closed on Delaroche's reputation, and the canvas fell from grace; its subsequent story is a sensational plot rich in drama (see p. 17). Rehabilitation came late, but *Lady Jane Grey* has now been firmly reinstituted in a firmament from which she shall no more descend. AR

1. Alley 1959, p. 298.

2. Salon of 1812, Liénard 1819, J.-B. Liénard, *Jeanne Gray*, No. 779 (probably the same picture); Bouton 1822, no. 160; De Jonnès, 1833, no. 1337. List compiled by Jon Whiteley, Christ Church, Oxford, in a letter to Cecil Gould, National Gallery, 7 November 1975. Unpublished, dossier NG53. See also Ziff 1977, p. 127, n. 29.

3. De Staël 1790. Inspired by *The Tragedy of Lady Jane Gray* by Nicholas Rowe which opened in London at the Drury Lane Theatre in 1715 and was regularly revived on the London stage until 1774 (See Spies 2009).

4. Harris Nicholas 1825, translated into French by E. Frère, 1832.

5. *Explication des ouvrages ... des artistes vivans, exposés au Musée Royal*, le 1er Mars 1834, Paris, Vinchon edn, 1834.

6. *Illustrated London News*, 5 February 1848, quoted in Bann 1997, p. 94

7. London, Minneapolis, New York 2003, no. 55, p. 121.

8. Painted for the Duke of Bedford, now in Tate. See London, Minneapolis, New York 2003, no. 55, p. 121.

9. Until 1829 Delaroche's maternal uncle J.-A. Joly was in charge of the Cabinet des Estampes at the Bibliothèque nationale de France.

10. In itself inspired by J. Thornthwaite's engraving of *Mrs [Elizabeth] Hartley in the character of Lady Jane Grey*, published in the 1776 edition of Nicholas Rowe's 1715 play, as an illustration for the second scene of act V. Spies 2009, n. 59.

11. Spies 2009, p. 45.

12. Spies 2009, p. 45.

13. Ziff 1977, p. 119.

14. Gautier 1834, p. 18.

15. Robert Smirke, *Queen Elizabeth appointing her Successor*, engraving by J. Neagle, 1796. Ziff 1977, p. 132: 'By 1834 it was common knowledge that the *Death of Elizabeth* had been based on a picture by Smirke.'

16. London 1994, p. 13.

17. Ziff 1977, p. 129.

18. The costumes worn by the ladies-in-waiting are outdated, and do not correspond to the fashion of the 1550s. Delaroche, meticulous in his historical reconstruction, was probably unaware of this.

19. 'The figure of the lady in waiting who faints and leans against a pillar recalls in its costume and its disposition certain works of Holbein.' T. Gautier, 'Paul Delaroche', first published in *L'Artiste*, 1858, in London 1975.

20. Gautier 1834.

21. Bann 1997, p. 119.

22. See Thomson 1981.

23. Infra-red examination by R. Billinge, 26 August 1994, report in conservation dossier, NG53.

24. The drawing was presented to the National Gallery by L.-R. Burket in 1985 and transferred to the British Museum in 1994.

25. Roy and Kirby 1995.

26. We are grateful to Sébastien Allard, Curator of Nineteenth-Century Paintings, Musée du Louvre, for this suggestion.

27. The drawing, in the Louvre, shows details of the bed and gothic medallion, which Delaroche was to reuse in cat. 14, see Bann 1997, p. 101. See also Nantes and Montpellier 1999, p. 55.

28. Siegfried 2000, p. 70.

29. Spies 2009, p. 50.

30. Gautier adds: 'C'est une remarque que tout le monde a faite, et qui ne contribue pas peu à donner au tableau un aspect morne et insignifiant', see Gautier 1834.

31. T. Gautier, 'Paul Delaroche' (1858), see London 1975.

32. Siegfried 2000, pp. 70–1.

33. Lithograph, from *Le Panthéon Charivarique*, *Ecole Nationale Supérieure des Beaux-Arts*, Paris (est. 5632).

34. London 1997, p. 12.

35. 'Accroché à la place d'honneur, au détriment de Delacroix, d'Ingres et de Decamps, [...] à la place réservée aux maîtres'. Gautier 1834.

36. *Le Magasin Pittoresque, 2e année* 1834, p. 273.

37. Amaury-Duval, quoted in London 1994.

38. T. Gautier, 'Paul Delaroche' (1858), see London 1975.

39. 'M. Delaroche (...) a tellement lessivé, savonné, ciré et brossé l'horreur, qu'il lui a donné de la gentillesse: les scènes les plus terribles deviennent agréables à l'œil, tant il en dispose coquettement tous les funèbres accessoires'. See Gautier 1994, p. 188.

40. See footnote 14.

41. 'Salon de 1834', *Le Cabinet de Lecture*, 9 March 1834, p. 13, in Ziff 1977, p. 133.

42. 'Salon de 1834', in *Etudes sur l'Ecole Française*, vol. 1, p. 241. In Ziff 1977, p. 133.

43. T. Gautier, 'Paul Delaroche' (1858), see London 1975.

44. A drawing in the Musée du Louvre shows Sir John Brydges walking down the stairs of the scaffold, followed by two men carrying the coffin, and the rest of the protagonists (Musée du Louvre, RF33136).

45. The list of engraved or lithographed reproductions after Delaroche produced and published by the firm Goupil has been established by P-L Renié in Nantes and Montpellier 1999, pp. 200–18.

46. Delaroche was the first ever artist whose work was published as a catalogue raisonné illustrated with photographs, Delaborde and Goddé 1858.

47. For an exhaustive list, see dossier for NG53 held at National Gallery. There is a faithful reduced autograph copy of the composition in Guildhall Art Gallery, Corporation of London (No. 1052, 44 × 53 cm, acquired 1926); cat. 83 is a good example of a variation after the Delaroche painting.

48. Spies 2009, p. 51. *Elisabeth d'Angleterre* by J.-F. Ancelot was first staged in 1829, with a tableau based on Delaroche's painting of 1827.

49. Spies 2009, p. 52.

50. 'Au Ballet', in Janin 1858. 'La toile qui s'était abaissée, au même instant, se releva! Cette fois l'échafaud était tout dressé! Une jeune femme blanche et pâle, à genoux, les yeux bandés par un beau mouchoir de soie, et les mains tendues au billot, cherche à convenablement se poser pour recevoir le coup fatal! Sur l'échafaud, une main prévoyante a jeté de la paille fraîche ... es femmes, à droite de la victime, laissent tomber, de leurs mains défaillantes, le collier et les bijoux dont elle s'est dépouillée; un vieillard, en cheveux blancs, plus pâle que la victime elle-même, la soutient en chancelant, et tout au fond, dans l'ombre, un homme vêtu de rouge, attentif à la scène, cherche, en un coin, la hache avec laquelle il doit frapper ... Quel étrange tableau vivant ... A la fin la toile est tombée ...' *Jane Grey, Tragédie en cinq actes et en vers, par M. Alexandre Soumet et Madame Gabrielle d'Altenheim*, Paris Odéon, premiered on 30 March 1844. See Ziff 1977, p. 134.

51. *Jane Grey, Tragédie en cinq actes et en vers, par M. Alexandre Soumet et Madame Gabrielle d'Altenheim*, Paris Odéon, premiered on 30 March 1844. See Ziff 1977, p. 134.

52. Nus and Brot 1856, based on Brot 1835. We are grateful to Martin Spies (Spies 2009, p. 52) for alerting our attention to these plays.

53. Here Gautier plays with the double meaning of the French word 'toile', meaning both painter's canvas and theatre curtain, see T. Gautier, 'Paul Delaroche' (1858), see London 1975.

PAUL DELAROCHE (1797–1856)

[54] *Strafford on his Way to Execution*, 1835

Oil on canvas, 249 × 310 cm
Private collection

Provenance: bought by the Duke of Sutherland and his brother Lord Francis Egerton from the artist; bought by John Francis Queeny of St Louis, Missouri from the Duke of Sutherland's sale in 1913; private collection.

ACHILLE MARTINET (1806–1877), AFTER PAUL DELAROCHE (1797–1856)

[55] *Charles I insulted by the Soldiers of Cromwell*, 1842

Engraving on paper, 43 × 53.2 cm
Private collection

On 8 January 1836, the Duke of Sutherland wrote to his mother: 'We saw on Monday one of the finest modern pictures I ever saw – it is by P. de la Roche [sic] and the subject is Ld. Strafford Going to His Execution – he says that the picture he has to do for F[rancis] of K. Charles I will be as good.'[1] The purchase of these two major works by the two brothers who owned the finest private collection of paintings in Britain at the time was a significant step in establishing Delaroche's reputation beyond France. Evidently *Charles I* was little more than a promissory note by this date, though Lord Francis Egerton had been sufficiently impressed by Delaroche's assurances to reserve it in advance. He may well have seen a preliminary sketch, in which the broad lines of the composition are established.[2] *Strafford on his Way to Execution*, however, was already on show in the studio. Though no indication of ownership was given when the two works were exhibited at the 1837 Salon, it may be assumed that by then both were destined for the Sutherland family.

The genesis of *Strafford* reflects Delaroche's long-standing interest in the personal dramas of some of the unfortunate victims of early modern English history. But it also reveals the greater freedom for his talents when he became Professor and master of a studio at the Ecole des Beaux-Arts late in 1833. Jules Goddé notes that 'this picture was completely sketched out in 1834 by M. Henri Delaborde, after a watercolour sketch that belonged to M. le vicomte de la Villestreux, and a wax maquette executed by Paul Delaroche, who only took the picture up again in the summer of 1835, on his return from Italy'.[3] Having finished *The Execution of Lady Jane Grey* by the end of 1833, Delaroche had turned to another English historical subject which he would make distinctively his own. The execution of the main counsellor of Charles I in 1641 was familiar to the many French readers who had studied the history of the Stuart dynasty. But the striking reference to Strafford's unjust fate in Alfred de Vigny's novel *Cinq-Mars* (where Delaroche found the material for his *Richelieu* of 1829) might also have resonated in his mind.[4]

As with *The Princes in the Tower*, Delaroche made a maquette for the work, which is now lost. The 'watercolour sketch' mentioned by Goddé could well be the study now in a private collection.[5] Goddé reveals that the soldier at the extreme right, who is not present in this sketch, was modelled by General Pierre Boyer (1772–1851), a veteran of Napoleon's army who was currently *Inspecteur-général* of the French gendarmerie and an amateur painter. Aside from this contemporary link, Delaroche remained mindful of his sources in English historical prints. James Northcote's *Tower of London*, engraved by William Skelton, had shown the bodies of the two Princes in the Tower being conveyed down a flight of steps (p. 67, cat. 16). Delaroche would have had this in mind when he sketched a possible sequel to *The Execution of Lady Jane Grey* in which the coffin of the young woman is brought down the stairs of the Tower, with the Lieutenant leading the procession.[6] In *Strafford*, the sense of arrested downward movement gives the bowed figure of the victim an added poignancy. The blessing of Archbishop Laud, Strafford's fellow prisoner in the Tower, is delivered through an iron grille, a motif that Delaroche has converted from Victor Schnetz's *Farewell of Consul Boethius to his family*, shown at the Salon of 1827 (Musée des Augustins, Toulouse).

The degree to which Delaroche's decision to embark on *Charles I* was influenced

by the interest of Lord Francis Egerton is hard to assess. He may well have had preliminary drawings to show his future patron, since one is still held by the Louvre.[7] Linda Whiteley has found that, before 1830, there was a drawing in the collection of Louis-Auguste Coutan. While the centred composition is a departure from the dynamic cross-movement of *Strafford*, it recalls the poignant contrast between an impassive victim and an aggressive crowd that Delaroche had explored in *Death of President Duranti* (1827, now destroyed). His vignette of *Joan of Arc*, engraved by Thompson for the illustrated edition of Barante's *Histoire des Ducs de Bourgogne* (1837), depends on a similar opposition, and *Marie-Antoinette before the Tribunal* (cat. 59) offers a late example. Among contemporary critics, Heinrich Heine was not alone in noting that the composition resembled a tavern scene in the manner of Jan Steen, though (in his judgement) Delaroche had not lived up to the aspiration to be a 'graceful and elegant Dutchman'.[8] The painting hung for many years in the dining room of Bridgewater House, but has not been visible since undergoing bomb damage in the Second World War (see p. 22). Its present restoration promises to bring back into public view the last of Delaroche's major paintings on English historical themes.

Aware of the disasters that could overcome unique paintings, Delaroche took great care to secure fine engravings of his work. For both *Strafford* and *Charles I*, he reserved his reproduction rights. The meticulous print by future academician Achille Martinet was published in 1842 by his dealer Goupil. SB

55

1. Quoted in Ward-Jackson 1985, p. 147.
2. Musée du Louvre, Département des Arts Graphiques (RF 35067).
3. Delaborde and Goddé 1858, plate 19.
4. See Bann 1997, pp. 146–7. Vigny pictures Richelieu hearing of the death of Strafford and musing on the inequity with which selfless service to an absolute monarch is rewarded.
5. Illustrated in Bann 1997, p. 148.
6. Musée du Louvre, Département des Arts Graphiques (RF 35136).
7. Musée du Louvre, Département des Arts Graphiques(RF 35067).
8. Quoted in Bann 1997, p. 152.

PAUL DELAROCHE (1797–1856)

[56] *The Girondins' Last Farewell, 31 October 1793 (Le dernier adieu des Girondins le 31 octobre 1793)*, 1856

Oil on canvas, 58 × 99 cm
Dépot du Musée Carnavalet – Histoire de France, Paris. Conciergerie – Centre des monuments nationaux (P.2111)

Provenance: acquired from the artist by Benoît Fould. Bequeathed in 1968 by Madame Bechmann.

This was one of Delaroche's last pictures, and his final historical painting. In the valedictory and commemorative painting of his studio, a posthumous tribute commissioned by his dealer Adolphe Goupil from Delaroche's pupil Louis Roux (fig. 35), Delaroche is seated at his easel working on it, with the *Young Martyr* directly behind (cat. 60). As in the case of *Marie-Antoinette before the Tribunal* (cat. 59), the work has to be seen at least partly in the context of recent histories of the Revolution of 1789 and, in particular, of the *Histoire des Girondins* by Alphonse de Lamartine, whom Delaroche met in Rome in 1844.[1] The Girondins were a political group of the 1790s who took their name from the members for the department of the Gironde, in the west of France, around whom the group centred. At first strongly radical in their views, they became more moderate during the Terror, and were finally denounced as reactionary. In June 1793, the Girondist deputies were arrested and imprisoned in the Conciergerie. They are shown here receiving news of their execution, which took place at the end of October, shortly after that of Marie-Antoinette.[2]

In earlier works, Delaroche, referred obliquely to recent history, often by analogy, with subjects taken from English history. By the mid-century, perhaps partly in response to recent historiography, scenes from more recent French history became frequent at the Salon. Delaroche made one drawing of this subject, bought by the Duchesse d'Orléans as early as 1838. In 1846, he took up the subject again, in a fine watercolour now in Edinburgh (fig. 31). Norman Ziff suggests that the composition (already broadly established in the watercolour) owes something to Charles Müller's *Call for the Last Victims of the Terror* (Musée de la Révolution Française, Vizille), though in that work the overturned chair, a common emblem of disorder, is the only note of disharmony, and the aristocratic prisoners themselves are elegantly grouped round a central seated figure. In Félix Philippoteaux's *Last Banquet of the Girondins* (Vizille), the group, as here, is united, preferring death to dishonour, but it is a picture which does not underline their fate, as Delaroche's images of martyrdom invariably do. The almost supernatural lighting in the present picture makes it clear that this is such an image.

Delaroche's painting has elements in common with the box-like settings of his work of the early 1830s, and in particular *The Assassination of the Duc de Guise*; the overturned chair reinforces the similarity. The upraised arms, on the other hand, in an action reminiscent of David's *Oath of the Tennis Court* (Musée National du Château de Versailles), serve to reinforce the notion of the Girondins' commitment to their original ideals, and yet the composition itself is very different. In marked (and deliberate) contrast to that work, the desultory character of the grouping, facing a shared martyrdom, has its own pathos, suggesting perhaps the inevitable dissolution of the early republican ideals. LW

[FIG. 31] Paul Delaroche (1797–1856), *Sketch for* The Girondins, 1846. Pen and black ink, sepia wash and watercolour heightened with white on paper, 13.8 × 26 cm. The National Gallery of Scotland, Edinburgh (D5430)

1. Nantes and Montpellier 1999, no. 99.
2. There is a sheet of studies in a private collection on which an execution subject (Marie-Antoinette, or possibly Madame Elisabeth), appears in conjunction with some lines transcribed from Lamartine's history.

EDOUARD GIRARDET (1819–1880), AFTER PAUL DELAROCHE (1797–1856)

[57] *Beatrice Cenci on the Way to her Execution*, 1859

Mixed media print on paper, 46.4 × 50.5 cm
The British Museum, London (1859.0514.802)

The story of Beatrice Cenci is that of a young girl from a high-ranking Roman family of the late sixteenth century, brutally treated by her father and banished, with her stepmother Lucrezia, to imprisonment in a high, remote castle as punishment for her denunciation of his abuse.

Plotting with her brothers, together with Lucrezia and an accomplice, to murder her father, she was, with the family, condemned to death. At some time in the eighteenth century, a painting of uncertain attribution, but then ascribed to Guido Reni (Palazzo Barberini, Rome), was said to represent her, and became the source for much romantic interest in her story, particularly in the nineteenth century. Shelley wrote a play on the theme; Stendhal took up the subject; Dumas recounted it in his *Famous Crimes*; Dickens mentioned it; nearer to the time of Delaroche's original painting (of 1855); Nathaniel Hawthorne referred to it in *The Marble Faun*, and the sculptor Harriet Hosmer took her as subject, as did the photographer Julia Margaret Cameron.[1] As Belinda Jack has remarked, not all the writers and artists fascinated by the story were prepared to confront its darker elements; Beatrice was a victim of incest and perpetrator of parricide, though she herself was very soon venerated as a martyr; a mass is still celebrated yearly for her in Rome, on 11 September.[2] Delaroche's image may hint at something more complex than simple martyrdom; Beatrice is walking in a sombre procession of hooded figures, a lighted taper behind her, her veil thrown back and the light of martyrdom already upon her, yet she has the air of both victim and penitent. The hope of redemption is signified by the prominent cross she holds – a cross which reappears in several of the numerous small drawings, largely of veiled or hooded figures, with which Delaroche prepared this work. No longer staged, certainly, in the manner of some earlier works, it nonetheless has something of a processional character which evokes theatrical performance, perhaps even an operatic chorus. The preparatory drawings themselves, many of which are now in the Louvre, closely resemble those with which Delaroche prepared his last religious paintings (those for *Good Friday*, for instance); like this one, they are works of a new, deep and generalised pathos. LW

1. See Jack 2003, ill. 2, pp. 84–5.
2. See Jack 2003, p. 2.

PEINT PAR PAUL DE LA ROCHE — GRAVÉ PAR EDOUARD GIRARDET

BEATRICE CENCI

Imprimé & Publié par GOUPIL & Cie le 1er Avril 1859
PARIS _ LONDON

PAUL DELAROCHE (1797–1856)

[58] *Saint Cecilia and the Angels*, 1836

Oil on canvas, 202 × 162 cm (approx)
Victoria and Albert Museum, London (553-1903)

Provenance: Pourtalès; Delessert sale, Paris 1869, no. 36; James Reiss collection; his daughter, Mrs Henry Jephson, by whom given in 1903.

'The beautiful legend of Saint Cecilia is one of the most ancient handed down to us by the early church.'[1] Mrs Jameson, the nineteenth-century historian of sacred art, recounts the legend without attempting, as she says, to separate truth from poetic fiction. A young woman in third-century Rome, secretly Christian, and of exemplary piety, 'composed and sang ... with such ravishing sweetness that angels descended to listen to her'. Married at sixteen, in obedience to her parents' wishes, she converted her husband to her beliefs, whereupon an angel appeared and crowned the pair with roses. Refusing to sacrifice to Jupiter, as was required by Roman authorities, her husband was imprisoned, and then put to death. Soon afterwards, after prolonged attempts to alter her persistent beliefs, she too was condemned. Her executioner's hand trembled as he struck the blow, with the result that she survived for three days longer, singing as she died. Since music was a constant element in her story, Cecilia became its patron saint. She was not shown with a musical instrument before the early sixteenth century, however, but thereafter was rarely seen without one. Perhaps the sweetness and antiquity of the legend inclined Delaroche to adopt an archaic – one might say Gothic – manner here, in treating the story of a martyr which, in certain elements, may have brought to mind that of Lady Jane Grey.[2]

His three great secular martyrdoms of these years, drawn from English history, show a marked debt to Northern art; this one, in contrast, reveals the impact of Italy, the result of a recent journey in preparation for a substantial commission (from which he later withdrew), to decorate the church of the Madeleine in Paris. After wandering through Tuscany, admiring and recording examples of early fresco, he travelled to Rome, where he met Louise Vernet, a young woman whose appearance struck many as angelic, and whose form and features reminded Ingres's pupil Eugène Emmanuel Amaury-Duval of early Christian art. Delaroche, too, must have seen something of this, painting her, in 1835, as an angel, and reusing her features in this work.[3] She was also a talented musician who caught the admiring attention of Hector Berlioz, and was thus appropriately cast by Delaroche in her role in this picture. Louise Vernet was the daughter of Horace Vernet, Director of the French Academy in Rome. She and Paul were married in the chapel of Saint Cecilia in the church of S. Luigi dei Francesi in Rome, a chapel decorated by Domenichino with scenes from the life of the saint, including probably the most famous of all depictions of her martyrdom.

The theme of the music-making saint is commonplace, but was given an unexpected twist by Delaroche, who borrowed elements from the theme of the Annunciation in his composition: a kneeling angel on one side, the seated Saint Cecilia on the other. The work itself introduces a new vein of ideal spirituality into Delaroche's work, one particularly associated, it would seem, with his wife and family, and to which he returned, in darker mode, after her early death. As Bruno Foucart comments,[4] his example was to be more influential than any other, not excepting Ingres and his pupils, upon a new, intense and original school of religious painting in France. LW

1. Jameson 1857, pp. 583–609.

2. Like Strafford and Charles Insulted by the Soldiers, this painting was destined to hang in one of the great nineteenth-century collections of Old Master paintings: in this case, that of the Comte de Pourtalés, in his splendid neo-Renaissance Paris town house.

3. Though sometimes compared with the features of Saint Cecilia (as one might expect), Louise Vernet's own features, as recorded in the previous year, more closely resemble those of the kneeling angel in the foreground.

4. Foucart 1987, p. 252.

PAUL DELAROCHE (1797–1856)

[59] *Marie-Antoinette before the Tribunal (Marie-Antoinette devant le Tribunal)*, 1851

Oil on canvas, 239 × 170 cm
The Forbes Collection, New York (PS3024)

Provenance: collection Count Hunolstein;[1] collection M. Perkins; collection Thomas Lucas; bought by present owner, London, Sotheby's.

Delaroche's work entered a new sombre phase after the death of his wife in December 1845. Some three years later, the political events of 1848 – the February revolution which ended the July Monarchy, followed by the workers' uprising in June – were to leave him in a deeply pessimistic state of mind. However, as Ziff comments, the present work cannot be taken as a comment on contemporary events, since he began preparatory drawings for this subject in 1847. In fact Delaroche's own early interest in the fate of the royal family during the Revolution of 1789 is evident from the thumbnail sketch which appears on the sheet bearing early studies for *Lady Jane Grey* (cat. 66), and exemplifies his general and abiding attraction to the theme of martyrdom, not necessarily from a politically committed standpoint. Fig. 33, showing Marie-Antoinette in prison, suggests a possible link in his mind between this subject and that of *Strafford on his Way to Execution* (cat. 54).[2]

As was his habit, Delaroche followed documentary sources for the present painting as far as possible. The contemporary account in the *Moniteur* described the former queen thus: 'During her interrogation, Marie-Antoinette preserved almost throughout a calm and assured countenance ... upon hearing the judgement, she allowed no change of expression to appear, and left the chamber without a word, either to the judges or to the public.' Of his own commitment to an unvarnished truth, particularly with regard to Marie-Antoinette's appearance, Delaroche claimed that therein lay the essence of the picture's beauty. In his pursuit of an authentic representation, he must have studied a print after a drawing by Pierre Bouillon (fig. 32), made at the time of the trial;[3] the plain features of the queen and the appearance of the crowd are comparable, though Delaroche, with characteristic dramatic economy, has eliminated the pleading gesture; and has brought her forward so that now, as so often in his pictures, we, the viewers, are the chief spectators.[4]

He may have known the print published in France in 1796, after William Hamilton's 1794 painting *Marie-Antoinette led to her Execution, 16 October 1793* (Musée de la Revolution française, Vizille), in which she is interpreted sympathetically, in a radiant light, with the uplifted gaze of a martyr. The brutish crowd of Hamilton's picture, pressing forward, intent on regicide, may have suggested to Delaroche some of the elements here, but with his abiding concern for the truth (particularly, as he said, in the case of such recent history), he has not presented the former queen in an idealised manner. He conveys by other means the sense that this is indeed a martyrdom: the composition recalls, irresistibly, images of Christ at the Tribunal. Thus, as he had done for *Lady Jane Grey*, for *Charles I insulted by the Soldiers of Cromwell* (see p. 112), and arguably, even for *Strafford on his Way to Execution*, which has something of the character of a Station of the Cross, he endows a literal representation with a symbolic meaning – in a manner not altogether different from the English Pre-Raphaelites. LW

[FIG. 32] Pierre Bouillon (1776-1831), *Trial of Marie Antoinette*, 1793. Pencil on paper, dimensions unknown. Musée Carnavalet, Histoire de Paris

[FIG. 33] George Keating (1762-1842), *Marie Antoinette, late Queen of France in the Conciergerie*, 1796. Engraving, 38 × 31.7 cm. Musée National des Châteaux de Versailles et de Trianon, Versailles

1. Count Paul Vogt von Hunolstein owned a collection of Marie-Antoinette's letters, and published a biography of her in 1864. For an account of the early exhibition history of this picture in America, see Nonne 2002

2. Beth Wright first published this telling comparison in Wright 1997, pp 35–6.

3. Ziff 1977, pp. 237–8.

4. A copy by Delaroche, presumably after a print, is in the Département des Arts Graphiques, in the Musée du Louvre (RF 35419).

PAUL DELAROCHE (1797–1856)

[60] *Young Christian Martyr (La Jeune Martyre)*, 1854–5

Oil on canvas, 170.5 × 148 cm
Musée du Louvre, Paris (RF 1038)

Provenance: Bought by Adolphe Goupil (15,000 francs) for reproduction, 1855; sold to Baron Adolphe d'Eichtal (36,000 francs), 1857; given to the Louvre by the three children of d'Eichtal in memory of their father, 1895.

The largest painting produced by Delaroche during his final years, the *Young Christian Martyr* is also a summation of the theme of female victimhood that was broached in *The Execution of Lady Jane Grey*. The drawings from the story of Saint Perpetua (see fig. 18, p. 44) indicate that he gave consideration to the legends of the early Roman martyrs, probably on his visit to Rome in 1843–4. A more contemporary source for the memorable composition might be John Everett Millais's *Ophelia*, which was shown at the Royal Academy in 1852 and travelled to the Paris Exposition Universelle in 1855. But Elisabeth Foucart-Walter is right in questioning the usefulness of this comparison.[1] For the contemporary critic Théophile Gautier, the work came as little less than a revelation. After seeing this 'last painting of Paul Delaroche' in the Goupil Gallery early in 1857, he made ample amends for the scathing comments he had made on early works such as the *Lady Jane Grey* some twenty years before. Praising the 'tender, vaporous, *hazy*' effect, reminiscent of the Italian Renaissance painter Correggio, he concluded: 'If [Delaroche] could count eight or ten figures like that one in his work, [he] would [have] nothing to fear from the competition of the greatest masters.'[2]

How Delaroche came to paint this anonymous martyr from 'the time of [the Roman Emperor] Diocletian'[3] is minutely described in a contemporary article. The picture was inspired by 'a kind of dream', which came to the artist while he was suffering from severe fever in December 1853. In a letter of January 1854, he pronounced himself well enough to start sketching the motif, first in a charcoal study, and then on a 'small white canvas'.[4] This invaluable letter expands on Delaroche's conception of the theme. The young Roman woman, who refused to sacrifice to the 'false gods', has been condemned to death and cast into the Tiber with her hands bound. '[T]he sun has set behind the sombre and bare banks of the river; two Christians, who are going silently on their way, notice the corpse of the young martyr which passes in front of them, carried by the waters.'[5]

This may well be the fullest commentary on the genesis and theme of a painting that Delaroche ever wrote. Yet a comparison of the different extant versions of the work reveals a number of problems in following its gestation. The initial charcoal study has probably disappeared, though there are several related pencil studies, mostly for the figure with bound hands, in the Louvre collection (RF 34811, 34812, 34813, 34817, 34819). Delaroche's 'small canvas', probably the painting sold in 1857 as the 'first thought' of the composition, cannot be traced either.[6] However, the painting in the Louvre is without any doubt the work seen by Gautier in 1857, before it was sold to Baron d'Eichtal. A note in the sale catalogue of June 1857 confirms that Goupil owned it, and reserved the rights of reproduction. The steel engraving, by Herman Eichens, duly appeared in 1861. Nonetheless, a work on such a scale was certainly not painted for the exclusive purpose of being reproduced, as were several of the small versions of Delaroche's major paintings that had previously left his studio. The size and the quality of the Louvre work imply that, though unsigned, Delaroche considered it as the definitive version. Its appearance in a prominent position in Louis Roux's retrospective painting of the studio (1858) supports this inference (fig. 35, p. 156).

This recognition affects the status of the other existing versions of the *Young Martyr*. There is no difficulty in authenticating the work 'begun by Delaroche but completed by [Charles] Jalabert' in the Walters Art Museum, Baltimore. Jalabert was one of Delaroche's most faithful pupils, and often worked in his studios at Paris and Nice. Moreover the Goupil account books record its sale in 1868.[7] But the fine version in the Hermitage poses a problem. Evidently both signed and dated, it cannot date from 1853, as previously recorded.[8] There can be no reason to reject Delaroche's own clear account of the work having been begun early in 1854. Measuring 73.5 × 60 cm, the Hermitage version is larger than the 'first thought' canvas (33 × 25 cm) and the Eichens engraving (65.2 × 53 cm), but less than half the size of the Louvre version. It does not appear to have passed through Goupil's books. If we are to trust the autograph, it might have been painted to give to a friend in 1854/5. SB

1. Foucart-Walter in Nantes and Montpellier 1999, pp. 326–7.
2. Gautier 1857, p. 146.
3. As described in Paris 1857b, p. 3.
4. Ulbach 1857, p. 368.
5. Ulbach 1857, p. 369.
6. Paris 1857b, p. 5.
7. Getty Research Institute, Goupil 3271, Book 4, p. 52, row 9.
8. See Ziff 1977, p. 302. A close inspection of the date on the painting in fact reveals that the last digit is difficult to interpret.

PAUL DELAROCHE (1797–1856)

[61] *Saint Veronica (Sainte Véronique)*, 1856

Oil on wood panel, 28×49 cm
Musée du Louvre, Paris (RF 1938–82)

Provenance: Delaroche-Vernet Collection; bequeathed to the Musée du Louvre, Paris, in 1938.

This is one of Delaroche's last religious images, painted in the year of his death. A small devotional work intended for private use, it is also a highly unusual depiction of the saint. In traditional iconography, Veronica plays a proselytising role.[1] When the image of Christ imprints itself on the veil with which she washes his face on the road to Calvary, she is compelled to publicise the miraculous gift. In Francesco Mochi's colossal sculpture in Saint Peter's, Rome, dating from the 1630s, she races ecstatically forward flourishing the sacred likeness for all to see. In an 1847 pen and ink sketch by Delaroche (Musée du Louvre, Paris), probably for a lost painting, a stately Veronica advances on a kneeling throng of supplicants proudly brandishing the 'true image' before her.[2] Here, however, she lies prostrate beneath the veil. Her head is turned away, eyes closed, as if the image of the suffering Christ were too overwhelming to contemplate. Triumphant exposition gives way to intensely private grief, or ecstasy. The recumbent pose, swathed in drapery, is indebted to the sculptor Stefano Maderno's marble *Saint Cecilia* of 1600 (fig. 34), which Delaroche would have seen in Rome in the mid-1830s as he studied masterpieces of Christian art in preparation for his unexecuted Madeleine project. Some twenty years later he recalled the pose, and the poignant expressivity Maderno achieved by focusing on the flow of drapery around and across the saint's body, discovering in it a solution to the aesthetic problem he had set himself here: how to unite absolute stillness with intense emotion.

[FIG. 34] Stefano Maderno (1576–1636), *Saint Cecilia*, 1600. Marble, Santa Cecilia in Trastevere, Rome

Ziff has commented that 'if Veronica's veil were not present in the painting ... it would be impossible to identify the subject'.[3] But that veil is no less unorthodox a component of the painting, and further evidence of Delaroche's willingness near the end of his life to experiment with the conventions of devotional imagery. In most depictions of Veronica the sacred cloth is 'subject to the ordinary conditions of ambient light ... [illuminated] by an implied light source outside the picture'.[4] As it hangs here from a tabletop, however, the cloth is also the principal source of illumination within the picture. As if lit from within, it casts a glow on Veronica's cheek, neck and upper back. The tense outline of her form achieves its plasticity from the radiance of Christ's face. That he is the source of illumination is made clear by a small preparatory study in pencil (Musée du Louvre, Paris) where lines representing rays of light emanate from the face.[5] There, startlingly, the veil hangs not on the side of a table but of a bed at the foot of which Veronica has fallen; it is as if she is presented to us not as Veronica alone but also as the Bride of Christ about to consummate her marriage, or as the Fallen Woman of the New Testament, Mary Magdalene. It is perhaps not surprising that in the painting that followed, Delaroche chose to suppress this suggestion – although Bernini, among others, had made it before him – of an intimate conjunction between religious and erotic fervour. It suggests as well that, had he lived, his religious art might have continued to develop in unexpectedly syncretic directions.

Bann, for whom the picture is a 'singular intervention in the history of religious art', has intriguingly proposed a relationship between Delaroche's depiction of Veronica's veil, the most famous image in the Christian tradition 'not made with hands', and his keen interest in photography and other forms of automatic reproduction.[6] It is, then, a key image in any discussion of the relationship in the mid-nineteenth century between painting and the radical new technologies photography brought to bear on image making. At the same time, and even though it remained in the private collection of the artist's family until entering the Louvre in 1938, the painting seems to have influenced fellow painters as well, not least Delaroche's most talented pupil, Jean-Léon Gérôme. His *Execution of Marshal Ney* of 1868 (cat. 86) adopts the prostrate pose of Veronica, as well as the motif of a recumbent figure swathed in drapery, and uses it in reverse for the figure of the fallen Napoleonic hero. CR

1. On the iconography of Saint Veronica, see Kuryluk 1991, p. 142.
2. Illustrated in Bann 1997, fig. 163, p. 266.
3. Ziff 1977, p. 261.
4. Bann 1997, p. 267.
5. Illustrated in Bann 1997, fig. 164, p. 266.
6. Bann 1997, p. 265.

WILLIAM SKELTON (1763–1848), AFTER JOHN OPIE (1761–1807)

[62] *The Execution of the Queen of Scots*, 1795

Etching and engraving on paper, 46.8 × 33.4 cm
The British Museum, London (1858.1009.137)

WILLIAM BROMLEY (1769–1842) AFTER JAMES NORTHCOTE (1746–1831)

[63] *Feckenham by Order of the Queen visits Lady J. Gray [sic] in the Tower*, 1792

Etching and engraving, 45.2 × 33.4 cm
The British Museum, London (1858.1009.128)

CHARLES GRIGNION (1717–1810) AFTER SAMUEL WALE (?1721–1786)

[64] *Death of Lady Jane Gray [sic]*, engraved for William Henry Mountague, *A new and universal History of England to the end of the year 1770* (London: J. Cooke, 1771)

Engraving on paper, 35.5 × 22 cm
Private collection

PIO FEDI (1816–1892) AFTER PAOLO VERONESE (ABOUT 1528–88)

[65] *The Martydom of Saint Justina* (after the painting in the Galleria degli Uffizi, Florence)

Etching and engraving on paper, 41 × 57 cm
The British Museum, London (1857.0411.126)

The exhibition of *The Execution of Lady Jane Grey* at the 1834 Salon provoked a trenchant criticism by Gustave Planche, who claimed that there was 'a striking analogy' between the painting and Skelton's engraving after Opie's *Queen of Scots* (1795), originally published in David Hume's *History of England*. Planche was justified in claiming that Delaroche used English print sources, and right to make a similar point about the *Death of Elizabeth*.[1] But in the case of *Lady Jane Grey*, the accusation of plagiarism was misplaced. Delaroche had certainly looked at a variety of existing sources, as was his usual practice. But these were not necessarily prints, nor do they appear to have been exclusively from English publications.

There was no portrayal of Jane Grey's execution in the illustrations to Hume. Her preparation for martyrdom was represented there by the steadfast way in which she rejected the monk Feckenham's attempts to make her recant her Protestant faith. There was, however, an English tradition of depicting the prelude to her execution, which took place on a raised scaffold, with Jane herself in a standing, rather than kneeling position. Grignion's print after Wale, a founder member of the Royal Academy, shows her being helped to the block in this fashion, as does the unattributed *Death of Jane Grey after an English painter* in *Magasin universel* (see cat. 76). The large sheet of drawings from before July 1830, where Delaroche sketches the final composition (see cat. 66), also features a study to the right with a standing figure, which compares with the portrayals in Wale and Grignion.

Delaroche determined to adopt the

62

63

64

65

kneeling position. He also rejected the vertical emphasis essential in illustrating a book production, which is responsible for the unpleasant effect of compression in Skelton and Opie's *Queen of Scots.* His composition evokes instead the great tradition of martyrdom paintings initiated by the Venetian Renaissance painter Paolo Veronese, and continued in Northern Europe by Peter Paul Rubens. The conquests of Napoleon had resulted in the temporary presence at the Louvre of one of the largest of these, Veronese's *Martyrdom of Saint George*, taken from the church of San Giorgio in Braida in Verona. Napoleon's commissaries also removed from a Flemish chapel Rubens's *Martyrdom of Saint George* (now Musée des Beaux-Arts, Bordeaux), in which a bending figure secures the saint's arms.[2] Particularly pertinent to Delaroche's project is Veronese's rendering of the death of a female saint, *The Martyrdom of Saint Justina* (Galleria degli Uffizi, Florence). Here the gesture of the outstretched arms of the saint, who is flanked by figures on either side, does present a 'striking analogy' with Delaroche's horizontal composition. If Delaroche was not acquainted directly with these paintings, he could have known them through reproductive prints such as Fedi's. SB

1. Planche 1855, p. 240.
2. Bann 1997, p. 127.

PAUL DELAROCHE (1797–1856)

[66] *Studies for Jane Grey and for 'The Dauphine and Louis XVII'*, before July 1830

Graphite on paper with bistre, 22 × 28.5 cm (RF 35133)

Provenance: Delaroche-Vernet-Sancholle-Henraux, presented in 1971

[67] *The Execution of Lady Jane Grey*, 1832

Watercolour and bodycolour on paper, 18.4 × 21.9 cm
The Whitworth Art Gallery, Manchester (D.1937.11)

Provenance: Jess Haworth Bequest, 1937

[68] *Study for Jane Grey*, 1832/3

Graphite and stump on paper, 15 × 13.5 cm
The British Museum, London (1994.0514.54)

Provenance: collection of L.K. Burket. Transferred from the National Gallery in 1994

[69] *Study for Jane Grey (squared)*, 1832/3

Graphite on paper, 12.1 × 14 cm (RF 35134)

[70] *Study for two hands*, 1832/3

Graphite on paper, 6.6 × 11.1 cm (RF 35135)

Provenance for cats. 69, 70: Marie Delaroche-Vernet-Henraux, presented in 1971

[71] *Studies for Jane Grey (with Ladies-in-Waiting and Executioner squared)*, 1832/3

Graphite on paper, 23 × 20 cm (RF 1727)

Provenance: Delaroche-Vernet Bequest, 1887

[72] *Studies for Jane Grey (Executioner)*, 1832/3

Graphite on paper, with bistre, 23 × 27 cm (RF 35132)

Provenance: Delaroche-Vernet-Sancholle-Henraux, presented in 1971

Cats. 66, 69, 70, 71, 72: Département des Arts Graphiques, Musée du Louvre, Paris

The documents assembled here suggest a tentative chronology for the development of *The Execution of Lady Jane Grey*. This sequence of drawings retraces a process of refining the composition over a period of around four years. Yet it cannot be assumed that Delaroche originally intended to associate his record of a decapitated queen with this comparatively little-known victim. As well as recognising the precedent of Mary Queen of Scots, he evidently envisaged depicting the execution of one of Henry VIII's wives: his study of the king enthroned (cat. 49) carries the name of Cath[erine] How[ard], and his provision of the executioner with a sword in the Manchester watercolour (cat. 67) might relate to the legend that Anne Boleyn chose to be beheaded in this way. Nonetheless the large Louvre drawing (cat. 66) is remarkable in including early studies for all the main features of the final composition. It also presents a sketch for 'La dauphine et Louis 17 au Temple', which indicates a terminal date for the whole sheet. The Duchesse d'Angoulême, who was sister to the boy king Louis XVII and shared his confinement in the Temple prison during the Revolution, ceased to be 'Dauphine' (i.e. wife of the heir to the French throne) in July 1830, after which date her father-in-law, Charles X, was succeeded by Louis-Philippe.[1]

This juxtaposition of a scene from revolutionary history with a less finished sketch clearly anticipating *Jane Grey* suggests that

66

Delaroche originally planned two pendants, both involving innocent royal victims. But the early dating of the sheet prompts a question. If Delaroche sketched *Jane Grey*, with its main features, before July 1830, how may we account for the lengthy interval before its completion? Cat. 67 is securely dated 1832, as is the portrait of Mlle Anaïs (cat. 73) which probably signals Delaroche's first prolonged acquaintance with the young actress. The issue therefore boils down to examining why his project was interrupted between 1830 and its completion in 1833.

Up to early summer 1831, Delaroche was preoccupied with the paintings that he sent to the Salon of that year (including *Cromwell and Charles I* which was not ready for the opening on 1 May). A letter of 25 April 1832 to his studio assistant Henri Delaborde, who was staying with his family in Meudon outside Paris, alludes to a further cause of delay in the year that followed. A deadly cholera epidemic ravaged Paris throughout spring 1832, and Delaroche remained in the city to nurse his sick brother Jules. Delaroche's letter announces that Jules is convalescing, but adds: 'I have not looked at my picture since you left and I will not return to it again until I can work on it like a mason.'[2] Conditions in Paris would, however, deteriorate further in the early summer. The first uprising of Louis-Philippe's reign took place, sparked off by the funeral procession of the Napoleonic general Lamarque on 6 June, and involving widespread disruption throughout Paris.

What then was the picture that Delaroche intended to resume when conditions improved? It is likely that the reference was to the major commission accepted in 1830 for a picture representing *The Takers of the Bastille* at the beginning of the French Revolution. This large work (now in the Petit Palais, Paris) appears to have been commenced with little enthusiasm, and was completed as late as 1839 with the assistance of another of Delaroche's assistants, Joseph-Nicolas Robert-Fleury.[3] The question then follows: at what stage did Delaroche decide to put the commission aside, and turn his attention to *The Execution of Lady Jane Grey*? The

67

68

69

70

decision could well have been associated with his first prolonged meetings with Mlle Anaïs, when she posed for her portrait as a fashionable young actress. It is likely that these sittings took place in the latter months of 1832, since this period coincided with her elevation to a new status as a *sociétaire* of the Comédie-Française. Cat. 67 suggests that she then agreed to pose for the figure of Jane in a dress of sixteenth-century French style. The tiny Baltimore drawing (fig. 17) that features the same period dress captures a moment of repose for the sitter, which the artist has instilled with his own sense of intimacy.

The two letters despatched by Delaroche to Anaïs (cat. 75) relate to a further important phase in the composition. The shorter of the two dates from the run of the play, *Les Enfants d'Édouard*, which opened on 18 May 1833. The longer and more explicit letter could well relate to the earlier months of 1833, since there is a reference to Anaïs's fireside. It is argued elsewhere (p. 42) that this letter was sent to arrange a sitting in Anaïs's apartment, with 'Charles Guyot' possibly modelling the role of the Lieutenant of the Tower. If this is so, cats. 68, 69 and 70 can all be related to this stage. Cats. 69, though very similar to 68, has been squared up to facilitate transfer of the motif to the larger scale of the painting. Cat. 70 is involved with the tricky foreshortening of Jane's outstretched arms.

To complete this timetable, there is unequivocal evidence that *The Execution of Lady Jane Grey* was expected to appear at the 1833 Salon, which opened on 1 March. The critic Théophile Gautier, writing in the same month, went so far as to accuse him of 'coquettishness with his Jane Grey so lauded in advance'.[4] Gautier was, however, expecting Delaroche to repeat his old trick of arriving late at the exhibition, and exciting popular demand, as had been the case with *Cromwell* in 1831. A further notice in a contemporary journal, dated 23 June, can only have rekindled the suspense by revealing that the painting was being 'finished at this moment' – too late for the Salon – but had supposedly been snapped up by Count Demidoff for the enormous sum of 20,000 francs.[5]

An intriguing footnote to this schedule exists in the form of another letter, which was briefly summarised in a late nineteenth-century catalogue of autographs, and which, in view of the preceding testimony, must surely have been assigned to the wrong year. According to this source, Delaroche wrote on 22 June 1832 to 'Madame Wyatt' that 'the presence of her daughter [was] indispensable for him to complete his picture of Jane Grey'.[6] If we assume that the date was in fact 1833, the implications of the message are fascinating. It is possible that Delaroche's correspondent was the 'Mme Wyatt, née de Vivefay' who exhibited at the 1831 Salon, and that the daughter mentioned was the future artist Emma-Cornélie Wyatt de Vivefay who became a well-known copyist under the Second Empire. Delaroche's acquaintance with the English artist Matthew Cotes Wyatt is attested by the 1822 entry in the Meyrick Visitors Book (cat. 11). But even if there is no direct link between the French-born lady

71

artist and the dynasty of English architects to which Matthew belonged, Delaroche would surely have recognised the rich Tudor connotations of the name Wyatt. The poet Sir Thomas Wyatt was imprisoned in the Tower under suspicion of being the lover of Anne Boleyn, and his sister Anne Wyatt was the lady-in-waiting who accompanied the unfortunate victim to the scaffold, and received her last confidences. Delaroche clearly wanted the most prominent of his grieving attendants to be finely characterised, with her upturned face entirely visible. It is tempting to imagine that Miss Wyatt did respond to the letter, since her name fitted the bill to perfection.

At any rate, the remaining studies involving the executioner and the grieving ladies (cats. 71, 72) did not require the presence of Mlle Anaïs; they would have been completed at Delaroche's studio in the rue des Marais St Germain. The lady-in-waiting with her face to the wall is clearly foreshadowed in cat. 66. But the detailed sketch of the lady with upturned face in cat. 71 may date back to a sitting with the daughter of Mme Wyatt. It suggests some acquaintance with Tudor costume, though for Jane Grey's precise period it is anachronistic. The distinctive head-dress might derive from a print after Holbein's rendering of the daughters of Sir Thomas More, and so would belong a generation earlier. The striking outfit of the executioner as it appears in the final painting allies Italianate features (such as the red tights) with genuine period features such as the jaunty cap. The large sheet of variant drawings for this crucial figure (cat. 72) shows that a live male model was introduced, after the grosser, sword-bearing figure of the Whitworth study had been discarded. Delaroche took great pains to define the meditative pose from which he contemplates his task.

Delaroche had been elected to the Académie des Beaux-Arts on 3 November 1832, but his only representation at the 1833 Salon was through Louis Henriquel-Dupont's aquatint after *Cromwell*. As recounted here, he had sold the painting most advantageously, but he had failed to meet the deadline for a late arrival, despite the rumours of its imminent appearance to which Gautier alludes. His nomination as Professor at the Ecole des Beaux-Arts on 15 October 1833, which secured him a new studio in the second courtyard of the Institut (the present seat of the French Academy), eventually gave him the chance to show off the completed *Lady Jane Grey* in this prestigious setting. His pride in the painting is signalled in a letter to the collector and painter Count Turpin de Crissé, who was invited to view it before the next Salon opened in March 1834.[7] SB

72

1. References in the French literature of the period habitually make it plain that this title refers specifically to the Restoration period which ended in July 1830: e.g. Balzac 2008, p. 438, where 'Mme la dauphine' is cited in connection with the 1829 Paris Salon.

2. Bibliothèque de l'Institut, Paris, Fonds Delaborde, ms 2156, f.141.

3. Ziff 1977, p. 84. The painting is indeed described as having been 'begun in 1830' in Paris 1857a, p. 36.

4. Gautier 1834, p. 149.

5. *Journal des artistes*, 1833, p. 463. This was certainly an exaggeration. The sum of 8000 francs is a more credible figures (see p. 102).

6. See Charavay 1896, n. 37780. I am most grateful to Eric Bertin for drawing my attention to this item, as well as locating the published sources in the previous two notes.

7. See letter (undated) in Fonds Turpin de Crissé, Musée des Beaux-Arts, Angers.

73

PAUL DELAROCHE (1797–1856)

[73] *Portrait of Mademoiselle Anaïs*, 1832

Coloured chalks on paper, 28.5 × 25 cm
Private collection, by family descent
Provenance: in the sitter's family.

HENRY SCHEFFER (1798–1862)

[74] *Portrait of Mademoiselle Anaïs*, 1833

Oil on canvas, 68.5 × 52 cm
Collections de la Comédie-Française, Paris (I 200)
Provenance: Collection Etienne Arago; gift of Madame Veuvre Laugier, 1892.

[75] Two letters from Paul Delaroche to Mademoiselle Anaïs, 1833

Folded sheets, text opening 15 × 22 cm
Private collection
Provenance: les autographes, Paris 2000 (Thierry Bodin).

In the late 1820s, Delaroche established himself as a fashionable portraitist. His virtuoso painting of *The Marquis de Pastoret* (1829, Museum of Fine Arts, Boston) joined a family portrait collection to which both David and Ingres had already contributed masterpieces. His *Portrait of Mademoiselle Sontag in the Role of Donna Anna* (1830, State Hermitage Museum) showed that he could also capture the glamour of a notorious operatic diva. When this oil painting was shown at the 1831 Salon, it was accompanied by a set of other unspecified 'portrait drawings' which attested to his new skill with coloured chalks.

The portrait of the actress Mademoiselle Anaïs, recently rediscovered in the keeping of a descendant, is one of the most charming of the series. It probably dates from the latter part of 1832, since Delaroche was occupied with nursing his sick brother during the serious cholera epidemic of the spring months. Anaïs learned during the course of the year that she had obtained the coveted position of *sociétaire* at the Comédie-Française, and could look forward to a life of financial independence. This portrait could well have been commissioned to celebrate her new status. She is dressed in the height of fashion, in a style that recalls the contemporary female portraits of Achille Devéria. The elegant Louis XV chair in which she sits would have been a long-term studio property, which implies that the sitting took place in Delaroche's studio at 17 rue des Marais St Germain (now rue Visconti). It is clearly the chair that supported the Marquis de Pastoret, and that stands out prominently in the left foreground of Louis Roux's evocation of Delaroche's last studio at the rue de la Tour des Dames, painted after his death (see fig. 35).

Delaroche was probably introduced to Anaïs by his friend and studio partner Eugène Lami, who appears to have known her for some years. This portrait would have been one of his regular commissions. Anaïs was naturally conscious of her image, and in the following year she commissioned the oil painting by Henry Scheffer which conveys something of the same innocent charm. But her professional relationship with Delaroche rapidly changed into something more serious. Anaïs had been selected to play the important part of Richard, Duke of York, in the production of Casimir Delavigne's *Les Enfants d'Édouard,* the tragedy based on Delaroche's painting shown at the 1831 Salon, which opened at the Théâtre français in Paris on 18 May 1833. It has been known for some time that she possessed one of

74

Delaroche's drawings, which she gave away to a fellow actress in 1836. The hypothesis that she was the model for *The Execution of Lady Jane Grey* was first raised on the basis of this connection.

However, the clear proof that Delaroche was passionately attached to Anaïs during this critical period had to wait for the discovery of the two letters exhibited here. Arguments relating their content to a possible scenario for the development of the painting can be found elsewhere in this catalogue (see p. 132). Here they are published for the first time in translation. The second letter is the shorter of the two, but the reference to a ticket for *Les Enfants d'Édouard* – and the fact that Delaroche uses the word 'actor' (*comédien*) in the masculine (as appropriate for a transvestite role) – implies a date after 18 May 1833. The first letter might date from some months earlier, as the rendezvous is by Anaïs's fireside. Its content is also more challenging:

1. *If you wish me to tell you my thoughts very frankly, my darling, I desire to pass the evening with you, to tell you as much as I can that you are my angel, my happiness and my life! To work on your portrait and give you the occasion to exchange some spiteful little remarks with your friend Eugène if I can bring him along to you together with my good Charles Guyot. So then till this evening at your home by the corner of your fire and on my knees before your eyes which will cry no longer. To you my life Paul D.*

You will scold me on the dirtiness of my sheet of paper, I have not been able to find any other.

2. *I await the ticket that you promised to Guyot. Will you, little darling, send it if you have it, and if not let me know how he can get it this evening. Till this evening, my love, my excellent little actor! And your head? Paul*

If I did not have people around me I would have been to see you.[2] SB

1. See Bann 1997, p. 122.
2. See p. 167 for this transcript in French.

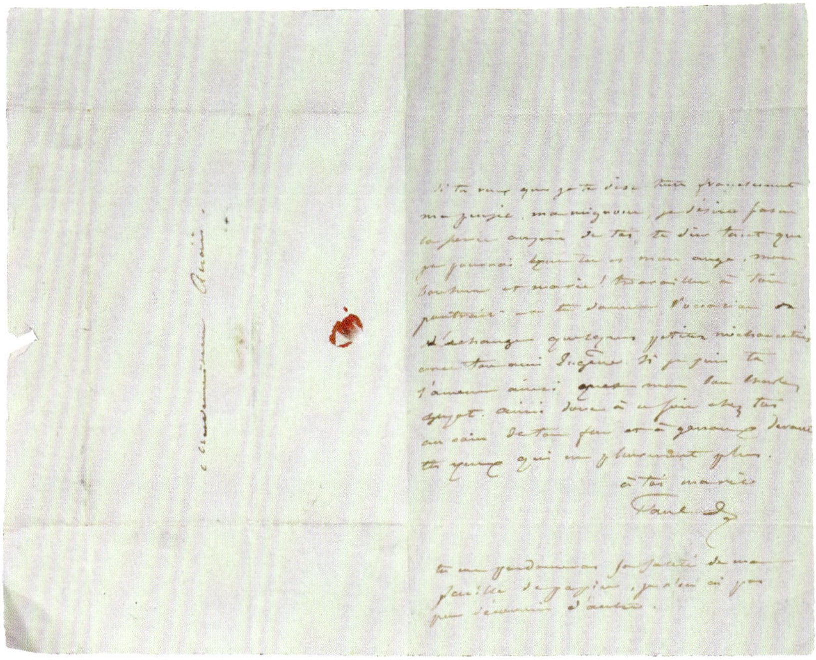

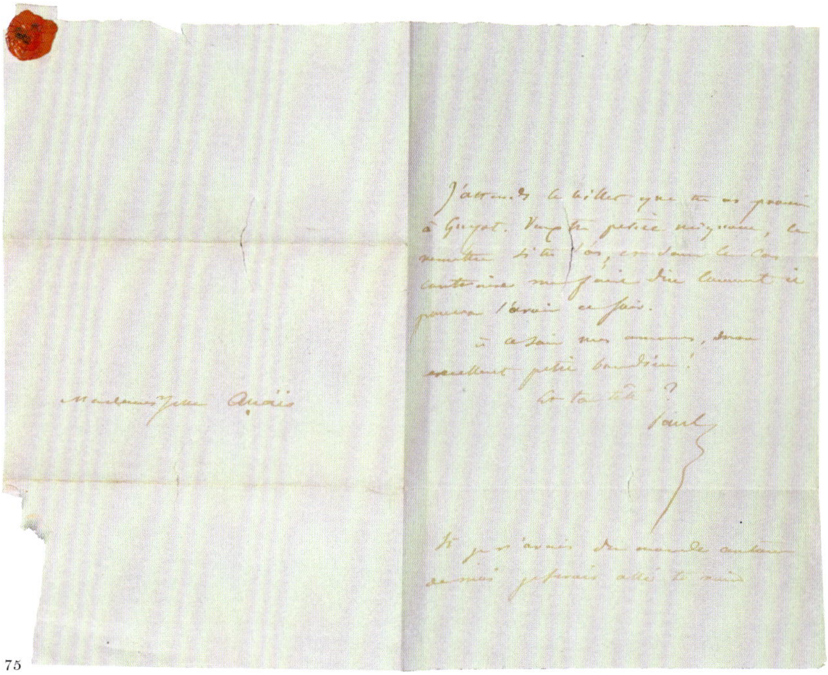

75

UNKNOWN ENGRAVERS

[76A] *Death of Jane Grey after the Painting by Paul Delaroche (1797–1856)*

Wood engraving on paper, 14×16.5 cm

[76B] *Death of Jane Grey after an English Painter*

Wood engraving on paper, 12×15 cm
From *Magasin universel*, 5 June 1834
Private collection

GIUSEPPE GATTI (1807–1880) AND GAETANO DURA (1805–1878) AFTER DRAWING BY ACHILLE DEVERIA (1800–1857)

[77] *Giovanna Grey*, about 1837

Lithograph on paper, 34×27 cm
Private collection

PAOLO MERCURI (1804–1884), AFTER PAUL DELAROCHE (1797–1856)

[78] *Jane Gray* [sic], about 1857

Engraving *avant la lettre*, 43×28 cm
Private collection

Delaroche's *Execution of Lady Jane Grey* had evidently been bought by Count Demidoff long before the opening of the Salon on 1 March 1834 (see p. 110). After the exhibition closed, it remained in his private collection until it was exhibited at Delaroche's retrospective of 1857. Yet its fame spread rapidly through prints and new versions of the subject. As early as 5 June 1834, the widely circulated French illustrated magazine *Magasin universel* published a print after a drawing of the exhibited work, opposite a well-informed article comparing an 'English painter's' treatment of the theme. Delaroche himself had taken the pains to publish a lithograph of his *Joan of Arc* in 1824, and contributed a print of *Mazarin* to the new journal *L'Artiste* in 1830.[1] In the case of *Lady Jane Grey*, however, he was determined to have an engraved reproduction of the highest quality to perpetuate the work. The brilliant young Italian engraver Paolo Mercuri, who was then settled in Paris, received the commission from Delaroche's dealers, Rittner and Goupil, before the end of the year.

Thereafter the production of the engraving proceeded at a snail's pace. Demidoff expressed surprise that it was not ready by January 1835, and claimed (erroneously) that, as its owner, he had the 'monopoly' of prints reproducing the work.[2] Mercuri worked slowly, with the result that the plate was still not finished fifteen years after, by which stage he had moved to Rome. From around 1850, the correspondence between Mercuri in Rome and Delaroche and his dealers in Paris, reveals that progress on the print was still slow, but continuous. Neither Delaroche nor Rittner lived to see its first showing in proof at the retrospective of 1857. But there can be little doubt that Delaroche was partly responsible for the time-consuming exchanges of the final few years, when proofs were regularly arriving in Paris for him to review.[3] He was eager that the engraving should improve upon the painting, correcting some of its apparent faults. The treatment of Jane Grey's head, for example, becomes less angular than previously, and her right arm is more accurately foreshortened. The print exhibited here derives from the collection of the Delaroche-Vernet family.

Achille Devéria's design for the lithograph of 'Giovanna Grey' makes no claim to be a reproduction of Delaroche's painting. Devéria had previously produced his own print version of *The Princes in the Tower*, and this Italian version of Jane Grey harks back to his earlier images of Tudor decapitation: a second *Jane Grey* (from the lithographic press of Noël, 1834) and an *Execution of Catherine Howard* (1835). All these prints must have traded on the notoriety of Delaroche's painting. The fact that 'Giovanna Grey' was issued in the 'Picture Gallery' of the most important lithographic press in Naples was a tribute to Delaroche's growing European fame. SB

1. See Beraldi 1981, p. 5, p. 167.
2. See Nantes and Montpellier 1999, p. 249.
3. See Bergeon 1994.

MAGASIN UNIVERSEL
SALON DE 1834. — M. PAUL DELAROCHE.
MORT DE JANE GREY.
MAGASIN UNIVERSEL

76

Galleria pittorica
GIOVANNA GREY

77

78

LITHOGRAPHER UNKNOWN, AFTER PAUL DELAROCHE (1797–1856)

[79] *Portrait of Anatole Demidoff (Monsieur le comte de Demidoff)*, 1839

Lithograph on paper, 30 × 24.5 cm, printed by Auguste Bry[1]
Bibliothèque Nationale de France, Paris (Dc 166 nv)

Anatole Demidoff (1813–1870), the first owner of *The Execution of Lady Jane Grey*, and later to become the husband of Napoleon's niece Princesse Mathilde Bonaparte, belonged to an extremely rich family from St Petersburg. His father Nicholas, a collector, like himself, settled eventually in Tuscany, where his charitable work eventually gained him the title of Count of San Donato, and where his villa became home to a collection which his son greatly increased.

Demidoff was a collector of catholic tastes. He very much admired the art of his own times in Paris, forming a large collection of modern paintings, including works by Bonington, Delacroix, Granet and Ary Scheffer. Immensely pleased with his purchase of *Lady Jane Grey*, he waited for it with unconcealed impatience while it was in the early stages of preparation for Paolo Mercuri's reproductive engraving. It may have been through Paul Delaroche's early friendship with the sculptor Félicie de Fauveau that Demidoff commissioned from her designs for the frames of his paintings when they were installed in his Florentine villa of San Donato.

In a painting now destroyed, Eugène Delacroix depicted Demidoff as a very young man, sitting rather stiffly on a sofa in the Paris apartment of the Comte de Mornay, with whom Delacroix had travelled to Morocco in the previous year. The present print presumably records a lost drawing which must have belonged to the lively series of portraits, often in coloured chalks (cats. 35, 73), in which Delaroche captured the faces and characters of his own immediate circle, and may have been one of the last of these. It records Demidoff's appearance a year or so later than does Delacroix's picture. The decoration so prominently displayed here is not, apparently, the honour said to have been obtained for him through the good offices of Delaroche himself.[2] LW

1. The *Bibliographie de la France* lists a portrait of Demidoff published by Auguste Bry on 27 July 1839 (n. 664).

2. *Revue des deux Mondes* 1835, pp. 595–6.

d'après Paul
Delaroche
L.R.F. 16.1838.
Imprimé par Auguste Bry, rue Favart, 8.

EUGENE LAMI (1800–1890)

[80] *The Salon of Countess Samoïloff (Le Salon de la comtesse Samoïloff)*, 1835–7

Oil on canvas, 26.5×34 cm
On the verso, the wax seal of Prince Paul of Yugoslavia
Private collection, by courtesy of the Galerie Terrades, Paris

Provenance: collection Anatole Nicolaïevich Demidoff; his nephew, Paul Pavlovich Demidoff, Prince of San Donato; his daughter, Princess Maria Pavclovna Demidoff of San Donato, Princess Abamalek Lazarev; her nephew, Prince Paul of Yugoslavia, then by descent.

This enchantingly composed evocation of Countess Samoïloff's salon in the then very smart rue de la Pépinière, in Paris, epitomises the Italian critic Mario Praz's notion of *stimmung*, the sense of intimacy created by a room and its furnishings. The hostess, graceful and lively, wears a dress inspired by mid-eighteenth-century fashion, a taste revived in the 1830s and 1840s, and echoed by the clock, the glass and the chair in the foreground. The two pieces in the background, on the other hand, suggest the abiding Russian liking for the Empire style.

In some disgrace after an affair with Tsar Nicolas I, Julie Samoïloff left her native St Petersburg and settled for a time in Milan, where Rossini, Donizetti and Bellini were among the visitors to her salon. The Russian painter Karl Briullov apparently loved her all his life. Her likeness, in idealised form, appears in his painting *The Last Day of Pompeii*, a work commissioned by their fellow countryman Anatole Demidoff, and one of three major pictures owned by him which were shown at the Salon of 1834. It seems most likely that Demidoff also commissioned the present picture from Lami, Baudelaire's *poète du dandysme*, who had been Delaroche's fellow-pupil at Gros's studio.

All three men appear in this group: Demidoff, in languid pose, at the table to the left of the hostess; Lami himself, beside him, drawing beneath the lamp (a chance to observe his features, see cat. 37), and Delaroche to the right of the fireplace, slightly towards the background. Standing beside Countess Samoïloff is the Count de Mornay, whom she eventually married, and with whom she had recently travelled to Morocco. The entire scene, distinguished and informal, faintly *ancien régime* in manner and mood, suggests a world in which Delaroche found himself for a short time in the 1830s, and to which certain of his portraits, and particularly his pastels, seem to belong. LW

JULES-GABRIEL LEVASSEUR (1823–ABOUT 1900), AFTER EUGENE BUTTURA (1812–1852)

[81] *Portrait of Paul Delaroche*, 1853

Engraving on paper, 28 × 21.5 cm
Private collection

PAUL DELAROCHE (1797–1856)

[82] *Study for the Head of Christ for La Madeleine, Paris (Portrait of Eugène Buttura)*, about 1835

Oil on canvas, 51.4 × 61.5 cm
National Galleries of Scotland (NG 2817)

Provenance: Galerie Elstir, Paris.

Delaroche was elected to the Académie des Beaux-Arts on 3 November 1832, and on 15 October 1833 he was named professor at the Ecole des Beaux-Arts in Paris. Less than a month later, he received one of the most prestigious state commissions of the period, when he was invited to undertake the entire mural scheme of the new church of La Madeleine in central Paris. Deeply conscious of his lack of acquaintance with the great Italian masters, he left France for a long visit to Italy in June 1834. But on his return to France a year later, he discovered that the prime space in the apse of the church had been given to a pupil of Ingres, Jules Ziegler. He decided to withdraw from the project and returned the substantial advance.[1]

Several oil sketches and drawings that Delaroche produced for this major scheme are still extant. Perhaps the most eloquent is this study for a Head of Christ, probably intended for one of the compositions where Christ is seen in profile, as a preacher or taking a meal with his disciples.[2] In keeping with his earlier practice, Delaroche chose a model from his own circle. He selected his striking young pupil Eugène Buttura, who would proceed to win the Grand Prix de Rome for historical painting in 1837.

Delaroche's closeness to several of his former pupils is attested by his correspondence. In Buttura's case, the legacy is the sympathetic drawing of his former teacher that was completed in 1849. Levasseur, who translated it into a fine engraving, was himself the pupil of Delaroche's most faithful reproductive engraver, Louis Henriquel-Dupont. Published after Buttura's death, and just three years before that of Delaroche, this print remains the most sympathetic portrait of the master. LW

1. See G. Brunel, 'Delaroche et le projet de la Madeleine', in Nantes and Montpellier 1999, pp. 87–103.

2. Nantes and Montpellier 1999, pp. 90–1.

81

EDOUARD CIBOT (1799–1877)

[83] *Anne Boleyn in the Tower of London shortly after her Arrest (Anne Boleyn à la Tour de Londres dans les premiers moments de son arrestation)*, 1835

Oil on canvas, 162 × 129 cm
Musée Rolin, Autun (982.3.1)

Provenance: appeared on the Paris art market in 1975, and in London in 1977. Acquired on the London art market in 1982.

Pierre-Nolasque Bergeret's *Anne Boleyn condemned to Death* (Musée du Louvre, Paris) shown at the Salon of 1814, must be among the earliest of nineteenth-century French paintings to indicate a growing taste for subjects from English history. Like *Lady Jane Grey*, it introduces the notion of martyrdom; in the entry that Bergeret submitted for the Salon catalogue (the *livret*), he quotes from a letter addressed to Henry from Anne: 'you have always elevated me; from a simple young girl to the rank of countess; from countess to queen; from queen, you wish to make me a saint'. Delaroche for a time took an interest in Henry VIII and his 'victims' (cat. 49), shortly before beginning work on the painting of another unhappy queen, Lady Jane Grey, who was executed 18 years after Anne Boleyn. However, as Isabelle Julia suggests, it was probably the music of Gaetano Donizetti's opera *Anna Bolena*, performed in Paris in 1831, which lent additional pathos to the subject, a pathos Cibot explores, concentrating on a single element in Delaroche's more complex composition. Cibot gives the theme of the grieving women a dramatic significance of its own, while still emphasising, as Delaroche had done, the contrast between the young queen, quietly contemplating death, and the grief, too deep to be witnessed, of the lady-in-waiting, who hides her face. The missal, open at a page showing the crucifixion of Christ, recalls the prayer book which is such a prominent feature of *The Princes in the Tower* (cat. 14), and, as in that picture, is more than a symbolic token; it acts as part of a temporal narrative; laid aside, it may suggest only a brief extent of time remaining. LW

LOUIS GALLAIT (1810–1887)

[84] *The Last Homage Paid to Counts Egmont and Hoorne*, 1855

Oil on canvas, 69 × 98.5 cm
Koninklijk Museum voor Schone Kunsten, Antwerp (1582)

Provenance: bought at the sale of Madame Louise Maskens, 18 April 1895.

Louis Gallait began his training with Philippe-Auguste Hennequin, a former pupil of David, but it was probably the time he subsequently spent in the studio of Matthieu-Ignace Van Bree which determined his taste for subjects from sixteenth-century history. He settled in Paris for a time in the early 1830s, where an early Salon success, his *Oath of Vargas* (Wallace Collection, London), shown in 1835, earned him the first of nine commissions from Louis-Philippe for the Musée Historique at Versailles. It must have been the example of Delaroche's series of major paintings drawn from the history of the Civil War in England which led Gallait to turn to a period within his own national history offering comparable subjects.

During the period of the Spanish occupation of the Netherlands, the Counts Egmont and Hoorne, although Catholic, and loyal to Philip II, were nonetheless involved in a series of religious and political struggles, and strongly opposed the exercise of the Inquisition in their own country. Egmont travelled to Spain in 1565 hoping to reach a settlement with the king, and was honourably received. However, two years later, Philip's envoy the Duke of Alba arrived in the Netherlands to suppress all opposition to Spanish rule. He arrested Egmont and Hoorne, and later signed the warrant for their death – a death which Egmont faced calmly, predicting the eventual liberation of his country. This was the heroic subject taken up by Goethe in his 1787 drama *Egmont*, and implicit in the incidental music which Beethoven composed for it in 1810. Gallait's carefully documented work lays stress on the factual aspects of this closing scene, but for him, and for his fellow countryman, the present political context – the newly acquired independence of Belgium after the revolution of 1830 – would have given a particular symbolic resonance to the subject.

The present picture is a reduction of the large painting shown at the Salon of 1851, and now in Tournai. The form of the composition, and the macabre representation of the severed heads, reunited with the bodies of the two victims, immediately recall Delaroche's *Cromwell and Charles I* (cat. 23) as the Goncourt brothers were quick to point out. However, Gallait, who admired Ary Scheffer as well as Delaroche, uses a technique which is more obviously painterly, in a manner close to the colourful romanticism of the 1820s. Where Delaroche in comparable subjects is literal, almost neutral, in his rendering of the material appearance of things, Gallait, on the other hand, while basing his account on Henne and Wauters's *Histoire de la ville de Bruxelles* of 1845, reconstructs and dramatises the scene in the light of his own interpretation of the event. The Archers' Guild comes to pay its respects to the victims as a candle is lit behind them, while the brutality of the Spanish presence is symbolised by two figures already relegated to the background: one, supposedly, a spy of the Duke of Alba, the other, unmistakeably, a Spanish soldier whose fierce yet guarded look is directed not at the victims, but at the members of the Brussels guild who, gravely mourning the dead, now with them dominate the scene. LW

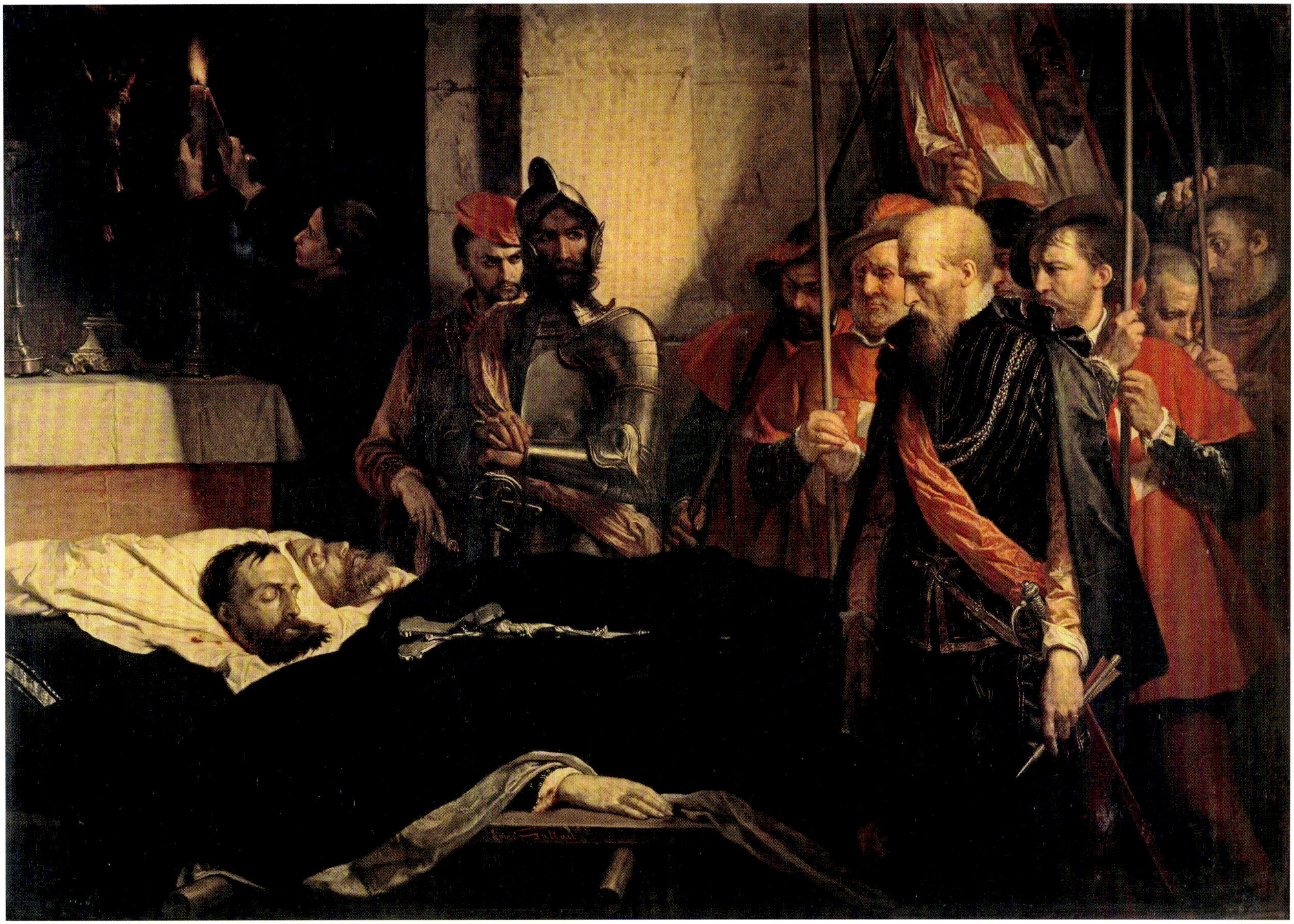

JEAN-PAUL LAURENS (1838–1921)

[85] *The Hostages* (*Les Otages*), 1896

Oil on canvas, 140 × 146 cm
Musée des Beaux-Arts, Lyon (B502)

Provenance: bought by the City of Lyon, 18 May 1898.

The relationship of this painting to Delaroche's *Princes in the Tower* has often been asserted. At Laurens's 1997–8 retrospective, it was declared to be 'not out of the question to see *The Hostages* as [his] personal translation of [Delaroche's] theme', given 'the absence of another noteworthy historical event of a similar kind'.[1] It is certain that the last years of the nineteenth century saw a revival of interest in Casimir Delavigne's play *Les Enfants d'Edouard* based on Delaroche's painting of 1830. This was performed at the Théâtre de la République, Paris, in 1897, and discussed in a thoughtful review on the subject of 'popular theatre'.[2] Yet it is inadequate to view Laurens's work as merely a 'personal translation' of a 'theme'. John Everett Millais's *Princes in the Tower* (1878) had employed a vertical format, expressing the sense of menace through the light that emanates from the top of a steep staircase. Laurens has contrived a no less ingenious variation on Delaroche's innovative use of space, using the well in the left foreground to suggest an unfathomable threat comparable to the aura of Delaroche's barred door. There is also reason to suppose that Laurens had a quite different historical event in mind, though he did not make the fact public.

A contemporary review comes close to revealing this source. Paul Adam wrote of the painting's first showing: 'Such are the *Hostages* whom the decorative resourcefulness of M. Jean-Paul Laurens has summoned up from history, just like the Byzantine Irene.'[3] The reference is presumably to an earlier Byzantine scene by Laurens, *Saint Jean Chrysostome et l'impératrice Eudoxie* (1893, Musée des Augustins, Toulouse), and it is indeed in an episode from Byzantine history that the source for *The Hostages* might be found. Laurens could have discovered the celebrated historian Amédée Thierry's description of the fate of two 'young princes of royal blood' at the hands of the Hun Attila, as recounted in the Latin chronicle of Priscian.[4] Raised as hostages at the Byzantine court, these young Huns had evidently become Christian (see the cross of the elder prince). They were summarily crucified on their return, and 'thus [Attila] inaugurated his reign'.[5]

Laurens's visual homage to Delaroche is encapsulated in his own clever transplantation of the Shakespearean plot, with the wicked Attila taking the place of Richard III. The fact that he did not advertise his source (and maybe did not want it to be discovered) reveals the extreme pressure to achieve originality that history painters were experiencing towards the end of the century. SB

1. Paris 1997, p. 114.
2. Dinamis 1897, p. 693.
3. Adam 1896, p. 111.
4. Thierry 1856, p. 50.
5. Thierry 1856, p. 51.

J-P Laurens.

JEAN-LEON GEROME (1824–1904)

[86] *The 7th of December, 1815, nine o'clock in the morning (The Execution of Marshal Ney) (Le 7 décembre, 1815, neuf heures du matin [L'Exécution du Maréchal Ney])*, 1868

Oil on canvas, 64 × 103.5 cm
Sheffield Galleries and Museums Trust (VIS.1844)

Provenance: sold by Goupil, 1871; with Boussod and Valadon, 1880; sold Christie's, London, 21 May 1881; Agnew's.

Born in 1824, Gérôme became a pupil of Delaroche in 1840, and accompanied him to Italy in 1843 when he decided to close his Paris studio. His career duplicated that of his master, since he became a professor at the Ecole des Beaux-Arts in 1864 and was elected to the Académie des Beaux-Arts in 1865. His marriage to the daughter of Adolphe Goupil in 1863 strengthened his long-term connection with the gallery and print publisher that had so effectively supported Delaroche's work. Through his extraordinary success in conquering new markets for his work, notably that of the United States, he took to a new level the worldwide diffusion that Delaroche had already begun to achieve. His pictorial innovations were also rooted in the compositions of Delaroche, who (in the words of one contemporary) was 'the director of [his] inspiration'.[1]

Gérôme's *Execution of Marshal Ney* perhaps provides the most striking example of his ability to reinterpret and transform a composition by Delaroche. Originally exhibited at the Paris Salon with an obscure title that provided only a date and time of day, the work depicts an event early in the French Restoration. The heroic marshal, known as 'the bravest of the brave', had been executed for defecting to Napoleon during the 'Hundred Days' when the Emperor had escaped from confinement on Elba, and temporarily resumed his reign. The kinship with one of Delaroche's most celebrated works, *The Assassination of the Duc de Guise* (1834), is plain to see. In both works, the foreshortened figure of the corpse lies stretched out in the right foreground, while the perpetrators of the deed retreat to the left. After Delaroche's death in 1856, Goupil had in fact commissioned another painting of an assassination, Gérôme's *Death of Caesar*, with the aim of reproducing it photographically as a pendant to the *Duc de Guise*.[2] In *Marshal Ney*, Gérôme again signalled his debt to the master.

But the painting is not just an updating of a sixteenth-century scene. Wolfgang Kemp has outlined the distinctive way in which it addresses the position of the spectator. '[T]he viewer is placed in position to grasp the "pre-pictorial" event ... His position is that of an eyewitness ... He is someone who comes upon the scene almost by accident and must first make sense of what he sees.'[3] Kemp contrasts this effect with Pierre-Paul Prud'hon's allegorical painting *Justice and Vengeance pursuing Crime* (1808, Musée du Louvre, Paris), where we are left in no doubt about the moral issue that is being acted out before us. It makes sense to refer back this feature of *Marshal Ney* to Delaroche's *Duc de Guise*, where the composition also invites the impression of 'com[ing] upon the scene almost by accident'. The distinction also brings us back to Stendhal's comment about the impact of Delaroche's *Death of Elizabeth* in 1828: 'Thus the spectator believes himself to be taking part in this terrifying spectacle.'[4] Stendhal interprets Delaroche's originality in terms of a clash between two contemporary styles of theatre, 'classic' and 'romantic'. Yet by the time Gérôme painted *Marshal Ney*, the camera had substantially altered the whole experience of spectatorship, lending new intensity to the 'eye-witness' experience.

The first appearance of Gérôme's painting at the 1868 Salon gave rise to controversy. Ney's son evidently wished it to be excluded from the exhibition. But John House has suggested that the real issue involved was its association with the works on the subject of *The Execution of Maximilian* begun by Edouard Manet in 1867, which did not get as far as the Salon because of their political sensitivity.[5] As was the case with the firing squad confronting the unfortunate Emperor of Mexico – a victim of French foreign policy – the soldiers despatching the hero in Gérôme's painting were clearly dressed in French uniforms. SB

1. Montgailhard 1906, p. 26 (summarising the view of the painter Lecomte de Noüy).
2. Chesneau in Paris 1859, p. 35.
3. Kemp 1985, p. 118.
4. Stendhal 2002, p. 152.
5. See J. Wilson-Bareau in London 1992, p. 100. The reconstructed second version of Manet's painting is in the collection of the National Gallery.

FREDERICK GOODALL (1822–1904)

[87] *Puritan and Cavalier*, 1886

Oil on canvas, 113 × 184.8 cm
National Museums, Walker Art Gallery, Liverpool (WAG 2926)

Provenance: Sam. J. Blackwell sale, Christie's, 21 July 1922, lot 158, bought Sampson; presented by George Audley, 1925.

The three great subjects from the English Civil War, *Cromwell and Charles I*, *Strafford on his Way to Execution*, and *Charles I insulted by the Soldiers of Cromwell*, were the last of Delaroche's subjects from English history. In mid-nineteenth-century England, his Civil War subjects, two of which were in distinguished English collections, were by then extremely well known and admired. This came about as a result of the exhibition of several of his works in London,[1] as well as through their widespread diffusion in the form of engravings. The publication of Thomas Carlyle's *Letters and Speeches of Oliver Cromwell*, published in 1845, no doubt played a part in encouraging interest in the 'psychological' aspects of Cromwell's character, and the period, in all its aspects, rapidly became a favourite subject for painters. Delaroche's three scenes from the period must have been particularly fascinating precisely on account of his representation of the private, inner responses of his protagonists, a representation of the unseen rendered the more convincing by his mastery of the visible.

No one has yet studied the impact of Delaroche's work on the English Pre-Raphaelites; though we know that Dante Gabriel Rossetti admired him, it may be that their comparable concern with an absolute truth to appearances developed independently. Frederick Goodall, son of Turner's engraver Edward Goodall, and great-grandson of a French émigré printmaker,[2] was a member of a group of painters known as the St John's Wood Clique, a group which included William Frederick Yeames, whose *And When did You Last See Your Father* (1878, Walker Art Gallery, Liverpool) has come to epitomise mid-Victorian history painting. Goodall too turned to scenes from Stuart history, but always preferred more cheerful moments, while preparing his canvases with Pre-Raphaelite fidelity.

On his *Raising the Maypole at the Restoration of Charles II*,[3] begun in 1850, he wrote: 'I spent some time at the British Museum searching for prints to procure the true costume for the period.'[4] In 1852, in order to begin work on *The Happier Days of Charles I* (1855, Bury Art Gallery and Museum), in which the king and his family are seen enjoying a day out on the Thames, he spent several months on a houseboat: 'I spent the greater part of that summer making studies for it of water-lilies, willows and swans' and 'several weeks at Windsor Castle, making studies from the Van Dyck picture of Charles I, Henrietta Maria and their Children'. Turning next to a subject from Tudor history, *Cranmer at the Traitor's Gate* (exhibited at the Royal Academy in 1855), he made many studies of the Tower of London, and 'Mr Meyrick, the great collector and authority upon arms and armour, helped me with the loan of helmets, fine swords and other implements.'[5] Ernest Gambart, who bought the picture, had by then become a close friend of Goodall. He was a former employee of Paul Delaroche's dealer Adolphe Goupil, and from 1850 onwards began putting on exhibitions of French paintings in London. By the time he and Goodall travelled together to Paris, visiting the studios of a number of Gambart's artist friends, including that of Delaroche's father-in-law, Horace Vernet, Delaroche himself had died, though Gambart must often have spoken of him. Enriched by an uninterrupted series of successes at the Royal Academy, and also, no doubt, by Ernest Gambart's practice, like Goupil's, of publishing reproductive engravings after his work, Goodall later built a house to designs by Norman Shaw, furnished it appropriately, and probably used it as the setting for the present picture, for which his son and daughter posed. Edward Morris suggests that it may be seen as an 'amusing parody of the many Civil War scenes painted by artists such as those in the St John's Wood Clique'.[6] Goodall's telling play on the use of empty space – the little dog (a King Charles spaniel, of course) and a reduction of the dramatic suspense of the Princes in the Tower to a mere game of hide-and-seek, makes this a work which assumes an immediate familiarity with several of the major pictures in this exhibition, and which shows that a late Victorian audience could be expected to understand and smile at a playful reference to the now entirely familiar dramatic art of Paul Delaroche. LW

1. *Strafford on his Way to Execution* and *Charles I insulted by the Soldiers* were both exhibited in London at the British Institution in 1838; *Cromwell and Charles I* at the Royal Academy in 1850.
2. A Goodall family historian, Neil Slark, wrote in 1981: 'Edward's wife, Eliza Ann le Petit, was the granddaughter of a French refugee who was one of the first printers in colour in England', adding, in a footnote: 'I have not been able to establish any connection with William Le Petit, the landscape engraver, though I suspect one exists.' Quoted in Slarke 1981, p. 4.
3. Presumably the work, signed and dated 1851, which was sold at auction at Hampel, Munich, 4 July 2008, lot 571.
4. Goodall 1902, p. 34.
5. Goodall 1902, p. 36.
6. Liverpool 1992, p. 50.

[FIG. 35] Louis Roux (1817–1903); this photograph shows Roux's lost painting of *The Studio of Delaroche*, about 1856. *The Girondins* (cat. 56) is on the easel in the centre of the painting. Painting, probably oil on canvas, dimensions and current painting location unknown.

Paul Delaroche: Chronology

ANNE ROBBINS

1797 Hippolyte-Paul Delaroche is born in Paris on 17 July, the second son of Marie-Catherine Bégat (1762–1828) and Grégoire-Hippolyte Delaroche (about 1750–1824), and brother to Jules-Hippolyte Delaroche (1795–1849). In a family of artists, dealers and art administrators, both children are destined early to an artistic career.

1816 Delaroche enrols in the studio of the landscape painter Louis-Etienne Watelet (1780–1866), and in September is admitted to the Ecole des Beaux-Arts. With his older brother already training as a history painter, it is decided that Paul should study landscape painting.

1817 At the Ecole des Beaux-Arts, Delaroche takes part in the contest for the Prix de Rome in Historical Landscape, a new category awarded for the first time that year. He fails at the second elimination trial.

1818 He registers in the studio of the Neoclassical painter Baron Antoine-Jean Gros (1771–1835), which Gros had taken over from his master Jacques-Louis David three years earlier, and works with fellow pupils Eugène Lami (1800–1890), his close friend, and Richard Parkes Bonington (1802–1828).

1820 Delaroche leaves Gros's studio. He paints a *Pietà* for the Duchesse d'Orléans (Musée Condé, Chantilly).

1822 He lives at No. 9, rue Childebert (since destroyed) in the Latin Quarter, in the bohemian environment of a boarding house called La Childeberte, and uses co-lodgers as models, including Adolphe Roger and Jean-Frédéric Schall, as well as other students from Gros's studio. In April, he shows at the Paris Salon for the first time, with three paintings on subjects from the Old and New Testaments. Earlier in the year he travels to London and visits the Meyrick collection of armour.

1824 Delaroche lives at 12 rue de Seine, Hôtel de La Rochefoucault. He shows four paintings at the Salon including *Saint Vincent de Paul Preaching* and *Joan of Arc* (see fig. 11), which receives much critical attention.

1827 He lives with Eugène Lami at No. 17 rue des Marais Saint-Germain, now rue Visconti. He visits London again. In November he exhibits at the 1827/8 Salon, including *The Death of President Duranty* (destroyed 1871) a commission for the Conseil d'Etat [Council of State], and *The Taking of the Trocadéro*.

1828 *The Death of Elizabeth* (Musée du Louvre, Paris), the first in a series of paintings illustrating English subjects, finally arrives at the 1827/8 Salon. Both it and *The Death of President Duranty* are highly praised. In April, Delaroche is made a Chevalier of the Légion d'Honneur. He visits Belgium.

1830 In March, he receives official commissions: a ceiling for the newly created Musée de la Marine and *The Taking of the Bastille*, a large decorative painting for the Paris Hôtel de Ville (Petit Palais, Paris). He produces early sketches for a painting on the subject of Lady Jane Grey.

In late July, the July Revolution sees the overthrow of the conservative government of the Bourbon monarch Charles X, and the ascent to the throne of his liberal cousin the Duc d'Orléans, as Louis-Philippe. During the revolutionary days Delaroche and Lami take part in the defence of the Louvre alongside Ingres and Delacroix.

1831 He exhibits seven paintings at the Salon, including the pendants *State Barge of Cardinal Richelieu on the Rhône*, painted 1829, and *Cardinal Mazarin's Last Sickness*, 1830 (both Wallace Collection, London). Two major paintings are of English subjects: *The Princes in the Tower* (Musée du Louvre, Paris) and *Cromwell and Charles I* (cat. 23), a state commission.

1832 Delaroche spends the year in Paris, initially nursing his brother, who is suffering from the cholera which is sweeping the city. He embarks on a relationship with Anaïs Aubert (1802–1871), known as Mademoiselle Anaïs, a noted actress and member of the Comédie-Française, and friend of Eugène Lami. She sits to Delaroche for her portrait (cat. 73) and is the model for his Lady Jane Grey in the painting completed the next year. In November, he becomes the youngest elected member of the Académie des Beaux-Arts.

1833 On 18 May, he attends the premiere of the play *Les Enfants d'Edouard*, by Casimir Delavigne. The play is dedicated to him and based on his *Princes in the Tower*. Mademoiselle Anaïs plays the part of Richard, Duke of York. In October, Delaroche is nominated Professor at the Ecole des Beaux-Arts, with a new studio on the premises. His pupils will include Thomas Couture, Jean-Francois Millet and Jean-Léon Gérôme. In November he receives a commission to decorate the central nave of the Madeleine church in Paris (see cat. 82, *Study for the Head of Christ*). Part of the commission is removed from him the following year, and after a dispute he withdraws from the project altogether in 1836.

He completes *The Execution of Lady Jane Grey* (cat. 53), elaborated over the previous three years.

1834 In March, *The Execution of Lady Jane Grey* prompts scenes of hysteria and collective emotion at the opening of the Salon. Critics are more measured, accusing the artist of plagiarism of English visual sources. *Cromwell and Charles I* is shown at the Lille Salon. In May, Delaroche is made an Officer of the Légion d'Honneur. In June, seeking ideas for the Madeleine project, he departs for Italy with Henri Delaborde and Edouard Bertin to study the great religious art of the past. In July and August he visits Florence, Pisa, Arezzo and Siena, and spends time at the Monastery of Camaldoli in the Tuscan Apennines. In October, he settles in Rome, where he pays regular visits to the Académie de France. In December he announces his engagement to Louise Vernet (1814–1845), daughter of the painter Horace Vernet (1789–1863), who is Director of the Académie de France in Rome.

1835 On 28 January, Delaroche marries Louise Vernet at San Luigi dei Francesi, Rome. At the Paris Salon, his *Assassination of the Duc de Guise*, on a popular historical and theatrical subject, is awarded a first class medal and meets with unprecedented success. Warders are placed on either side of the painting. Having returned to Paris, Delaroche and his new wife move to a house at No. 7 rue de la Tour des Dames, in the 'Nouvelle Athènes' area.

A contract is made between the printmaker Mercuri and the firm Rittner and Goupil for an engraving of *The Execution of Lady Jane Grey* (although it is published only in May 1857).

In June, he delivers an oration at the funeral of his master Gros, and takes over Gros's studio: it soon becomes the most popular of the July monarchy. *The Princes in the Tower* and *The Execution of Lady Jane Grey* are exhibited at the Douai Salon, northern France.

1836 Delaroche declines to sit on the Salon jury, in protest at the voting procedures, which allow architects to vote on the admission of paintings. He is commissioned to paint a mural in the lecture theatre (Hémicycle) of the Ecole des Beaux-Arts, the '*Artists of All Ages*'. On 1 December, his first son, Horace, is born.

1837 Delaroche shows at the Salon for the last time with his *Saint Cecilia* and the large paintings *Strafford* and *Charles I Insulted* (cats. 58, 54, fig. 7), together with three portraits.

Halfway through, he requests that *Charles I* be displayed where *The Execution of Lady Jane Grey* had hung three years earlier, attracting considerable success. Despite this effort, the painting only encounters a lukewarm reception from the public, and harsh reviews from critics.

1838 In April Delaroche receives a commission for five historical paintings on Frankish and Carolingian kings for the pavillon du Roi at Versailles. To prepare for this task, he travels to Italy for the second time and collects information about Byzantine art in Venice and Ravenna.

1839 Delaroche returns from Italy in March. By now, his studio comprises 85 pupils. At the request of the Russian collector Anatole Demidoff (who had bought *The Execution of Lady Jane* Grey in 1833), he paints the *Portrait of Peter the Great* (Hamburg, Kunsthalle), and his self portrait (private collection, Paris). He writes a report on photography for the scientist and statesman François Arago (1786–1853).

1841 Delaroche's second son Philippe is born on 21 February. In July, the Hémicycle de l'Ecole des Beaux Arts is inaugurated. Delaroche receives payment of 80,000 francs for the project, which he worked on with four assistants.

1842 He paints the *Childhood of Pico della Mirandola* (Musée des Beaux-Arts, Nantes), showing the Renaissance humanist as a child on his mother's lap. Ignoring the advice of his father-in-law Horace Vernet, he refuses commissions for the court of Tsar Alexander in Saint Petersburg, preferring to focus on his family and the running of his studio.

1843 Delaroche paints *A Mother's Joy*, a tondo inspired by the paintings of Raphael (Collection Musée J.P. Pescatore, galerie d'Art de la Ville de Luxembourg). He spends part of the summer in Normandy with his family. In October, an incident of hazing in his studio forces him to close it, despite protests from his pupils. Free from this commitment, he embarks on his third trip to Italy, where he spends a year.

1844 The first performance of Alexandre Soumet's play *Jane Grey* at the Odéon theatre in Paris takes place on 30 March. Delaroche spends the summer and early autumn in Rome. Inspired by Italy, he determines to resume work on the Versailles commission once back in Paris. He is joined by his pupil Jean-Léon Gérôme. In November, the family returns to Paris.

1845 He completes *Napoleon at Fontainebleau* (Museum der Bildenden Künste, Leipzig), a commission showing the Emperor meditating on his forthcoming exile, of which he will produce seven versions.

On 18 December, his wife Louise dies, aged only 31. Deeply affected, Delaroche paints her on her deathbed, with an aureole above her head, like a saint (1845; Musée des Beaux-Arts, Nantes). More than 4,000 people attend her funeral.

1846 Delaroche declines to apply for the Direction of the Académie de France in Rome. He paints mostly portraits.

1847 *Charlemagne crossing the Alps*, at Versailles, is completed with the participation of Gérôme.

1848 In March Delaroche is elected to the committee in charge of the painting displays for the Salon. From spring to July he stays at Le Havre, Normandy, with his sons. He is anxious about the revolutionary events in Paris which end the Orléans monarchy and lead to the creation of the Second Republic. In August he is in Aachen, where his son Horace receives treatment for a circulatory disease.

Twenty-seven years after Napoleon's death, Delaroche paints *Napoleon crossing the Alps* (Musée du Louvre, Paris). In September, he is elected a municipal councillor for Paris.

1849 Delaroche spends spring in Aachen, then travels to Frankfurt, Weimar, Leipzig and Dresden, and on to Switzerland. He visits the Duke and Duchess of Saxe-Weimar and other courts. By October, he is in the south of France. He begins to spends his winters in Nice near his friends, the Princess de Beauvau-Craon and her sister Countess Delphine Potocka. His brother, Jules-Hippolyte, dies.

1850 He spends summer in Craon (Mayenne), at the home of the Princess de Beauvau, with Horace, whose poor health prevents him from travelling to Aachen for treatment. The autumn is spent in Burgundy and Nice. He may have visited England during this year.

1851 By the end of March, *Marie-Antoinette before the Tribunal* (cat. 59) is complete. Delaroche paints portraits of his sons (both in private collections).

1852 Delaroche visits Belgium, and spends September in Paris.

1855 Delaroche chooses not to exhibit at the Exposition Universelle. He paints *Young Christian Martyr* (cat. 60), 'the saddest and holiest of all my compositions'. For critics, the painting reveals a new direction in style and inspiration for Delaroche. On 16 December a fire in the hémicycle of the Ecole des Beaux-Arts partly destroys Delaroche's mural. He immediately embarks on the restoration, which is completed after his death by Robert-Fleury.

1856 Delaroche completes *The Girondins' Last Farewell, 31 October 1793* (cat. 56). He starts painting four scenes depicting the Virgin Mary at the time of Christ's Passion, in small dimensions. Of these, only one will be brought to completion.

On 4 November Delaroche dies aged 59 in the house at 7, rue de la Tour-des-Dames, Paris. At his bedside are his son Horace and his fellow artists Charles Jalabert and Jean-Léon Gérôme. The funeral takes place three days later and Delaroche is buried next to his wife in the Cimetière du Nord, now Cimetière Montmartre, in Paris.

1857 From 7 April to 5 May a posthumous exhibition of Delaroche's work, the first retrospective of this kind ever organised for an artist, is held at the Ecole des Beaux-Arts in Paris. On 12–13 and 15–17 June the contents of his studio and his art collection are sold (fig. 35).

1858 A catalogue raisonné of his work, with text by Henri Delaborde and Jules Goddé and photographs by Robert Jefferson Bingham, is published.

Lenders to the Exhibition

ANTWERP
Koninklijk Museum voor Schone Kunsten Antwerpen

AUTUN
Musée Rolin

BOURG-EN-BRESSE
Musée de Brou

CARDIFF
Amgueddfa Cymru —
National Museum Wales

EDINBURGH
National Gallery of Scotland

LIVERPOOL
Walker Art Gallery, National Museums Liverpool

LONDON
The British Museum
Victoria and Albert Museum
The Wallace Collection

LYON
Musée des Beaux-Arts de Lyon

MANCHESTER
The Whitworth Art Gallery

MONTPELLIER
Musée Fabre

NEW YORK
The Forbes Collection

NIMES
Musée des Beaux-Arts de Nîmes

NOTTINGHAM
Nottingham City Museums and Galleries

OXFORD
Ashmolean Museum

PARIS
Bibliothèque nationale de France
Musée Carnavalet / Conciergerie / Centre des monuments nationaux
Comédie-Française
Fonds national d'art contemporain (Cnap), Ministère de la culture et de la communication
Musée du Louvre
Galerie Talabardon et Gautier
Galerie Terrades

ROUEN
Musée des Beaux-Arts de Rouen

RUEIL-MALMAISON
Musée national des châteaux de Malmaison et de Bois-Préau

SHEFFIELD
Graves Gallery, Museums Sheffield

And lenders and private collectors who wish to remain anonymous.

SPECIAL EXHIBITION
A Masterpiece Recovered:
Delaroche's *Charles I Insulted*
Private Collection

These exhibitions have been made possible with the assistance of the Government Indemnity Scheme which is provided by DCMS *and administered by* MLA.

Bibliography

ACKERMAN 1986
G. M. Ackerman, *The Life and Works of Jean-Léon Gérôme*, London and New York 1986

ADAM 1896
P. Adam, 'La peinture au Salon des Champs-Elysées', *Gazette des Beaux-Arts*, vol. 2, 1896, p. 111

AIX EN PROVENCE 1992
D. Coutagne and I. Néto Daguerre (eds), *Granet Peintre de Rome*, exh. cat. (Musée Granet) Paris and Aix-en-Provence 1992

AIX EN PROVENCE 2008
D. Coutagne, *François-Marius Granet (1775–1849), Une vie pour la peinture*, exh. cat. (Musée Granet) Paris and Aix-en-Provence 2008

ALFORD 2008
S. Alford, *Burghley: William Cecil at the Court of Elizabeth I*, New Haven and London 2008

ALLEVY 1938
M-A. Allévy, *La mise en scène en France dans la première moitié du dix-neuvième siècle*, Paris 1938

ALLEY 1959
R. Alley, *Tate Gallery Catalogues: The foreign paintings, drawings and sculpture*, London 1959

ANON 1893
Anon, *An Englishman in Paris*, (7th edn) London 1893

ASCHAM 1570
R. Ascham, *The Scholemaster*, London 1570

AYLMER 1559
J. Aylmer, *An Harborowe for Faithfull and Trewe Subiectes*, London / Strasbourg 1559

BALZAC 2008A
H. de Balzac, '*Béatrix*' (1838–44), in *La Comédie humaine*, vol. 12, Paris 2008

BALZAC 2008B
H. de Balzac, 'Z. Marcas' (1840), in *La Comédie humaine*, vol. 17, Paris 2008

BANN 1984
S. Bann, *The Clothing of Clio: On the Representation of History in Nineteenth-century Britain and France*, Cambridge 1984

BANN 1997
S. Bann, *Paul Delaroche: History Painted*, London and Princeton 1997

BANN 1999
S. Bann, 'Envisioning Rome: Granet and Gibbon in dialogue', in C. Edwards (ed.), *Roman Presences: Receptions of Rome in European Culture, 1789–1945*, Cambridge 1999, pp. 35–52

BANN 2000
S. Bann, 'The Image of History', *Word & Image*, vol. 16, no. 1 (January–March) 2000, pp. 1–6

BANN 2001
S. Bann, *Parallel Lines: Printmakers, Painters and Photographers in Nineteenth-Century France*, London and New Haven 2001

BANN 2002A
S. Bann, 'History and the Image; from the Lyons School to Paul Delaroche' in C. Anderson (ed.), *The Built Surface*, Aldershot and Burlington vt 2002, pp. 278–93

BANN 2002B
S. Bann, 'Remembering Louise Vernet', *Art History*, vol. 26, no. 1, (February) 2002, pp. 1–25

BANN 2003A
S. Bann, 'Oscillations of the I: Academic Painting after the French Revolution (Louis Hersent, Léopold Robert, Paul Delaroche)', in S. Deines et al (eds), *Historierte Subjekte – Subjektivierte Historie*, Berlin and New York 2003, pp. 205–23

BANN 2003B
S. Bann, 'Questions of Genre in Early Nineteenth-Century French Painting', *New Literary History*, vol. 34, no. 3 (Summer) 2003, pp. 501–11

BANN 2005
S. Bann, 'Delaroche, Napoleon and English Collectors', in *Apollo*, October 2005, pp. 24–31

BANN 2006
S. Bann, 'Paul Delaroche's Early Work in the Context of English Painting', *Oxford Art Journal*, vol. 29, no. 3, 2006, pp. 341–9.

BANN 2007A
S. Bann, 'The Studio as a scene of emulation: Marceline Desbordes-Valmore's *L'Atelier d'un peintre*', *French Studies*, vol. 61, no. 1 (January) 2007, pp. 26–35

BANN 2007B
S. Bann, 'This man is Cromwell. Paul Delaroche's painting of 1831 and its critical reception', in P. Seddon (ed.), *Between Two Heads, Four essays on Cromwell, Charles 1st and Delaroche*, exh. cat. (Musée des Beaux-Arts, Nîmes and Centre for Contemporary Visual Arts, University of Brighton), Brighton 2007, pp. 27–37

BANN 2008
S. Bann, '*L'Atelier de Bervic* par Louis Henriquel-Dupont', *Revue de la Bibliothèque nationale de France*, vol. 30 (October) 2008, pp. 57–62

BANVILLE 1859
T. de Banville, *Esquisses parisiennes*, Paris 1859

BARANTE 1835
P. de Barante, *Mélanges historiques et littéraires*, 3 vols, Paris 1835

BARANTE 1842
P. de Barante, *Histoire des Ducs de Bourgogne de la Maison de Valois*, 6th edn, 8 vols, Paris 1842

BARRINGER 2001
T. Barringer, 'Rethinking Delaroche/Recovering Leighton', *Victorian Studies*, vol. 44, no. 1 (Autumn) 2001, pp. 9–24

BAUDELAIRE 1968
C. Baudelaire, *Curiosités esthétiques*, ed. J. Cain, Paris 1968

BELLIER DE LA CHAVIGNERIE 1868
E. Bellier de la Chavignerie, *Dictionnaire général de l'Ecole française*, Paris 1868

BENOIST 1994
L. Benoist, *La Sculpture romantique*, Paris 1994

BERALDI 1981
H. Beraldi, *Les Graveures du Siècle*, 10 vols, reprint, Nogent-le-Roi, 1981

BERGEON 1994
A. Bergeon, 'Le temps ciselé, correspondences autour d'une oeuvre gravée: éditeurs, artistes, critiques (1829–1859)', *États des lieux*, vol. 1, 1994, pp. 37–88

BERTIN 1997
E. Bertin, 'Les Peintures d'Ingres IV: Un prétendu modèle pour la Stratonice', *Revue du Musée Ingres*, vol. 70 (April) 1997

BIRRELL 1931
F. Birrell (ed.), *Diary of a Scotch Gardener at a French Court at the End of the Eighteenth Century, by Thomas Blaikie*, London 1931

BISSON 1942
L.A. Bisson, *Amédé Pichot*, Oxford 1942

BORDES AND CHEVALIER 1996
P. Bordes and A. Chevalier, *Catalogue des peintures, sculptures et dessins, Musée de la Révolution française, Vizille*, Vizille 1996

DE CAILLEUX, NODIER AND TAYLOR 1820–1878
J. Taylor, C. Nodier and A. de Cailleux, *Voyages pittoresques et romantiques dans l'Ancienne France, par MM.Ch. Nodier, J.Taylor et Alph. de Cailleux*, 21 vols, Paris 1820–78

CHARAVAY 1896
E. Charavay, *Lettres autographes et documents historiques, 271 (May–June) 1896, n. 37780*

CHAUDONNERET 1980
M-C. Chaudonneret, *Fleury Richard et Pierre Revoil: la peinture troubadour*, Paris 1980

CHAUDONNERET 1983
M.C. Chaudonneret, 'Tableaux troubadour' in *Revue du Louvre*, 5/6, 1983, pp. 411–14

CHAUDONNERET 1999
M-C. Chaudonneret, *L'Etat et les artistes: De la Restauration à la monarchie de Juillet*, Paris 1999

CRESPIN 1565
J. Crespin, *Actes des martyrs deduits en sept livres depuis le temps de Vuiclef et de Hus iusques à présent*, Geneva 1565

DAVEY 1909
R. Davey, *The Nine Days' Queen*, London 1909

DELABORDE 1857
H. Delaborde, 'Paul Delaroche', *Revue des deux mondes*, 1 March 1857, pp. 5–32

DELABORDE AND GODDE 1858
H. Delaborde and J. Goddé, *Oeuvres de Paul Delaroche*, Paris (includes slightly revised version of Delaborde 1857, and *Catalogue raisonné* (illustrated with photographs by R.J. Bingham, unpaginated)

DELAROCHE-VERNET 1910
H. Delaroche-Vernet, 'Ernest Hébert. Lettres à Paul Delaroche', *Revue de Paris*, vol. xvi, no. x, 1910.

DELAVIGNE 1846
C. Delavigne, *Œuvres complètes*, Paris 1846

DE LISLE 2008
L. de Lisle, *The Sisters who would be Queen*, London 2008

DENTON 1998
M.F. Denton, 'The Gendering of Genres in Post-Revolutionary French Painting', *Art History*, vol. 21, no. 2 (June) 1998, pp. 219–46

DE STAEL 1790
Madame de Staël, *Jane Gray, tragédie en vers*, Paris 1790.

DINAMIS 1897
C. Dinamis, 'Le Théâtre populaire', *Revue d'art dramatique*, New series, 2: 12, 1897, pp. 691–3

DOHERTY 2006
B. Doherty, '"The Colportage Phenomenon of Space" and the Place of Montage in The Arcades Project', *Germanic Review*, vol. 81, no. 1, Winter 2006, pp. 38–59

DUFFY 2009
S. Duffy, 'French artists and the Meyrick Armoury', *Burlington Magazine*, vol. cli, no. 1274, May 2009, pp. 284–92

DUMAS 1866
A. Dumas père, *Mes Mémoires*, Paris 1868

DUMAS 1968
A. Dumas père, *Mes Mémoires*, vol. v, ed. P. Josserand, Paris 1968

DUMAS 1974
A. Dumas père, *Théâtre complet*, vol. i, ed. F. Bassan, Paris 1974

DUPONCHEL 1829
H. Duponchel, 'Des bals costumés de S.A.R. Madame la duchesse de berri comparés aux diverses mascarades qui ont eu lieu en cour depuis le 14e siècle', *Revue de Paris*, April 1829, p. 244

EDINBURGH 2002
H. Rosslyn and A. Maggi, *Rosslyn, Country of Painter and Poet*, exh. cat. (National Gallery of Scotland), Edinburgh 2002

EVENDEN 2004
E. Evenden, 'The Michael Wood Mystery: William Cecil and the Lincolnshire Printing of John Day', *Sixteenth Century Journal*, vol. 35, no. 2, 2004, pp. 383–94.

EVENDEN 2008
E. Evenden, *Patents, Pictures and Patronage: John Day and the Tudor Book Trade*, Aldershot 2008

FAIRFIELD 1972
L.P. Fairfield, 'The Mysterious Press of "Michael Wood" (1553–1554)', *The Library*, 5th ser., vol. 27, no. 3, 1972, pp. 220–32

FOUCART 1987
B. Foucart, *Le Renouveau de la Peinure Religieuse en France (1800–1860)*, Paris 1987

FOXE 1563
J. Foxe, *Actes and monuments of these latter and perillous dayes touching matters of the Church ... Gathered and collected according to the true copies [and] wrytinges certificatorie, as wel of the parties them selues that suffered, as also out of the bishops registers*, London 1563

FOXE 1570
J. Foxe, *The first [and second] volume of the ecclesiasticall history contayning the actes and monumentes of thynges passed in euery kynges tyme in this realme, especially in the Church of England*, London 1570

FREEMAN AND MAYER 2007
T. Freeman and T.F. Mayer (eds), *Martyrs and Martyrdom in England c.1400–1700*, Woodbridge 2007

GARRETT 1938
C.H. Garrett, *The Marian Exiles*, Cambridge 1938

GAUTIER 1834
T. Gautier, 'Salon de 1834', *La France Industrielle, Exposition permanente des produits des arts et de l'industrie français*, April 1834

GAUTIER 1857
T. Gautier, 'Une Martyre: Dernier tableau de Paul Delaroche', *L'Artiste*, vol. 6, no. 3, 15 February 1857, pp. 145–6

GAUTIER 1994
T. Gautier, article for *La Presse*, 10 March 1837, in *Théophile Gautier critique d'art*, ed. M-H. Girard, Paris 1994

GERNSHEIM 1956
H. and A. Gernsheim, *L.J.M. Daguerre: the history of the Diorama and the Daguerrotype*, London 1956

GILLET 1934
L. Gillet, 'Un Tableau romantique', *Le Trésor des musées de province*, Paris 1934

GOODALL 1902
F. Goodall, *The Reminiscences of Frederick Goodall, R.A.*, London 1902

GOTLIEB 2000
M. Gotlieb, 'Poussin's Lesson: representing representation in the Romantic Age', *Word & Image*, vol. 16 no. 1 (January–March) 2000, pp. 124–43

HALEVY 1861
F.E. Halévy, 'Paul Delaroche', *Souvenirs et portraits: Études sur les beaux-arts*, Paris 18613

HARRIS NICHOLAS 1825
N. Harris Nicholas (ed.), *The Literary Remains of Lady Jane Grey; with a memoir of her life*, London 1825, trans. E. Frère, Paris 1832.

HASKELL 1975
F. Haskell, 'Un monument et ses mystères: L'art français et l'opinion anglaise dans la première moitié du xixe siècle', *Revue de l'art*, no. 30, 1975

HASKELL 1976
F. Haskell, *Rediscoveries in Art: Some Aspects of Taste, Fashion and Collecting in England and France*, London 1976

HASKELL 1993
F. Haskell, *History and its Images*, New Haven and London 1993

HAYNES 1740
S. Haynes, *A Collection of State Papers ... From the Year 1542 to 1570*, London 1740

HEINE (NO DATE)
H. Heine, *Lutèce*, Paris

HEMMING 1979
F.W.J. Hemming, *The King of Romance: A Portrait of Alexandre Dumas*, London 1979

HOWARD 1822
G. Howard, *Lady Jane Grey and her Times*, London 1822

HUGO 2009
V. Hugo, *Les Misérables*, 2 vols., Paris 2009

IVES 2009
E.W. Ives, *Lady Jane Grey: A Tudor Mystery*, Oxford 2009

JACK 2003
B. Jack, *Beatrice's Spell: The Enduring Legend of Beatrice Cenci*, London 2003

JAMESON 1857
A. Jameson, *Sacred and Legendary Art*, 2 vols, London 1857

JANIN 1858
J. Janin, *Les Symphonies de l'Hiver, Paris, Morizot*, 1858.

JOANNIDES 1975
P. Joannides, 'Some English Themes in the Early Work of Gros', *The Burlington Magazine*, vol. 117, no. 873, December 1975, pp. 774–85

KAHNG 2007
E. Kahng, *The Repeating Image: Multiples in French Art from David to Matisse*, London and New Haven 2007

KEMP 1973
M. Kemp, 'Scott and Delacroix, with some assistance from Hugo and Bonington', in *Scott Bicentenary Essays*, Edinburgh 1973, pp. 214–2

KEMP 1985
W. Kemp, 'Death at Work: A Case Study on Constitutive Blanks in Nineteenth-Century Painting', *Representations*, vol. 10 (Spring) 1985, pp. 102–23.

KURYLUK 1991
E. Kuryluk, *Veronica & Her Cloth: History, Symbolism, and Structure of a 'True' Image*, London 1991

LACAMBRE 1984
J. Lacambre, 'Un style international en 1850; à propos de l'exposition Delaroche', *Revue du Louvre et des Musées de France*, no. 5/6, 1984, pp. 337–40.

LAMOUREUX 2000
J. Lamoureux, 'Delaroche et la mort de la peinture', *Word & Image*, vol. 16, no. 1 (January–March) 2000, pp. 116–23

LA ROCHELLE 2009
A. Lys (ed.), *Marie Stuart – une figure Romantique? La destinée artistique de la reine d'Écosse au xixe siècle*, exh. cat. (Musée des Beaux-Arts) La Rochelle 2009

LARROUMET 1904
G. Larroumet, *Derniers portraits*, Paris 1904

LEBLANC DE FERRIERE 1834
A. Leblanc de Ferrière, *Jeanne Gray, drame en trois actes et cinq tableaux*, Paris 1834

LEE 2007
Y.-K. Lee, 'Ingres au Salon de 1834: Le Martyre de Saint Symphorian', *Bulletin du Musée Ingres*, vol. 79, 2007

LEMOISNE 1912
P.-A. Lemoisne, *Eugène Lami 1800–1890*, Paris 1912

LEMOISNE 1914
P.-A. Lemoisne, *L'œuvre d'Eugène Lami*, Paris 1914

LENORMANT 1833
C. Lenormant, *Les Artistes Contemporains. Salon de 1831*, Paris 1833

LEVINE 1973
M. Levine, *Tudor Dynastic Problems, 1460–1571*, London 1973

LIENARD 1819
J.B. Liénard, *Jeanne Gray ou le Triomphe de la religion sur l'amour*, 1819

LIVERPOOL 1992
E. Morris and F. Milner, *And When Did You Last See Your Father?*, exh. cat. (Walker Art Gallery) Liverpool 1992

LOACH 1999
J. Loach, *Edward VI*, London 1999

LOCKHART 1914
J.G. Lockhart, *Memoirs of Sir Walter Scott*, 5 vols, London 1914

LONDON 1930
National Gallery Millbank: Review of the Acquisitions during the Years July, 1927 – December, 1929, London 1930

LONDON 1975
C. Gould, *Delaroche and Gautier: Gautier's Views on the Execution of Lady Jane Grey and on other compositions by Paul Delaroche*, exh. cat. (National Gallery), London 1975

LONDON 1992
J. Wilson-Bareau (ed.), *Manet: The Execution of Maximilian: Paintings, Politics and Censorship*, exh. cat. (National Gallery) London 1992

LONDON 1994
S. Duffy et al, *Anatole Demidoff, Prince of San Donato (1812–1870)*, exh cat. (Wallace Collection) London 1994

LONDON 1997
S. Duffy, *Paul Delaroche 1797–1856: Paintings in the Wallace Collection*, exh. cat. (Wallace Collection) London 1997

LONDON, MINNEAPOLIS, NEW YORK 2003
P. Noon (ed.), *Constable to Delacroix: British Art and the French Romantics*, exh. cat. (Tate Britain, Institute of Arts, The Metropolitan Museum of Art) London 2003

LYON 2007
Le Temps de la peinture, exh. cat. (Musée des Beaux-Arts) Lyon 2007

MACCULLOCH 1996
D. MacCulloch, *Thomas Cranmer: A Life*, London 1996

MACCULLOCH 1999
D. MacCulloch, *Tudor Church Militant: Edward* vi *and the Protestant Reformation*, London 1999

MAGGI 1999
A. Maggi, 'Poetic stones: Rosslyn Chapel in Gandy's Sketchbook and Daguerre's Diorama', in *Architectural History*, vol. 42, 1999, pp. 263–83

MALFATTI 1956
C.V. Malfatti (ed.), *The Accession, Coronation and Marriage of Mary Tudor as related in Four Manuscripts of the Escorial*, Barcelona 1956

MASCALCHI 2005
S. Mascalchi, 'Un'artista riconsiderata e un cornice ritrovata', in *DecArt 4*, December 2005, pp. 50–9

MASTRUZZO 2000
G. Mastruzzo, 'The hidden name of our story: Hayez and Delaroche', *Word & Image*, vol. 16, no. 1 (January–March) 2000, pp. 91–105

MEISEL 1983
M. Meisel, *Realisations: Narrative, Pictorial and Theatrical Arts in Nineteenth-Century England*, Princeton 1983

MERLE 1842
J.T. Merle, 'Mlle Anaïs (dans les Enfans d'Edouard)', *Galerie des artistes dramatiques de Paris, dessinés d'après nature par A. Lacauchie*, vol. ii, Paris 1842

MIRECOURT 1854
E. de Mirecourt, *Le Baron Taylor*, Paris 1854

MIRECOURT 1871
E. de Mirecourt, *Delaroche Decamps* (3rd edn), Paris 1871

MONTGAILHARD 1906
G. de Montgailhard, *Lecomte de Noüy*, Paris 1906

NANTES AND MONTPELLIER 1999
C. Allemand-Cosneau and I. Julia (eds), *Paul Delaroche: Un peintre dans l'histoire*, exh. cat. Nantes (Musée des Beaux-Arts) and Montpellier (Musée Fabre) Paris 1999

NEW HAVEN AND LONDON 1991
P. Noon, *Richard Parkes Bonington: 'On the Pleasure of Painting'*, exh. cat. (Yale Center for British Art) New Haven and London 1991

NICHOLS 1850
J.G. Nichols (ed.), *Chronicle of Queen Jane*, London 1850

NONNE 2002
M. Nonne, 'Les droits douaniers américains et les marchands de tableaux franïcais au xixe siècle', *La Revue du Musée d'Orsay*, no. 14, Spring 2002, pp. 102–8

NOTTINGHAM 2002
M. Cambridge, *Richard Parkes Bonington; Young and Romantic*, exh. cat. (Nottingham Castle Museum) Nottingham 2002

NUS AND BROT 1856
E. Nus and C-A. Brot, *Jane Grey. Drame historique en cinq actes*, Paris 1856

PARIS 1857A
Charles de Mourgues Frères, *Exposition des œuvres de Paul Delaroche*, exh. cat. (Palais des Beaux-Arts) Paris 1857

PARIS 1857B
Catalogue des tableaux, dessins et croquis de M. Paul Delaroche, Hôtel des commissaires priseurs, Paris 1857

PARIS 1859
Salon de 1859, Paris 1859

PARIS 1979–80
E. Vergnolle, *Le 'gothique' retrouve*, exh. cat., (Caisse Nationale des Monuments historiques et des Sites) Paris 1979, pp. 105–119

PARIS 1991
B. Chénique, 'Géricault une vie', in *Géricault*, exh. cat. (Grand Palais) Paris 1991, pp. 261–308

PARIS 1997
L. des Cars and A. Dahuerre de Hureaux, *Jean-Paul Laurens 1838–1921 peintre d'histoire Paris*, exh. cat. (Musee d'Orsay) andToulouse (Musee des Augustins) Paris 1997

PARIS 2008
A. Dion-Tenenbaum, 'Le Quadrille de Marie Stuart', in T. Crépin-Leblond, ed., *Marie Stuart: Le Destin français d'une reine d'Ecosse*, exh. cat. (Musée national de la Renaissance, Château d'Ecouen, Musée Conde,) Paris 2008, pp. 104–111

PICHOT 1825
A. Pichot, *Voyage historique et littéraire en Angleterre et en Ecosse*, Paris 1825

PICHOT 1826
A. Pichot, *Vues pittoresques de l'Ecosse*, Paris 1826

PLANCHE 1855
G. Planche, *Études sur l'Ecole française (1831–1852): Peinture et Sculpture*, 2 vols, Paris 1855

PRAT 1997
L-A Prat, 'Deux dessins pour *Les Enfants d'Edouard: Bonvin ou plutôt Delaroche (1797–1856)*', *Revue du Louvre et des Musées de France*, no. 2, 1997, pp. 67–70

POUGETOUX 1994
A. Pougetoux, 'Peinture "troubadour": histoire et literature. Autour de deux tableaux des collections de l'impératrice Joséphine', *Revue du Louvre et des Musées de France* 1994, vol. 44, no. 2, pp. 51–60

POUGETOUX 1995
A. Pougetoux, 'Un autoportrait d'Henriette Lorimier', *Bulletin des Musées de Dijon* 1995, pp. 47–51

PUPIL 1985
F. Pupil, *Le Style troubadour: ou la nostalgie du bon vieux temps*, Nancy 1985

RIOPELLE 1999
C. Riopelle, 'Florence, 1820–1824', *Portraits by Ingres: Image of an Epoch*, exh. cat. (The Metropolitan Museum of Art) New York 1999

ROBINSON 1846–7
H. Robinson (ed.), *Original Letters relative to the English Reformation ... chiefly from the Archives of Zurich*, 2 vols, Cambridge 1846–7

ROME 2003
O. Bonfait (ed.), *Maestà di Roma da Napoleone all'Unità d'Italia: D'Ingres à Degas – Les artistes français à Rome*, exh. cat. (Académie française de Rome) Rome 2003

ROUEN 1983
M-P Foissy-Aufrère, *La Jeanne d'Arc de Paul Delaroche: Salon de 1824*, exh. cat. (Musée des Beaux-Arts) Rouen 1983

ROY AND KIRBY 1995
A. Roy and J. Kirby, 'Paul Delaroche: A Case Study of Academic Painting', *Historical Painting Techniques, Materials, and Studio Practice*, Symposium, University of Leiden, The Netherlands, 26–9 June 1995

RUSSELL 1987
F. Russell, *Portraits of Sir Walter Scott: a Study of Romantic Portraiture*, London 1987

SAMUELS 2003
M. Samuels, 'Illustrated Historiography and the Image of the Past in Nineteenth-Century France', *French Historical Studies*, vol. 26, no. 2, Spring 2003, pp. 253–28

SANCHEZ AND SEYDOUX 1999
P. Sanchez and X. Seydoux (eds), *Les Catalogues des Salons I (1801–1819)*, and *Les Catalogues des Salons ii, (1819 [supplément] – 1834)*, 2 vols, Paris 1999

SECHAN 1883
C.P. Sechan, *Souvenirs d'un homme de Théâtre*, 1831–1855, Paris 1883

SHELTON 2000
A. Carrington Shelton, 'Ingres versus Delacroix', *Art History*, vol. 23, no. 5, December 2000, pp. 76–92

SHELTON 2005
A. Carrington Shelton, 'Le Martyre de Saint Symphorian at the 1834 Salon', *Ingres and his Critics*, Cambridge 2005

SIEGFRIED 2000
S.L. Siegfried, 'Ingres and the theatrics of history painting', *Word and Image*, vol. 16, no. i, (January–March) 2000, p. 70

SILLARS 2006
S. Sillars, *Painting Shakespeare: The Artist as Critic, 1720–1820*, Cambridge 2006

SLARKE 1981
N.G. Slarke, *Frederick Goodall, R.A*, Oundle 1981

SPIES 2009
M. Spies, *Victorian Visions of Lady Jane Grey*, unpublished dissertation, University of Ghent 2009

STARKEY AND GROSVENOR 2007
D. Starkey and B. Grosvenor, *Lost Faces: Identity and Discovery in Tudor Royal Portraiture*, London 2007

STENDHAL 2002
Stendhal, *Salons*, eds Stéphane Guégan and Martine Reid, Paris 2002

STOW 1592
J. Stow, *The annales of England faithfully collected out of the most autenticall authors, records, and other monuments of antiquitie from the first inhabitation untill this present yeere 1592*, London 1592

STRONG 2004
R. Strong, *Painting the Past, The Victorian Painter and British History*, London 2004

TANYOL 2000
D. Tanyol, '*Histoire anecdotique* – the people's history? Gros and Delaroche', *Word & Image*, vol. 16, no. 1 (January–March) 2000, pp. 7–30

TAYLOR 2001
P. Taylor, *Thomas Blaikie, the Capability Brown of France*, East Linton 2001

THIERRY 1856
A. Thierry, *Histoire d'Attila et de ses successeurs*, 2 vols, Paris 1856

THOMSON 1981
R. Thomson, *French Nineteenth-Century Drawings in the Whitworth Art Gallery, Manchester*, Manchester 1981

ULBACH 1857
L. Ulbach, 'Paul Delaroche', *Revue de Paris*, vol. 36, no. 1, (April) 1857, pp. 349–72

VAUTHIER 1918
G. Vauthier, 'Rapport du comte de Forbin sur le Salon de 1824', *Bulletin de la Société de l'Histoire de l'Art Française 1915–1917, Paris 1918, p. 172*

VIEL-CASTEL 1831
H. de Viel-Castel, 'Cromwell, par M. Delaroche', *L'Artiste*, vol. 1, no. x, 1831, pp. 268–70

VIGNE 1998
G. Vigne, 'Scandale au Salon de 1834!', *Papiers d'Ingres*, Collections graphiques du Musée Ingres de Montauban, vol. 20, 1998, pp. 1–9

VOS 1989
A. Vos (ed.), *Letters of Roger Ascham*, New York 1989

WARD-JACKSON 1985
P. Ward-Jackson, 'A.E. Carrier-Belleuse, J.-J. Feuchère and the Sutherlands', *Burlington Magazine*, vol. 127, 1985, pp. 147–539

WHITMAN 1903
A. Whitman, *Samuel William Reynolds*, London 1903

WRIGHT 1981
B.S. Wright, 'Scott and Shakespeare in Nineteenth-Century France: Achille Déveria's Lithographs of "Minna and Brenda" and "Les Enfans d'Edouard"', *Arts Magazine*, vol. 55, no. 6 (February) 1981, pp. 129–33

WRIGHT 1997
B. S. Wright, *Painting and History during the French Revolution: Abandoned by the Past*, Cambridge 1997

WRIGHT 2000
B. S. Wright, 'Delaroche's *Cromwell* and the historians', *Word & Image*, vol. 16, no. 1 (January–March) 2000, pp. 77–90

WRIGHT 2007
B. S. Wright, 'The Space of Time: Delaroche's Depiction of Modern Historical Narrative', in *Nineteenth Century French Studies*, vol. 36, nos. 1–2 (Fall/Winter) 2007, pp. 72–93

WRIGLEY 2000
R. Wrigley, 'Paul Delaroche's Italian noviciate', *Word & Image*, vol. 16, no. 1 (January–March) 2000, pp. 106–15

WYATT 2005
M. Wyatt, *The Italian Encounter with Tudor England: A Cultural Politics of Translation*, Cambridge 2005

YATES 1934
F. Yates, *John Florio: The Life of an Italian in Shakespeare's England*, Cambridge 1934

ZIFF 1977
N. D. Ziff, *Paul Delaroche: A Study in Nineteenth-Century French History Painting*, Ann Arbor 1977

ZIMMER 2006
T. Zimmer, '*L'Ensevelissement du Christ* (1851–52) d'Hippolyte, dit "Paul" Delaroche', *Recherches en histoire de l'art*, vol. 5, no. x, 2006, pp. 137–144

ZIMMERMAN 2003
M. F. Zimmerman, *The Art Historian: National Traditions and Institutional Practices*, London and New Haven 2003

Photographic Credits

AIX EN PROVENCE © Musée Granet, Aix-en-Provence: fig. 9

ANTWERP © Lukas – Art in Flanders VZW: cat. 84

AUTUN © Ville d'Autun (France), Musée Rolin / photo S. Prost: cat. 83; © akg-images / André Held: fig. 5

BALTIMORE © Collection of the Maryland State Archives: fig. 17

BOURG-EN-BRESSE © Monastère royal de Brou / photo Hugo Maertens, Bruges: cat. 6

CARDIFF © Amgueddfa Cymru – National Museum of Wales, Cardiff: cat. 2

DETROIT © The Detroit Institute of Arts, Detroit, Michigan / Bridgeman Art Library, London: fig. 14

EDINBURGH © National Galleries of Scotland: cat. 82; fig. 31

LIVERPOOL © Walker Art Gallery, National Museums Liverpool: cat. 87

LONDON © Suzanne Bosman: fig. 6; © By permission of The British Library, London: fig. 35; © The Trustees of The British Museum: cats. 15, 16, 17, 18, 21, 24, 25, 57, 62, 63, 65, 68; © The Honourable Society of the Inner Temple: fig. 2; © The National Gallery, London: cat. 53; fig. 4; © By courtesy of the National Portrait Gallery, London: fig. 3; © National Portrait Gallery, London / Art Archive: fig. 29; © NI Syndication: fig. 8; © V&A Images / Victoria and Albert Museum, London: cat. 58; © By kind permission of the Trustees of the Wallace Collection, London: cat. 11, 12; fig. 15; © The Wallace Collection, London / Bridgeman Art Library, London: fig. 26

LYON © Musée des Beaux Arts de Lyon / photo Alain Basset: cat. 5. © RMN, Paris / René-Gabriel Ojéda / Thierry Le Mage: cat. 85

MANCHESTER © The Whitworth Art Gallery, University of Manchester: cat. 67

MONTPELLIER © Musée Fabre, Montpellier Agglomération: cat. 51

NEW HAVEN, CONNECTICUT © Yale Center for British Art, New Haven, Connecticut: fig. 1

NEW YORK © The Forbes Collection, New York: cat. 59

NIMES © Musée des Beaux-Arts de Nîmes / Giraudon / Bridgeman Art Library, London: cat. 23

NORWICH © Norwich Castle Museum & Art Gallery: fig. 12

NOTTINGHAM © Nottingham City Museums and Galleries: cat. 4

ORLEANS © Musée des Beaux-Arts d'Orléans / photo François Lauginie: fig. 20

OXFORD © Copyright in this Photograph reserved to the Ashmolean Museum, Oxford: cats. 28, 39

PARIS © Bibliothèque Nationale de France, Paris: cats. 19, 27, 52, 79; © Collections de la Comédie-Française / photo P. Lorette: Ecole Supérieure des beaux arts: fig. 30; cats. 30, 33, 74; © Galerie Talabardon & Gautier: cat. 35; © Musée Carnavalet, Histoire de Paris / Photo Bridgeman Art Library, London: fig. 32; © Centre des monuments nationaux, Paris / Patrick Cadet: cat. 56; © RMN, Paris / Hervé Lewandowski: cats. 14, 60, 61; Thierry Le Mage: cats. 41, 42, 43, 44, 45, 46, 47, 48, 66, 69, 70, 72; Thierry Ollivier: cat. 71; René-Gabriel Ojéda: fig. 10; © Art Archive / Musée du Louvre, Paris / Gianni Dagli Orti: fig. 28

PRIVATE COLLECTIONS © Photo courtesy of the owners: frontispiece; cats. 7, 8, 9, 10, 13, 20, 22, 26, 29, 31, 32, 34, 36, 37, 38, 40, 49, 50, 54, 55, 64, 75, 76, 77, 78, 81; figs. 7, 16, 18, 19, 21, 23; © Photo Bridgeman Art Library, London: fig. 22

PRIVATE COLLECTION BY FAMILY DESCENT © Photo courtesy of the owner: cat. 73

PRIVATE COLLECTION COURTESY OF GALERIE TERRADES © Photo Thierry Jacob, Paris: cat. 80

PROVIDENCE, RHODE ISLAND © Museum of Art, Rhode Island School of Design: fig. 24

ROME Church of Santa Cecilia in Trastevere, Rome © akg-images / Nimatallah: fig. 34

ROUEN © Musée des Beaux-Arts de Rouen: cat. 3; © Art Archive / Musée des Beaux-Arts de Rouen / Gianni Dagli Orti: fig. 11

RUEIL MALMAISON, chateaux de Malmaison et Bois-Preau © RMN, Paris / Daniel Arnaudet: cat. 1

SHEFFIELD © Sheffield Galleries and Museums Trust / The Bridgeman Art Library: cat. 86

STOURHEAD / THE NATIONAL TRUST © David Cousins / The National Trust: fig. 25

TROYES © Musée des Beaux-Arts de Troyes: fig. 13

VERSAILLES, Musée National des Châteaux de Versailles et de Trianon, Versailles © RMN, Paris / Gérard Blot: fig. 33

WASHINGTON DC © National Museum of American History, Smithsonian Institution: fig. 27.

Appendix

Transcription of two letters sent to Mademoiselle Anais From Paul Delaroche (see cat. 74)

1. Si tu veux que je te dise très franchement ma pensée, ma mignone, je désire passer la soirée auprès de toi, te dire tant que je pourrai que tu es mon ange, mon bonheur et ma vie ! travailler à ton portrait et te donner l'occasion d'échanger quelques petites méchanchetés avec ton ami Eugène si je puis te l'amener ainsi que mon bon Charles Guyot. Ainsi donc à ce soir chez toi au coin de ton feu et à genoux devant tes yeux qui ne pleureront plus.

à toi ma vie
Paul D

Tu me pardonneras la saleté de ma feuille de papier, je n'en ai pas pu découvrir d'autre.

2. J'attends le billet que tu as promis à Guyot. Veux tu petite mignone, le remettre si tu l'as, et dans le cas contraire me faire dire comment il pourra l'avoir ce soir.
à ce soir donc, mon amour, mon excellent petit comédien!
Et ta tête ?
Paul

Si je n'avais du monde autour de moi je serais allé te voir.

Index

Italic references indicate illustrations